Books in this Series by Alexander John Shaia

Heart and Mind Community: Six-in-One Guide, Convener Text, 2020

Heart and Mind: The Four-Gospel Journey for Radical Transformation, Second Edition, Print & Kindle, 2017

Heart and Mind: The Four-Gospel Journey for Radical Transformation, First Edition, Kindle, 2014

Heart and Mind: The Four-Gospel Journey for Radical Transformation, First Edition, Print, 2013

The Hidden Power of the Gospels: Four Questions, Four Paths, One Journey, San Francisco: HarperOne, 2010

Beyond the Biography of Jesus: The Journey of Quadratos, Vol. II, 2008

Beyond the Biography of Jesus: The Journey of Quadratos, Vol. I, 2006

Other Books by Alexander John Shaia

Returning From Camino, Second Edition, English Print & Kindle, 2019
　Rückkehr Vom Jakobsweg, German Print, 2019
　Al Regreso Del Camino, Spanish Print & Kindle, 2019

Radical Transformation

THE FOUR-GOSPEL JOURNEY OF
HEART AND MIND

Radical Transformation

The Four-Gospel Journey of Heart and Mind

ALEXANDER JOHN SHAIA
with
MICHELLE L. GAUGY

ISBN 13: 978-1-7348234-0-0
ISBN 10: 1-734-82340-2

Copyright © 2020 by Alexander John Shaia and Michelle L. Gaugy
First Shaia-Sophia House hardcover printing, 2020

All rights reserved. Other than for the purposes and subject to the conditions prescribed under the *Copyright Act*, no part of this publication may be reproduced, stored in a retrieval system, or transmitted in any form or by any means, electronic, mechanical, photocopying, recording or otherwise, without the prior permission of the publisher.

Shaia-Sophia House
San Antonio, Texas, USA

Unless otherwise stated, biblical quotations are taken from the *New Revised Standard Version* (NRSV) of the Bible, copyright © 1989 by the Division of Christian Education of the National Council of Churches of Christ in the U.S.A. Used by permission. All rights reserved.

"Psalm 19," "Psalm 22," "Psalm 121," "Psalm 122," "Psalm 126," "Psalm 131" "Psalm 133," from *Opening to You*, Viking Penguin © 2002 by Norman Fischer. Rights held by author. Used by permission.

"Warning" and "Wilderness Prayer" from *In Wisdom's Path: Discovering the Sacred in Every Season* © Jan L. Richardson. Orlando, FL: Wanton Gospeller Press, 2012. www.janrichardson.com. Used by permission.

"Coleman's Bed" from *River Flow: New & Selected Poems 1984–2007*, 2nd Edition, by David Whyte © Many Rivers Press. Used by permission of Many Rivers Press.

*To the many anonymous women and men
who millennia ago heard the Gospel,
chanted its words,
and walked the journey,*

*and in memory
of my sitto Butrus, jiddo Shaia
and Emily Westfield
grand-daughter of slaves.*

Contents

Foreword	xiii
Preface	1

ONE
    THE STORY OF QUADRATOS   9

TWO
    THE KEYS   25

THREE
    THE FOURFOLD JOURNEY OF TRANSFORMATION   45

FOUR
    CLIMBING THE GREAT MOUNTAIN OF MATTHEW   63

FIVE
    CROSSING MARK'S STORMY SEA   133

SIX
    BEING IN JOHN'S GLORIOUS GARDEN   189

SEVEN
    WALKING LUKE'S ROAD OF RICHES   299

EIGHT
    EIGHT ESSENTIAL AND CONTINUING PRACTICES   387

NINE
    PARADIGMS AND PROMISES   417

Connect with Quadratos	431
Bibliography	433
Index A: Scripture Cited, Listed Alphabetically by Book of the Bible	449
Index B: Scripture Cited, Listed Alphabetically by Chapter/Page in *Radical Transformation*	453
The Four-Gospel Journey: Northern Hemisphere	458
The Four-Gospel Journey: Southern Hemisphere	459
Acknowledgements	461
Author and Collaborator	463

Your pattern is perfection
It quiets the soul that knows it
And its eloquent expression
Makes everything clear
So that even the simple are wise.

Psalm 19, translation by Norman Fischer

From this it is clear that the Word,
the artificer of all things,
being manifested to [all]
gave us the gospel,
fourfold in form
but held together by one Spirit.

Bishop Irenaeus of Lyon, 180 CE

The heart of human identity is the capacity and desire
for birthing. To be is to become creative and bring forth
the beautiful.

John O'Donohue

FOREWORD

Alexander John Shaia has produced, over a number of years, a body of work that provides Christians and seekers alike a spiritual practice of transformation with great promise and power. As I consider the scope of his work, I am reminded of another contemporary spiritual practice that I witness daily—walking the labyrinth.

Grace Cathedral, in San Francisco, was the birthplace of the modern labyrinth movement. When the Rev. Lauren Artress, an Episcopal priest and canon of the Cathedral, began this work in the early '90s, there were really only a few medieval labyrinths left in Christendom, remnants of a vigorous spiritual practice of a millennium ago. Now there are labyrinths in thousands of churches worldwide.

My office in Diocesan House, next to the Cathedral, looks out on one of our two labyrinths. Any time of day, through my windows, I see people walking. Actually, "walking" doesn't really convey how people use the labyrinth; some skip, walk backwards, run. Some carry bells, which they sound as they walk slowly, meditatively. Although there are numerous guides on how to walk, none of these people seem to be following any guidelines whatsoever.

Around the side of the Cathedral, on California Street, there is a small entrance. Inside, there are several icons—John Donne, Martin Luther King and Mary Magdalene, among others. As with the labyrinth, people come in all day to pray, light a candle, or just to be quiet before one or more of these sacred images. This informal use of icons is another spiritual practice, placed directly into the hands of people, and available for all, including those who won't show up in any church, mosque or synagogue on a day of community worship.

As with the renewal of walking meditations and praying with icons, Dr. Shaia has mined Christian tradition to bring forward a spiritual practice of transformation and make it fresh and alive for today. Known as The Four-Gospel Journey, its potential is already becoming manifest, as individuals, groups and entire communities are using it all over the world, and the word is spreading.

I live in one of the most secularized areas on Earth, but it should not be concluded from that fact that the San Francisco Bay Area is spiritually arid—quite the contrary. Instead, there is a palpable spiritual hunger here, and it is exciting that this hunger for transformation might be fed in such a foundational, substantial way—by reconnecting with the gospels of the New Testament.

Dr. Shaia reveals how the traditional four gospels constitute a progressive practice of spiritual transformation, for individual seekers and whole communities. In this way of understanding, our sacred texts are given back to the Church and to all as living guides, re-centering human life on wisdom, compassion and service, and rooted in a mystical relationship with Christ—the center of a person, the center of a community, the center of the universe.

And what is the nature of the spiritual transformation found at the heart of this process? It is the restoration of our Unity in God, who pervades, infuses and contains the Universe and all within it. And this Four-Gospel Journey is a large step on the way to restoring Unity, and anything that helps us to move further along is a significant step in the right direction.

I use the phrase "given back" with respect to the four gospels because we, in the western Church and culture, have been on a century-long "quest for the historical Jesus." That is, our scholars have been assiduously sifting through the canonical gospels, and the many non-canonical gospels, attempting to determine what sayings can be attributed with some confidence to the person, Jesus of Nazareth. This quest has paid off in spectacular ways, and has also led to some unfortunate assumptions that have left us impoverished in our religious culture and practices.

Primarily, an over-emphasis on the historical Jesus blinds the Church to the progressive nature of Christ—moving *with* the Church and *with* the world through time. Reconnecting to this dynamic living Christ will help us find meaning in today's dilemmas and respond compassionately

FOREWORD

here and *now*. This Four-Gospel Journey offers a vital step toward such integration. By rediscovering early Christianity's pattern and sequence of four, Dr. Shaia shows how their most important practices—Sunday worship, preparation for Baptism, and the Feast of Easter—were founded on a dynamic process of transformation, understood to be an embodied experience of the living Christ. Seen in this way, the selection of precisely four gospels, rather than fewer or more, is apt; four—like the seasons—expresses a turning, cyclical dynamism.

In this work is a new understanding of an ancient truth. Dr. Shaia believes that those who selected the Canon (the approved list of the books comprising the New Testament) had a divinely inspired search. But that search was far more than only choosing the most theologically sound gospels. They were also looking for something practical and effective—four gospels that when placed together serve as a seamless text of transformation, a present moment practice of living with Christ.

So with The Four-Gospel Journey, Dr. Shaia has given us back our central sacred text, not as a conflicted or faulty historical record but as a vibrant, luminous path of transformation. And living this truth of Christ, ever present in an eternal now, we understand that this practice of transformation asks to be enacted anew today.

Dr. Shaia writes that he is hearing from people using this practice and how they are adapting it to their own needs. The creative appropriation is already underway! I expect that all of us, Dr. Shaia included, will be delighted by the surprises that await as Christians and seekers alike open themselves to the reshaping and re-centering of their lives by walking this path.

Already in the Diocese of California, a group of us, clergy and lay, are beginning to imagine how this return of The Four-Gospel Journey might be incorporated into our life and spiritual practice, and become the significant piece of religious renewal it promises.

As with the labyrinth and the icons in Grace Cathedral, I believe we will see seekers and Christians and all who have God-shaped holes in their hearts, make this path their own, in their own surprising ways.

I shall hope, and pray.

I invite you to enter a patient time of reading, a deep listening, so that you, too, might receive this gift of the four traditional gospels—a vibrant, deeply satisfying practice, filled with luminous joy and peace, speaking to your life today, wherever you live, whatever you believe, and offering a wise way to meet the dilemmas you face. Such is the good news!

+ Marc Handley Andrus
Episcopal Bishop of the Diocese of California, USA

PREFACE

Whatever our challenges today—personal, communal, spiritual, or even planetary—we can think of ourselves as being at an immense crossroads. This is a moment that offers enormous possibilities for transformation and at the same time looming obstacles and inherent dangers. At such a juncture, we need clear vision, fresh thinking and wise hearts to help us not only navigate our lives but do so with a sense of equanimity and love. We need treasured guides that have stood the test of centuries, and are also astute enough in the present moment to truly provide worthy counsel for today's crises and tomorrow's unexpected dilemmas.

As Christians, I believe we need our sacred texts to live in a way that helps us to unite our hearts *and* minds—to combine devotion and practice with critical thought and loving-kindness. There are those who believe that in order to achieve such union we need a more "historical" gospel, more closely based on Jesus' original words.

Others ask for a new gospel entirely—one founded on continued revelation in contemporary writing and poetry, possibly including music and other elements. However, I believe that the answer we seek can already be found in the four traditional gospel texts of Matthew, Mark, John and Luke—an answer that requires no change at all, but only a fresh way of understanding.

In this book, you will gain that fresh understanding and see that the four gospels can be used as an extensive spiritual and psychological map. Although this may seem like a strictly modern view, it is actually The Way of Jesus that was followed by our early Christian ancestors.

Since this Way encompass four paths, I have named it *Quadratos*. Although the journey is sequential, cyclical and never-ending, as the seasons of nature are, this is a new poetic word to refer to the ancient, fourfold journey of growth and radical transformation known by all major religions and schools of psychology.

In reading, you will also discover that this pattern is found throughout nature, cultures, and other structures worldwide. Because of its universality, it is my great hope that the Journey of Quadratos will be used as a productive tool by any who wish to find hope and meaning, and a common life together.

When you commence this exploration of Quadratos, you may find it initially challenging to set aside, at least for a short while, what you previously have known about the gospels, so that you might see them anew. Particularly if the words and stories are revered and familiar, learning something unexpected about them may require a degree of effort.

Luke's gospel contains the metaphor of new wine needing a new wineskin. I believe it's fair to say that for many The Four-Gospel Journey will feel similar. Its perspective and language will likely feel like a "new skin" and take time before it becomes comfortable.

Quadratos is not a mere re-working of the Gospel as it has been taught for many, many years. It is a genuine metamorphosis—one I believe to be entirely consistent with early Christianity's view—but nonetheless, far different from Christian thought and interpretation of the last few centuries.

This fourfold journey teaches us that growth often comes from necessity, and its arrival not only yields benefit, but also exacts cost; most often discomfort and adjustment, sometimes severe etc.

Indeed, even my personal journey as an author has been bumpy and I think requires some important clarifications at this juncture. I have been speaking about this topic for well over a decade and the first incarnation of this book, *Beyond the Biography of Jesus Vol. I*, was published in 2006.

Over these many years, I have heard concern from some of my Jewish readers about what they perceive as an unfair characterization of Judaism contained in this account. The pain, covert and overt, that has been inflicted on Jewish people by Christians over many centuries is real. In no way do I wish to add to this pain, so it is imperative that I be clear about the particular historical moment addressed in this book.

PREFACE

Like all people, all religions and all societies go through times of deterioration, which are often—even usually—followed by learning better ways to respond to the myriad pressures of their societal and historical circumstances. This book reveals the deep pattern of Quadratos as evident within the four traditional gospel texts and follows Christianity's journey through the pattern as it gradually emerged from the matrix of first-century CE Judaism.

From all the extensive research I have done, it is clear to me that the great and glorious heart of the Judaic faith that I know well and highly respect is not remotely reflected in the events that took place in the years of the first century CE, through the destruction of the Temple in 70 and the chaotic decades thereafter. In this period, the central and most powerful parts of the Temple—the priests—had become rigid and oppressive, almost cult-like.

They were obsessed with control, demanding obeisance to rigid laws and huge prices for sacrificial animals. They had become a religious bureaucracy. Many of the priests had sold out to the Roman Emperor in attempts to maintain their power and financial gains, and they were tenacious and united against all threats. In the early part of the century, Jesus the Christ was naturally in serious conflict with these Temple authorities, calling them to account for their behavior.

Then, in the aftermath of the loss of the Temple, Judaism was thrown into a maelstrom of conflict and anxiety as it struggled to survive and find a new equilibrium. With all the priests massacred, the Pharisees emerged as the best available leaders and worked tirelessly to hold Judaism together.

Yet, in the last decades of the first century some Pharisees, believing that what was needed in the time of crisis was a purer and unadulterated Judaism, stridently advocated the removal from the synagogues and Jewish life of any who believed the Messiah had already come. At the same time, it was Pharisees like Hillel the Elder (Hillel HaGadol), sage and scholar, whose wisdom led the Jewish faith strongly through this period of great trial, and it is their efforts that birthed the rabbinical movement that holds Judaism firmly to this day.

Therefore, in the early part of the first century CE, Jesus the Christ was in resolute opposition to the Temple authorities, particularly the Priests and

Sadducees. Then in the last decades of the first century, some Pharisees sought to forcefully discriminate against Messianic Jews, which resulted in deeply traumatic impacts as they transitioned into becoming "Christians." It is *these aspects of Judaism* which I discuss and refer to in this book. And we will see these effects clearly in all four gospel texts, and especially in John and Luke.

Were there other helpful and more mystical sects of Judaism at the time? Definitely, there were. But these sects were marginalized, just as Jesus and the followers of Jesus were, and had no real access or input to the Jewish power base. The understandings of Judaism and Jewish scripture described in this book come specifically from this low period immediately before and after the destruction of the Temple. Judaism has long since passed through this period, which was, thankfully, historically brief.

As an important note, Roman Catholicism, my own tradition, has suffered from many "low periods", including the blaming of Jews for Jesus' death, the Spanish Inquisition and the horrific response to the Protestant Reformation. Religions are inspired by God, but human beings are always fallible and sometimes go gravely astray. We pray the missteps are brief, but we must not blink when we examine history, otherwise we will never learn the lessons that those errors hold for our future challenges.

The book begins with three introductory chapters. The first deals with my personal odyssey leading to the discovery of the gospel as a fourfold journey. The second lays out the five keys to understanding this new integrative perspective, and the third holds an overview of the full journey, and each gospel as one of its four paths. Also included in the third chapter is some discussion of the ubiquity and universality of the Quadratos pattern.

Depending on your reason for reading, you may or may not find the information in the early chapters helpful when you begin. Some readers enjoy or need background to appreciate this new view of the gospel. Others wish to simply move forward and experience the journey and may find some of this to be excess information, or information too soon.

PREFACE

Four gospel chapters follow in the sequence of the spiritual journey and of Quadratos: Matthew, Mark, John, then Luke. Each chapter opens with the imagery of a poem rather than jumping straight into linear words. Each of the four gospel texts, which I have designated as one of four paths, is then discussed in terms of its individual role in the transformational journey.

I give the historical background of the gospel and then move through the text from beginning to end. Excerpts are quoted and ancient and contemporary insights provided. Differences between the gospels are noted and explained. Each chapter closes with a prayer, a summary, and spiritual exercises—recommendations for practice that build sequentially from each gospel path to the next.

Following the fourth path—The Gospel of Luke—you will find a separate chapter with eight practices for individuals and communities to consider incorporating into their journey. These are also a "summary" of the behavioral changes provided by the Quadratos Journey. Should you wish to get a preview of where we're headed you can always jump forward to these. Finally, the last chapter gives concluding thoughts for moving forward on the journey.

Some readers will choose to steadily read all the way through the book. However, you may observe that a gospel calls out to you at a particular moment. If it does, pause, reflect, and study that part. Be present with your heart and your mind. Heed your inner voice and allow all those extra pages to wait their turn. There is time.

This book is not an overnight read—rather, it can truly become a journey. I think of it more as a process. And I am pleased to share with you that, over the years since this book first appeared in print, readers have discovered many ways of experiencing this journey and have written to me about them. Here are examples, which I hope will invite your own creativity, and stimulate you as you begin:

- Couples and friends have chosen to read the book aloud to each other, stopping between short sections to reflect, share and pray.

- Some individuals and communities have chosen to associate their reading and reflection with the seasons: Matthew for autumn, Mark for winter, John for spring and Luke for summer.

- For the greatest depth, formation and transformative power, there is the *Heart and Mind Community: Six-in-One Guide*. This process has been in development since 2007, and used with hundreds of small communities worldwide. Read the testimonials on the website.

  The compendium has one guide for each of the four gospel-path chapters, as well as one on preparing for the journey, and another on the eight continuing practices. Designed for use by a community of two or more, the Guides are proving to be of inestimable value for both individual and community transformation.

  For more information or to acquire, see www.quadratos.com/shop/guides/

This Four-Gospel Journey is the core of my Christian faith, because for me it holds an *experience* of a dynamic, living Jesus the Christ and offers the capacity to address the most pressing and recurring questions we face as humans in a way that is pragmatic, inclusive and loving. In Quadratos, Matthew, Mark, John, and Luke are given a framework. They are integrated into one seamless account, and that sequential journey facilitates a process of spiritual, emotional and intellectual transformation. And that enables them to serve both individuals and communities in a way I believe they were intended to do.

Finally, the combined gospels go far beyond the sequential journey they form. Together they are *the* sacred text and contain the deeper message of the Gospel itself, which is the universal, human and eternal message of Love. And this Love can be expressed as: *All Live Within One*, have always done so and will always do so, from the beginning to the end of time, without end. Amen.

PREFACE

No matter how we communicate our sense of God, the core pattern of the journey remains. The Cosmos is One, and also within One. We are One and within One and we inextricably belong to each other, as we do to All.

I believe that as we make this ancient fourfold journey, we each will grow further in an understanding of these new relationships and will begin to inhabit them. Our hearts and minds will unite, and we will truly give birth to the new heaven and earth that we seek.

Could it be just this simple—to see anew and to walk?

Be Safe. Be Well. Walk with Peace, Love and Courage.*

Alexander John Shaia
Santa Fe, New Mexico

Feast of All Saints & All Souls
20th Anniversary of The Four-Gospel Journey
01 November 2020

---

* Bedouin blessing for one who is leaving on a sacred pilgrimage.

Chapter 1
THE STORY OF QUADRATOS

When I was seven years old, racists burned my grandmother's house to the ground. They waited until nightfall so they could slip through the shadows. Then they scoured her house, dug in her closets, opened her wooden chest, stripped the mantels of her beloved mementos, and put everything into a big pile in the living room. All the Catholic artifacts, statues, and family pictures from her tiny home were added to the stack. Placing the crucifixes atop the heap, they poured on kerosene, lit matches, and fled.

Fire engulfed the structure in minutes. Summoned from my bed, I rushed to her house with my family and watched the conflagration, despairing, certain that my grandmother was inside, perishing in agony. We all called her "Sitto," which is Arabic for grandmother, and she was especially beloved to me.

Since she walked with a cane, I was sure there was no way she could have escaped the terrible fire. However, hours later she appeared, having fortuitously been taken to church by a friend that evening. Her restoration to us was joyful, but I will never, ever forget the smell of the charred wood, nor my fear, nor the palpable experience of hate that surrounded me that night. Indelibly imprinted on my seven-year-old heart was the clear understanding that being "outside" meant the risk of pain and terror, and perhaps even the loss of life itself.

Why was Sitto's home burned? Because in that 1950s southern community, all of us in the Shaia family were certainly outsiders. My grandparents had emigrated from Lebanon, and we were Maronite Catholics. At that time, Birmingham, Alabama, was less than one-half of one percent Catholic, and Maronites were a tiny, obscure minority even among those Catholics. I was truly a minority of a minority within an immigrant minority in a city that was, in those days, not kind to minorities.

Step by Step

When it came time to write this book, I felt that the fire of my past was the perfect image for the beginning of this spiritual journey. You may share some of these feelings if you think of the terrible pain of the last unforgiven argument you had with a loved one and then try to imagine it magnified by dozens, by hundreds, and by thousands outward—into your family, your community, your country, and your world.

As simplistic as it sounds, at their core, aren't most of the conflicts in the world unforgiven arguments? The beginnings of change often come from the charred embers of loss or the hard, rocky ground of necessity. Mine did. I vowed to commit myself to: "No more and never again."

To give an example of the kind of transformational spirit for which we are striving, I'd like to tell you about my family's Sunday dinner five days after the fire. We always met on Sundays at Sitto's house—everyone: parents, brothers, aunts, uncles, cousins, the whole extended crowd—and usually we sat around the big, old mahogany table, which was covered for the occasion with embroidered linen and china.

My recollection isn't clear whose house we went to that week, but I do remember that the tables were planks on sawhorses, the chairs were folding metal, and the tablecloths were paper. The grown-ups sat in the middle, the kids around the edges. Sitto, as always, was at the head of the makeshift main table, and when the room hushed, she led us in saying grace.

Afterward, there was silence, and then her eyes, clear and direct above the glasses perched midway down her nose, slowly moved to meet the eyes of every person in the room—even ours, the children. We all waited patiently in the silence. Finally, she spoke. Her voice was soft, and she said only two words, though she repeated them until she was sure we understood and accepted them: "No hate. No hate...." And I felt the burden lift from the heart of my family.

So, despite the intolerance and misunderstanding that pervaded Birmingham in those days, within the circle of my large Semitic family I had a childhood filled with beauty, mystery, and love. "Semitic" describes the culture shared by the settled village people of Israel, Jordan, and Lebanon, as distinguished from the nomadic Bedouin and Arab traditions. Even transplanted to America, our culture had changed little from that lived by my ancestors.

My grandparents, aunts, and uncles were as familiar to me as my parents, and my cousins felt like my brothers and sisters. Family and faith made

ONE—THE STORY OF QUADRATOS

up the cornerstones of our "village." We spent every Sunday together—usually at my grandmother's, as I said—and the rhythms of that day never changed: morning mass, shared breakfast, an elaborately prepared lunch, all followed by an afternoon of leisurely conversations, cards, and sports. At nightfall, each family made its way home, knowing that the next Sunday, and the next and the next, would be the same.

My mother's mother, my "sitto," and my father's father, my "jiddo," were the beacons of my childhood. They were also the heart of our entire family, and they lived until I was in my late twenties. Sitto was the anchor of compassion for us all, and I never heard her speak an unkind word of another human being.

Jiddo, well known in our community, was a peddler and folk healer. Tradition forbade him from healing his own family, but there was a constant stream of friends knocking on his back door. He smelled of the earth and mystery, and though he could neither read nor write, he was certainly the first mystic I knew.

These elders immersed me in the richness of their Middle Eastern heritage, which was in many ways still their primary world. The stories and word pictures painted by Arabic idioms, beautiful words drawn from the language and traditions of centuries, filled our daily life and instilled in me a poetic heart. I learned to be comfortable with ambiguity, for when I requested the English translation of an Arabic phrase, Sitto's patient reply was: "Oh, honey, Arabic is poetry. It won't come out in English."

In my late teens, I left this closeness and entered the University of Notre Dame, intending after graduation to go on to seminary. The shift to that academic environment made me feel as though I had fallen from a high cliff. Nothing made sense to me. I was engulfed by a maze of intellectual and philosophical discourse.

Students stayed up all night talking about whether God was dead. This wasn't even remotely credible. I was part of God. How could God be dead? *I* would be dead. Immense words and theories swirled around me, but no one was cooking spicy Sunday dinner and holding hands in prayer.

My fellow students were good people, even friends. They were smart, knowledgeable, and articulate, but they weren't speaking of the God I knew. The God I understood was founded in poetic mystery, not reason. Worship was an experience I could feel in my body, not an ideology. Confused and lonely, again I felt I was standing outside.

I floundered in this new, complicated environment, and neither my Semitic understandings nor the academic concepts I was studying addressed the challenges I faced. I often went to the Grotto, which sits behind Notre Dame's Basilica and is a replica of Lourdes. It has a bank of a thousand vigil candles flickering with the light of individual hopes.

I would add my own and pray for guidance. For me, it was a place of quiet solace and reflection. Eventually, I switched my major from theology to cultural anthropology with a focus on indigenous peoples and their rites of initiation.

These traditions were closer to my own early culture and I found them beautiful. They also seemed more flexible, more adaptable to change than the Western systems of thought that had seemed so frustrating to me.

The indigenous cultures also described a consistent journey of spirit, even though each people had their own cosmology and stories and their own vocabulary and worldview. In every society, a multistage process was required to make the transition from childhood to adulthood.

The first stage always called for "entering"; it involved ignorance and loneliness. The second always held pitfalls or trickery. The third brought dawning understanding, even ecstasy. The fourth held the final keys to maturation, which were carried back into the community in some way.

Although I wasn't sure why, I found these simple yet arduous steps held an emotional logic that "made sense" to me.

Feeling much more grounded by my anthropology studies, I then found professors at Notre Dame who helped me synthesize the richly embroidered past of my heart with the intellectual abundance of Western Christianity. Henri Nouwen and Morton Kelsey validated my mystical sense of God at a time when many considered such a point of view irrational.

ONE—THE STORY OF QUADRATOS

John S. Dunne opened a bridge for me between Western and Eastern theologies and led me to discover the mysticism in many Western religious perspectives that I had believed empty of it. Joseph Campbell lectured on sacred scripture as a mythic journey, and his words opened new ideas in me that connected with my anthropology studies.

C. G. Jung's writings, which I discovered through my coursework, helped me join the mythic (though unreflective) Semitic and Middle Eastern traditions in which I had been raised with the postmodern western world in which I now lived.

My time at Notre Dame set me on a path of seeking how to balance critical thought with deep feeling, as well as how to bring soaring vision to ordinary and practical life. Then, in my senior year I took a class on liturgy from Mark Searle and learned about the ancient four-gospel reading cycle that had been rediscovered by the scholars of the church and just restored to use in Sunday worship.

I was so taken by the idea that the early church had had a beautiful and systematic design for *all four gospels* that I determined to pray them that way myself on a weekly basis. And I have done so from that day forward.

After my graduation from Notre Dame, full of confidence—and following a custom in existence for every Alexander in my family (save three) since the year 1300—I entered seminary to become a priest. But this long-anticipated plan did not work at all. The church was my spiritual home, yet seminary failed to nurture my spirit as I had expected.

I sought expansiveness and joy; instead I found a narrow and lifeless training that lacked the deep resonance of centuries. However, priesthood was the rock on which I had invested the entire vision of my future life—not to mention all the expectations of my huge extended family. I felt there was no way I could turn my back on it or them. Not only would I would be shamed and bereft, but I would have to start over again and somehow rediscover a way to accomplish the things that mattered to me.

Although that seemed a prodigious task, I anxiously hoped that a larger life awaited me outside those walls. So, after much prayer and soul-searching, I left and began a new journey. As I drove away in grief for the loss of my dreams, I stopped, turned back, and remembered Sitto's little house in flames. I thought, "This time, my own home is burning, but *I* set the fire." Then I faced forward again and settled in for my long drive.

I soon found a position on the staff of a Catholic parish. At that time, the Roman Church was in the midst of dramatic changes. Among those changes was restoration of the ancient rite of Christian baptism, a much more extensive and lengthy process than the simple pouring of water. I was asked to help implement this change, and my parish duties became focused on this practice and the spiritual renewal it promised.

My anthropology studies allowed me to immediately see its profound links to other wisdom traditions I had studied. This high Catholic ritual was a fourfold rite of initiation and maturation! Here, in Western language and culture, was the same grace, deep truth and power that I had found when I studied the practices of indigenous peoples.

The Roman Catholic Church has ornate names for the four steps of the full baptism process: inquiry, catechumenate, purification-enlightenment, and mystagogia. But these complicated words defined the same basic stages I had seen so often in indigenous cultures.

The candidate for baptism enters the process, goes through a time of prayer and study to achieve spiritual/personal growth, gains illumination or understanding, and then deepens the understanding and carries it back to the community in some way. Whether people underwent the ritual in the lengthy manner of ancient times or in the shorter version we were restoring, it was clear that, precisely as in native cultures, a journey of radical transformation was what was happening.

In the United States, the Roman church began to teach all dioceses how to reincorporate the ancient baptism process. I was appointed a teacher of the rite and spent a decade facilitating this renewal all across North America. As I did so, I became more and more convinced of the ritual's wisdom and broad efficacy. I even wished its stages could somehow be incorporated into "regular," ongoing church life, not just baptism.

I began to wonder if the four-stage, or four-step, or four-path structure itself, which I had found in such diverse cultures, might be significant, and perhaps hold its own truth.

Then, ten years after I graduated from Notre Dame, I entered a doctoral program in clinical psychology. I was still trying to meld critical thought and deep feeling—more specifically, to meld my spiritual inclinations with what I had learned about human behavior. I had two fortuitous occurrences.

First, in my clinical studies I was immersed in new discoveries on trauma, learning how trauma impacts our bodies, our emotions and our critical thinking. Indeed, when I studied the literature on healing from trauma, I encountered a four-step therapeutic process that moved the client from an initial "frozen" state through wide swings in emotion/thought to an equilibrium and finally to a balance that incorporated awareness and use of the entire cycle into everyday life.

Second, I met and trained with Dora Kalff, a Swiss Jungian analyst, devout Christian, and practitioner of Tibetan Buddhist meditation. She had combined a therapeutic technique known as "Sandtray" with the principles of Jungian psychology and the meditational practices of Tibetan Buddhism.

Frau Kalff called her synthesis "Sandplay." In Sandplay, a therapeutic client creates a scene or picture in a tray of sand by shaping the sand and (or) placing figures and objects in it. Over the course of making a series of these scenes, the client reveals a personal narrative that unfolds on a level beneath conscious awareness. Healing comes through the subconscious process of creating and "telling" the story using visual and three-dimensional imagery.

When I began my clinical practice, I chose to use Sandplay as a primary therapeutic method for my work with trauma patients. And I became a senior practitioner and certified teaching member of the International Society for Sandplay Therapy. I consulted on myriad cases throughout North America, as well as Europe and Asia.

Over and over, I saw an identical fourfold pattern sequentially disclosing itself. Sandplay psychotherapists often identify one of the earliest scenes made by clients as a "Numinous Tray"—one that holds images indicating their intent to submit to an inner journey. This tray is followed by a series of scenes describing increasing tension, polarization and conflict. In the third phase, a scene will appear that is called a "Self Tray," which reflects an experience of union. Eventually, a series of trays will show a return to everyday life, but with a larger sense of consciousness that includes obligations beyond those of the personal self.

As a practitioner and consultant, I have seen hundreds upon hundreds of Numinous Trays and Self Trays and the trays that followed them. It didn't matter if the clients were children or women or men. It didn't matter if the figures they chose were icons from current culture, mythical figures, or phantasmagorical creatures, nor did it matter if twigs or seashells or bright, glittery stones surrounded them.

In every single instance, the outer story told by the images matched the inner story experienced by the client, and the pattern was invariably fourfold and sequential. This happened with or without the conscious intention, or even awareness, of the individual. To me, the conclusion seemed inescapable. Here was the same journey I had seen before, containing the same four paths—this time in the practice of psychology, and in a totally contemporary and cross-cultural setting.

Wondering further about the pattern I seemed to be encountering everywhere, I began investigating spiritual writings. In *The Different Drum: Community Making and Peace*, psychiatrist M. Scott Peck describes four stages of community formation: pseudo-community, chaos, emptiness, and, finally, genuine community. Then I read *Original Blessing*, by theologian Matthew Fox. *Original Blessing* announces four paths of religious progression, which Fox names Via Positiva, Via Negativa, Via Creativa, and Via Transformativa.

Next, I turned back to the classics of Western spirituality, and found the same sequence in Ignatius of Loyola's Spiritual Exercises and Teresa of Avila's *The Interior Castle*—although she made more divisions, breaking the pattern into seven parts or castles, rather than four.

In like fashion, author Lauren Artress in *Walking a Sacred Journey*, describes the labyrinth as a walking meditation that reflects the same pattern although its sequence may be broken into either four or seven sections.

At this point, I considered the faiths themselves, particularly the Jewish roots of Christianity, and remembered that the Passover celebration ritually recounted a four-part tale of Judaism's liberation: being freed from slavery in Egypt, wandering in the wilderness, arriving in the Promised Land, and finally creating a fruitful home there.

Then, looking beyond Christianity, though the vocabulary is quite different, I discovered the same journey in the Four Noble Truths of Buddhism (Impermanence, Suffering, Non-Attachment and the Eightfold Way of Right Relationship), the inner sequence of Hinduism's epic accounts of Shiva, Parvati and Ganesha, the mystical Sufi teachings and worldwide anthropological descriptions of a shaman's training and initiation.

I also learned that storytellers identify four parts in the great myths and epics of ancient literature—parts named by Joseph Campbell—as hearing the summons, enduring the obstacles, receiving the boon, and returning to community. At that point, I became virtually certain for myself that this fourfold inner pilgrimage is a universal truth whose imprint can be found across time, geography, culture and religious tradition. Every single pattern asks the journeyer to begin and start some form of inquiry.

Next comes a time of trial, often involving pitfalls and sometimes trickery, but always bringing new and hard-won understanding. The gift of enlarged comprehension, wholeness, and greater perspective is third, sometimes coming suddenly, often with the sense of outside assistance. The fourth step requires actual practice of the wisdom gained, with some component of bringing that knowledge back to the community or to those who come after the journeyer.

Epiphany

I continued to practice and teach, still on my own spiritual journey, never dreaming that what I was observing and learning would become this book. Then suddenly, a decade later, in the year 2000, on a cold, star-filled night in northern New Mexico, my entire world changed.

I was on sabbatical and had chosen New Mexico as an appropriately peaceful place to study and meditate. On the night of November 1, in the midst of the Christian Feasts of All Saints and All Souls, I found myself reading *The Four Witnesses*, a just-released book authored by Robin Griffith-Jones, an Anglican priest and Oxford University scholar.

It was through Jones' book that I learned how deeply and empathetically the Gospels of Matthew, Mark, John, and Luke had been directed to specific communities of early Christians. I read the story of each long-ago audience, noting their distinct historical, geographical, and cultural differences. Each community had wrestled with a unique and critical spiritual question.

As I read, I felt a rising sense of familiarity. I *knew* these questions. In fact, I knew them very well. The fourfold spiritual journey appeared in my mind. I saw the procession of indigenous peoples growing into their communal lives. I saw initiates moving into the mature practice of their various faiths. I saw troubled men, women, and children shifting objects in sand as they worked through trauma.

Invariably, each person moved through four paths, and each path mirrored one of the emotional and spiritual challenges faced by a specific early Christian community to whom one of the four texts responded. Suddenly, my enjoyment of the still night on the high plateau disappeared. My thoughts became a frenzy of swirling progressions. The pattern of four seemed to be everywhere. It was clear—and amazing.

I grabbed my Bible, turned first to The Gospel of Matthew, and started to read. I read for most of the night, the passages illuminated by my new perspective. The familiar words—the import of the texts—that I had read hundreds of times before—were transformed before my tired eyes.

Suddenly, I realized that each gospel was organized around a different metaphorical landscape. Matthew, writing after the Great Temple of Jerusalem had fallen, uses the metaphors of mountain and rock and stone. Mark, directing his gospel to Christians under the sentence of death, uses the metaphor of wilderness and Jewish historical equivalents for wilderness—deserts and bodies of water.

John's gospel, likely written as a meditation on Christian baptism, uses the metaphor of garden, often explicitly, the Garden of Eden. The

ONE—THE STORY OF QUADRATOS

Gospel of Luke, written to maturing Christian communities throughout the Mediterranean, has a core metaphor that is less apparent—the road: everything in Luke happens travelling *between* places.

As I read, I realized that even the writing style of each author seemed to synchronize with the message held by that particular gospel. The Gospel of Matthew is a bit flowery and has a lot of reassuring adjectives. Mark has absolutely no extra words at all: it is short, almost hard, and completely to the point. John is glorious metaphysical poetry, while Luke is practical, matter-of-fact, almost chatty. These discoveries awed and excited me. But a deeper revelation was still to come.

I thought of the many times I had puzzled over the ancient Sunday reading cycle. I had prayed the cycle for many years; I found it deeply meaningful and loved it profoundly. But I had often asked, *Why* was it read Matthew, then Mark, then John (during Lent and Easter), then Luke?

I always thought there must have been some good reason, yet no one had ever been able to give me one, and though I had searched, I had never found any explanation. Now my old questions kept intruding: Who had created it originally, and why? Did that sequence hold some special truth? My already overloaded brain added these further queries to the cerebral stew.

For a long time afterward, I thought of what happened next as my "discovery." I now realize that, in fact, I discovered nothing. Rather it was as if a deeper wisdom of the gospels found *me*. All of my upbringing and prayer and education and life experience had been preparation for the moment that came that night under the limitless stars.

To me it seemed as though thunder sounded and a door flew open, though there wasn't a cloud in sight. I believe I know how Archimedes felt when he discovered the displacement of water and shouted, "Eureka!"

Suddenly, I comprehended the original reading cycle in a completely new way. I trembled in the dark as I saw revealed the landscapes of faith, the ancient journey that our early mothers and fathers had walked—but which had been long forgotten. I saw the four texts as Christianity's great teaching of the universal journey.

Four early communities wrestled with *four* distinct sets of challenges when faced with *four* distinct sets of historical circumstances that prompted *four* deep questions requiring answers. There are *four* universal paths to spiritual maturity. There are *four* levels of healing needed after trauma in order to recover psychological balance. Early Christians commonly placed the *four* texts into a specific sequence and read them that way in most communities until the seventh century.

Without psychology, without all the self-knowledge we have gained in the last two millennia, clearly inspired by a much greater wisdom, the early fathers and mothers of Christianity managed to grasp and set out the universal progression in a clear and workable fashion.

The four individual texts, set in their ancient sequence, disclose what we can now know and celebrate as one seamless Gospel—the full internal/eternal journey, the great and immutable design, the heart and mind of God that moves all creation.

And oh, yes! They were so clearly the same four paths that had led me to this extraordinary moment. On that November night, as I reviewed the history of the early Christians, I also retraced my own. I realized that the deep counsel of Matthew's gospel had first reached me in college. So many customs, expectations, and beliefs had gone with me to Notre Dame.

That matriculation was the repository of unreal hopes—mine and the frozen dreams of the entire extended Shaia family. And just as surely as the Great Temple of Jerusalem, that repository crumbled when confronted with the powerful forces of my real life. Using my new perspective, I could see that the first path of my spiritual journey was strewn with the boulders of disappointment and confusion.

I realized that my departure from Matthew's text and my entrance into the bleak despair of the second path of Mark had been precipitated by the decision I had made to leave seminary and not enter the priesthood. The following years I was in the wilderness and desert of hard learning—wandering from one experience to another, staying in prayer, trying to turn each new effort into a sincere time of humility and obedience to spirit. Mostly, it was my hope that I would find a place with enough resonance and meaning to hold me. I searched for purpose while I prayed.

ONE—THE STORY OF QUADRATOS

Epiphany finally arrived in that wonderful instant when I comprehended a deeper purpose in the four texts and the reading cycle. The sonorous poetry of John's gospel echoed in my ears and coursed in my blood, raced through the bones and muscles of my body, filling my soul as I experienced the deepest joy imaginable.

After that night, I spent a long while resting in the wonderful complexities of this glorious garden, allowing my heart and my mind and all of myself to be immersed in the new truth.

Since then, that November moment in 2000, and after my immersion time, I have been walking, most of the time, on Luke's road in the fourth path. I have been learning more about my own growing maturity, and taking the message of the ancient gospel journey into larger reality.

I coined the word *Quadratos* to provide a concise and intuitive way to express an understanding of the fourfold process. My own comprehension of the Gospel as the Journey of Quadratos grows daily. Through my studies, my practice, and my own life, I have come to realize and appreciate with gratitude how solidly this map of the journey has been there for us, all this time, for us and leading us.

Now, in these tumultuous days, it is my ardent hope that you, too, may find your heart and mind and life deeply renewed—even radically transformed—by an ever-growing awareness of the Gospel as the Journey of Quadratos; and may you also find a commitment to its fresh and continual practice.

Chapter 2
THE KEYS

Our world is changing. It is slowly moving away from many years—at least a thousand—of being primarily focused on rationalism and science. Science has given us extraordinary progress in many areas, including our brains. However, room is now being made once again for the other parts of life and other ways of thinking—for music and art, for emotion and spirit.

Nonrational ways of receiving information and for integrating that information into life are beginning to be acknowledged, even in academic and scientific venues. This is an immense shift that affects every aspect of all cultures, including religion. So, quite naturally everyone feels varying degrees of discomfort, anxiety, and at times, very intense conflict. These symptoms can deeply affect Christianity and Christians as well.

My heart and my head ache as I listen to what often feel like endless arguments that are couched in the language of "let me tell you about the *true* Jesus." I understand the frustrations and grief that fill this long moment of moving between eras.

Yet it seems to me that such a moment asks us to explore new ways of describing our eternal truths—integrative ways that reflect both heart and mind. This is, after all, the glorious entirety of awareness to which the last two millennia have brought us.

When we join the advancements of our rational minds with the deepening experience of our hearts, we have the gift of an enlarged human consciousness and perspectives that are vastly more expansive and deepened. And if we are able to apply such expansive perspectives to the gospels, I believe we gain a new comprehension that replenishes us in the same way that hushed awe fills us when we see images of our indescribably vast cosmos.

To reach toward this kind of enlivening experience, it is first indispensable to expand our method of decision-making. When we move into the present millennium, integrating the rational and non-rational ways of thinking into our business and our lives, it helps us to achieve greater balance.

The limited, more reductionist way of thought that has predominated in so many thought systems for the last several centuries—a belief that truth will become known if we just break everything down into separate elements and study them and arrive at little truths and then extrapolate to the whole—simply does not serve us adequately today. This way of thinking successfully constructs automobiles and airplanes, but isn't effective for learning about God, or people, or any complex problem for that matter.

Deep and heart-filled work is complicated. We need our whole selves for that work—emotion, intuition, body and soul, together *with* our rationality. We also must search for far more than bits of data. The needs of our lives and our planet require that we seek out universal and integrative patterns—ones that have proven consistent in many areas—and that we do so in an interdisciplinary fashion without clinging to traditional boundaries.

This was precisely the kind of search I was led to make for much of my early life, and though the answer I received on that cold November night in New Mexico was not one I could ever have imagined, I can see now that it proceeded directly from the nature of the quest. I further believe that the pattern I eventually named the Journey of Quadratos is also true to this same way of thinking and problem-solving, this necessary "rejoining" of heart and mind.

And as I have continued to work with it and see its results, I also believe that it holds the potential to move the gospel beyond the quarrels and internecine divisions—particularly about language and meaning—that have become focused so strenuously upon it. Quadratos can provide a framework that accommodates, integrates and welcomes a wide and lively diversity within Christianity.

Today I speak about this new perspective as often as I am able. It has already begun to create change in parts of the United States, Canada, the U.K., Europe, South Africa, Australia and New Zealand. It has also begun to create change among everyday Christians, communities, spiritual directors and even in clergy formation across diverse denominations.

I am excited and hopeful about it as a perspective to be tried, chewed over, discussed and further researched by scholars of varying disciplines, so that together we may discover if this is really the substantial gift of Spirit to our time that I suspect it to be.

Unlocking The Four-Gospel Journey

One of the things that laid the ground for my epiphany—the "aha!" moment when everything "clicked" into place—was my many years of study in theology, psychology, anthropology and science. These studies had prepared my heart and mind well. Yet questions remained. How had the various elements come together through history to create what I was able to see today as a complete journey? Since that life-changing moment, mine has been a patient period of exploration and study, working backwards through time to as accurately as possible, discover and name the core elements and to correctly situate them in Christian thought.

There are five principal elements—*keys*—that together led to the formation of the gospel sequence and a full understanding of them unlock its perspective for our use. They are

I. The great name, Jesus the Christ;
II. The evangelist Paul, and the particular way in which he was an eyewitness;
III. The historical dilemmas of four early Christian communities;
IV. Early Christians' self-identification and practice as Followers of The Way; and
V. The choice of these particular four gospels and their sequencing into a Three-Year Sunday Reading Cycle.

Let us look at each of these as we progress through this ancient puzzle that these keys unlock.

Key I
The Great Name–Jesus The Christ

This first "key" was once a cornerstone of early Christian belief that has over the centuries been tragically left by the wayside. Today, in much of Christian conversation there seems to be an underlying assumption that Jesus was born, lived, died, was resurrected—and then somehow *diedagain*.

There is an overwhelming emphasis on the crucifixion and on "Jesus died for our sins." These beliefs tend to treat Jesus as though he is more dead than resurrected. But for Christians, our fundamental witness is that Jesus the Christ *lives*. Early Christians never made this mistake, in part because they never used only the name Jesus. They regularly used the full sacred name **Jesus the Christ** (or its abbreviation Christ Jesus), and they lived the truth of this name in their spiritual practices.

The apostle Paul is the earliest known Christian writer. In about 45 to 60 CE, Paul wrote extensively and translated many concepts from their original Aramaic (spoken in Palestine) into Greek, the language of commerce most widely understood in the Mediterranean region. It is generally believed that Paul's writings predate the first of the four traditional gospels by at least five years.

When he wrote, Paul chose the Greek word "Christos," which meant "the anointed one," to replace the Aramaic word "Messiah," which had a corresponding definition. Paul genuinely understood the full import of Jesus' life, death *and* resurrection. He knew the names "Messiah" and "Christos" were both inadequate—*no* words could express the full truth of the divine.

Although the meaning of "Christos" was important and would carry a strong part of Hebrew history forward, Paul knew Jewish theology very well. He fully understood the Hebrew concept of naming God as "I AM"—a reality both within and outside of time. He knew he had to do still more in order to faithfully transmit a more complete understanding of Jesus' message.

Therefore, Paul tried to build greater comprehension through everything he wrote that expanded the perception of "the anointed one." He knew he had the responsibility to carry the greatest of messages, not just to his fellow Jews, but to all people. Paul's example and precepts had, I believe, a radical influence on the development of Christianity, and as a result on gospel writing in general and on all four of the gospel writers, although we will see his direct impact most powerfully in The Gospel of John.

In 1 Corinthians, thought by some scholars to be the only letter solely composed by the apostle himself, Paul made it clear that he knew the Christ as preexisting the world. He wrote, "Yet for us there is one God, the Father, from whom are all things and for whom we exist, and one Lord, Jesus Christ, *through whom are all things* and through whom we exist" (1 Cor. 8:6). Also, that the Christ was "the spiritual rock" from which the Hebrews drank in the desert (1 Cor. 10:4). Other letters say that Moses "suffered abuse for the Christ" (Heb. 11:26).

And in Colossians we find written that **"[the Christ] is the image of the invisible God, the firstborn of all creation; for in [the Christ] all things in heaven and on earth are created, things visible and invisible, whether thrones or dominions or ruler or powers— all things are created through [the Christ] and for [the Christ]. [The Christ] is before all things, and in [the Christ] all things hold together." (Col. 1:15–17)**

These and many other of Paul's writings make it clear that he understood the Christ as an overarching, eternal, holy power without individual characteristics of any kind, existing in all dimensions, simultaneously within time and completely outside of time. For example, the Christ was present with Moses long before Jesus' physical arrival on earth. Paul knew and wrote of the Christ as an *eternal reality*, and he comprehended Jesus as an individuated embodiment of that reality.

Although Paul had frequent disagreements with Peter and the other apostles, who initially saw things in a more limited way, eventually Paul's views prevailed. By the time the four gospels were written, and throughout the early centuries of Christianity, the formal name used by all believers was the full three words long: Jesus the Christ.

If anyone were to have used a shortened version, it would still have held the unlimited and immutable reality of the full name. The power of Paul's persuasion is undeniably clear, because the new religion ultimately derived its name from the sacred title he devised, becoming "Christian," instead of what might have been more likely—Jesusian.

The deep understanding with which Paul imbued this prodigious name is a significant factor in the revolutionary story form of the "gospel." By the time the first gospel was orally composed during those horrendous days in Rome when being a Christian was a certain death sentence, Mark was really not telling the biography of Jesus at all.

In fact, Mark was recounting Jesus the Christ as a living, present-moment reality to his community, as the great name in effect *mandated* he do—even though it was some thirty years after Jesus' death and resurrection. And so were the gospel writers who came after Mark.

In general, scripture scholars for the past few centuries have failed to note the fact that readers in those early days knew and accepted and acknowledged the resurrection without hesitation. Therefore, the great name Jesus *the* Christ automatically meant the gospel accounts in these communities were heard (or chanted or read) as present- moment realities happening in their midst and not primarily historical recitations.

Key II
Paul's Eternal Witness

Another element in the composition of these four gospel texts is that each text intertwines two forms of eyewitness; Paul's sense of the "present moment" with accounts formed from historical remembrances. We might well call a gospel text the holy embrace of Peter the historical eyewitness with that of Paul the eternal eyewitness.

It is an important corrective to the search for a more pure historical Jesus to recall that Paul—the most effective evangelist of the first century—never saw the historical Jesus. Paul had a personal inner experience of Jesus the Christ that transformed his life.

It is precisely this experience outside of time or location that aids Paul in being *the* great evangelist. Paul's proclamation is that anyone may have a direct experience of Jesus the Christ because the Christ is, quite simply, not located in any particular place or historical moment.

Paul moves this new tradition forward by always focusing on a present-moment reality. And this reality is open to all people, beyond any tribe and across all time and space. Paul literally preached a message of Jesus the Christ "here" and "now."

I believe that Paul's impact is the most significant unrecognized factor in gospel interpretation. If we recognize Paul's contribution and give it its proper importance, it follows why each of the four chosen gospels were the ones composed in those Christian communities where Paul lived and taught for a considerable period of time.

Paul's preaching of Jesus the Christ as a living here and now reality set the standard for Christian scripture. It became an additional change agent that required a gospel to be far more than a recitation of sacred history.

Honoring this key of here and now, the gospel stories I retell in this book are placed in present tense. Quoted scripture, however, has not been altered. Note your experience in reading Jesus' words and actions as a present-moment reality.

Key III
Four Historical Dilemmas
& The Gospel of Here and Now

The next element is of enormous significance, and it provides the reasons why these specific gospels, with their specific "discrepancies," were composed. The major differences or discrepancies between the four gospels have been a matter that has puzzled Christians for a long, long time.

For example, careful readers know that the story of Jesus' birth varies dramatically in each account, and even disappears entirely in the Gospel of Mark. The arrest, trial, crucifixion, and resurrection accounts are equally disparate, as are many other details. Each gospel uses very different language, selectively highlights parts of Jesus' life and teachings, and employs a distinct metaphorical "landscape."

The traditional belief has been that the gospels represent four stories of the birth, life, death and resurrection of Jesus the Christ, and that furthermore, since the gospels were all written well after the fact, these discrepancies are nothing more than to-be-expected variations between eyewitnesses. This argument has been largely accepted for generations because it appeals to our hearts, and we can acknowledge it because we have a deeply felt sense of truth in these texts that goes beyond pure logic.

In the face of more recent scholarship, however, this view falters. In the last several decades, scholars using archaeological and linguistic evidence have posited three other theories: claiming that the traditional texts are inaccurate historical documents to begin with; or they are biased and inaccurate documents developed by competing factions as Christianity grew; or the texts are so corrupted by apocrypha and mistranslation as to be meaningless. And any acceptance of these theories would remove the gospels from a useful role as either historical or faith documents.

Yet, all of these beliefs are essential contributions to the religious conversation. The limitation of all of them, with respect to our core issues of concern, is that none of them is sufficient to resolve our uncertainty about gospel controversies, our need for awe, or our spiritual need for meaning.

While they may not completely defeat the gospels, neither do they bring the gospel words—or the words of any other early writings—into manifest reality in our daily lives, emotionally, intellectually, and spiritually.

The Four-Gospel Journey, in contrast, offers a starkly different answer— one that speaks to both head and heart. This view began with the work of scholars who pointed to some of the differences in the texts deriving, in part, from the historical realities of the communities to which they were addressed.

However, Quadratos moves further, analyzing the specific discrepancies and understanding them as not only correct, but precise, purposeful and useful. They issue from the way each gospel was composed.

In the hundred years after Jesus' death, each of the four traditional gospels was written during unique historical circumstances for a specific group of early Christians in a distinct geographical location. In each case, the writer reframed the core story of Jesus' life, death, and resurrection, emphasizing and even altering its elements to give that particular gospel clear relevance and *guidance* for the singular historical realities and dilemmas of its audience.

For example, Mark was the first gospel composed. It combined elements originating from the apostle Paul's writings with stories of Jesus and shared by groups of desperate Messianic Jews condemned to death by Emperor Nero in first-century Rome.

Those courageous believers would meet as they could in homes or cells and try to allay each other's fears and bolster their slim hopes through the ancient tradition of storytelling. As they did, their extreme emotional realities—their agony and their ecstasy—became folded into their recounting of the life and inspiration of a living Jesus the Christ.

This way of storytelling combined present-moment realities with prophetic and practical lessons. The accounts were instructive, interesting—even exciting, and completely distinct from Greco-Roman prose and other religions' ways of storytelling. This new form of narrative, which became known as a gospel (meaning "good news"), profoundly helped the desperate community experience the Christ's continuing and living presence in their struggles.

Mark then put this form into writing; he made the gospel form official. His written story of Jesus the Christ was different from a lecture or a formal sermon. Just as the oral form had done, Mark's words enabled people to see themselves in the accounts that were written down.

When the stories were read aloud or chanted as prayer, which was their usual use in those early times, people listening could understand that Jesus was not simply an historical figure, but was an ongoing experience within each person, a doorway to the lessons, compassion, strength and sense of purpose they needed to maintain their faith. This gospel form quickly found a home in Messianic hearts and took root.

When Mark chose language and metaphors to hearten the Messianic Jews in Rome, and later when Matthew, and Luke and then John followed Mark's pattern and shaped many of the "facts" of the story so that their account would be meaningful to their audience, they did not betray the truth of the message of Jesus the Christ.

On the contrary. When they mixed the historical Jesus with the dilemma of the community, they formed a vehicle for a living participation with the Christ. The changes, and specifically the "discrepancies," made it possible for a particular early Christian community to live their daily lives with the sure knowledge and experience that God was with them in their time of trial.

Throughout this book, I will refer to Matthew, Mark, John, and Luke as though they *personally* wrote down every word of the gospels that bear their names. Actually, many scholars now think it more likely that the gospels began as an oral tradition, and that each "author" represents words originally developed and taught aloud for many years.

In the case of each gospel, sometime during the first century CE someone, (or maybe a group with full inspiration and deep compassion) crafted an entire body of teachings into a written document that was specifically refined to meet the needs of a particular community at a particular point in history. Perhaps this was indeed the "author." But maybe it was a scribe, or even a group of students.

In early tradition, the Greek word *kata*, "according to," was attached to each of the four gospels. It may have signified a kind of warranty that the gospels were "according to" the named author (regardless of who actually recorded the words) and thus the material in them was faithful to his accounts; alternatively, it may have meant that the author actually transcribed the account himself.

Key IV
The Way: A Fourfold Journey of Transformation

Early believers in Jesus the Christ called themselves Followers of The Way. We have tended to understand this identification as generic: simply people who followed Jesus. But I suggest something entirely different. I suggest that they knew that a Christian life was not a static reality; it was rather, a process continually unfolding before them as they walked their truth.

I further posit that the Followers of The Way were guided by a clearly understood journey that, while not precise, was laid out in an ever-repeating cycle of four steps, or paths. While the evidence for these benefits comes in part from my background in anthropology and in part from much intuitive logic as opposed to a trail of written documents, I believe it is nonetheless clear.

The explanation for its beginnings comes from Christianity's deep Jewish roots. My anthropological studies tell me that indigenous cultures worldwide have consistently had fourfold maturation rituals. So, first of all it is likely that the tribal predecessors of Judaic culture provided the structural underpinning for subsequent, more sophisticated Jewish practices.

Both Jewish and Christian scholars have made significant discoveries about the way the ritual of Passover was celebrated in first-century Jewish life—including Jesus' lifetime—and until the destruction of the Temple in 70 CE. Many people today assume that the lengthy Passover ritual as described in the Haggadah has "always been that way."

But it hasn't. The Haggadah was not written down until many years after the Great Temple was destroyed. Prior to that, the Passover celebration was a more informal home event with ritual words passed down for centuries from person to person. Over the two centuries before Jesus, the celebration had taken on quite a bit of Greek Socratic (Hellenistic) influence, which suited Jewish social tradition quite nicely, so what had begun as the recitation of a story had morphed into almost a question and response ritual.

On the morning of Preparation Day for the celebration, the head of the household took a lamb to the Temple for slaughter. Then, he would bring the meat home so that it, together with the other prescribed ritual foodstuffs, could be properly prepared. Eventually, when it was time for the meal, those gathered would be called to table for a joyous repast.

But the feast included an important ritual. Someone at table would query those gathered, following an informal script that revolved around four questions that not only told the great Story of Exodus, but also applied it to the participants' present lives.

So, we might imagine: "This is the story of our slavery, and today we are enslaved…" "We wandered for forty years in the arid desert, and today we find that we are wandering, unable to make a decision …" "But at *last* we arrived in the Promised Land, and we're planning … this year, God-willing." Followed by, "Since then we have been committed to making ourselves and our people thrive in God's promise of this Land—and look around this table and see the kernel of the community that needs our love, every day."

From this deep annual ritual and the understandings flowing from it, we can well imagine how this core metaphor became a spiritual springboard for *every* Hebrew's journey with God—a journey of freedom and liberation, one with four sequential paths that continually repeated in the lives of every individual and in the life of the community.

So there is the key—and it is a far-reaching link, indeed. The explanation for early Christians' natural comfort with being Followers of The Way was specifically and profoundly rooted in their Jewish traditions and, almost certainly, the principal of four-ness, found in ancient rituals from prehistory. The sequence was well-known to them, and the road well-marked.

Yet, as Christians did in so many other ways, they expanded the journey from that of their mother tradition, pushing beyond a focus on tribe and bloodline. Christians took their strong, familiar framework of family and community relationships and of freedom and melded to it an identifiable, cyclical *inner* journey of transformation available to everyone, incorporating the living reality of Jesus the Christ.

Soon, The Way came to be understood by early Christians as an ongoing gradual process of maturation into an image of the eternal Christ in whom they believed they were already made. Within just a few years of Jesus' death and resurrection, understandings of the journey were seen in practices incorporated into Christian symbols and rituals.

The cross began to be drawn with four equidistant points instead the three-pointed shape onto which Jesus was nailed. By the early second century, Sunday worship was regularly conducted in four parts: gathering together, chanting scripture, breaking bread and sending forth.

Most significantly, baptism (the initiation ritual for becoming a Christian) became a four-step process, equipping new members for their like journey with Jesus the Christ. In these early centuries, an individual emerged from the waters, a deep pool in the shape of a four-pointed equidistant cross, to hear the entire assembly cry out their name followed either by "a Christ" or "in Christ."

Imagine what that felt like—coming up from near-drowning—to hear everyone assembled calling your name: "Rachel, a Christ!" "Michael, in Christ!" It must have been an extraordinary experience. Christians were certain that the Christ lives—and lives in them.

As time passed, The Way—the on-going, fourfold journey of living with Jesus the Christ—gradually came to have formal names. Within two centuries the word "sanctification" was sometimes being used. Or—as a process of transformation into an actual part of Christ—the process was called "divinization" or "deification."

Finally, the word "theosis" often came to be used for both cases, and was especially used in Eastern Christianity to refer to a process of spiritual transformation. Today, the word "theosis" is being recaptured as a meaningful shorthand that refers to a gradual and ongoing spiritual journey to be ever more one with God/the Christ.

Key V
The Four-Gospel Journey & Sunday Reading Cycle

In 315 CE, Emperor Constantine legalized Christianity. As Roman oppression lifted, communication became easier among various Christian communities and Christians realized that wide differences in belief existed between them. Theological arguments erupted. Over the fourth century, various councils were held, beliefs were standardized, and practices were developed, refined, and formalized. Gospels were one of the many things systematized. At the time, there were at least fifty texts called a gospel!

A number of historians have suggested that sexism, power, and privilege had a great hand in the winnowing to four texts. And of course all of these could have been factors. Nonetheless, one question remains a puzzlement: why were multiple gospels selected? If the point was to tell the story of Jesus' life, death, and resurrection, one account would be sufficient to accomplish that purpose.

Or, if more than one account was desired for some reason, one would think they should substantially agree with each other. However, four texts—Matthew, Mark, John, and Luke—were affirmed as "true" gospels, and they have significant discrepancies. Why were four accounts chosen, and why these four? There are no known written documents that definitively answer these questions, but there are some significant clues.

We do know that Irenaeus, the bishop of Lugdonum (Lyon, in today's France), attached divine and universal significance to the number four. In 180 CE, he pronounced, "The Gospels could not possibly be either more or less in number than they are. Since there are four zones of the world in which we live, and four principal winds … it is clear that the Word … gave us the gospel, fourfold in form but held together by one Spirit."

Also, the four texts together were entitled *Euaggelion*, which means "the good news of the kingdom." Furthermore, Eusebius, bishop of Caesarea and a church historian, labeled Matthew, Mark, John, and Luke "the holy quaternion of the gospel" (singular) in about 300 CE.

Most importantly, in those early centuries, as Christian evangelists walked from village to village, it seemed that these four gospels (of all the accounts then available) were the ones most often shared to open new hearts and minds. Believers chose to pray and pass these words on to others. The early communities appear to have found a power in these four gospels that was not present in the other texts.

It is my belief that the efficacy of these particular gospels in the transformation of people's lives, transmitted using the vitality of the oral 'here and now' gospel form, went hand-in-hand with the rapid and powerful spread of a new way of living called the Christian faith.

Subsequent to the various councils, five lectionaries (books of mandatory Sunday readings) were adopted—one in each region of Christendom. While each region had variations in the chosen text from Sunday to Sunday, the five were broadly consistent.

From the fourth through the seventh centuries, in Sunday services throughout the Christian world, all four gospels were chanted or read aloud in a similar progression over a three-year cycle. This also maintained a Judaic custom called the Palestinian Cycle that called for chanting the entire Torah over three years of Shabbat.

The widespread use of this reading progression meant that hearing the four gospels in a sequence was a bedrock element of early Christian practice. The first year was dedicated to The Gospel of Matthew, the second to Mark, and the third to Luke. These gospels have clear story lines, and are called "synoptic" gospels.

John's gospel—less a story and more a series of thematic meditations—was reserved for a special purpose. From the late second century onward, the major portions of The Gospel of John were read primarily during Lent and Easter. However, during the Seasons of Christmas, Epiphany, and the Sundays after Pentecost, small portions of John were interspersed amongst readings from the other three gospels to more deeply illuminate and complete their messages.

Exactly how did the idea of combining a general belief in the fourfold journey with the selection of specified gospels in a clear sequence occur? Did they see the journey reflected in these four gospels, as I have? Maybe this was a customary way the four were already read? Were lots drawn? I do not pretend to know.

Happenstance or calculation, an individual or a committee? My belief is that people who were charged with discernment and decision-making converged with a sequence of spiritual practices already known to work well. The pressures, realities, and needs of the society at that particular point in history played their part, as they always do. Then grace intervened and the pattern was set.

I doubt we will ever be certain how the pattern came to be created, but undeniably the four-gospel journey set in the three-year Sunday cycle held a great design, and that design went far beyond the stories and lessons told by the individual gospels. This great pattern seemingly worked very well for hundreds of years. Then, abruptly it was cast aside.

Sometime in the 600s, the Christian church apparently decided that it needed a simpler story. Christendom had been under attack for two centuries from northern warlords, and its cities were crumbling wrecks. Weakened churches were largely the only remaining centers for education, food distribution, and often law and order.

I don't know which of the several popes who ruled very briefly and followed the long reign of Gregory the Great actually changed the reading cycle, but one of them did. I suspect that the impulse came from Gregory's influence, which derived from his reliance on the views of the holy monk Benedict of Nursia, the founder of the Benedictine Order.

Benedict believed in and taught "nothing too harsh and nothing too burdensome." It is easy to see that in a time when few people could read and when the church was totally overcome with demands and was focused on people's survival, a short, straightforward Jesus story would seem very appealing, and this is the probable basis for the change.

Regardless of the precise history and the exact theological reasons, which we will never know for certain, both the beautiful and complex three-year cycle, and the four-gospel journey it held were abandoned. To replace them, the first uniform lectionary for Western Christendom was issued: fifty-two Sunday lessons selected from all four gospels that, in combination, told a succinct sacred and linear biography of Jesus' life and teachings.

Gradually, understandably and unfortunately, Christianity became concentrated on the details of Jesus' personality and life, a focus which remains today. Subsequent centuries saw the rise of education, the invention of the printing press, the wide dissemination of books, and the Protestant Reformation.

People began reading the scriptures, fresh translations appeared, and many Reformation congregations returned to reading the entirety of the four gospels at Sunday services, although none of them followed the ancient sequence except inadvertently. Sadly, no one seemed to know of the ancient three-year reading sequence. The great design had been lost.

More centuries passed. In the 1940s, the Roman Catholic Church re-opened its immense library for general research. The ancient three-year cycle was rediscovered; and after much study, but seemingly without grasping the pattern's deeper significance, the Roman Catholic Church reinstated the three-year cycle in 1969. They saw it as a way that all four gospels would be read, communicated, used for worship—and that a more complete text of the gospels might aid their members' spiritual lives.

TWO—THE KEYS

Within ten years, the Episcopal, Anglican, Lutheran, Presbyterian, United Church of Christ, Disciples of Christ, and Methodist churches followed suit. Today, these Christian churches, with minor exceptions, all read the same gospel passages on Sunday mornings, yet lack connection to the deeper intention in the cycle and its transforming potential.

Unbeknownst to me, at the time of that long ago "aha!" in the high desert, the pattern disclosed then was only a beginning. My studies since have led me to discover its long history and the five keys, which when understood together, offer us a deep perspective that might entirely transform the gospels—even for those of us who know the words by heart.

The great name of Jesus the Christ and the "here and now" witness of Paul keep the living presence of the Christ awake and vital in our understanding and our practices. The historical dilemmas of the four early Christian communities lovingly answered in the texts of Matthew, Mark, John and Luke speak with equal compassion as they help us forge a deeper life as we journey along each of the four paths today.

The Followers of The Way become our early predecessors, laying out the steps we can be guided by now, following in a practice that joins heart *and* mind. And the early leaders of Christianity? What gifts of foresight, practice and inspiration blessed them to formally choose these four texts and establish the Sunday cycle? Though that mystery will likely never be fully explained, our thanks and blessings can certainly be prayed.

Let us now move away from history, and next turn to an overview of the four gospel paths themselves.

Chapter 3

THE FOURFOLD JOURNEY OF TRANSFORMATION

*T*he opening portion of this chapter is designed for "handy reference." You may wish to read it now or come back to it later. It provides a summary of the entire Journey of Quadratos as disclosed by each of the four gospel paths and its corresponding gospel text. The texts, their core metaphors and historical dilemmas are briefly discussed. The historical challenges are also put in relationship to our present-day spiritual lives, so that the complete sequence—and its transformative role—can easily be seen.

In the second section of the chapter, the universality of the fourfold sequence is reviewed and discussed. The pattern is shown in church life, in literature, in the arts, in nature and in science—the entirety of life. I also talk about the impact of the pattern on society, and what the consequences are of its lack.

For those who wish to proceed directly into the journey itself, by all means, skip this section and move ahead to the next chapter. For the rest, an overview of the First Path is our beginning point.

The First Path: How Do We Face Change?
Climbing The Great Mountain of Matthew

Matthew's gospel was written to the Messianic Jews of Antioch two to five years after the destruction of the Great Temple of Jerusalem and the massacre of all its priests. The Temple, its rules and priests had represented the center of their lives, and now many were certain that God had abandoned them. They felt alone and frightened. The Jewish community was undergoing intense grief and teetered on the edge of being torn apart by the tremendous struggles that naturally ensued.

Matthew used the image of a mountain as a deeply poignant and evocative metaphor throughout his gospel because Mount Moriah, the site of the Temple, had been the holiest place in Judaism for millennia. He knew the power this image represented for his fearful and faltering readers, and he used it to bring them to a new truth.

Through it, he revealed a revolutionary teaching of Jesus the Christ to Antioch's Messianic Jews: they *no longer needed* a bleating lamb, a particular place, a physical temple, or even the mediation of priests as a condition of faith. In Matthew's account, Jesus the Christ taught of a new temple. This new temple was located within each individual and it mandated that the condition of one's heart and behavior was a matter of personal responsibility.

Matthew's gospel illustrates how well he understood times of confusion and trial and how skillfully he was inspired to answer those dilemmas through the gospel narrative. In this gospel Joseph and Mary are engaged to be married when Joseph suddenly discovers that Mary is with child, and not by him. Hurt and confused, but wanting to avoid disgrace, he plans to dismiss her quietly.

> ***But just when he has resolved to do this, an angel of the Lord appears to him in a dream and says, "Joseph, son of David, do not be afraid to take Mary as your wife, for the child conceived in her is from the Holy Spirit. She will bear a son, and you are to name him Jesus." (1:20-22)***

Joseph does as the angel commands—and we know the rest of the story. But the larger point is that the angel comes to Joseph in stillness, in the midst of his confusion, and Joseph is willing to honor the message he receives, even though it contradicts family practice and tradition. Change often requires this kind of attentive listening, as well as additional resources of courage.

In the first path of our own spiritual journey we ask, *How do we face change?* We usually find ourselves in much the same place as the Messianic Jews. We have been going about our lives in an unreflective way. Suddenly, we are brought up short by the crumbling of a part of our life we have taken for granted. Maybe a loved one dies, or our finances fail, or we are betrayed. None of the habits and assumptions we've built up—assuming they will protect us—helps us.

We don't know what to do. We feel lost—lonely and estranged. Attempting to find a solution, we whirl around in desperation, trying this, avoiding that. Finally, we take a small step out of our confused and self-involved spin and begin the journey.

But we are immature and ignorant, and when we enter the unknown, inevitably we fall short. We begin again. Eventually, by some grace we accept the necessity of change and life's uncertainty and find ourselves on the second path.

The Second Path: How Do We Move Through Suffering?
Crossing Mark's Stormy Sea

The City of Rome at the time of Mark's gospel was a terrible place for Messianic Jews. Made scapegoats by Nero and held responsible for an immense seven-day fire that had burned much of Rome, they found themselves at the mercy of the centurions who went through the city knocking on doors in search of Jesus' followers. Once found, these believers and their entire families were taken away, horrifically tortured, and murdered before crowds in the Circus Maximus.

The entire Jewish community was in chaos, filled with bitterness and despair. Believers in Jesus as the Messiah were asking themselves if their belief was true and whether it was worth the sacrifice of their lives and their children's lives. Mark's stark language and his metaphorical images of wilderness and trackless sea reflected the bleakness of their terrible dilemma.

Each of the messages Mark offered held both despair and hope. His account of Jesus' life and teachings assured his readers that their suffering—or even death—fulfilled a plan greater than their individual lives. He helped the Messianic Jews believe they could trust that God had not abandoned and would not abandon them. He assured them that their time of suffering would eventually end. Even the lives lost, he told them, held value and meaning and would benefit future generations.

Mark's gospel included many vivid images of endurance through faith, but the best known are probably those of Jesus and his disciples making multiple nighttime crossings of the Sea of Galilee during violent storms. The disciples quake in terror while Jesus the Christ sleeps peacefully, eventually waking to quell the tempest. On the final crossing, Jesus completely loses patience with the fearful disciples, saying,

> *"Do you still not perceive or understand? Are your hearts hardened? Do you have eyes, and fail to see? Do you have ears, and fail to hear? And do you not remember?"*
> **(8:17–18)**

The second path can be very bleak and frightening, and we often long for an all-powerful person or substance to remove our pain and terror. The disciples have seen Jesus stop the storm, and they want him to do it again; but he refuses. The inner strength we find in faith will carry us through all adversities if we trust it—if we *remember*, as Jesus instructs.

The second path requires great endurance. Our question is, *How do we move through suffering?* While most of us are probably not facing imminent physical death, we still quake at the strangeness of the new reality we have entered at this stage of our journey. It feels alien and filled with fear, but we can't turn around and go back because we know the old ways won't work.

Our ego-self, author of all our well-worn patterns of behavior and thinking, finds itself under assault and desperately tries to re-establish control. Persistent, it sets up deceptions which we must unmask and ignore if we are to continue on. Competing voices and values tear at us. We feel lost and even feel as though we might die. Somehow, though, we remain on a course to a distant future, a place we cannot yet discern. The glimmers of hope and faith that we remember and find in prayer and meditation sustain us. We clutch them with grim determination.

The Third Path: How Do We Receive Joy?
Being in John's Glorious Garden

The Gospel of John stands apart from the other gospels in many ways. Rather than employing a story line of Jesus' life to accomplish his objectives, John used long, philosophical narratives with the primary metaphor of garden—specifically, the Garden of Eden. It is likely that these discourses were used as meditations—part of believers' preparations for Christian baptism in the city of Ephesus.

THREE—THE FOURFOLD JOURNEY OF TRANSFORMATION

By the time this gospel was written at the end of the first century, the Followers of The Way called themselves Christians. They also came from many backgrounds, not just Judaism. Ephesus was a thriving port city and the new faith spread rapidly. Enthusiasm was great and spirits were high—but the euphoria of those high spirits was now slipping into self-righteousness and division. John sought to establish a common and deeper grounding for the followers of the young Christian faith and warned them of the dangers presented by their zeal.

The kinds of experiences John refers to in his gospel are written from a frequently symbolic and mystical perspective. They are literally "not of this world", unconcerned with anything except higher consciousness, and can feel unconventional, which is also true for much of the third path.

Since mystical experience was not a valid Greek conception, it is somewhat unusual for John to have focused so powerfully on it. However, he clearly understood that human experience of an epiphany of wholeness and greater love is not only completely unforgettable, but very significant. And it is this extraordinary inner knowing of *all-in-union* that is the joy of John's garden—and also the template for our further practice.

> ***"And I will ask the Father, and he will give you another Advocate, to be with you forever. This is the Spirit of truth, whom the world cannot receive, because it neither sees him nor knows him. You know him, because he abides with you, and he will be in you." (14:16-17)***

When The Gospel of John was placed in the Sunday cycle, it was broken into parts and put amid the recitation of each of the other three gospels. This placement tells us that if the Christians of the third and fourth centuries did in fact establish the reading cycle with conscious intention, they knew the rigors of the spiritual journey well—and had a terrific (if intuitive) grounding in basic psychology.

This inner knowing of *all-in-union* is the joy of John's garden—and is also the template for our further practice. They understood that if the journey was sustained, a moment of revelation would undoubtedly arrive, but that the wondrous, revelatory moment would be simultaneously glorious—and perilous. The seeker would receive an epiphany, but there was grave danger that he or she could quickly "lose it" or significantly misconstrue it. John's gospel words incorporated into the cycle in this fragmentary way—throughout the journey—sounded a recurring and carefully calculated call of joy and wholeness—and caution.

Yet, there are other times that arise in our lives, well-comprehended by the wisdom of those early Christians, when the separated sections of John's meditations suddenly cohere into a revelatory whole—a complex and glorious vision, an ecstatic, poetic song of the soul. After the trials represented by the gospels of Matthew and Mark, the things that have seemed separate—the pieces of ourselves, the pieces of our lives, and the pieces of the gospel—suddenly, and usually unexpectedly, come together. Almost miraculously, everything makes sense.

We want only to sit in the garden and open ourselves to this wondrous and radiant experience. In us, all around us, the mystery of union unfolds, and we feel—deeply—the truth of oneness with Spirit. Ecstasy fills us, or perhaps the deepest calm we have ever known.

Having come through the pain and uncertainty of the second path, the full Gospel of John can feel like nothing less than a perfectly timed, life-giving oasis. Lest we become too possessive of this oasis, our necessary meditation for the third path is, *How do we receive joy?*

We learn that we need to stay awhile. We must abide with an inner stillness and reflection, allowing parts of us still mired in shame and unworthiness to come forward and join the divine embrace. Everything we see wears the face of love, as gratitude awakens and grows.

Gradually, we feel an opening to fresh questions, and we realize that our new truth comes with responsibilities, though we glimpse them only vaguely. We realize that if we do not meet these responsibilities, our revelation will sour and remain immature. We have more to learn and so must make the next choice. We decide to leave this still-unfinished, though blissful, state and continue the internal/eternal journey.

THREE—THE FOURFOLD JOURNEY OF TRANSFORMATION

The Fourth Path: How Do We Mature in Service?
Walking Luke's Road of Riches

The Gospel of Luke was written as a two-volume document in the last part of the first century to assist and instruct various communities of Christians throughout the Mediterranean region. Although growing and thriving in their faith, many Christians carried new pain as they were formally cast out from Judaism, their mother faith. Penalties and legal sanctions against the practice of Christianity that had existed only in Rome spread outward after the schism with Judaism in the mid-80s, and the Roman Empire became a much more active oppressor.

These two historical events presented significant obstacles to the emerging Christianity communities. How were they to respond to hurt? To injustice? Part of Luke's answer was contained in the metaphor that is primary in this gospel. Everything in The Gospel of Luke happens "on the road" while traveling. The destination is not the focus at all. It is entirely secondary.

Luke called the early Christians to practice. He asked them to change their previous ways of responding to difficulty and crisis, telling them to model their lives on the example set by Jesus and the apostles. He encouraged them to offer compassion when faced with oppression and to demonstrate the values of Christianity by the witness of their lives.

He instructed them to trust in their spiritual practice, and have faith that the changes they sought would ultimately arrive. Luke asked Christians to forsake any bitterness over their separation from Judaism, and to avoid direct combat with the Romans. His narrative reiterates, over and over, that the only proper course for Christians is "to be" the change they desire.

Luke filled his gospel with stories of compassion and service to an extent not found in any other gospel, and his Beatitudes were revelatory. However, his simplest instruction was provided in **10:25-28.**

> *A lawyer tests Jesus, "Teacher, what must I do to inherit eternal life?" Jesus responds, "What is written in the law? What do you read there?" The lawyer answers, "You shall*

love the Lord your God with all your heart, and with all your soul, and with all your strength, and with all your mind; and your neighbor as yourself." And Jesus says to him, "You have given the right answer; do this, and you will live."

Further on, Jesus illustrates the same principle with the story of the Good Samaritan. But the entire truth is complete already: when we love our neighbor as we love ourselves we are compelled to live our lives in service. This is how our transformation truly occurs, allowing the meaning and purpose of our lives to unfold.

In the fourth path we ask, *How do we mature in service?* We are much like those early Christians. Our ego-selves need to become grounded. We have to learn more than theory. We must absorb the behavior of a new way. Our inner guidance continues to grow so that we may reduce, even eliminate, the old ego-self's protective and controlling reactions to events. This path of full psychological and spiritual transformation takes time.

As it becomes familiar, we discover that the new way is more fluid and less predictable than the ways we have known. Our daily practice becomes a faithful and ongoing study of joy, compassion, and integrity, and our sense of equanimity strengthens. We comprehend that the journey never ends. The fourth path eventually leads back to a new first path, filled with grief and promise. As we reflect back and peer ahead, we welcome this perpetual cycle of new beginnings and the fresh opportunities we will have to learn and deepen in a conscious way.

The Design Throughout Christianity

There are many ways in which the sequence remains in Christian practice. The full baptism ritual, which appeared formally in about 300 CE and is one of the most enduring celebrations of Christianity, perfectly mirrors the lessons taught in the fourfold sequence. Its structure has four steps: entering, prayer/growth, illumination, and commitment to service. These steps perfectly echo the guidance revealed in the gospel order of Matthew, Mark, John, and Luke. The Catholic ritual known today as the mass (called "the Breaking" and "the Eucharist" in earlier Western tradition) also reflects the sequence of four.

First the believer forms an intention and enters the sacred place (church) for mass, opening her heart to inspiration and challenges. Second, the words of scripture and sermon charge her with stringent self-examination. Third, she experiences the oneness of being All with God, called "communion." Lastly, the believer receives the final blessing, the *missa* (which means "to be sent"), mandating her to go out into the world in service.

Labyrinth walks also show us a reflection of the fourfold progression. Labyrinths originally entered Christian tradition in the twelfth century as an inner substitute for the outer pilgrimage to Jerusalem, which was simply too dangerous at the time for faithful believers to actually undertake. A genuine pilgrimage and a labyrinth walk both display a fourfold progression.

First: the pilgrim makes the decision to set out on her journey, or to cross the labyrinth's threshold. Second: the pilgrim embarks on the journey, following a circuitous path while paying careful attention and praying fervently. Third: upon arrival in the holy place, or center, the pilgrim spends time in reflection. Fourth, and last: the pilgrim returns home (or moves back out through the pattern) with his or her prayers focused on the integration of revelations gained into everyday life. This precisely mirrors the Journey of Quadratos.

So, we may see that the four paths have endured in Christianity, although for centuries they have remained beneath our awareness. We have walked them, often randomly, without conscious intention. And the paths can also be readily intuited in a variety of mystical and spiritual Christian texts by authors as diverse and venerable as the Desert Fathers and Mothers, St. Benedict, and St. Francis of Assisi.

More specifically, Hildegard of Bingen, in her *Book of Divine Works* (written in the twelfth century), discussed spiritual "progress" in terms of a cycle of four, which she called "the very pulse of life." She wrote that progress begins with a time of "purging and purification," followed by "confrontation with temptuous impulses," then moves into "vigorous life and enchanting fragrance," and finally reaches "the ripeness of nature and the perspicacity of the increasingly alert and mature human being."

The Quadratos pattern is also closely matched by the "Spiritual Exercises" developed by St. Ignatius of Loyola in the sixteenth century. This is a series of exercises, meditations and prayers that has gained immense popularity in recent years, even outside Christianity. Designed to be led by a spiritual director over a thirty-day retreat, the retreatant is to focus on Ignatius' exercises (although the gospels are also used in the process).

The first week is spent in deep contemplation of God's love and in praying to be purified and rid of "disordered attachments"—anything that stands in the way of doing God's will. In the second week, the life of Jesus the Christ is contemplated, with the objective of moving beyond mere history into a sense of Jesus' life as a present, participatory reality. The third week is devoted to a complex understanding of pondering the intensity of God's unconditional love. The final week shares in the joy of resurrection and synthesizes the experience so that a whole vision may be achieved. The objective is a daily life that glorifies God and extends love to others.

St. Teresa of Avila, also in the sixteenth century, described the identical spiritual journey in her work *The Interior Castle*, although she divided it into seven steps, or "castles," instead of four.

As mentioned in Chapter 1, we find the four stages in the contemporary books of Matthew Fox and M. Scott Peck. And though they did not explicitly name the passages fourfold, the writings of both Henri Nouwen and Thomas Merton— particularly some of their more autobiographical works, such as Merton's *The Seven Storey Mountain* and Nouwen's *The Inner Voice of Love: A Journey through Anguish to Freedom*—are filled with their personal progression through these very paths. We can also see how their lives bore witness to using their spiritual maturity in commitment to issues and needs in the larger human community.

THREE—THE FOURFOLD JOURNEY OF TRANSFORMATION

The Universal Design
Always Present

Four stages, four gospels. We surrender, we struggle and endure, comprehension finally dawns, and we gradually learn the practices that make our understanding or our discovery repeatable, consistent, and real—and then we bring our works and our words to each other. I believe that this pattern is not only that of spiritual transformation. I believe it is the identical fourfold sequence that describes the process an artist uses to create—and a scientist to discover.

I think that it is the core pattern of all social, political, and institutional change, as well as that of our civil discourse. I find it both humbling and inspiring to know that we walk to the same ebb and flow we hear in Mozart, read in Shakespeare, and see in Michelangelo.

I've mentioned finding the progression of four in indigenous cultures, in other religions, in various psychological and philosophical writings, and in my clinical Sandplay practice. But these are only a few places the sequence can be discovered. Truly, it is ubiquitous. In literature from worldwide cultures, the "Hero's Journey" invariably follows the identical arc.

Classic structures for opera, symphony, and theater all demonstrate this same pattern (though in modern times change has appeared). And though the divisions into four are not quite as crisp and clear, the same process and trajectory can readily be discovered in a wide range of contemporary social programs, such as the "twelve steps" of recovery, sequential plans for increasing creativity, and programs for developing community.

When we examine the underpinning of the process, the structure of four-ness itself, we find still more mirrors, and at a much more fundamental level. When Bishop Irenaeus of Lyon said in defense of the Gospel as four texts, "The natural activity of the Lord is fourfold," he was basing his premise on the great amount of "four-ness" readily observable in the natural world.

He wrote of "four zones of the world ... four principal winds" and, in another text, "quadriform animals." And all of us (except those located at the equator and poles) can bear personal witness to these great truths when we experience the turning of the four seasons of the year. Each year crispy autumn becomes dark winter, yielding to the new life of spring and eventually the sere, hot days of summer.

Almost two millennia after Irenaeus wrote, distinguished scientists Geoffrey West and James Brown published research in 2004 in *Physics Today* that further supports the significance of four-ness. West and Brown investigated the laws governing the "scaling" of the following systems for humans, animals, and plants: metabolic rate, life span, growth rate, heart rate, DNA nucleotide substitution rate, length of aortas and genomes, tree height, mass of cerebral gray matter, density of mitochondria, and concentration of RNA. (Scaling is the relationship between different internal systems and the whole as plants/animals change size.)

Remarkably, the researchers found that all these systems change with size on a ratio of one to four. Coincidentally, the article is entitled *"Life's Universal Scaling Laws"* (italics mine).[2] At an earlier lecture for the 2001 Stanislaw Ulam Memorial series, Dr. West stated, "It appears that nature's magic number is four." It is probably only a bit of an overstatement to say that we, and our world, are both built on and "nested in" units of four-ness.

The pattern of Quadratos truly appears as a universal, and the thread of four runs through almost every aspect of existence. Whether we accept or decline the invitation to make it *conscious*, every one of us will be—indeed, already is—in submission to the monumental sequence. However, this does not in any way mean that Quadratos is precise, or smooth, or simple, or linear. It is cyclical. In fact, it is *multi*-cyclical. Life questions arise in one path and begin to find resolution in the subsequent path just as they simultaneously yield to myriad new questions in another. We have traveled and will travel each of the paths many times.

We will grow from the dependence of childhood to the autonomy of adulthood, sometimes alone and sometimes with company. We will be healthy and we will be sick. Life's seasons will constantly change and call

---

[2] Geoffrey B. West and James H. Brown, "Life's Universal Scaling Laws," *Physics Today*, Sept. 2004, 36–42

out to us with their individual necessities. Different aspects of our life will consistently appear at varying points of the sequence.

For instance, our personal life may be occupied with the challenges of one path, our professional life with another, while our communal life is on yet a different path altogether. The resultant tumult can be very difficult to discern and to negotiate. Life, and the grace available to it, is rarely linear and well defined.

The Quadratos journey is as complex as we are. While most of us use our voice to speak, we also understand that the endless variations of tone and pitch make each of our voices unique. In the same way, our spiritual walk is both constant and infinitely variable, shared but at the same time singular. Nonetheless, throughout our journey the underlying pattern persists, and for all of us, the rhythm beats in a measure of four.

The Tragedy of Three

For far too long, Western religions—and, more recently, psychology—have been centered on a three-step pattern. Although there are many different vocabularies, generally mainline Christian theology and spiritual direction describe a progression of purgation, illumination and union. Psychology uses surrender (or commitment), testing (or trial), and illumination (or resolution). Regardless of what words are used, union or resolution—all you have to do is maintain "it." Not only is this mistaken, in our present world it easily becomes a dangerous and damaging misconception.

Three-step processes produce electrifying conversion stories and seemingly instantaneous changes which look great and warm our hearts. Quadratos shows what happens after the dramatic change, however. Sadly, and almost inevitably, the old habits, attitudes or behaviors return—usually with a vengeance. Alternatively, overly spiritualized worlds in which everything remains "nice" on the surface are constructed and maintained. Sometimes even entire communities participate in these regressions on the journey.

In either form, nothing approaching true transformation is possible, because pain, anger and alienation underlie every single action. Overall, individuals are generally in worse condition than before they began the journey, primarily because they carry a heavier burden of disappointment and even shame. Therefore, individuals in this condition are a greater detriment to their relationships and their work. Genuine community is completely out of the question.

By the time we reach the end of John's gospel, we will understand why it is only by the completion of the third *and* fourth paths that we ensure our journey engages the responsibilities of true love and transformation, and reaps tangible benefit for others as well as for ourselves. Quadratos provides a way for us to understand the cultural necessity—even urgency—for increased numbers of people to move through the third path and truly walk the fourth.

A more conscious awareness of the fourfold map has finally found its way back to us. Now the ancient and sacred Gospel can be seen as an integrated and inspired blueprint of our spiritual journey. And as we bring greater awareness of the map to practice, we will be more fully engaged in Christianity's most noble purpose—and that of all humanity—ongoing transformation through love.

The Journey of Quadratos awaits. Let us enter it together, and begin its first path, *Climbing the Great Mountain of Matthew.*

Chapter 4

CLIMBING THE GREAT MOUNTAIN OF MATTHEW

WARNING

*Before you enter this terrain
there are a few things
you should know.*

*There is no entry fee,
but it will cost you plenty
to make this journey.*

*Pack a lunch. Lose your map.
Travel lightly. The weather
is unpredictable.*

*I am prone to sudden washouts,
to the startling crumbling of earth.
It's good to watch your step,
but what is underneath is strong
and you are welcome to settle there,
to rest the night
or stay for a season.*

*Be careful at dusk.
It's when the beasts come to the water,
and it's not that they would devour you,
but they are protective of their terrain
and will not easily yield.
I can tell you
they will never be utterly tamed,
but with choice morsels
and soothing words,
you may have them
eating from your hands.*

*If these warnings sound harsh, good;
this terrain is not
for the faint of heart
or for those who would travel
its contours crudely,*

*littering its landscape
and stripping its soil.*

*But I think you are made
of stronger stuff
and more tender,
that you already know
the lay of this land;
how its treasures will yield
to your searching fingers,
how its wellsprings will ease
your traveller's thirst,
how its brambles and thorns
will give way
to the waiting hidden garden
where grows the sweetest,
most exquisite fruit
waiting to be consumed.*

Jan L. Richardson

How Do We Face Change?
The First Path

We begin our journey with Matthew, the gospel that answers the question, *How do we face change?* As we set out, what can we expect? To begin with, we can anticipate a certain internal sequence to this first path. And though each person's walk may vary in its chronology, every aspect of the sequence must be experienced.

And this is true regardless of how we make our way through the process. No ignoring, evading, or avoiding will be possible. The good news is that you have accomplished the first phase already—and probably the second also—without even realizing it!

That is because we ourselves, just as we are today, comprise the first part of the path. This concept is fundamental and very important, but it frequently gets ignored. We each begin this walk with the unique elements of our own individual nature and a life that has been lived and experienced.

FOUR—CLIMBING THE GREAT MOUNTAIN OF MATTHEW

Each of our personal stories, even if unreflective until now, is integral to the process. It is the matrix from which our new lives will be formed. Our singular selves and histories, in this very moment, press the first footprint onto the path.

Feelings mark the second phase. A sense of estrangement, loneliness, or discomfort arises. The specific feelings and timing may differ, but discomfort will be a universal feeling. And though we are aware of these inner tremors, we may not clearly understand that they signal the opening of an inner rift. Their rocking, gentle at first, but then increasing, alerts us to a disconnection between our interior and exterior lives—often extreme and sometimes total.

Our first and completely natural instinct is to push these feelings away. We have busy lives and no desire to disrupt them. We dismiss the feelings as minor and related "only" to a specific outward event—a disappointment or a loss. We attempt to ignore them. In the short term this may be a successful strategy for us, especially if they are indeed minor.

However, if the underlying dislocation is genuine and more extreme our feelings become much more difficult to set aside. We find ourselves in a great dilemma. The small self we have been, spiritually and psychologically, is simply not up to dealing with the life we have. Increasingly, as challenges mount so does our inclination to blame them on things outside ourselves. Victimhood looms and our future dims. The quandary in our hearts and souls calls out for relief.

Some of us are more attuned to the inner call, but many of us may be aware consciously only of the ways the dilemma manifests *outwardly*—broken relationships, abuse, depression, and fear. Yet, as awful as we feel, it is the terrible pain we undergo that provides our impetus for change. We begin to be willing.

Willingness is the seed from which change can sprout, and once it has been planted our journey of spirit will genuinely begin. We feel as though our beginning goes in fits and starts, and that it is a struggle that lasts for quite some time.

We may change partners, change substances, read the latest self-help book or withdraw from the world. Yet, eventually we will be called onward. At some point, we will discover that the time and effort we spent skirmishing amongst temporary "solutions" were experiences we needed to open us further.

Once we are sufficiently receptive, the invitation arrives as the third part of this path. It comes in myriad ways, differently for each of us. Our spouse says, "I need to talk with you," and simultaneously our stomach plummets while our heart leaps at the hope for a renewed relationship. The doctor pronounces, "I'm afraid I have to tell you …" and we struggle for the hope of healing.

Financial reverses become opportunities to examine and adjust how we are living out our value system, while a call from the school principal can beckon us to improved communications with our child. Within grief and confusion, we are able to also discern a greater and more productive possibility for our lives.

Nonetheless, we must deal with the shock we felt when the invitation first arrived—and it can throw us into the kind of despair that makes our shoulders slump way down and our chin drop to our chest. Yet even this despair has a good purpose. It can lead us to further willingness—this time to make a reluctant yet vital admission: *we are unable to "go it alone."*

Our pain joins our sadness, our humility and our faint hopes, and an amazing spiritual alchemy transpires. An internal decision mysteriously forms. Our personal history bends with reluctant compliance and becomes perfumed with the extra-special component I identify as grace. From the deepest part of our being, like the sounding of the bell that calls us to worship, "I will" is pronounced to the invitation for journey. A far vista appears on the horizon, and its beauty beckons our soul.

So, we set forth, holding a kernel of belief that we can actually manage to reach that distant, beautiful place that has called to us, though we do not yet understand how. Almost immediately, the fourth phase steps right

FOUR—CLIMBING THE GREAT MOUNTAIN OF MATTHEW

into our path: increased challenges. That shouldn't be a surprise. We're new at this after all. Ignorance and a lack of skill are naturally going to lead us into missteps and, sometimes greater difficulties.

It is also a troubling time. Our initial resolve begins to weaken. Powerful longings to return to our old emotional home fill us, no matter how clearly we see its cracks and crumbling walls. None of our usual logic and solutions work. They never did work too well, and now they are ineffective with our new problems. Confused and squirming, in one way or another we inevitably betray the intention of the journey—yet even this betrayal is a necessary step.

In our floundering, we start to soften a bit and discover a new, often awkward self-compassion. Employing it, we begin to identify the inner sources of our errors and slowly correct their influence on our actions. Each self-correction merits congratulation and gives us greater inner confidence. Our increasing inner knowledge enables us to continue despite frustration, and to do so with conviction instead of resignation. This is the fifth and concluding part of the first path: the ability to restore our course when we fail. It is also the most vital.

For some people, the initial self-awareness on the first path may last for a very long time. Whether long or short, it has substantial trial and error within it. Over the course of our lives, we will come to know the first path well. As we cycle over and over again through the Quadratos process, we will grow to recognize the signs of its arrival. Although the stumbling struggle of beginning sometimes goes more smoothly for us than at other times, when we are in deep crisis the struggle can still have the full awkwardness and pain of our first experience of the first path.

Within The Gospel of Matthew, we will uncover a profound guide who will awaken us to all of the hope and challenge of Quadratos' first path.

Our exploration of the gospel will begin with a study of its historical context, which starts long ago with Jerusalem's Great Temple and its importance to the Jewish people of the first century. Then we will move on—to Matthew's words and counsel.

Before we enter these ancient times, let us prepare some "common ground." Although our outer lives could not be more different from those of people in the first century, we still have "temples" today. Each of us has beliefs, aspects of our lives we regard as fundamental, on which we rely for our interior stability. These beliefs may center around health, our body, love, family or finances. We derive joy and meaning from these interior beliefs. We think, we hope, they will never change.

When we look back on them or tell their stories, we edit charitably—simplicity and satisfaction reign. Sometimes our "temples" are inherited; they can easily become family traditions. Sometimes we build them. We count on them. No matter what our temples are, we consider them central, solid, and sacred. We yearn for them to be secure and expend great effort in attempts to make them so. They have genuine roles in our lives—but we are sometimes forced to discover that they have no real permanence.

Across time and culture people have felt a desire for permanence. In reflections of their desire, they have imbued physical landscapes—particularly high mountains and standing rocks—with meaning. Mountains connote the eternal; they represent basic and unchanging security. Governments and companies regularly use them as iconic images to instill confidence and faith—think of insurance companies, banks, and the Rock of Gibraltar. Spiritual traditions have built pyramids and stone circles, raised altars on cliffs, put their temples on rock, and incorporated metaphors of security and permanence into their foundational theologies.

Nonetheless, at some point even rocks crumble. All of us come to the experience of enormous loss. Whatever it is that we believed would stand forever trembles and falls. Dark chasms and precipices appear with the suddenness and drama of a volcanic eruption. It is precisely at this point that we find ourselves standing on the first path, barefoot and covered in ashes.

This is where the millennia disappear and we are on "common ground." Our hearts could just as well be in first-century Jerusalem.

FOUR—CLIMBING THE GREAT MOUNTAIN OF MATTHEW

Earliest Days
The Great Temple in Jerusalem

In the first century CE, the Temple of the Jewish people was in Jerusalem high atop the pinnacle of Mount Moriah. This had been its sacred location for a thousand years and a place of Jewish destiny for two thousand. The Temple was the religious, political, and financial heart of the Jewish faith and of all its traditions. It was deemed central to life itself.

The high altar of the Temple was believed to stand on the precise place where Abraham, the father figure from whom all Jews (and Muslims and Christians) count their lineage, built the altar on which to sacrifice his precious son Isaac. A careful reading of the text reveals Abraham's trust in God and confidence that his God would not require his son to be sacrificed (a new human understanding of God in that era). Abraham's confidence in this new understanding of God secured the covenant between Yahweh (the Hebrew name for God) and the Jewish people; and by that covenant they had come to understand themselves as "chosen."

A thousand years later, King David was led to that same mountain. There he built a great city that he named Jeru-Shalom, place of peace, now Jerusalem. The site of Abraham's surrender to Yahweh's will—Moriah's peak—was designated as the location for the sole, monumental temple of the Jewish people. Although David never built the edifice, his son Solomon fulfilled his father's dream, completing the immense structure that became known as the First Temple (or Solomon's Temple) about 900 BCE.

Over the centuries that followed, the Jewish people came to believe Solomon's Temple and the sacrifices offered there were, quite literally, the things that guaranteed God's relationship with them. In the hour before dawn each day, the high priest prayed and solemnly poured the blood of a fresh-killed lamb over the high altar. His actions reaffirmed and re-secured Abraham's covenant, providing assurance that the sun would rise that morning.

The whole Jewish order of creation depended on that prayer of that high priest, standing at that altar, in the still hour before dawn of that day—and of each and every day. It was a deeply accepted belief that when the Messiah came in accordance with the prophecies, he would come to this exact spot: to the holy place of Abraham's and the high priest's sacrifice.

And he would come as a direct result of the perfection and fidelity of the religious practices of the priests and the chosen people they led.

Then, in the sixth century BCE the Babylonians overran Jerusalem, destroying large portions of the First Temple, capturing the priestly class, and removing them into exile. Undaunted, their beliefs and traditions secure, the Jews laid the stones anew and rebuilt the Temple a mere hundred years later. This building, erected on Solomon's foundation, was called the Second Temple.

Late in the fourth century BCE, when Alexander the Great conquered the region, a new and more hopeful reality began for the Jews. Alexander allowed much greater freedom of religious practice. Indeed, his relationship with the people of Abraham was so benevolent that in the first year of his reign, the Jews named all of their first-born sons Alexander, introducing that foreign name into the Semitic world.

Unfortunately, the harmonious years were brief. Alexander died only seven years after conquering Palestine, and his entire empire was quickly divided among regional kings. Palestine's new rulers, who came from the Greco-Syrian region, continued Alexander's benevolence through their early reigns. However, as time passed matters began to change. Successors imposed increasingly harsh restrictions on Jewish life and worship, and attitudes toward the Jews shifted dramatically.

Eventually, there was desecration. The Greco-Syrian kings raised statues to their own gods on the high altar of the Second Temple and held athletic competitions in its heretofore sacred courtyards. Nonetheless, the Jewish people and their priests held fast to their pride and faith.

They knew that the Temple's basic foundation had survived for a thousand years despite all trials. They were certain it would continue to stand and would forever provide the security and promise of Abraham's covenant. As a great and chosen people, they were confident they would prevail against every onslaught. Their sense of security could not be shaken.

In the mid-second century BCE, the Maccabean brothers led a Jewish revolt and re-secured the Temple. Subsequently, it was ritually cleansed, and an eight-day Feast of Rededication (which Jews now celebrate as

Chanukah) was held in 164 BCE. Within twenty years of the Temple's reclaiming, an independent Jewish state was completely in place, and the chosen people were once again free to follow their traditions. But this surcease was to be brief.

In 63 BCE, Syria and Palestine were absorbed into the Roman Empire and a brutal occupation began. People throughout the expanded empire were heavily taxed nearly to starvation. Rome ignored, even mocked, the independence of the Jewish people and installed a single Roman to serve as both high priest and *ethnarch* (provincial king) over the region. Although the Jewish resistance and outcry against this step caused the positions of priest and ethnarch to be separated back into two, Rome persisted in its unceasing political pressure. The critical roles of both king and high priest became virtual puppet positions of the Roman Empire, filled only by those who accepted and followed Roman directives.

The Jewish people remained undaunted. Though small in number and resources, they firmly continued to believe that they could throw off the Roman emperor as their forebears had thrown off Pharaoh more than a thousand years before. Their high estimation of their own power and destiny was unambiguous and frequently claimed.

The Roman governor watched the community with a wary eye, and at each Passover—the springtime remembrance of the Jewish liberation from Egypt—the governor became very nervous. As a huge and fervent throng came to make their annual sacrifice at the Temple, tensions inevitably rose.

Approximately ten years before Jesus' birth there were serious riots during Passover. The Jews actually took back control of Jerusalem and held it for fifty days until the Feast of Shavuot, the celebration of Moses hearing Yahweh's voice on Mount Sinai. On that fiftieth day, Rome sent in its centurions.

Although the outcome was briefly in question, Rome's greater power ultimately prevailed, and Jerusalem was returned to the empire's control. But hundreds of Roman soldiers and thousands of Jewish rebels and innocent pilgrims lost their lives in the conflict.

Despite their defeat, the Jewish community spent the next six decades completing a major expansion of the Second Temple, their zeal and determination undiminished. This was done in the midst of Rome's brutal occupation—and was perhaps even encouraged by it. King Herod—himself half-Jewish—led the construction, hoping to win the Jewish people's affection. Indeed, when the Second Temple was completed in about the year 50 CE, it was thereafter called Herod's Temple, and it was considered the architectural jewel of the eastern Mediterranean.

Once again, high on its hill, the Temple was the repository of Jewish faith and hope. Certainty about the permanence of this Temple was widespread, as was an increasing belief that the Jewish Messiah would soon come. Fueled by pride, long-burning resentments against Roman rule increased and smoldered, occasionally breaking out in violence.

By the year 60, small Jewish uprisings had proliferated, and over the next decade fighting broke out across Palestine. A full-scale revolt appeared imminent. In 70, as tensions boiled, the newly elected Roman emperor, Vespasian, decided to permanently deal with this group he viewed as combative and problematic. Not satisfied to merely add to the Jewish body count, and determined to destroy the Jewish power base completely, Vespasian prepared the most devastating blow possible.

On the precise anniversary of the date that Babylon destroyed Solomon's Great Temple, the Roman guard—under the command of General Titus, Vespasian's son—arrived in full and terrifying force. In disciplined and thundering cadence, the massed troops marched to the center of Jewish life, Herod's Second Temple, and undertook to level it completely.

There is no known equivalent to what Rome did that day. The Temple's high altar, the heart of worship, was shattered into tiny pieces. While some troops burned all of the Torahs and scrolls and destroyed the holy vessels, others took down the massive walls stone by stone and completely removed them from the city.

This time, Rome wanted no ambiguity and no contentious survivors in exile. Titus' men massacred virtually all of the Temple authority—the priests, the scribes, and their families and tribal members. They slaughtered tens of thousands of Jews. Emperor Vespasian wanted absolute certainty that not one scrap of scroll nor any tiny vestige of the Temple remained. There would be nothing at all left upon which the proud Jewish people could pin their hopes.

Much of Jerusalem was sacked that day, but the Temple was a different matter. The soldiers' instructions were specific and crystal clear: no looting of the Temple was permitted—only its total annihilation. When the troops were done, nothing more than a flat platform and a bereft community survived. Vespasian's horrifying and decisive action accomplished its goal. The Temple, all of its authorities, and all of its worship had ceased to exist.

Even the earlier fall of the First Temple had not fractured Judaism as did this second and total destruction. This loss threatened the foundations of Hebrew cosmology and wiped out almost every leader of the faith. Everything the Temple and its priests had represented in the hearts and spirit of its people had to somehow be rebuilt if the Jewish faith was to survive. In this time of great danger, a rebirth was necessary.

Birthplace of The Gospel of Matthew
Great Antioch on the Orontes, 70s CE

After the massacre, the few remaining Temple leaders fled to the city of Antioch. Its Jewish community, though in total chaos and preoccupied with great challenges, became the new center for the remnants of the Hebrew faith. It was also the crucible of inspiration for Matthew's gospel.

Antioch, a great center of the Greco-Roman world, lay about three hundred miles due north of Jerusalem, only a week's journey away. Because there were several cities named Antioch throughout Asia Minor, Matthew's Antioch, which stood on the banks of the Orontes River, was called Great Antioch.

The Orontes opened to the Mediterranean Sea, providing a sheltered deep-sea port and a strategic location for Rome's military control. A contemporary map reveals that the Orontes is today known as the Asi River, and the Turkish city of Antakya now lies over the remains of Great Antioch.

RADICAL TRANSFORMATION

In the year 70 CE, Antioch's Jewish population was exceeded only by that of nearby Jerusalem. The city's synagogue was grand and had special status. It contained items originally from Solomon's Temple (the First Temple) that had been secreted away to Antioch when the Babylonians pillaged.

Prideful worshippers, perhaps presumptuously, even referred to Antioch's synagogue as a "second temple." Additionally, Antioch's large base of Jewish leaders included many descendants of Temple authorities who had fled there after the unsuccessful Passover uprising some eighty years earlier.

This city was a natural crucible in which Judaism could begin to reorganize and recast itself. Reform efforts began in the chaos of a bitter factional struggle that raged throughout the faith. Four factions arose and fought for the heart of the Jewish community.

One segment believed that all hope was lost and was certain that an apocalyptic end time had arrived. They maintained that the destruction of the world—either by flood or by fire—was imminent, and that the Temple's destruction had been the first sign of the final days.

The Pharisees, a body of religious lawyers who had risen to greater power when the priests and scribes were slaughtered in Jerusalem, headed a second group. Some of them maintained that the Great Temple's destruction had resulted from God's wrath brought on by laxity of religious observance. These Pharisees, therefore, sought to unify Judaism through a more diligent observance of Mosaic law and ritual practice. They maintained it was *only* by these means that the Temple would be restored and the promised Jewish Messiah would finally arrive.

Another faction, perhaps numerically the largest, was confused and unsure of what to believe or which way to turn. Many of these people simply wanted to get on with their lives. Others were fearful of any course and waited for the "right" answer to appear—one that would provide them with a sense of stability and safety.

The final contingent was the Messianic Jews. Though small in number, the members of this group were determined. They viewed their context and their problems as starkly different from those of the other factions.

They believed that their Messiah had already come and that Jesus was that Messiah. Their challenge lay in trying to understand what the Messiah expected of them in the wake of the loss of the Temple, the priests and their accustomed rituals. They additionally had the difficulty of navigating through their families and the city's Jewish community, the majority of whom did not share their beliefs.

Today, we recognize this final group as the early Christians, and they were Matthew's intended audience. He directed his gospel specifically to them in their time of chaos, trial, and difficult beginnings. Matthew wanted them to understand that their Messiah who had come, Jesus the Christ, had a new teaching.

This Messiah taught about a new temple—one to be built within the heart of each follower as a direct and personal relationship with God, supported by a community of like believers. No longer was a huge edifice or a special location needed. Matthew's inspired gospel became the prayer and practice of the Messianic Jews, and it formed their spiritual foundation.

In this book, I use the words "Messiahnians" and "Messianic Jews" to refer to these early followers who believed that Jesus was their Messiah. I also use the expression "Christus followers," the language found in early documents. These terms are applied primarily in the periods prior to the formal break with Judaism (therefore in discussions of the Gospels of Matthew and Mark).

Facing the Mountain
Approaching Matthew Today

Even though Mark was historically the first gospel written, Matthew was the gospel placed first in the ancient Sunday reading cycle. A gospel of endings and new beginnings, Matthew offered Sunday listeners the beginning of a divine process.

This gospel put forward to its first hearers—the Messianic Jews of Antioch—a message of hope and fresh promise. It presents the same to us. It clearly conveys an understanding of the first spiritual path of

Quadratos. Matthew's metaphors of mountain and rock perfectly describe our own landscape in this first phase.

As we make our way up our own mountains, we trip over pebbles, jump over rocks, and try to climb over the boulders of our actions, preconceptions, and fears. How often do we continue to believe in their permanence and solidity, even as we watch them shift and crumble, both from their essential instability and in the face of our stubborn persistence?

The patterns in which Matthew structures his lessons are as inexorable as the lessons we must ourselves learn in the first path. They circle back over and over again, each building on the previous lesson and leading to the inevitable, unavoidable conclusion.

As we study this gospel sequentially, we'll see how Matthew's writing specifically addresses the first path, using every segment of Jesus' life to direct us to the development of our own inner resources. We'll particularly note his emphasis on the qualities of self-honesty, self-compassion in the face of loss, and trust in the divine.

Fallible Icons
The Genealogy

Inspirations and reassurances begin immediately in the opening chapter of Matthew's gospel, principally provided by a lengthy recounting of the genealogy of Jesus the Messiah. No other gospel has this recitation. (Luke has a genealogy, but it is much less prominent and contains different names.) By starting out in this manner, Matthew accomplishes a dual purpose for the Messianic Jews of Antioch.

He holds up the entire line of names, allowing them to roll sonorously off the page in a majestic procession of historical Jewish icons. This told the Antiochians that they came from a great and long line of people who had suffered tremendous loss, but who had prevailed. It reminded them that they were descended from Abraham, with whom God had directly covenanted, and that they had inherited the warrior might of King David. They, too, were special, and they, too, were strong. This function of the recitation is explicit—clear to us even today.

Also, explicit to the Messianic Jews were the losses, betrayals, and historic twists and turns represented by the names in the list. The labyrinthine narratives signaled that they, too, needed to expect the unexpected and should not be overcome by fear. It reassured them that their forebears had not only survived, but had even discovered treasure in their reverses and thrived.

Indeed, a further message within the genealogy emphasized that there are instances when challenging traditional structure, rather than maintaining it, can bring great honor. This was profound counsel and deep affirmation for the Messiahnians. It also came at a time when they found themselves unwelcome and disrespected by their more conventional Jewish counterparts.

These messages held by the genealogy are less obvious to a present-day reader. Some of us may recognize the names, but we generally associate them with the pinnacles those icons reached by the end of their successful life journeys. Matthew's audience, however, knew the entire stories—successes and failures—of these real, struggling human beings. Chronicles of Jewish heroes and heroines comprised the glorious heritage repeated regularly throughout their lives. They had grown up knowing the full drama of each person named.

There is no way that in these pages we can replicate the quality of knowing that comes from oft-repeated tales learned from birth. However, we have selected a few stories and fleshed them out from information that can be found in the Hebrew scriptures. As we go through the genealogy, we'll see how the icons become human—fallible and beset by woes, just as we are. This lets us absorb Matthew's message with an understanding that more closely approximates that held by the Messianic Jews.

Matthew's first line, a summary sentence, goes straight to the heart of the entire recitation. It begins with the central belief that Jesus is the Jewish Messiah, and immediately moves on to combine his name with those of the greatest of the great leaders, David and Abraham. To Matthew's original listeners these words intoned, in effect, "This is your heritage; this is your belief, and this is the core of its truth."

> ***An account of the genealogy of Jesus the Messiah, the Son of David, the son of Abraham. (1:1)***

Matthew's lineage recites the direct line of Abraham: to Isaac, one of Abraham's sons; then to Jacob, Isaac's son; and then to Judah, one of Jacob's sons; and methodically on, clear to Solomon—and eventually to Joseph, husband of Mary, who was the mother of Jesus. What can we learn from this genealogy?

Following early tribal tradition, Abraham has two wives, Sarah and Hagar. Hagar has a son, Ishmael, but Sarah is sadly barren until very late in her life. Then an angel appears and tells Abraham that Sarah will conceive. She would have gloried in this news earlier in her life, but at her advanced age the prospect seems so ridiculous that she laughs when she hears the angel's prophecy. Nonetheless, a son, Isaac, is born to her.

After his birth, ill will between the wives begins, growing to such a degree that Abraham, at Sarah's insistence, casts out Hagar and Ishmael. (Ishmael was later named the patriarch of Islam.) Abraham's choice of Isaac over Ishmael flew in the face of tribal tradition, which clearly held that the birth of a son, particularly a first son, was a concrete sign of God's blessing, just as the lack of a son was a curse.

The human dilemmas in this story are huge. Sarah, miserable and "cursed" with barrenness most of her life, suddenly as an old woman has to contend with an infant. Abraham has a houseful of angry, fighting women and has to throw one of them out, along with a blessed son! Together, Abraham and Sarah, while comfortable and settled in their life in Ur, subsequently find themselves forced to leave everything they know and move to Palestine, a land completely alien to them. Their lives are filled with unanticipated losses, predicaments, and change.

The lineage continues with more elements considered highly nontraditional. According to ancient tribal custom, eldest sons always inherited and younger sons frequently received little or nothing. Yet for generations, Matthew's list does not contain a single eldest son.

Abraham completely breaks with custom when he makes Isaac his inheritor instead of Ishmael, his eldest son. Jacob, the second son of Isaac, tricks his way into his inheritance in place of Esau, his elder brother. In turn, Jacob names his fourth son, Judah, as heir, bypassing three older sons and again deviating from the community's beliefs and expectations.

FOUR—CLIMBING THE GREAT MOUNTAIN OF MATTHEW

Abraham was the father of Isaac, and Isaac the father of Jacob, and Jacob the father of Judah and his brothers. (1:2)

Judah has three sons: Er, Onan, and Shela. Although Er and Onan married, they are killed before either of their wives bear children. Judah, attempting to lift the curse of (male) childlessness from his family, orders Tamar, Er's widow, to stay unmarried until Judah's youngest son, Shela, is old enough to marry her.

Tamar acquiesces, but when Shela matures, Judah reneges. Tamar, needing children (preferably sons) to provide for her in her old age, takes action. She veils herself and, in disguise seduces Judah. Being smart and prudent, she also persuades Judah to give her his signet (seal) and staff before he lies with her.

When she becomes pregnant, Judah sentences her to death for the shame she had brought on his name through her disobedience and promiscuity. When Tamar proves Judah's fatherhood with the signet and staff, Judah revokes his sentence and welcomes her back. She bears him twin sons, Perez the elder and Zerah.

... and Judah the father of Perez and Zerah by Tamar. (1:3)

Matthew's "calling of the roll" moves through many brave and iconoclastic men and women and eventually gets to King David, his wife Bathsheba, and Solomon. This was a story that all Jews of the time knew very well indeed. They were rightfully and immensely proud of David, even though he had significant human flaws and a life rife with betrayals.

After all, he had built their holy city Jerusalem, united and expanded the Promised Land, and ruled benevolently. Yet Matthew's wording also specifically identifies David as an adulterer (saying that he fathered Solomon "by the wife of Uriah"). David's shame, however, went far beyond the betrayal of marriage vows.

King David sleeps with Bathsheba, wife of his faithful servant Uriah, impregnating her, while Uriah gallantly fights one of David's wars. Worse, he tries unsuccessfully to deceive Uriah about the paternity of the child, and when the deception fails, he sends Uriah back into the heart of the battle in a move tantamount to murder. Worse still, his hope that Uriah will die on the battlefield comes true.

With Uriah's death, David is able to marry Bathsheba, but the child that comes of that union dies. This was a sure sign that God had cursed them. David, in his old age, passes over his eldest son (by a prior wife) and chooses another child, Solomon, to inherit his throne. Solomon becomes the Jewish icon who represents wisdom. It is he who held the honor of building the Great Temple.

> ***... and David was the father of Solomon by the wife of Uriah. (1:6)***

Matthew's choice of the genealogy is a wonderfully wise and compassionate opening for the Messianic Jews of Antioch. With the rhythms of a chant, it speaks a proud and ancient history and brings that history forward into a hopeful future. Most of the names seem foreign to our eyes. But to the eyes, ears, and hearts of Matthew's audience, the litany must have seemed like the rising of a giant army of affirming angels carrying a message far more potent than a mere procession of names.

Even more importantly to people who knew the stories, the genealogy certainly did not read like a list of devout and holy people with circumspect lives of perfection, humility, and generosity. These were *imperfect* humans—indeed, their very imperfection was often the source of their heroism and their reputation. They had been tested. In lives that twisted and turned, they had suffered great periods of loneliness and estrangement. They had known confusion and conflict. Yet these heroic figures had endured—and their path of trial had led directly to the coming of the Jewish Messiah.

Matthew's genealogy completely contradicts those amongst the Pharisees who believed the Messiah would come only from perfection, a blessing from God for flawless behavior and diligent religious practice. More than anything else, the genealogy affirmed the Messianic Jews. It inspires them with their great lineage and encourages them to eschew the beliefs and customs of others in the Jewish community who sternly held to a legalistic, perfectionist notion of the Messiah.

We share so many of the lessons of Matthew's genealogy on the first path. Remember the beginning of this chapter? We each start with a history—a particular matrix that is only and individually our own. This is the hard ground on which we stand, facing the mountain arising before us. We have, however, an inheritance greater than just ourselves. We each have prophets and warriors in our past, people of great depth and endurance and spirit.

We are following in the footsteps of the daughters and sons of our own Davids and our own Abrahams. As we begin our journey, we will be wise if we take the time to identify these significant people in our history. We need to establish our heroes and heroines, our inspirational figures. We may be able to find them within our direct lineage, or we may discover a kinship further afield in our human family. In either case, what we are looking for are real humans whose frailties, challenges and successes have relevance to our own.

We will find these inspirations especially useful during the stumbles of the first path. However, as we continue we will likely wish to revisit and even expand the search for our personal genealogy. Doing so, we will learn more about ourselves. We will better discover which heroes and heroines we need and want to keep around us for support. Will we require the fortitude of Sarah, the careful prudence of Tamar, the self-forgiveness of David, the wisdom of Solomon? Or the practical nature of our grandmother? Or Nelson Mandela's unfailing ability to smile?

Receiving the Call
The Announcement of Jesus' Birth

Matthew concludes the genealogy with the story of Joseph, and clearly shows that the historical line of the Messiah came through Joseph, even though he was not Jesus' biological father.

> *... and Jacob the father of Joseph the husband of Mary, of whom Jesus was born, who is called the Messiah. (1:16)*

Matthew is not relating a biography of Jesus. He is telling a story of faith and of faith tested. His focus is on Joseph, a man who finds himself with a great dilemma. Joseph is betrothed to Mary, which by Judaic law means they are married but not yet living together. And Joseph discovers Mary is pregnant.

Joseph is devout. He prays regularly, tries to help others, and follows all the rules. He is considered "righteous." He absolutely knows that Mary's child cannot possibly be his. He feels betrayed and trapped. We can assume that his mind swirls with questions and protests, and we can be sure he begins an internal search. Why has this pain come to him? Has he committed some terrible wrong to be so punished?

Joseph's predicament was more than personal. Semitic life demanded adherence to custom. Villages were governed by social approval, and neighborly gossip was the arm of correction. If a couple argued at the breakfast table, the village knew every word and gesture by lunchtime. The small, tight society had clear expectations of behavior and response. Deviation caused shunning by the entire village, a fate genuinely worse than death, since the shame would forever taint the family name and lineage.

Descended from David and by extension linked to the Messiah, Joseph bore an even greater responsibility to the community. Should he risk ruining his family's honor and continue this marriage to a now-pregnant woman? Or should he cast out the woman who has betrayed him? While neither option offers a painless solution, Joseph initially gives in to tradition, and decides he will quietly end the marriage.

> *Now the birth of Jesus the Messiah took place in this way. When his mother Mary had been engaged to Joseph, but before they lived together, she was found to be with child from the Holy Spirit. Her husband Joseph, being a righteous man and unwilling to expose her to public disgrace, planned to dismiss her quietly. (1:18-19)*

History indicates that as a conventional and "righteous" man, Joseph unreflectively lives the life expected by his society. Suddenly, an "angel … in a dream" comes to him and instructs him that he is not to cast Mary out, but to keep the child, raise the boy as his own, and name him Jesus. Undoubtedly, as he receives these divine instructions he feels everything he knows of the world collapse.

Yet Joseph faithfully complies, and in doing so becomes a powerful exemplar of courage and trust. Antioch needed this example of acceptance which said, "Stay open to the inner messages of God. It is important that the feelings that may arise within you that contradict those messages—your assumptions and fears—are not allowed to impede you. Neither should the demands of your people and their traditions. If God asks, you must be willing to move forward, no matter the cost."

> *But just when he had resolved to do this, an angel of the Lord appeared to him in a dream and said, "Joseph, son of David, do not be afraid to take Mary as your wife, for the child conceived in her is from the Holy Spirit. She will bear a son, and you are to name him Jesus, for he will save his people from their sins." All this took place to fulfill what had been spoken by the Lord through the prophet: "Look, the virgin shall conceive and bear a son, and they shall name him Emmanuel," which means, "God is with us." When Joseph awoke from sleep, he did as the angel of the Lord commanded him; he took her as his wife, but had no marital relations with her until she had borne a son; and he named him Jesus. (1:20–25)*

The focus on Joseph instead of Mary in the nativity of The Gospel of Matthew is the first place where the gospel inconsistencies truly illuminate the Quadratos journey. We are not yet aware of our new life being birthed, but our lives haven't been working out too well. Consciously or not, we are awaiting the invitation.

Or maybe we have received it, but we haven't wanted to acknowledge it. We are like Joseph, questioning our situation and circumstance. And, also like Joseph, we must trust in the call. The fog will lift and the next part of the path will unfold. Remember, Joseph did not seek his dream—it sought him—and only with a similar calm and stillness can we discover the holy condition of our own journey.

It takes time to learn these new ways. Our experience is limited, and it may prove inadequate to generate genuine conviction. When we encounter doubt and anxiety, we can muster up those heroes and heroines for support as we grasp for solid footing. We can call friends who are more experienced on the journey. We can read and meditate on this Gospel over and over again as needed. And we can pray. Matthew reminds us through Joseph that "God is *with us!* God is *with me.*"

Homeward Star
The Nativity of Jesus the Christ

Matthew next tells the story of Jesus' birth. The account opens with the name of King Herod—historically a very dangerous figure—and then goes on to the sighting of a new star and the tale of "the Magi," wise ones coming from the East. Signifying the rising of the sun and the direction the priests faced for morning sacrifice, the east represents the direction of new beginnings, of hope arising from the face of darkness.

Also, a Greek belief of the time held that all people received a star at birth—a gift that served as a guiding spirit, similar to many people's trust today that each of us has a guardian angel or spirit surrounding us.

King Herod, consumed by fear over the threat of the Messiah, a new and unknown element, asks Jewish scribes and priests where the Messiah is to be born. In a subterfuge, Herod then relays this information to the Magi, asking them to find the child and report back the precise location so that he can also go and "pay him homage." The Magi leave King Herod, see the guiding star, follow it, and are led directly to the newborn Jesus.

> *In the time of King Herod, after Jesus was born in Bethlehem of Judea, wise men from the East came to Jerusalem, asking, "Where is the child who has been born king of the Jews? For we observed his star at its rising, and have come to pay him homage." When King Herod heard this, he was frightened, and all Jerusalem with him; and calling together all the chief priests and scribes of the people, he inquired of them where the Messiah was to be born. They told him, "In Bethlehem of Judea; for so it has been written by the prophet: 'And you, Bethlehem, in the land of Judah, are by no means least among the rulers of Judah; for from you shall come a ruler who is to shepherd my people Israel.'" Then Herod secretly called for the wise men and*

> *learned from them the exact time when the star had appeared. Then he sent them to Bethlehem, saying, "Go and search diligently for the child; and when you have found him, bring me word so that I may also go and pay him homage." When they had heard the king, they set out; and there, ahead of them, went the star that they had seen at its rising, until it stopped over the place where the child was. (2:1-9)*

The Magi are deemed the wisest of individuals. Led by the star, following heavenly and prophesied signs, they arrive at Joseph's home. In Matthew's gospel, despite the story depicted in holiday school plays and children's books, Mary and Joseph live in their home in Bethlehem, where they are presumably comfortable. They do not wander looking for a place to have their child, nor do they take refuge in a stable or a manger.

And the Magi also bring gifts—powerful and symbolic gifts of gold, frankincense and myrrh, which come to Mary and Joseph much as the earlier dream had come to Joseph. Their gifts, brought from the East, are all profound references to the Great Temple. Frankincense and myrrh have been the precise and essential components of the most important Temple rituals. They were as costly as the gold of the Temple's vessels. The highly aromatic resin of myrrh was added to the oil used for royal and priestly anointing. Frankincense was burned only for the highest sacrificial offerings.

With these precious materials, Matthew symbolically transfers the components of the old physical Great Temple to the infant Jesus, the Messiah and emissary of the new, inner temple. Through the stories of extraordinary messengers—angel and Magi—Matthew makes sure that every Messianic Jew in Antioch clearly understood that Yahweh had granted his blessing and power to the new Lord. For added emphasis, Matthew incorporates another dream vision which cautions against a return to Herod's realm.

> *When they saw that the star had stopped, they were overwhelmed with joy. On entering the house, they saw the child with Mary his mother; and they knelt down and paid him homage. Then, opening their treasure chests, they offered him gifts of gold, frankincense, and myrrh. And having been*

warned in a dream not to return to Herod, they left for their own country by another road. (2:10-12)

How does the story of the Magi at Jesus' birth fold itself into our lives? First is the image of the star. This is an enduring metaphor for a spirit that guides us. It can be found firmly embedded in our language and our psyches through all these ages. The word "disaster" literally means "dis-star"—to be separated from one's star, from one's inner guidance. It is important for us to recover this understanding now. We face *disaster* when we are separated from our deep wisdom.

And disaster is not too strong a word: although new inspiration is rarely welcome at first, we ignore it at our peril. Dangers abound. Herod was implacable in his determined efforts to locate the threat represented by Jesus. He wanted to protect the center of his power. Similarly, our fears and ignorance threaten the nascent life within us. Fear moves in hidden places and holds secrets. It is quiet, sneaky, and unrelenting.

The fears we feel at our personal new birth mirror the difficulties of Jesus' arrival. Our inner birth, equally unexpected, is also a home birth. The spiritual journey begins in the middle of our ordinary life. We have no exotic locales to distract us. We are usually alone, or feel so. What we have thought to be our normal world has crumbled, turned completely upside down, and become chaotic. Still, we have somehow heard our invitation to a new life, mustered our courage, and—despite our trepidation—moved ahead.

But our difficulties have continued unabated. The messengers of the King of Fear within us are still on the hunt; they dog our every step. However, in the midst of our disorientation, the Magi will pay us a visit as they did Jesus. We don't know what form they will take or what specific gifts of wisdom they will bring. The presents the Magi offer may be small—a piece of the past resolved—or very large—an unshakable communication with Inner Spirit—but we can count on them being precious and powerful.

We will find that these presents are tools for our journey. They will hold the same prominence and solemnity of the ancient gold, frankincense and myrrh. We are asked to keep expectant watch for the arrival of our own personal Magi. And when we receive their messages, we must be attentive, so that their wisdom can unfold for us as we travel.

Returning to Pain
The Flight to Egypt and Galilee

After Jesus' birth, an angel comes again to Joseph telling him to take Mary and the tiny, defenseless new baby away from the comfort of their home. Even more distressing, he is instructed to take them to Egypt, the country of Jewish slavery—a place of deep danger, of historical alienation and pain.

Joseph must surely feel that he has, once again, received an enormous, incomprehensible—even mistaken—charge. However, the move is necessary to protect the child from Herod, who is determined to find the baby and kill him. In his efforts, Herod has slaughtered all male children two years old and younger throughout the region of Bethlehem.

Joseph accedes to these instructions, yet his trials are not over. Though Herod dies and Joseph might safely return home to Bethlehem, once more an angel appears to him in a dream, this time telling him he is *still* to remain away, separated from his parents and siblings.

Matthew's audience would have understood how extreme this command was. All custom and the deepest responsibilities felt by a man of his time dictated that leaving one's family was an act tantamount to abandonment. It was considered a sure sign that one's ancestors had been cursed and one's descendants would be shamed. For a third time, Joseph was asked to bear the burden of an incomprehensible and terrible requirement.

Yet, once again Joseph obeys. Leaving Egypt, he chooses Nazareth in Galilee as his new destination. Nazareth is a distant northern region that southerners like Joseph consider a crude, heathen, poverty-stricken, undesirable place. The Messiahnians would have empathized with Joseph, since their decisions had thrown them into a state that felt equally unfamiliar, emotionally away from friends and cherished traditions. Their inner lives were in similar turmoil.

Now after they had left, an angel of the Lord appeared to Joseph in a dream and said, "Get up, take the child and his mother, and flee to Egypt, and remain there until I tell you; for Herod is about to search for the child, to destroy him." Then Joseph got up, took the child and his mother by night, and went to Egypt, and remained there until the death of Herod. This was to fulfill what had been spoken by the Lord through the prophet, "Out of Egypt I have called my son." When Herod saw that he had been tricked by the wise men, he was infuriated, and he sent and killed all the children in and around Bethlehem who were two years old or under, according to the time that he had learned from the wise men. Then was fulfilled what had been spoken through the prophet Jeremiah: "A voice was heard in Ramah, wailing and loud lamentation, Rachel weeping for her children; she refused to be consoled, because they are no more. When Herod died, an angel of the Lord suddenly appeared in a dream to Joseph in Egypt and said, "Get up, take the child and his mother, and go to the land of Israel, for those who were seeking the child's life are dead." Then Joseph got up, took the child and his mother, and went to the land of Israel. But when he heard that Archelaus was ruling over Judea in place of his father Herod, he was afraid to go there. And after being warned in a dream, he went away to the district of Galilee. There he made his home in a town called Nazareth, so that what had been spoken through the prophets might be fulfilled, "He will be called a Nazorean." (2:13–23)

The angel's instruction to Joseph that he take his wife and tiny baby, leave the comfort of his home and flee to Egypt is one of the most profound of Matthew's passages, perhaps because we can relate so deeply to the truths it holds. Our angel, a wisdom voice, will also come to us in stillness. It will tell us that we must hurry back into our own personal Egypt, our place of inner wounding.

It will tell us that we must psychologically take our whole selves—both our inner child-self *and* our inner parental aspect—when we make that most difficult trek. In this exile, we will live with an awareness of pain, gradually opening to the *new* Christ energy within, so that by such grace, our fears and wounding no longer paralyze us, halting our journey.

And it might take a while. The strength of our resolve may well turn out to be measured like Joseph's, in patience and fidelity and by our willingness to endure and remain vigilant as time passes and old understandings die. We too will likely have to go from the first exile into a deeper and wilder place. Only through our commitment to this process can we safe-keep the precious nativity we hold. This is the first and critical part of the agreement we made with ourselves when we accepted Quadratos. We took on the responsibility to make the journey, and we also vouchsafed to be its guardians.

Will we yield to wisdom's voice and accept the necessary exile? Will we risk living in foreign and very uncomfortable places? Will we honor the promises we made to ourselves? The Magi and Joseph all went into the unknown, following a star, listening to an angel. Our course up the veiled mountain likewise feels unknown, mysterious, and frightening, but it is the gestation of the Messiah's birth in us. Quadratos tells us that our feet fall securely on a well-worn path.

Courage! Trust! Walk onward.

Repentance and Blessing
Jesus' Baptism

Next in the gospel is John the Baptist, who appears in "the wilderness of Judea." Antiochians knew that this wilderness lay below and south of the old Temple mount in Jerusalem, in the direction of Egypt. They remembered the fate of the Temple, the murder of the priests, and the ensuing despair encountered by the Jewish people. They also knew the hopelessness and wildness into which the great city had fallen. Yet John the Baptist calls out that the kingdom of heaven—the reign of Spirit—is near. And he calls for repentance!

These words must have puzzled the Jews in Antioch. They may well have asked, "What could he possibly mean? Wasn't the destruction of our Temple enough? How deep must our suffering be, and how can our despair bring the Messiah closer to us?" Could John's words mean that we, ourselves, must repent? But why? Surely the disasters that befell us were not of our making! This confusion was precisely Matthew's intention.

In Matthew's gospel, John uses the word "repent." The choice is significant. The root of "repentance" is the Greek word *poina*, which means "pain." Historically, this word took three linguistic forks. One was *poine*, referring to legal compensation and, later, to expiation and punishment. Another was *poena*, meaning the taking of vengeance. The third, *poenire*, took the meaning of conscience and absolution, becoming the word "repentance" (and also becoming part of "penitentiary," which originally meant "house of correction").

Matthew's choice of words conveys an understanding that repentance is a correction of one's heart and mind—an act of personal, voluntary, inner change. This is quite different from the frequently held view that repentance connotes punishment or vengeance.

I believe that Matthew intended the Jews of Antioch to understand that they had to repent in order to mark the change from their old ways to new practices that would generate greater meaning and vitality in their lives.

> **In those days John the Baptist appeared in the wilderness of Judea, proclaiming, "Repent, for the kingdom of heaven has come near." This is the one of whom the prophet Isaiah spoke when he said, "The voice of one crying out in the wilderness: "Prepare the way of the Lord, make his paths straight." (3:1–3)**

John's further ritual of repentance—the baptisms—took place at the Jordan River, just east of the city of Jericho, precisely where the Hebrews had crossed into the Promised Land. It's important to understand that the ritual of washing in this gospel is *not* the baptism practiced by Christians. The ritual Matthew refers to is first-century Judaic baptism, a cleansing performed for ritual purification. Present-day Judaism calls this a *mikvah* bath.

Gathered at the river were multitudes from Jerusalem and Judea, places of power and privilege. Among them were Sadducees and Pharisees, members of elevated levels of society. By including these, Matthew takes careful and precise aim. These two groups in Antioch supported the "old order." The remnant Sadducees advocated a return to Temple worship, while some Pharisees, who were becoming Judaism's primary authority, sought to unify the Jewish people through codified beliefs and standardized rituals.

In Matthew's telling, John the Baptist stands at the Jordan's ancient crossing place and asks for a journey that will require a profound emotional reversal of the odyssey the Jews had made. John cries out, "Repent!" and calls for a commitment to go back into the wilderness, to make radical change and correction.

He invites the gathered multitudes to enter the river and accept a new time of exile from their historic communities. Going further, John specifically challenges the elite groups, inveighing against them as a "brood of vipers," warning of "wrath" and fire and burning, even denying their claim to the lineage of Abraham.

In this way, Matthew warns the Jews of Antioch that if they hold to the old Temple and its traditions, they choose a sure path to destruction—one that equals the quick and painful death of a viper's bite. No past glories would protect them. All vitality would perish.

At the same time, Matthew uses John's voice to send a dramatic message of hope: "The new temple has arrived. Abraham's true lineage is through Joseph to Jesus. Leave. Face completely away from the comfort of the old, accept your insecurities, and walk forward. Enter the water and repent. Be corrected. You will be cleansed of your desires to hold on to your yesterdays. Repent and allow Spirit's heart within you to beat anew!"

> *Now John wore clothing of camel's hair with a leather belt around his waist, and his food was locusts and wild honey. Then the people of Jerusalem and all Judea were going out to him, and all the region along the Jordan, and they were baptized by him in the river Jordan, confessing their sins. But when he saw many Pharisees and Sadducees coming for baptism, he said to them, "You brood of vipers! Who warned*

> *you to flee from the wrath to come? Bear fruit worthy of repentance. Do not presume to say to yourselves, 'We have Abraham as our ancestor'; for I tell you, God is able from these stones to raise up children to Abraham. Even now the ax is lying at the root of the trees; every tree therefore that does not bear good fruit is cut down and thrown into the fire." (3:4-10)*

Matthew recounts that Jesus arrives "from Galilee" in the north, where Joseph and Mary lived in exile, to join John's baptismal gathering at the Jordan. John feels himself unworthy to offer a mikvah bath to his Messiah, seeing him as an exalted presence, and thus he resists performing the ritual. Jesus, however, makes the point that renewal is a necessity for everyone, even himself, and insists that John serve. John consents, and Jesus enters the water.

Coming up out of the water Jesus beholds a great vision. The heavens open and the Spirit of God arrives "like the dove." Again, Matthew carefully chooses a highly resonant metaphor for the Antiochian Jews. They were surely reminded of the dove that returned to Noah on the ark holding an olive leaf in its beak, heralding the appearance of "new land" after the devastation of the great flood.

Matthew uses the language of Genesis, amplifying its vision with even more images of hope and love. Genesis describes the world as flat and enclosed within a dome that separates us from surrounding and threatening water. If the dome opened, there would be a deluge and the earth would be destroyed, as it was in Noah's time.

By his reference to the alighting dove, Matthew is implicitly offering a fresh vision designed for wavering Hebrew hearts, particularly for those who believed that the end of the world was imminent: "If you repent, the truth of a loving God will awaken in you. You will know you are called 'beloved.'"

> *Then Jesus came from Galilee to John at the Jordan, to be baptized by him. John would have prevented him, saying, "I need to be baptized by you, and do you come to me?" But Jesus answered him, "Let it be so now; for it is proper for us in*

this way to fulfill all righteousness." Then he consented. And when Jesus had been baptized, just as he came up from the water, suddenly the heavens were opened to him and he saw the Spirit of God descending like a dove and alighting on him. And a voice from heaven said, "This is my Son, the Beloved, with whom I am well pleased." (3:13-17)

What does John's clarion call to "Repent!" mean to *us* on the first path of Quadratos? It reminds us that we each have inner voices of Sadducees and Pharisees that roil and breed ceaselessly within us like a nest of "brooding vipers."

When we hear them, they often seem to be in a superior or elevated position, yet their true faces are our own wounds, anxieties, and even fear of change. Held in their grip, we are inflexible and incapable of renewal. We know only one answer and are unable to entertain a new question. The poison in their terrible fangs will quickly kill any possibility of the new life we are trying to discover—quickly, silently, and certainly.

When we receive the invitation for change, we find ourselves in much the same position as Antioch's Messianic Jews to whom the strong words of this gospel were written. Our fear and rigidity takes many forms. Do we think the end times have arrived and there is nothing to live for? Do we believe that whatever devastation has occurred has happened because we did something wrong or not right (the words "if only," "should have," and "ought to" echoing in our minds)? Do we fall into despair or resignation or denial, substituting work or addiction or other escapes to avoid dealing with our dilemma?

John the Baptist spoke to Antioch and now speaks to us. We need to make the vital decision to become aware of these outworn inner voices and recognize that they no longer serve us—then respectfully set them aside. We too have to "repent" and have the willingness to grow and walk in a new direction.

In Jesus' insistence that John perform the baptism, we are reminded that the Christ is an exemplar of our own individual journey. The need for renewal and inner correction is to be expected and welcomed. And if we are able to find support, assistance and community participation, so much the better. Confronting the dilemmas of the past and attempting to correct their effect in us has particular prominence on the first path of Quadratos.

One of the greatest blessings we discover is that as the process of transformation circles back through our lives again and again, we can increasingly detect our need for renewal. Our expanded awareness is accompanied by greater capacity and comfort in completing the task. Over time, these "upgrades" can even become pleasurable—or at least satisfying.

Just as Matthew has done, we should call particular attention to the role of taking concrete—even public—action to mark our decision to enter a journey. Many established religious rituals began with this purpose, but we can certainly craft our own. Even if they remain private, or are shared only with a single friend, these acts reinforce our intention and provide an external marker to which we can refer in times of trial. If we choose a more public acknowledgment we benefit even more, because our chosen community will stand beside us and can be marshaled in our support.

The most important communication Matthew sends to us across the centuries comes at the very end of Jesus' vision. It is the gorgeous word spoken by the voice from heaven to Jesus, who stands in our stead. "Beloved," the voice pronounced: "Beloved, with whom I am well pleased."

What a remarkable message to hear in our first path, when we are not always feeling very pleased or particularly lovable. We need this message; we need to hold it tightly and to remember it. This is the firm foundation of Quadratos and of our journey: we are not alone and we are loved. We are the Beloved. These are the words that can sustain us as we continue to make our way up the treacherous and rocky path.

Saying No to Illusion
The Temptations

The gospel next recounts that immediately after receiving his vision and hearing God's blessing, Jesus was led into the wilderness. Again,

FOUR—CLIMBING THE GREAT MOUNTAIN OF MATTHEW

Matthew is directing his words to the internal experience of the Messianic Jews, who had voluntarily entered a spiritual wilderness. Their choice to follow Jesus as the Messiah had led to the sacrifice of friends, family, community, and tradition. Their feelings of isolation and abandonment were strong.

> *And a voice from heaven said, "This is my Son, the Beloved, with whom I am well pleased." Then Jesus was led up by the Spirit into the wilderness to be tempted by the devil. (3:17–4:1)*

After fasting for forty days in the wilderness, Jesus becomes famished and in his deep exhaustion, "the tempter" arrives. When the tempter comes to Jesus, he immediately challenges Jesus to make bread from stones to assuage his hunger. Jesus ignores the challenge, completely rejecting the tempter; he refuses to participate in a meaningless demonstration of power and maintains that better nourishment would be found through Spirit, in "every word that comes from the mouth of God."

This is a message from Matthew to the Messiahnians wearied after the fall of the Temple, that they are equally at risk of a similar temptation, of picking up the old ways. In the first century, bread was everyone's daily staple, and Matthew intends the stones to represent the building blocks of the old Temple which lay scattered.

> *He fasted forty days and forty nights, and afterwards he was famished. The tempter came and said to him, "If you are the Son of God, command these stones to become loaves of bread." But he answered, "It is written, 'One does not live by bread alone, but by every word that comes from the mouth of God.'" (4:2–4)*

The tempter comes a second time and places Jesus atop "the temple." This time, he asks Jesus to prove his divinity by throwing himself from the great height without harm. In effect, the tempter whispers to Jesus, "Surely your God is not a God of such pain. Surely 'the Beloved' would not have to suffer so."

Matthew speaks directly to the newly converted Messiahnians in this passage, knowing that they were particularly vulnerable to this temptation.

They must have found it very difficult to reconcile the pain that they were experiencing with their understanding of being "loved by God."

> *Then the devil took him to the holy city and placed him on the pinnacle of the temple, saying to him, "If you are the Son of God, throw yourself down; for it is written, 'He will command his angels concerning you,' and 'On their hands they will bear you up, so that you will not dash your foot against a stone.'" Jesus said to him, "Again it is written, 'Do not put the Lord your God to the test.'" (4:5-7)*

In the third trial, Matthew offers another clear-eyed vision of the temptations the Messiahnians faced. The devil places Jesus on a very high mount and shows him "the kingdoms of the world and their splendor." He offers Jesus the glittering temptation to set himself above others as a "special" or a specially anointed man.

This temptation of self-righteousness—a risk to which all "new believers" are particularly susceptible—would have resonated with the Messianic Jews in their time of external chaos and internal trial. In this allegory, preying on the anxiety of fear and separation, Jesus is promised great treasures if only he will take a few small steps toward worshipping the devil.

> *Again, the devil took him to a very high mountain and showed him all the kingdoms of the world and their splendor; and he said to him, "All these I will give you, if you will fall down and worship me." Jesus said to him, "Away with you, Satan! for it is written, 'Worship the Lord your God, and serve only him.'" Then the devil left him, and suddenly angels came and waited on him. (4:8-11)*

Matthew's temptations were not just on target for Antioch—they are wisdom stories for us on the first path of Quadratos as well. Emotionally, we find ourselves in a strange and unaccustomed place—climbing a mountain path, lost in a wilderness. Most of us have been taught by our families and culture that we must pass some kind of rigorous test to become worthy to hear the deep voice of love, that love is something we need to *earn*.

Matthew reverses this belief. He tells us that hearing the "voice of love" requires nothing more than opening our hearts to an ever-present invitation. God's call challenges us to walk through a bleak landscape so that we may get to the place where that love will mature. The fearful tests we undergo set in as we gradually remove the deeply entrenched obstacles within ourselves to hearing the voice of love with more clarity. From this perspective, each crisis we meet is a fresh invitation. As we make our small steps, the elation that arises with our fresh discovery helps to sustain our resolve.

Just as Jesus became susceptible to temptation when he was famished and exhausted, we do too, as we make our way through challenges. When we feel we have reached the limits of what we can do or endure, three temptations become clearest to us:

First Temptation: *Denial* The illusion proffered by the first temptation might be called, "Why deny myself this pleasure?" It asks, "Why settle for stones? Why not take that drink? Why not escape my intention by burying myself in family or work?" We need to recognize the real fears and insecurities that reside within these questions and the pitfalls that acting on them represents.

Second Temptation: *Self-Indulgence* The second temptation whines. Its imploring voice says, "Surely this path is not about suffering?" When we listen to this voice, we try to maintain our lives in a rosy world where we never face our pain, only deny it. We indulge in fantasies and long for worlds without unfairness or conflict. Sometimes we slip into the role of victim and identify all of our pain as coming from outside ourselves, from "them." Our confused ego-self offers us this illusion as it struggles to stay in control.

If we allow this cycle to continue, the tragic next step is an inevitable whisper that urges, "If this is from God, then God has abandoned us, and we should abandon God." All of us who have suffered loss or trauma or tragedy will recognize the power of this suggestion and the risk of accepting it; but if we are to move toward our inner freedom, we must resist.

Third Temptation: *Sense of Being Special* The third temptation may be the most pernicious, because it can be sneaky—very, very sneaky. Its vehicle is self-righteousness. It tells our ego-self that it can be in charge, "special," elevated above others, a "king." This temptation subverts our elation. It converts our sense of being "beloved" into a false belief of being "*most* beloved."

The instant we begin to believe that our personal and hard-won certainties are the truth for anyone other than ourselves, we have fallen prey to this temptation and have, in effect, begun to "worship" the devil. Why? Because we have allied ourselves with the devil of division, who thrives when we diminish the experience and inner wisdom of others. This is a grim course leading inevitably to the type of grandiosity that seeks the elevation of self at the expense of others—and the avoidance of pain through a false sense of merit or privilege.

The effects of this third temptation are visible throughout the world on a daily basis. It can begin with something as simple as the desire of a child for a particular kind of clothes or toy, so that he or she will feel more "special," be more popular—and hence "better"—than his or her peers.

If this sense of specialness grows unchecked, the adult will likely be convinced that outer signs and material goods equate to happiness and entitlement. Communities divide rather than unite as walls go up around "gated developments." Mental and emotional gates follow the physical gates. And on both sides of the walls, people speak of "them."

In religion we see the same pattern. One church, or synagogue, or mosque—self-elevated and thereby separated from full human community—condemns the practices of another by predicting God's wrath and shunning or sometimes even killing the members of another sect it perceives to be an offender. In global politics, one country calls another "evil" and acts on that perception; yet in its self-righteousness, it employs policies as extreme as those of the opponent it denounces, even making war. All of this is the "temptation" that Jesus resists and that Matthew's inspired prose condemns.

These words are not ivory-tower idealism of any kind. Of course, there are real differences between people. Genuine and valuable distinctions exist, created by true merit as well as earned rewards, and there are a multitude of problems generated by these differences for which pragmatic solutions must be found.

However, this does not alter the truth that when our inner selves convert any distinctions into a perceived right to diminish others, we are not on a holy path. Instead, we are submitting to the mighty enticements of the third temptation, and we are serving the tempter. God, whom we seek and serve, does not devalue our differences. God holds us all as equally beloved.

Another caution: Any time that we find ourselves praying a prayer of restoration, asking for a return of the past, or of our old comfortable ways and thoughts—even if it is a very small request—it is wise to stop immediately and reflect upon our motives. Most often, self-reflection will reveal that such prayers are really an attempt to quell our uncertainty.

While this is understandable in these early days on the first path, and we should view our yearning self-compassionately, we need to realize that we cannot go back. It can be useful to understand that our uncertainty is necessary and holy. If we could manage to dispel it, we would also destroy Mystery—the very thing we seek. Therefore, as uncomfortable as we may feel, Mystery is the deep companion of our journey and cannot be cut down to human size. It cannot be made comprehensible and monolithic. It is Mystery. It is God.

The genuine path that opens before us does not lead in the direction of greater control, but rather toward a new kind of intimacy. It releases us into learning to live within great unknowing, instead of being frightened of incomprehension and attempting to exert power over it. Our journey will be walked *through* unknowing, and it is the ways in which we choose to contend with our fears about this that will constitute the greatest perils of our pilgrimage. Matthew's allegories of Jesus and the tempter awaken us to the most significant of these risks.

Climbing with a Practical Heart
The Sermon on the Mount

Chapters five through twenty-five of Matthew's gospel comprise the heart of what have come to be called Jesus' "wisdom teachings." The opening portion of this enormous section—chapters five, six, and seven—is known as *The Sermon on the Mount*. Among its many passages, it contains the *Our Father* or *Lord's Prayer*. Its core teachings, *The Beatitudes*, are found in chapter five. We will study these closely.

Chapters eight through twenty-five are largely composed of lessons called "parables," which amplify and elucidate the previous instruction. Matthew included them as additional tools for those in Antioch, and designed them as conundrums, an ancient method of wisdom teaching. Each is intentionally structured to confound, to tie the rational mind into knots, and to assist in the deconstruction of old ways of thinking.

The theory holds that while the mind is thus occupied, something may be loosened in the heart, thereby allowing for the grace of fuller understanding. The parables are lengthy and we will not study them here. However, I strongly recommend that you read them. They can be valuable in wrestling with the new ways that begin to arise in the first path—and they are filled with beautiful poetic passages.

In chapter five, we see that Matthew, ever cognizant of symbolic efficacy, and especially that of the Great Temple, sets Jesus' great sermon atop a high mount in Galilee. We should note, however, that this mountain has no name. It is not one of the traditional Jewish holy places, and there is no physical structure of any kind. The Messiah, seated—the expected posture of an elder teaching in the Temple—begins to speak. Furthermore, Jesus' words of wisdom do not remonstrate or demand in the style of the Temple priests, but instead tumble out poetically and lovingly, in a new way of teaching.

The section begins with the lyrical verses of the Beatitudes. Their lilting words transmit a nine-fold blessing from Jesus to his disciples and to the Messiahnians whom Matthew addresses. Each of the nine couplets invokes supportive and constructive attitudes of heart—practical assistance for beginning and withstanding the inner challenges of a spiritual journey.

FOUR—CLIMBING THE GREAT MOUNTAIN OF MATTHEW

When Jesus saw the crowds, he went up the mountain; and after he sat down, his disciples came to him. Then he began to speak, and taught them, saying:

"Blessed are the poor in spirit, for theirs is the kingdom of heaven. Blessed are those who mourn, for they will be comforted. Blessed are the meek, for they will inherit the earth.

Blessed are those who hunger and thirst for righteousness, for they will be filled. Blessed are the merciful, for they will receive mercy. Blessed are the pure in heart, for they will see God.

Blessed are the peacemakers, for they will be called children of God. Blessed are those who are persecuted for righteousness' sake, for theirs is the kingdom of heaven.

Blessed are you when people revile you and persecute you and utter all kinds of evil against you falsely on my account. Rejoice and be glad, for your reward is great in heaven, for in the same way they persecuted the prophets who were before you." (5:1-12)

After reciting the Beatitudes, Jesus continues. His teaching is clear, uncompromising and is not recorded in any other gospel. He lays out new ways of evaluating and dealing with traditional practices. Like a repeated chant Jesus states, "You have heard it said to those of ancient times…" and then inserts a particular religious or cultural practice. His following words form his expanded interpretation of the practice — beginning with the words, "But I say to you…".

These became a new directive—a very explicit instruction manual crafted by Matthew using the revolutionary words of Jesus the Christ. And the instructions directly addressed Antioch's Messianic Jews, who found themselves deeply embattled by the regressive voices attempting to pull them back to yesterday's Temple and its practices.

Matthew's intention is twofold. First, he uses wording that makes it clear that perfect religious practice does not bring the Messiah. That is one purpose of the repeated, chant-like recitation of the words "you have heard it said." The Messiah has already arrived, so anyone still calling for perfection was clearly wrong. Messianic Jews could relinquish any onerous burden of perfection (and any sense of shame that belief generated) with a clear conscience.

His second goal is to convince the Messiahnians of the need to think in new ways about rules of conduct. Just because a respected external authority has established a code of behavior does not make it necessarily correct. Meaningless acquiescence is not a holy course; a genuinely holy path requires individual responsibility, effort, and scrutiny. As Jesus the Messiah teaches, learning as well as reflection and evaluation reveal the essence of "rules," enabling our behavior to become a meaningful practice flowing naturally from love and compassion.

> *"Do not think that I have come to abolish the law or the prophets; I have come not to abolish but to fulfill." (5:17)*

> *"You have heard that it was said to those of ancient times, 'You shall not murder'; and 'whoever murders shall be liable to judgment.' But I say to you that if you are angry with a brother or sister, you will be liable to judgment; and if you insult a brother or sister, you will be liable to the council; and if you say, 'You fool,' you will be liable to the hell of fire." (5:21-22)*

> *"You have heard that it was said, 'You shall not commit adultery.' But I say to you that everyone who looks at a woman with lust has already committed adultery with her in his heart." (5:27-28)*

> *"Again, you have heard that it was said to those of ancient times, 'You shall not swear falsely, but carry out the vows you have made to the Lord.' But I say to you, Do not swear at all, either by heaven, for it is the throne of God, or by the earth, for it is his footstool." (5:33-35)*

> *"You have heard that it was said, 'An eye for an eye and a tooth for a tooth.' But I say to you, Do not resist an evildoer. But if anyone strikes you on the right cheek, turn the other also; and if anyone wants to sue you and take your coat, give your cloak as well; and if anyone forces you to go one mile, go also the*

second mile. Give to everyone who begs from you, and do not refuse anyone who wants to borrow from you." (5:38-42)

"You have heard that it was said, 'You shall love your neighbor and hate your enemy.' But I say to you, Love your enemies and pray for those who persecute you, so that you may be children of your Father in heaven; for he makes his sun rise on the evil and on the good, and sends rain on the righteous and on the unrighteous." (5:43-45)

The wisdom teachings in Matthew contain such an abundance of sensible counsel that we would do well to keep them close. They are a poetic guide to the promises and the dangers that greet us on the first path. The recommendations and responses they hold are truly Be-Attitudes, designed to move us forward. They challenge us to:

- Accept that we do not and will not know results in advance. We often feel "poor in spirit."

- Make farewell to our yesterdays and embrace the grief we feel.

- Be humble in our willingness to journey. Yielding to exile will yield riches of Spirit.

- Know that our true hunger and thirst are for Spirit, and only Spirit, despite all trials and temptations.

- Greet all we encounter, within and without, in mercy and reap the rewards of gratitude. Recognize that mercy derives from *merces*, a Latin word that translates as "reward." (It continued into French as *merci*, meaning "thanks," or "gratitude.")

- Be full of heart. Do not seek to remove any thought, any feeling, or any person from our inner life. Each is an aspect of Spirit. Welcome them all.

- Believe in "Jeru-Shalom" as a home of welcome that accommodates the true peace of respect for differing voices, if we will but listen.

- Accept inner and outer hardship as needed for the sake of living a new life in the presence of God. Power and applause are not what we seek. Our journey leads instead to humility and service.

- Anticipate lack of esteem. Be prepared instead for tension—even conflict—and meet it with respect and love.

The nine Beatitudes reflect diverse parts of a harmonious unity. These reflect and touch each other over and over again, without end, as we go through our lives. They are the very heart of Jesus' teachings, and the practice of these teachings opens us to compassion.

Are we willing to place these on our hearts, walk with them on our feet, hold them in our hands, and seal them in our thoughts? If we do, we will have more insight along our journey. They will become our guide and a sturdy walking staff on which we can lean in the arduous times we will face.

We can find equal relevance in the rest of the Sermon on the Mount provides equal relevance. All of us have "heard it said"—by parents, by friends, by society, by religious institutions—that we ought to "do this" or "avoid that." Unreflectively, we may have accepted or rejected these words.

Jesus asks us to become more conscious. He tells us that truth is not found on the surface. We are encouraged to explore the original purpose and meanings of the things we have been told, and to examine carefully their genuine truth and meaning in our hearts and lives today.

We have talked about the risk of returning to older, seemingly simpler ways, but an equal peril lurks within this first path: the urge to rush ahead. Our ego-self can just as readily deceive us into thinking that all of yesterday's wisdom is empty folly—that nothing we have ever learned or been told has merit or benefit; that we are without guidance. Rejecting everything and racing off to the "new and better" can be a sprint to isolation and despair. Following either one of these extreme positions is only a trick, not a truth.

Quadratos requires that we ignore these deceptions and stay present, digging deeper, exploring further. Although many people and institutions have become protectors of empty practices, there are many others who still hold truthful, living attitudes of heart. We are on a journey to discover which ones have real veracity for us and endeavor to claim them in our own personal way.

Meeting Betrayal with Friendship
The Passion

Each of the four gospels has an account of Jesus' final days and death. These accounts are commonly called *The Passion*, deriving from the Latin root *pati* which means "to suffer or endure." Each gospel recounts the Passion story in a different way—no less dramatic, no less inspirational, no less spiritually valuable—but very, very differently.

In each telling, the intensity of the Passion crystallizes the answers to the spiritual question offered by that gospel. The community to whom the story is directed understands Jesus the Christ's death and resurrection as the necessary and logical culmination of the lessons that precede it. Furthermore, the writer of each Passion carefully nests the account in circumstances that enable his particular community to poignantly and personally internalize Jesus' experience in their own historical circumstances.

In Matthew's gospel, remember that the Jewish community of Antioch was dispirited and anxious. Matthew's Passion account is directed to this small, beleaguered group of Messianic Jews and is designed to provide very precise guidance. Throughout this account, Jesus the Christ is the exemplar of remaining emotionally and spiritually present in a time of distress and uncertainty. Matthew's Passion brings the gospel's question into the realm of the very specific: In the midst of anxiety and fear, how do we embrace change with love rather than succumb to victimhood?

Arriving in Jerusalem

After preaching the Sermon on the Mount, Jesus continues to teach in Galilee and Judea, telling stories and challenging the authority of the Temple and its leaders at every turn. The chief priests and Temple elders in Jerusalem are quite naturally becoming increasingly incensed over the potential rebellion these teachings represent. They are afraid the power, authority, and prerequisites of the Temple are at risk.

Jesus finally arrives in Jerusalem itself, and the Temple leaders decide it is time to dispose of this upstart teacher. But they are apprehensive. Jesus is so popular that they fear riots might break out if they arrest him, and then Rome would hold the Temple responsible.

Overtaken by both urgency and opportunity, the authorities opt for a plan offered by Jesus' disciple Judas. The arrest is scheduled during the Feast of Unleavened Bread, the celebration today known as Passover. Though the chief priest and elders are reluctant to interfere with the festivities because they fear a riot. Judas' plan calls for confronting Jesus late at night and privately, when the public will hopefully have little, if any, reaction.

> *When Jesus had finished saying all these things, he said to his disciples, "You know that after two days the Passover is coming, and the Son of Man will be handed over to be crucified." Then the chief priests and the elders of the people gathered in the palace of the high priest, who was called Caiaphas, and they conspired to arrest Jesus by stealth and kill him. But they said, "Not during the festival, or there may be a riot among the people." (26:1–5)*

In the midst of this account, Matthew takes a few verses and makes a pointed digression. During a meal in the home of Simon the leper, an unnamed woman is described as anointing Jesus' head with expensive oil. Five verses later, Matthew recounts the large amount of silver that Judas Iscariot receives for betraying Jesus. It appears the entire purpose of this juxtaposition is to pose a question to the Messiahnians: "In times of difficulty and isolation, there will be choices to make. Will you pay the cost to honor the beliefs of your soul? Or will you collect the price of shame and betray them? The expense of either will be high, and you will have to decide."

> *Now while Jesus was at Bethany in the house of Simon the leper, a woman came to him with an alabaster jar of very costly ointment, and she poured it on his head as he sat at the table. (26:6–7)*

> *Then one of the twelve, who was called Judas Iscariot, went to the chief priests and said, "What will you give me if I betray him to you?" They paid him thirty pieces of silver. And from that moment he began to look for an opportunity to betray him. (26:14–16)*

The Last Supper

The Last Supper, clearly identified as the Passover meal, is held at an unidentified house. Conversation begins abruptly and focuses on impending betrayal, which Jesus accepts matter-of-factly.

In the custom of the time, meals were served in a single, common bowl. Tearing a piece of bread to use as a scoop, each person reaches into the bowl, gets food, then eats. Jesus announces that his betrayal will come from *"the one who has dipped his hand into the bowl with me."* Read literally, these words state that everyone at table that night will betray him; Jesus does not differentiate between Judas and the other disciples.

Jesus knows that none of the disciples are sufficiently ready, sufficiently mature in their faith, to be capable of constancy. He knows that they will cling to their old behaviors, the old order, and that many betrayals will occur, and more than once.

This is an inevitable and predictable part of the early stages of the spiritual journey—and *all* of the disciples are vulnerable. Jesus wants to prepare his followers for this reality. He wants to bring them forward to the much more important lesson of "what remains to be done *after* betrayal."

Everyone at the table, even Judas, responds, "Surely not I?" Matthew notes, however, one small—but extremely significant—difference concerning Judas. Eleven of the disciples address Jesus as "Lord," in recognition of Jesus' higher nature and authority, but Judas addresses Jesus as "Rabbi."

In that time, rabbis were not the specially educated heads of congregations they are now. Largely self-appointed teachers who had the capacity to attract a following, they were often completely unlettered. With this address, Judas therefore minimizes Jesus' station, treating him as simply another man. Judas could, with impunity, ignore and even disrespect a mere rabbi.

In all likelihood, this is more a message to the Messiahnians than an accurate historical detail. Matthew is probably much more concerned that those in Antioch acknowledge Jesus the Christ as "Lord" instead of "Rabbi" than Jesus would have been. Nonetheless, it is an important distinction in this gospel with respect to either Judas' lack of understanding or commitment.

> *On the first day of Unleavened Bread the disciples came to Jesus, saying, "Where do you want us to make the preparations for you to eat the Passover?" He said, "Go into the city to a certain man, and say to him, 'The Teacher says, My time is near; I will keep the Passover at your house with my disciples.' " So the disciples did as Jesus had directed them, and they prepared the Passover meal. (26:17–19)*

> *When it was evening, he took his place with the twelve; and while they were eating, he said, "Truly I tell you, one of you will betray me." And they became greatly distressed and began to say to him one after another, "Surely not I, Lord?" He answered, "The one who has dipped his hand into the bowl with me will betray me. The Son of Man goes as it is written of him, but woe to that one by whom the Son of Man is betrayed! It would have been better for that one not to have been born." Judas, who betrayed him, said, "Surely not I, Rabbi?" He replied, "You have said so." (26:20–25)*

Gethsemane, Arrest, and Trial

After the meal, Jesus goes with the remaining disciples to the Mount of Olives knowing he will be arrested there. Jesus reiterates that all of the disciples will desert him. Peter protests that he will never abandon Jesus no matter what others do. In response, Jesus predicts Peter's three-time denial "before the cock crows." Peter again promises his total fidelity, as do the rest of the disciples. Yet within a few hours, they would, indeed, all desert him. The irony of this repeated promise adds to the litany of betrayals we find in Matthew's story.

> *When they had sung the hymn, they went out to the Mount of Olives. Then Jesus said to them, "You will all become deserters because of me this night; for it is written, 'I will strike the shepherd, and the sheep of the flock will be scattered.' But after I am raised up, I will go ahead of you to Galilee." Peter said to him, "Though all become deserters because of you, I will never desert you." Jesus said to him, "Truly I tell you, this very night, before the cock crows, you will deny me three times." Peter said to him, "Even though I must die with you, I will not deny you." And so said all the disciples. (26:30–35)*

Jesus then goes with the disciples to Gethsemane, atop the Mount of Olives, to pray. The Aramaic word *Gethsemane* means a place where olives are pressed, and using it here as the named location clearly reinforces the core message of this gospel: the effort, strain, and attentiveness necessary to produce the oil of balm and anointing.

Selecting the three most loyal and experienced disciples—Peter, James, and John—Jesus takes them further, leading them away from the others. He requests they remain with him and stay awake as he prays. The Messiah throws himself on the ground and prays to his Father, "If it is possible, let this cup pass from me; yet not what I want but what you want." The three disciples, tired and distressed, prove unable to stay awake and fall soundly asleep. Jesus remonstrates with Peter that if he cannot even stay awake—clearly he is not yet strong enough to endure difficult tests of faith.

An often-debated question arises here about which cup Jesus prayed not to drink. Earlier at the Passover meal, Jesus had said he would not take wine again "until that day when I will drink it new with you in my Father's kingdom" (26:29). Yet in this verse, perhaps only an hour later, Jesus prays to let "this cup" go by if possible. Did he mean the cup of his imminent death, or a metaphorical cup of bitterness caused by the desertion of his intimate friends and disciples?

We cannot know this with absolute certainty. However, because Matthew consistently emphasizes betrayal and its consequences throughout the Passion (as well as Jesus' almost nonchalant acceptance of his fate), I firmly believe this prayer is metaphorical, asking for release from inner pain over the desertion, and is not Jesus' prayer to avoid physical death.

> *Then Jesus went with them to a place called Gethsemane; and he said to his disciples, "Sit here while I go over there and pray." He took with him Peter and the two sons of Zebedee, and began to be grieved and agitated. Then he said to them, "I am deeply grieved, even to death; remain here, and stay awake with me." And going a little farther, he threw himself on the ground and prayed, "My Father, if it is possible, let this cup pass from me; yet not what I want but what you want." Then he came to the disciples and found them sleeping; and he said to Peter, "So, could you not stay awake with me one hour? Stay awake and pray that you may not come into the time of trial; the spirit indeed is willing, but the flesh is weak." (26:36–41)*

When Judas appears at Gethsemane with a crowd sent by the Temple authorities, he identifies Jesus by kissing him, again using the word "Rabbi" and not "Lord." Jesus, however, addresses the disciple as "friend." By doing so, Jesus completely embodies the principles he taught in the Sermon on the Mount, returning nothing but the greatest love and respect even when it is not offered to him. He then calmly accepts his arrest. Could there have been a more dramatic example for the Messianic Jews of Antioch of responding to betrayal with equanimity and compassion?

FOUR—CLIMBING THE GREAT MOUNTAIN OF MATTHEW

> *While [Jesus] was still speaking, Judas, one of the twelve, arrived; with him was a large crowd with swords and clubs, from the chief priests and the elders of the people. Now the betrayer had given them a sign, saying, "The one I will kiss is the man; arrest him." At once he came up to Jesus and said, "Greetings, Rabbi!" and kissed him. Jesus said to him, "Friend, do what you are here to do." Then they came and laid hands on Jesus and arrested him. (26:47–50)*

Following the arrest, the chief priests along with the entire council hold a trial (quite different than the trial we will read of in The Gospel of John). Throughout this trial, Jesus remains silent. Finally, when placed under oath, he responds to the high priest and does not claim to be the Messiah. Jesus speaks instead of the "Son of Man," an implicit reference to the Hebrew book of Daniel (7:13), which contains a vision in which Daniel saw "one [who is] like a human being" acting as God's agent, winning a battle for God, and restoring harmony between heaven and earth.

The chief priests are enraged when they hear Jesus predict that "the Son of Man" will sit in a place of power. This vision implies that high priests' sacrificing animals on an altar will become unimportant, clearly denouncing the authority of the Temple and foretelling nothing less than a spiritual revolution.

In effect and under oath, Jesus had drawn a line, and historically he was proven correct. Ultimately, the presence of Jesus the Christ and the ensuing growth of Christianity (along with other more mystical Jewish sects) was a major factor in the crumbling of the Temple's inner authority. Only a few decades later, Rome completed the job by destroying the Temple's outer shell.

Matthew, always determined to communicate this parallel to the Messianic Jews, never misses an opportunity to reiterate: "Let your old beliefs and desire for a physical temple go. These allegiances are outworn. They are like a heap of dry bones. Lovingly let them be and continue on your path up a new mountain. Embrace the unknown. You are beloved. Do not fear."

> *Now the chief priests and the whole council were looking for false testimony against Jesus so that they might put him to death, but they found none, though many false witnesses came forward. At last two came forward and said, "This fellow said, 'I am able to destroy the temple of God and to build it in three days.'" The high priest stood up and said, "Have you no answer? What is it that they testify against you?" But Jesus was silent. Then the high priest said to him, "I put you under oath before the living God, tell us if you are the Messiah, the Son of God." Jesus said to him, "You have said so. But I tell you, From now on you will see the Son of Man seated at the right hand of Power and coming on the clouds of heaven." Then the high priest tore his clothes and said, "He has blasphemed! Why do we still need witnesses? You have now heard his blasphemy. What is your verdict?" They answered, "He deserves death." (26:59–66)*

Betrayals continue in the Passion story. Peter, the most intimate of Jesus' disciples, fearing arrest fulfills Jesus' prediction and denies knowing Jesus on three separate occasions. However, Matthew uses this example as an opportunity for a deeper teaching. Despite his betrayal, Peter subsequently experiences not only remorse, but more importantly, self-understanding. Consequently, he remains not only a full disciple but also a witness throughout the narrative.

This underscored Matthew's point to the Messianic Antiochians that facing one's weakness with honesty and mercy leads to greater strength. In the event this happened in their community, they should welcome rather than shun any individual who had the courage to behave as Peter has.

> *Now Peter was sitting outside in the courtyard. A servant-girl came to him and said, "You also were with Jesus the Galilean." But he denied it before all of them, saying, "I do not know what you are talking about." When he went out to the porch, another servant-girl saw him, and she said to the bystanders, "This man was with Jesus of Nazareth." Again he denied it with an oath, "I do not know the man."*

FOUR—CLIMBING THE GREAT MOUNTAIN OF MATTHEW

> *After a little while the bystanders came up and said to Peter, "Certainly you are also one of them, for your accent betrays you." Then he began to curse, and he swore an oath, "I do not know the man!" At that moment the cock crowed. Then Peter remembered what Jesus had said: "Before the cock crows, you will deny me three times." And he went out and wept bitterly. (26:69-75)*

Judas, meanwhile, also feels remorse over his betrayal of Jesus. Returning to the priests, he claims repentance and gives them back the silver he had been paid. They dismiss him contemptuously. In complete despair, Judas leaves and kills himself. Matthew has put Judas' and Peter's behavior in clear contrast.

Peter reflected on his actions; he "remembered what Jesus had said." He acknowledged Jesus' power as greater than his own. So even though he had briefly given in to his fears, he had the stability for self-forgiveness and the capacity to move forward. He could return to the Messiah and walk on despite his failings.

Judas, on the other hand, lacked the inner resources to reflect beyond his own misery. In Quadratos' terms, he was spiritually immature. He lacked Peter's humility. Instead, he remained trapped by the narrowness of his arrogance and rigidity and was unable to reflect and "remember" in the way Peter could.

When shame and despair overwhelmed him, and his conscience wanted to make a correction, he was unable to do so. He didn't know how. He returned to the only ways his ego-self knew—the old ways, personified by the "chief priests and elders." Caged in his fears, Judas was caught in self-hatred and not open to receive Spirit's love and forgiveness. Death was the only option allowed by the limitations of his closed imagination and heart.

Judas' suicide appears only in The Gospel of Matthew. It was a message to the Messiahnians, but it endures as one of the great teachings of Christianity: forgiveness and growth are always available for a believer in

Jesus the Christ. The voice of love is ever-present. *We* are the only ones who can close the door to forgiveness, and we close it on ourselves, through our own lack of understanding and self-compassion.

> **When Judas, his betrayer, saw that Jesus was condemned, he repented and brought back the thirty pieces of silver to the chief priests and the elders. He said, "I have sinned by betraying innocent blood." But they said, "What is that to us? See to it yourself." Throwing down the pieces of silver in the temple, he departed; and he went and hanged himself. (27:3–5)**

Subsequent events have a tone of increasing bitterness. The "chief priests and elders" persuade "the crowds" to demand that the Roman governor, Pontius Pilate, grant clemency to Barabbas, another prisoner and known criminal, and sentence Jesus to death. Pilate acquiesces.

Matthew frequently links "crowd" and "chief priests and elders." He uses this vocabulary at Jesus' arrest, and again at the sentencing. In other words, this "crowd" was not just any group of people from Jerusalem, or even an innocuous group of Jews, but *a specific group of Temple followers, doing the bidding of the Temple authorities*. This is a distinction critical for our comprehension of events that follow.

After his condemnation by Pilate, Jesus is taken away and flogged. But first, the soldiers place a scarlet robe on him. Although all four gospels record the robe, the color varies in each, reflecting the core message of that particular gospel. Matthew robes Jesus in the color of blood, wanting to call attention to the link between Jesus' imminent death and ritual sacrifice, a central component of Jewish traditional religious life.

As we noted previously, in the hour before each dawn, the chief priest poured the blood of a lamb over the high altar. Jews of that time believed that the life force of a creature or a person resided in their blood, which made it the most significant element of the animal and therefore of the sacrifice. The meat itself was discarded and burned.

Images of blood are woven throughout this gospel. The lengthy genealogy dramatizes the *bloodline* of the Messiahnians. When Herod searches for the infant Jesus, he sheds the *blood* of innocents. Judas' silver, received for betraying Jesus, became later known as *"blood money."* Pilate washes his hands of Jesus' innocent *blood*, and the Temple authorities and their crowd cried out: "His *blood* be on us and on our children!"

For centuries, this cry of blood from the crowd has been read as a curse, and used to justify the torture and killing of Jewish people. Did Matthew intend this as a curse on the Jews? All biblical texts have many possible readings, but because of the particularly horrible uses to which this phrase has been put, it is very important to analyze this thoroughly. I do not believe that Matthew intended to curse Jews or the Jewish religion at all.

My belief is based on several obvious realities. The first is the clear metaphorical meaning Matthew ascribes to the Temple authorities and the "crowd" of Temple followers around them. Throughout the gospel, these figures symbolize the old ways of thinking and doing. They represent groups and people who, over time, became complacent and allowed inspiration to diminish so that increasingly rigid structures were accommodated.

These same people became unreflective and obedient to authority and tradition for its own sake. So, when they cried out after Pilate's decision, their words represent the desperate words of a threatened belief system, which Matthew has characterized as "corrupt" and useless.

The second reason that I reject the all-too customary interpretation is because Matthew so completely expresses the first path of our spiritual journey. His Passion is a profound analogy. His account tells Jesus' story while simultaneously revealing its deeper revelation: spiritual growth requires something akin to a shedding of blood, a death and a renunciation of previous ways, discarding the useless inner life that did not serve.

Understood in this sense, the phrase "His blood be upon us and our children" would mean that Jesus' new blood would fall upon the crowd (and their descendants), and falling upon them, would bless them and change them. The new would transform the old.

I realize that this is an unorthodox reading of the crowd's cry. However, I find its message of encouragement and hope for the Messiahnians— that their Jewish brothers and sisters would eventually join them in their beliefs—to be far more consistent with Matthew's gospel than the traditional (and to me, hateful) interpretation.

The "curse" theory cannot be valid for an even greater reason: it would be completely antithetical to Jesus' behavior and teachings, and certainly to Matthew's inspired gospel that recounts them. Scholars agree that the Beatitudes contain the clearest example of Jesus' principal lessons, and these explicit instructions mandate that Matthew's messages throughout his gospel be interpreted in that spirit. Matthew wants the Messianic Jews to be transformed by love, not hampered by hate.

> *Now the chief priests and the elders persuaded the crowds to ask for Barabbas and to have Jesus killed. The governor again said to them, "Which of the two do you want me to release for you?" And they said, "Barabbas." Pilate said to them, "Then what should I do with Jesus who is called the Messiah?" All of them said, "Let him be crucified!" Then he asked, "Why, what evil has he done?" But they shouted all the more, "Let him be crucified!" So when Pilate saw that he could do nothing, but rather that a riot was beginning, he took some water and washed his hands before the crowd, saying, "I am innocent of this man's blood; see to it yourselves." Then the people as a whole answered, "His blood be on us and on our children!" So he released Barabbas for them; and after flogging Jesus, he handed him over to be crucified. Then the soldiers of the governor took Jesus into the governor's headquarters, and they gathered the whole cohort around him. They stripped him and put a scarlet robe on him, and after twisting some thorns into a crown, they put it on his head. They put a reed in his right hand and knelt before him and mocked him, saying, "Hail, King of the Jews!" They spat on him, and took the reed and struck him on the head. After mocking him, they stripped him of the robe and put his own clothes on him. Then they led him away to crucify him. (27:20-31)*

Crucifixion and Death

Except for his preparatory prayer in Gethsemane, Matthew gives no hint that Jesus suffers or even takes much note of the terrible events of the Passion. He responds simply and quietly to Pilate at his trial and, it seems, responds not at all to the flogging or sustained mockery.

When the time finally comes for his painful death, Jesus' demeanor still does not change. At Golgotha, the place of crucifixion, Matthew tells us that Jesus is offered gall, a bitter substance that deadens pain when mixed with wine. Jesus rejects the potion. He chooses to remain fully awake, to face and feel every moment with an open mind, heart, and body, not resisting pain.

His noble behavior demonstrates the legitimacy of his place in the genealogy as "the son of David, the son of Abraham." This serves as an excruciating message to Messiahnians: "Suffering is of value. This time is your necessary trial, your unavoidable inner death. Stay present. Stay awake to the experience. God will sustain you."

> *And when they came to a place called Golgotha (which means Place of a Skull), they offered him wine to drink, mixed with gall; but when he tasted it, he would not drink it. (27:33-34)*

Jesus hangs on the cross, withstanding the jeers and mockery of the Temple authorities. Matthew's Passion references the temptations when he describes how the priests, scribes and elders at the crucifixion challenge Jesus to come down and escape his torment.

Matthew makes an explicit parallel, equating the demands of the priests with the second temptation of the devil. He unequivocally avers that the Temple authorities are corrupt, no longer useful, and obstructing the new ways. "Do you think some Pharisees abuse their power in Antioch?" Matthew asks. "Look at how the old Temple structure abused the Messiah!" No opportunity is lost to make his point.

> *Those who passed by derided him, shaking their heads and saying, "You who would destroy the temple and build it in three days, save yourself! If you are the Son of God, come*

> *down from the cross." In the same way the chief priests also, along with the scribes and elders, were mocking him, saying, "He saved others; he cannot save himself. He is the King of Israel; let him come down from the cross now, and we will believe in him. He trusts in God; let God deliver him now, if he wants to; for he said, 'I am God's Son.'" The bandits who were crucified with him also taunted him in the same way. (27:39-44)*

As Jesus' last moments draw near, he calls out the first line of Psalm 22: "My God, my God, why have you forsaken me?" To be certain it is properly identified, Matthew puts it both in its original Aramaic and in its translation. Any devout Jew in the first century who had prayed all his life would have hoped to be able to pray this psalm at his death.

Its misinterpretation by some of the "crowd" is a pejorative comment by Matthew about the crudeness of their character and the lack of their piety.

> *And about three o'clock Jesus cried with a loud voice, "Eli, Eli, lema sabachthani?" that is, "My God, my God, why have you forsaken me?" When some of the bystanders heard it, they said, "This man is calling for Elijah." At once one of them ran and got a sponge, filled it with sour wine, put it on a stick, and gave it to him to drink. But the others said, "Wait, let us see whether Elijah will come to save him." Then Jesus cried again with a loud voice and breathed his last. (27:46-50)*

Only The Gospel of Matthew records the next phenomenon: a great earthquake and a simultaneous tearing of "the curtain of the temple" that occur precisely at the moment Jesus dies. This is a reference to the curtain that shields the entrance to the Holy of Holies in the Temple, making this a powerful and climactic image for the Messianic Jews.

The Messiahnians of Antioch could certainly relate to an earthquake. Every aspect of their lives was being shaken. Their connection to the divine must have seemed especially precarious. Without the Temple, could they still reach God, know God, and see God? The picture Matthew presented must have awed and frightened them.

FOUR—CLIMBING THE GREAT MOUNTAIN OF MATTHEW

Nevertheless, the stories they could find within this metaphorical imagery also fully affirmed their hope in the blessing at the heart of Jesus' teachings. The curtain in the Temple tore because it had lost its usefulness. The Messiah had come, and God was now omnipresent. The treasures, until then kept behind the curtain, now rested everywhere, accessible at any time and to all believers—not just the priests. Furthermore, this cataclysmic opening had also raised the saints, who would presumably now be available, directly, to them.

> ***Then Jesus cried again with a loud voice and breathed his last. At that moment the curtain of the temple was torn in two, from top to bottom. The earth shook, and the rocks were split. The tombs also were opened, and many bodies of the saints who had fallen asleep were raised. (27:50-52)***

How shall we summarize the significance of Matthew's Passion? In our own journey's beginning, we have been greeted with hope and grief, promise and resentment. That is the first path of Quadratos. We know that no matter the depth of our previous spiritual growth, crossing into a new unknown and standing on a threshold of radical change will always give us a sharp sting of anxiety.

Will we choose to keep walking even if others around us do not? Will we choose to be awake as we wind our way up the mountain? Will we choose to confront our fears, even unto the death of our small beliefs and to the uncompassionate corners of our most hidden hearts? Will we choose kindness—at this juncture, mostly for ourselves? And, as we are able, for others?

On this path, our first deep practice requires self-responsibility and presence. We need to be "with" ourselves—mind, body, and spirit—in a condition of self-honesty and openness. Although we must not descend into isolation, we also cannot allow ourselves to be distracted by anything or anyone. We can take no gall. Instead, our course is prayer, and the asking for wise counsel therein.

Our second practice is patience. As we make our way up the mountain, we will have many missteps, many "self-betrayals." We must expect this, and meet each of these with love rather than piling self-criticism and shame on our fragile heads.

Our third practice is self-compassion. Can we name ourselves "friend"? Can we comprehend that our journeys are as individual as we are, and even our mistakes are a part of the odyssey that Spirit has chosen for us? We must respect and honor the efforts we are making. We need to say over and over again, "Thank you." Our self-embrace will provide us the courage and freedom to continue.

Moving Past Tribe
The Resurrection of the Messiah

Just as each of the four gospels has a distinct Passion account, so too are there four very different resurrection accounts. In each gospel, the story of the resurrection serves to both resolve and carry forward into practice the core set of concerns on which the gospel is focused.

Matthew's resurrection account is a buoyant conclusion to his gospel. This gospel teaches the words of Jesus the Christ in inspiring, yet uncompromising prose. Throughout a purposeful journey, the travails and abuse of his trial and crucifixion, and even his death, Matthew shows us a tranquil and loving Jesus. Now, at the end of the gospel, the resurrection holds out the magnificent vision of a world that can become reality if the challenge of Jesus' transcendent example can be met.

After Jesus' burial, as both Mary Magdalene and Mary (the mother of James and Joseph) wait by the tomb, Matthew recounts a second earthquake and the simultaneous rolling back of the tombstone by an angel. Sitting on the stone, the angel proclaims Jesus' resurrection saying, "He has been raised from the dead, and indeed he is going ahead of you to Galilee; there you will see him."

Like the earlier combination of earthquake and curtain-tearing, this reiterates Matthew's central message: "God, the promise of the Messiah, has moved out of the Temple, out of the tomb. He lives and is with you. You are invited to a new and larger life."

> *After the sabbath, as the first day of the week was dawning, Mary Magdalene and the other Mary went to see the tomb. And suddenly there was a great earthquake; for an angel of the Lord, descending from heaven, came and rolled back the stone and sat on it. (28:1–2)*
>
> *The angel said to the women, "Do not be afraid; I know that you are looking for Jesus who was crucified. He is not here; for he has been raised, as he said.... 'He has been raised from the dead, and indeed he is going ahead of you to Galilee; there you will see him.' This is my message for you." (28:5–7)*[3]

In Galilee, the place of the promised second sighting, the disciples encounter the risen Jesus as the angel had promised. But this does not happen on either of the great historic Jewish mountains—not on Mount Moriah nor on Mount Sinai. It is simply "a mountain" in Galilee, significantly unnamed, just as the mountain is for the Sermon on the Mount.

Matthew, once again, is explicitly leaving the Temple mount in Jerusalem behind. The new mountain of the Messiah is not in a particular place. It is anywhere, and everywhere. It is within.

Since there is only a single appearance of the risen Christ in this gospel, Matthew clearly wishes his summary to be focused on the points he makes here. He chooses to reiterate and expand the same words Jesus referenced in his trial before the high priest—the revolutionary and extraordinary vision of the prophet Daniel.

---

[3] There is a small section (28:9–10) that tells of an encounter between the two Marys and the risen Jesus. It was almost certainly added to Matthew a century after the gospel was originally written. This is believed partly because its placement at this point in the text disrupts the gospel's otherwise seamless narrative. When this section is omitted and the gospel is returned to the original, Jesus appears only once, on an unnamed "mount in Galilee."

These final words defied the foundation of traditional Jewish Temple belief. When the resurrected Jesus appears in Galilee to his disciples, he decisively announces that the full power and unity of both heaven and earth are *his*, and his alone. He claims all divine and temporal authority. He speaks in the name of the one God, and he gives a command that must have completely astounded his listeners.

Jesus the Messiah, the risen Christ, tells the disciples to leave the mountain. He instructs them to take the power of God—the inner power they have gained and all that they have learned—out to every place and everyone.

He instructs them to teach discipleship—that same profound journey of intimate relationship with Spirit they have been learning from him—to one and all, near and far. He directs them to share the lessons of love. He tells them to tell others that the divine has only one source, and that every person is a son and a daughter of that source.

Messianic Jews surely found this instruction not only revolutionary but horrifying. They are Jews. They trust in an understanding as deep as their history, that *their* God is uniquely in their bloodline. After all, the covenant with Abraham has made them first among all people, specially privileged.

Now the Jewish Messiah has come—and of course they are certain that he has come for them. It must be almost impossible for them to believe that after two thousand years of their ancestors suffering, hoping, and waiting, they are not going to receive any exceptional acknowledgment. However, Jesus' instruction tells them they must renounce any sense of privilege that they might believe is theirs alone.

Even further, they are instructed to open their hearts and minds to all tribes—in effect, to give their privilege away to "all nations," even to the oppressors! It must seem impossible—almost absurd. After all, their world is rocking with inner and outer earthquakes, and the logical course in an earthquake is to hold on to what is solid, not to let it go.

How can *their* Messiah ask them to give up the belief in their privilege when they have already lost so much? This has to be a deeply dismaying challenge for the suffering Messiahnians.

The direct and simple beauty of the gospel's last line must have allayed the dismay and confusion somewhat. With the same full power and authority of heaven and earth used for his difficult instructions, Jesus the Messiah pronounces, "Remember."

He tells his followers never to forget that they are not alone. He is with them, loving them, always and forever. This is, indeed, the fitting and final message to which Matthew has brought everything in this gospel: "And remember, I AM with you always, to the end of time."

> *Now the eleven disciples went to Galilee, to the mountain to which Jesus had directed them. When they saw him, they worshiped him; but some doubted. And Jesus came and said to them, "All authority in heaven and on earth has been given to me. Go therefore and make disciples of all nations... teaching them to obey everything that I have commanded you. And remember,*
>
> *I am with you always, to the end of the age." (28:16-20)*[4]

When we are trying to relate this last section of Matthew's gospel to our own lives, it is natural at first to think in terms of how dissimilar our experience is today. After all, in the Mediterranean basin, early human groups were tribal, as they were in most parts of the world. Each tribe had its own god and the village beliefs determined their entire understanding of the world. The citizens of Antioch were essentially tribal, filled with fears and trepidation when encountering anything new.

Indeed, tribal culture still dominates in many regions of the world today. And tribal reactions relate to us—even in urban, first-world areas—more than we might realize. The "nation state" many of us live in now, larger and more cooperative than the tribe, is quite recent in the history of humankind.

---

[4] Present-day Bibles include the phrase "baptizing them in the name of the Father and of the Son and of the Holy Spirit" at this point in the text. This phrase, commonly referred to as "the baptismal commission," was added to the gospel some years after the original text was written because the concepts of Father, Son, and Spirit did not crystallize until after full separation from Judaism had occurred and self-identification of early followers as "Christians" had commenced.

I talked earlier about the close sense of "village" found in my extended Lebanese family. Right now, in tribes throughout the world, people are taught that they only "know" people from their own village, even if they can see the villages of outsiders in the distance. And today we tend to think that these sorts of beliefs are remote from us. Yet these tribal understandings shape everyone's early development, no matter where we live—whether in isolated rural areas or large, urban cities.

Today, most of us have told ourselves that our understanding is different, more developed or "sophisticated." Yet we retain many vestiges of the old patterns. We are frequently suspicious of those who differ from us in ways large and small. We keep company with those most like ourselves in custom and thought, and we speak of outsiders as "them"—in our families, our work, our churches, our countries.

So, while our fearfulness of Jesus' command may have lessened somewhat over the centuries, its basic challenge has not. We still need the words to inspire us, because their practice is still daunting, no matter how much we may believe in the principles of equality and oneness. We are, after all, on the first path.

The self-honesty we have begun to gain on our trek up Matthew's mountain has given us a small glimpse into our next challenge, Mark's stormy sea. Throughout Matthew we have been called—like Joseph, husband and dreamer—to accept emotional exile and make an original journey.

To accomplish this, we have had to put our usual ways of knowing aside and begin walking to an inner voice, as Joseph did. In these last lines of Matthew, we begin to realize that the cost to heed this inner voice will be enormous, but we can sense that the benefit will be likewise.

At the beginning of his gospel, Matthew recounts the story of the Messiah's lineage and the coming of a child to be named Emmanuel, which means "God is with us." The last line of the Gospel echoes that meaning, which has given us the power to continue and sustain our journey. It is an unequivocal promise: "Remember, *I am with you always*, to the end of the age." This is the answer to all of our questions and all of our fears. God is with us!

FOUR—CLIMBING THE GREAT MOUNTAIN OF MATTHEW

Now we move on, headed for Rome and the very stormy sea of the Gospel of Mark. We will walk with Matthew's final message as our staff, holding it firmly as we stride toward the waves that glint before us. The second path and its gospel will be another great challenge, but I promise you we will make our way through it.

Remember—there is not just one path. Nor are there two paths, or even three. There are four paths in the Journey of Quadratos. We can and will traverse the second path—and the third—and the fourth. We have the map. Do not forget: we are not alone—we are *never* alone. With God's promise in our hearts, let us move into Mark's gospel.

Prayer for The First Path

Psalm 121

I lift my eyes to the mountain peak—
Where does my help come from?
It comes from you
Maker of heaven and earth
Who holds my foot firm on the path up
Who's constantly present
Everywhere aware

Look!
With you there's no obscurity
Nothing is dim, asleep, inert
To those who question and struggle
You respond, keep hold, give cover
So that by day the sun won't burn
Nor by night the moon mesmerize

You guard against evil
Enfold and reveal the soul

Guard my arrival
Secure my departure—

Now
Always.

translation by Norman Fischer

EXERCISES FOR THE FIRST PATH

Create Temenos

Temenos is a Greek term. It literally translates "to make a cut or furrow in the ground." It was particularly used to indicate the unbroken cut that marked off the spiritual area where a temple was to be built. The unbroken trench thereby created was intended to assuage fear that the divinity might escape from the holy place.

The Greeks also understood that to go to a temple was risky behavior. One went there to ask a question, and asking meant that one did not know—a frightening admission for the ego-self. Each person therefore wanted to be sure that she or he was going to a place of genuine wisdom and safety before making the journey into the unknown. Temenos provided that assurance.

In our present-day world, temenos is a very useful way of understanding the balance between safety and risk. Too much safety easily leads to complacency. In our comfortable lives, we can readily slip into the illusion that security and a lack of challenge are our prerogatives.

If we face too much risk, we can discover the opposite imbalance which is a condition of emotional paralysis. Feelings of overstimulation or overwhelm can lead us into the opposite illusion that the journey is simply too painful and beyond our capacity.

The practice of the first path is a continual practice of fits and starts—of making progress and falling back. In this way we learn our emotional and psychological strengths and vulnerabilities. Next, we discover our personal and unique balance between appropriate challenge and a sense of overwhelm. It is incumbent upon each of us to create and sustain our own individual practice of *temenos*. I recommend three supports to aid in this effort:

- Gather the people, words, poems, stories, music and films that inspire you to trust, to set out on a new journey, and to welcome challenge. Especially collect stories and films of your heroes and heroines, saints and mystics, and world figures or a family member. Create a library of successful journeys that inspire you not only to begin but to keep moving.

- Secure a trusted adviser, spiritual guide, soul friend, or mentor.

- Begin a daily practice of reflection, meditation, and prayer.

Every effort you put forth toward creating these supports will result in untold riches and enormous benefits—not only in the completion of the Journey of Quadratos but throughout the rest of your life.

Welcome The Other

The Lakota people of North America have a concept called the *heyoeka*, or "the other." A person identified as a heyoeka, whether male or female, becomes an official "opposite," feeling and thinking and expressing what others will not. The heyoeka dresses in heavy clothes in the summer and lightweight fabrics in the winter, walks backward, laughs when others are sad, and is sad when others are happy.

His or her most important role is served when the people are in deliberation at council. As a decision begins to gain approval, the heyoeka must speak loudly and strongly to the opposite opinion. The Lakota believe that every voice and every position on an issue must be given a respectful hearing before the people can make a correct discernment.

Heyoeka is a specific name from a specific people, but this practice of offering respect to every voice and position is generally found throughout the indigenous people of the Americas. It was also known in the court of Europe (in limited form) as the role of "the wise fool."

Therefore, as you are setting out, create an intention to listen for the annoying, irritating opinion inside yourself, amongst your family members, your friends, your church, your region and country. When you hear it, when you sense that resistance inside yourself, begin the practice of extending respect to the other and the other's position.

Indeed, try to think about *all* positions, especially those you would normally reject automatically, even (or especially) if they make you uncomfortable or angry. Attempting to welcome these ideas does not mean following them—but it does mean trying to know them and trying to understand differing positions and the people who hold them. It is possible that one of these seemingly foreign ideas may provide the key to your next step—or even your entire journey.

HOW DO WE FACE CHANGE?
The Core Question of The Gospel of Matthew

The great, overarching message of Matthew is to set out on the journey with courage and trust. Matthew was writing to Messianic Jews who were in turmoil and had no idea they were to be among the founders of a new religion. His steadying words still echo with prophetic insight and pragmatic counsel invaluable to all who are on the first path of the Journey of Quadratos. How often are we, too, surprised by the completely unexpected way events turn out in our lives? Courage and Trust!

The Genealogy of Matthew, the story of Joseph, the arrival of the Magi, and Jesus' vision at his baptism tell us to search our individual histories, and also the experience and stories of others for inspiration. Each great example we find reminds us that arduous journeys are universally experienced, cyclical, can be accomplished, and are worthwhile. We learn to remain open to surprise and that great gifts will come from unexpected, seemingly improper, contradictory, or uncomfortable sources. Above all else, we are reminded that even when ash falls from the sky or the earth trembles—we are beloved.

Herod's example and Mary and Joseph's return to Egypt ask us to confront our fears about making a new journey and to learn from them. When we then return and recognize our places of deep wounding, Spirit will help us begin to loosen pain's hold and lead us to larger freedom. We need to disregard "what if?" and "should have" and "if only."

The tempter asks us to be mindful of our motives along the first path for many self-illusions can lead us astray. Self-righteousness and a sense of privilege are particular problems when we claim our beliefs as right for anyone other than ourselves or try to aggrandize ourselves at the expense of others.

The Beatitudes help us stay on the road if we keep them close at hand. They provide comfort and inspiration for the journey, useful practices to engage us, standards to emulate and beautiful words to pray.

The Passion account affirms that if we truly accept our invitation to the journey offered by Jesus the Christ, we can stay "awake" to the process, and if we do fall asleep, we can wake and begin again. Change can be embraced with a full heart. When difficulties befall, we needn't blame others, ourselves, or adopt a "why me?" attitude. And we may leave aside any paralyzing despair that would have us end the journey believing we are utterly alone, at fault and unworthy of forgiveness.

The Resurrection account tells us to take personal responsibility for our spiritual lives and accept the challenge to make our own journey. Certitude is not expected. Doubt goes hand-in-hand with trust and courage. We need to renounce any sense of being special that we may feel because of Jesus' presence with us. And we are learning that on the journey we need never feel alone. We have Jesus' promise: "Remember, I am with you always!"

Chapter 5

CROSSING MARK'S STORMY SEA

WILDERNESS PRAYER

I am not asking you
to take this wilderness from me,
to remove this place of starkness
where I come to know
the wildness within me,
where I learn to call the names
of the ravenous beasts
that pace inside me,
to finger the brambles
that snake through my veins,
to taste the thirst
that tugs at my tongue.

But send me
tough angels,
sweet wine,
strong bread:
just enough.

Jan L. Richardson

How Do We Move Through Suffering?
The Second Path

The second path is without a doubt the most agonizing of the four paths—so it is a very good thing that it is also the least complicated. In the first path, we had to learn and live with our greatest fears and insecurities. Now, in the second path they fight back. The profound question of the second path is, *How do we move through suffering?*

We feel as though we are in a small boat on a stormy sea—terrified, exhausted, fragile. The winds and water lash us as we are tossed about in a gray, horizonless, directionless world. Is help coming? There is no way to tell, and in any case, we are not sure how to discern what would help and what would harm us further. We are thirsty, but only saltwater surrounds us. We are filled with doubt that drains our strength like the deepest failure. We feel pretty certain we will die.

We know we can't return to the beginning. At this point, we probably could not even find that place—but we don't really wish to anyway. We want to get through this time. We have only one genuine possibility, and that is to fall back on ancient and proven practice. We pray. We meditate.

We stay attentive for a hopeful sign or voice—a navigational star, a neighborly and knowledgeable sailor who knows the waters better than we. We pray and listen more. Then we follow the instructions we receive, in whatever way we receive them, without question. We pray and listen still more. We surrender yet again to whatever greater knowledge is expressed to us. And we continue to pray.

The bleak condition in which we find ourselves now is precisely the same condition in which the early Christians of Rome in the middle of the first century found themselves—lost, alone, struggling to have hope. The Gospel of Mark was written as a compassionate beacon to light the way through their enduring journey of faith, and it now illuminates our second path.

Birthplace of the Gospel of Mark
Rome, Mid-60s CE

In the first century, Rome was the great Mediterranean center of power. Anyone who wanted to exert influence, or just wanted to be in the middle of things, had to go to Rome. By the year 60, Rome numbered some two million people, thirty to forty thousand of whom were Jews.

Even though that was only two percent of the population, the Roman government paid a significant amount of attention to this minority, ensuring and sustaining a long-established pattern of discord and contention. Roman Jews would live in relative peace for a time. Then a problem would arise and they would be evicted. They would return, enjoy a bit of peace, and then endure another eviction. Evictions took place in 139 BCE, and again in 19 and 49 CE.

In the year 41, Emperor Claudius came to power. He immediately restricted the Jews by prohibiting the use of public places for worship, which effectively shut down the synagogues. The Jews regrouped and began using private homes as gathering places for Sabbath worship and other Jewish feasts and celebrations.

Everything remained quiet on the surface until the year 49, when disturbances broke out in the Jewish quarter. Claudius responded and decreed the expulsion of all Jews from Rome. Although we lack clear historical evidence, we do know that tensions had been mounting in the quarter between traditional Jews and Messianic Jews who believed in the Christus (the Christ). I conjecture that the conflicts between these two groups were behind the expulsion.

After Claudius died, Nero became emperor in the year 54, and the Jews were allowed to return. The apostles Peter and Paul, the two most prominent figures of first-century Christianity, both lived in Rome during those mid-century years. Peter may initially have come in the 40s, been evicted, and returned in 54.

Paul is thought to have been brought to Rome as a prisoner, and lived there under house arrest, having arrived between 56 and 60. In the agonizing years of Mark's gospel, they both lived in Rome—probably in close proximity to each other in the Jewish quarter, a marshy area across the Tiber river from the hills on which the aristocracy resided in elevated splendor.

The Christian church was ultimately to be founded on the differing gifts of these two powerful leaders, but their approaches were so dissimilar that conflict between them was inevitable. By all accounts, until coming to Rome they had successfully avoided each other for years. Now they found themselves in the same city.

Both were members of a troubled minority in a time of great tumult at the center of power. Their personal and theological differences stood in stark contrast as each simultaneously vied for influence and loyalties in the Jewish community. It is strange irony indeed that the Christian church later gave them a shared feast day: June 29 is the Feast of Saints Peter and Paul.

Peter was a fisherman who grew up in Galilee, far from Jerusalem and its perceived high culture. He had known Jesus personally, and had been one of the inner circle of disciples. Peter was the titular (and cautious) leader of the Messianic Jews. Although we have almost no writings by him beyond two possible letters in the New Testament, tradition has frequently described his personality with words such as "gentle" and "accepting."

By contrast, Paul was a scholar and orator who wrote extensively. His are the first and oldest Christian writings we have, dating from approximately 45 to 60 CE, prior to the first gospel. Although he grew up in what is today known as Turkey, he was well educated and very much at ease in Greco-Roman culture. Paul had a fiery heart and tongue, and though he never personally knew the historical Jesus, he carried the message of the Christ across Asia Minor and Greece as a committed evangelist. Paul—unlike Peter—was a Roman citizen, although he was accused of being a dangerous radical and enemy of the emperor.

On July 19 in the year 64 CE, an immense fire erupted in Rome that blazed for five days, stilled, then ignited again and burned for another forty-eight hours. The flames raced through most of Rome, and when the conflagration finally ended, most of the city had been reduced to embers. Little remained—not even the stately hillside homes of the aristocracy were spared. Many people died.

Common gossip spread among the devastated Romans that Emperor Nero was responsible for the fire. Rumor was that he had started it so that his proposals to raze buildings and rebuild Rome in a grand, classical manner could proceed unhindered. The tales proliferated, and Nero soon found himself under attack by his senators. He needed to find the real culprits, or at least someone to blame, and he needed to do so quickly.

Fate—and ghetto geography—provided his answer. The Jewish quarter, untouched by the fire, made the Jews perfect scapegoats for Nero. The fact that the Jewish section was far away across the river and on the outskirts of Rome (which is why it didn't burn), was ignored. Word raced through the quarter that the Jews were about to become Nero's way out of his predicament.

Feelings resurfaced from the earlier disturbance and expulsion in 49. The Jews had been back in Rome for only ten short years. Understandably, they dreaded another eviction and dreaded even more the likelihood of worse punishments exacted by the desperate emperor. Fear and anxiety rose to near panic. Predictions of mass suffering and executions spiraled out of control.

Desperate to forestall what they were certain would be Nero's terrible wrath, it appeared that someone went to the emperor and confessed that a fringe group had indeed set the fire. They identified the culprits as the Messianic Jews, the Christus followers. Centuries later, it is impossible for us to know precisely what anxieties or divisions drove whoever to Nero with this story or what they expected that Nero would do.

Today, we know only Nero's horrific response. Nero immediately demanded that the Jewish community collaborate with Roman soldiers to identify those belonging to the Christus group. Presented with a completely untenable situation and trying to reduce casualties, the Jewish community agreed. A mini-genocide ensued. Roman soldiers knocked on every door of the quarter demanding to know if anyone in each house was a Christ believer. The answer determined the fate of the householder and everyone else in that house.

If a believer was identified, either by others in the community or his own admission, everyone in his house was seized and publicly executed. Normal execution involved leading victims to the floor of the Circus Maximus, shackling them, splattering them with blood, and then loosing starving dogs to eat them as Roman citizens watched. Today, twenty centuries later when we visit St. Peter's Basilica and walk on its great piazza or watch televised ceremonies held there, it is difficult to imagine that this was a place of terrible torture and slaughter.[5]

There was no exemption from horror. If the head of the household denied being a believer, he was nonetheless required to name someone who was. The named individual was summarily arrested and executed, with no opportunity for appeal or protest. Neighbor was forced to turn on neighbor. As the number of executions mounted, self-preservation was the order of the day. Reportedly, family members even turned in other family members. Fear and paranoia reigned.

---

[5] One archaeological opinion says that the Circus Maximus was temporarily moved across the Tiber river to the vicinity of Vatican Hill after the fire of 64 CE.

In the end, the Roman Messianic community was totally destroyed. Among its many casualties were the great leaders, Peter and Paul. Although Peter initially fled Rome to avoid the slaughter, accounts written years later tell that his escape was stopped—not by Romans, but by a vision of the Christ. The story goes that Christ appeared and asked, "Peter, where are you going?" Chastened, his conscience and faith reawakened, Peter reversed his footsteps and returned to Rome, where he was immediately arrested and executed. Later unsubstantiated accounts relate that he died after being lashed upside down on a post or cross.

Paul had already been charged as an enemy of the emperor and taken to Rome as a prisoner to await trial some years prior to the genocide. However, as a Roman citizen, he was permitted house arrest and had been languishing there, still awaiting trial. However, as a self-avowed leader of the Christus community, his guilt was deemed evident and no trial was required.

All Roman citizens were entitled to the dignity of a "quick" death and could not be tortured, so Paul was spared the agonies of the Circus Maximus. Reports say that he was beheaded. This is, in part, why many statues and paintings of Paul show him holding a sword. (The other reason is his zeal and fiery oratory.) Other purported leaders of the Christus group were set afire and used as human torches at Nero's debauched banquets for the aristocracy.

What could possibly have been worse for those who believed in Jesus as the Messiah? They identified themselves as faithful Jews. (It would be another twenty years before they fully self-identified as Christians.) They had been totally betrayed and abandoned by their community. Their families, their children, their elders—even Peter and Paul—had been gruesomely murdered.

We can only imagine the overwhelming extent of their isolation and pain, and undoubtedly there were times when the promise of the Christ, the prophesied Messiah, seemed hollow and empty. Terror, shame, abandonment and death are the context in which the Gospel of Mark was composed.

Adrift in the Storm
Approaching Mark Today

The Gospel of Mark is not only the earliest written; it is also the shortest of the four gospels. Correspondingly, this is the shortest gospel chapter of this book. This size does not imply that Mark, or the second path of Quadratos for that matter, holds any less importance than the other three. In fact, its concision has deep significance. Mark and the second path house some of our deepest and most complex feelings—our fears, our resentments and our early wounds.

Indeed, if we were to spend too much time annotating and examining this particular path, we would likely defeat, or at least conceal, its unique power and gift. We might easily fall into masochism, perversely relishing the struggle and elevating it beyond its place as part of a greater process. Therefore, as we move through the gospel, let us be content with its brevity.

Although Mark's gospel was the earliest written, it was placed second in the reading cycle, which supports my thesis about the purpose of the cycle. And it also completely matches our experience in the second path of Quadratos.

This path will knock on the door of our hearts and knock more than once. Some of the knocks will be as fearsome as those heard in Rome millennia ago. The way in which we will choose to answer is the profound question we meet in this part of our journey.

As we proceed through the gospel, we will have very little lyrical language for company. Mark's words are terse and spare. He gives us nothing but the barest outlines. He does not paint the landscape with flowery descriptions. His stories are stark and revelatory. Why? First, because he addresses Rome's Messianic Jews who lived under a death sentence. They had no use for hearts and flowers.

Second, because the core message of the gospel itself is simple, direct—even tough. That message is embodied in this gospel by a Messiah who fully understood the suffering of his followers—who came to earth, took human form, and withstood agonizing pain.

This Messiah wanted those who followed him to know that while their pain was necessary, because they were part of a much larger process, that he not only genuinely understood their suffering but was there with them as they suffered. Mark did not need an abundance of words to convey that.

Nonetheless, we will encounter some significant literary devices. Mark uses the metaphor of wilderness, as well as two equivalent-to-wilderness metaphors drawn from Jewish history and tradition: deserts and bodies of flowing water. In order to escape Egypt centuries earlier, the Jews had had to enter and traverse the Red Sea. It was their nemesis, the great barrier to their freedom. Seas in general were wild and unruly places, treacherous.

In Hebrew writings, seas, lakes, and rivers represented deep anxiety and even death, and so did the desert. The great flood of Noah was strong in memory, as were the myriad stories of the forty-year desert trial of the Jewish people, from which few survived to enter the Promised Land. Mark compassionately uses these three images—wilderness, deserts and bodies of flowing water—throughout his gospel to represent the inner landscape of frightening and uncharted territory.

Despite Mark's often bleak language, he does not—ever—write a phrase that is *only* painful, or terrible, or daunting. Nor does he depict trials that lead only into despair. We will see that each image of wilderness is coupled with an image of comfort or hope. John the Baptist eats both locusts (yuck!) and wild honey. When sin is confessed, cleansing is received. Heaven is torn apart and a dove descends. Jesus goes into the wilderness and encounters *both* beasts and angels.

The sparseness of language may make this coupling difficult to grasp at first. Our initial impression is anything but hopeful. Mark writes nothing but the barest outlines: no long descriptions, nor even a list of the temptations. He acknowledges the angels with little more than a nod. Patience and close reading, though, will reveal the pairings. Mark *always* includes hope.

As we enter this next stage of Quadratos—the deep chaos of the second path and our own stormy sea—this straightforward style can provide its own kind of comfort. It suits the needs of the place we are in and the ways we are able to hear. And Mark's specific words, through the principal parts of his gospel, will illuminate the path—expanding on and guiding us through this most difficult part of our journey.

What Good News?
Beginning the Gospel

Mark's gospel begins with a call to fill hearts with hope and gather strength. Clearly inspired, he announces, "Good news!" Yet Rome's Messianic Jews didn't have much to celebrate. Even though they had professed Jesus as Messiah, as asked by their faith, their obedience to his call threatened their lives and had resulted in the senseless slaughter of their family and friends.

"*What* good news?" they might well have asked. Yet—with his opening words, Mark insists that those hearing this text cast off all doubt. He reminds them of their most central truth and calls them to the glory and joy it holds—the glory and joy that summoned them to believe in the first place. From this point of beginning, Mark will carry the Christus followers into the deepest understanding of their beliefs, and the possibilities of meaning and purpose that lie within their great suffering.

> ***The beginning of the good news of Jesus the Christ, the Son of God. (1:1)***

One of the most startling differences between this gospel and that of Matthew is the complete absence of any kind of birth narrative, or indeed anything about Jesus' early life at all. Mark moves immediately to one of the most powerful, persuasive, and meaningful parts of the story of the Messiah for his audience—the account of John the Baptist and Jesus' baptism. Mark says that Jesus has arrived, and with nothing intervening, he starts to recount the specific events he knows will matter most to the Messianic Jews in Rome.

To open the baptism narrative, Mark significantly calls attention to the prophecy of a Suffering Servant foretold by Isaiah in the eighth century BCE, as the coming of one who would suffer for his people, who would "not grow faint or be crushed until he has established justice in the earth." (Isa. 40:3; 42:4) Mark also makes his first of eight separate references to the metaphor of "wilderness" in this initial twelve-verse passage.

> *As it is written in the prophet Isaiah, "See, I am sending my messenger ahead of you, who will prepare your way; the voice of one crying out in the wilderness: 'Prepare the way of the Lord, make [the Lord's] paths straight.' " (1:2–3)*

Multitudes answered John the Baptist's invitation at the Jordan River, just as reported in Matthew's gospel. But the focus is very different in this gospel. Although John the Baptist issued a call for repentance in both gospels, in Matthew his words were directed primarily to the Temple officials and privileged classes.

Mark, with a dissimilar audience and objective, establishes a ritual completely unlike the other. There is no mention of officials here. Mark's multitudes are simply "people" who came to the Jordan for baptism (the mikvah bath) and confession of their "sins." In this context, how does Mark intend the word "sin"?

Having been shunned by the larger Jewish community, the Roman Messianic Jews carried great burdens of shame. The scapegoating and divisions within their faith community, plus Nero's executions, had exposed them to the most brutal realities of human behavior. They harbored terrible feelings of disappointment and anger that ate at their inner lives and contaminated all their relationships.

These were the "sins" that Mark calls on them to confess as he describes John's baptism at the Jordan. Mark is showing them a way to release their pain and to begin a process of forgiveness—forgiveness of themselves, of their families, and of their community—so that they might move forward and once again live full lives.

> *John the baptizer appeared in the wilderness, proclaiming a baptism of repentance for the forgiveness of sins. And people from the whole Judean countryside and all the people of Jerusalem were going out to him, and were baptized by him in the river Jordan, confessing their sins. (1:4–5)*

John next announces that Jesus will soon arrive to perform baptisms, and not "with water, but ... with the Holy Spirit." The message was clear to the multitudes—and to the Roman Messiahnians. "Sin" had been cleansed, and repentance, the correction of one's heart and mind, could be claimed. Through confession and the mikvah bath, the barrier of unresolved inner burdens had been removed. One would be ready for the Christ, and even greater transformation.

> *[John] proclaimed, "The one who is more powerful than I is coming after me; I am not worthy to stoop down and untie the thong of his sandals. I have baptized you with water, but he will baptize you with the Holy Spirit." (1:7-8)*

In the verses that follow are several of those careful juxtapositions that we mentioned previously as being characteristic of Mark. All are written in his typically stringent language. Each begins with an image of great challenge and ends with an image of promise. Every word assures the listener that trial is always accompanied by hope.

They may rest eternally assured that God remains with them in their suffering and will never abandon them. The message's simplicity calls believers to use the gospel in a practical way—as a means to transcend despair. Implicitly, Mark charges "Read on!" "Chant on!" "Keep praying!"

Notice the structure of these consecutive verses. These couplings— their apposed concepts, their sequence, their one-by-one narration, and their stripped-down words—give the sense of a litany, or mantra. When we realize that first-century Messianic Jews probably did not read these words, but rather chanted them aloud, often over and over, we can begin to grasp their beauty and effectiveness. There are many more passages like these in Mark's gospel—some before these and others that follow them.

> *In those days Jesus came from Nazareth of Galilee and was baptized by John in the Jordan. And just as he was coming up out of the water, he saw the heavens torn apart and the Spirit descending like a dove on him. And a voice came from heaven, "You are my Son, the Beloved; with you I am well pleased." (1:9-11)*

And the Spirit immediately drove [Jesus] out into the wilderness. He was in the wilderness forty days, tempted by Satan; and he was with the wild beasts; and the angels waited on him. (1:12–13)

Now after John was arrested, Jesus came to Galilee, proclaiming the good news of God, and saying, "The time is fulfilled, and the kingdom of God has come near; repent, and believe in the good news." (1:14–15)

Our increased awareness of inner opposites and the tensions between them will define the second path of our spiritual journey. Mark's juxtapositions typify many of the divisions we are now beginning to feel. We started out hoping to gain larger life, more meaning, and more vitality—or at least to jettison the worst of our problems. We entered the process knowing it would be difficult.

We followed the instructions in this book: we found heroes and heroines, we created safe space, we sought wise advice, we opened ourselves as well as we could, we meditated and prayed. But so far, it seems that everything we have done has been unavailing.

We often feel disheartened as we move further into the second path, because the first path left us in a state of such high anticipation. With more questions than answers, we experience increasing despair and weariness.

I give you fair warning and fair promise: the real stripping is about to begin. Yet this peeling of layers, this shedding of old beliefs, habits, and assumptions, is necessary. Patience must become our core practice, and we need to recognize that "mindless" strength is its underpinning.

Our analytic skills will not help us in this place. We are beginning the process of what psychology calls "ego death." Mystics and shamans describe it as dismemberment, as being torn apart, limb from limb. In this time, psychologically, in all practical ways we are still unborn. Our *belief* in new life, not its experience, gives us legs to keep walking.

FIVE—CROSSING MARK'S STORMY SEA

At this point, many of us try to shorten the process finding it just too painful. We feel that the sooner we return to the "light," the better. Frequently, our struggling ego-self rushes to forgiveness. Having visited the painful parts of our personal history, we choose to end our work on our past, "deciding" to view troublesome people and events with loving equanimity.

These efforts initially seem positive and successful. We receive heaps of praise and support from others for our "forgiveness" and "changed attitudes"—but we are actually just making maneuvers to avoid our path. These are mere surface adjustments that accomplish nothing lasting, although it may take us some time to realize this.

The deep river of anger and fear and pain still runs within us, no matter how far we try to conceal it behind a facade of loving words. Our work does not end until we thoroughly strip ourselves to the core of our painful emotions. Before we can truly alter these feelings, we must embrace and fully experience them with sufficient patience, for sufficient time.

If, however, we choose to stay in this uncomfortable place, and use the Quadratos sequence of the gospels as a guide, we will see how the baptism in Mark's account builds on the instruction given in Matthew's. Having left our old ways, we must now confess our "sins."

Gradually, we learn that confession is not a recounting of *unearned* shame. It has nothing to do with the relentless inner punishment we often exact from ourselves when someone betrays us, or when we fall short of unjust parental or societal expectations. Rather, confession requires us to scrutinize our inner life, in part so that we may lift the weight of debilitating shame.

Making "a searching and fearless moral inventory of ourselves" constitutes the fourth step of twelve-step recovery programs. This inner examination is what we must do now. As much as we would like to avoid this process, we need to become aware of our limitations, our inner pain, and the transgressions we have committed upon ourselves and others.

At the same time, we must accept the equally significant challenge to identify our strengths, our gifts, and our good deeds. In this manner, we will also begin to better develop the ability to hear, know, and accept the clarity of our own inner voice.

As we take responsibility for our transgressions, we also need to assume "appropriate" guilt—in other words, fully understand and accept our wrongdoing—and then express, when that is possible and appropriate, our genuine desire for forgiveness. Also, when possible, we need to make restitution, taking care to do so in a self-compassionate way. In our rigorous striving for self-honesty, we learn to grant to ourselves the same understanding and latitude we freely grant to others.

When we take responsibility, we must also acknowledge "inappropriate" guilt. This is a deeper issue. Many of us hold shame resulting from our instinct to blame ourselves for burdens that are not truly ours. They can result from emotional or physical neglect, or physical, sexual, or psychological abuse. These are most often things we internalized as children, usually placed upon us by society or our parents, often unknowingly, sometimes not.

Whatever they are, if we are doing our deepest journeying, the second path is where we will discover their deadly impact on our lives—and where we will stop and take whatever steps are needed to heal them if we are to continue our spiritual quest. In this instance, the second path can become much lengthier.

Although we will be able to take much of this "inner inventory" by ourselves, we don't have to. We can, and should, enlist all the help we need. But when we are done, and begin to achieve sincere understanding through our evaluation, any aloneness will end, regardless. Because our next step is to stand humbly before another human being and fully, honestly, and voluntarily share ourselves with them.

Once we reach this difficult, poignant, and wondrous point—once we open ourselves to being truly known, we can begin the process of fundamental change. We can truly absorb and accept help and wisdom. We can begin to actually release our pain. At last! These steps of inner repair are the "sins" and the "repentance" revealed by the Gospel of Mark.

If we have more serious burdens of shame, such as those caused by childhood neglect and abuse, then we will absolutely need further help. We cannot turn away from this necessity. Our solitary perspective, even in prayer, will not be sufficient to move us through these difficult passages. Counselors who are specially trained in the work of reprocessing early childhood development and trauma or a variety of twelve-step groups such as Adult Children of Alcoholics are among the resources to seek out.

Yet, no matter what level of confusion or pain we uncover, it is important to remember that our suffering is temporary—and we have chosen to bare ourselves. We have done this because we know it is necessary to clearly reveal the Christ within in order to touch love.

Confusion and Discernment
On and Around the Sea of Galilee

Mark's next set of lessons uses topography to metaphorically frame his stories. He alternates his narratives between the wilds of the desert and the terrors of the Sea of Galilee. With the rhythm of the tides at the Sea of Galilee, Jesus prays, then goes out; returns to pray, then goes out again. Earlier in the chapter Jesus is baptized (prays), and then is driven out into the desert.

Next, we find that Jesus seeks solitude to pray, and then returns to minister to the crowds. He both circles and crosses the sea. Mark uses this pattern to reinforce some of his wisest counsel: "Amidst confusion," he advises, "amidst the demands of others and one's internal clamoring, stop. Leave. Go pray. Go chant. The true course is found in a quiet mind and centered heart."

> *In the morning, while it was still very dark, [Jesus] got up and went out to a deserted place, and there he prayed. And Simon and his companions hunted for him. When they found him, they said to him, "Everyone is searching for you." He answered, "Let us go on to the neighboring towns, so that I may proclaim the message there also; for that is what I came out to do." And he went throughout Galilee, proclaiming the message in their synagogues and casting out demons. (1:35-39)*

From chapters two through eight, Mark continues his narrative by describing Jesus' ten-city tour, historically known as the Decapolis (literally "ten cities" in Greek). As Jesus circles the shore of the Sea of Galilee, he makes no fewer than four crossings with his disciples.

The core teachings of this gospel are within these crossing accounts. The dramatic first account exemplifies all four. The Messiah demands that the group make the trip by night, creating an especially terrifying experience. A great storm arises, leaving the disciples trapped in their small boat, tossed around in the dark, unable to see, certain that their lives are in imminent danger.

What is Jesus' response to this terror and chaos? He sleeps peacefully in the rear of the boat on a cushion, while his disciples are seized by panic. Despairing, they finally rouse him and plead that he rescue them: "Teacher, do you not care that we are perishing?"

The hysteria felt by the disciples in the boat paralleled the emotional state of the Roman Messianic Jews. Stranded by their faith in the Messiah and assailed on all sides, their lives were also in peril. Like the disciples, they were very, very frightened.

We can almost hear their anguished queries: "Has the Messiah really come? Is the Messiah with us? Has God abandoned us?" Mark's inspired message assures them that the Christ is with them, just as Jesus had been with the disciples in the storm-tossed boat.

In the raging storm when the disciples beg in fear, Jesus' voice calls out: "Be still!" Immediately, the wind stops. Awed by this demonstration of Jesus' omnipotence, the disciples accept it as indisputable evidence of Jesus' divinity, discuss it, and rush to deify him.

Similarly, in each of the next three crossing stories when Jesus commands, any and all turmoil ceases. These demonstrations of divine power and authority amaze and comfort the disciples. Jesus' loud pronouncements restore order. Jesus *is* the all-powerful Messiah. Jesus *is* with them. Jesus *will* protect them. They have no reason to fear death!

However, the progression of the crossing stories demonstrates a greater message. Jesus continues to use his power to calm storms, yet in each crossing, Mark recounts that he grows increasingly impatient. His disciples simply presume that Jesus will perform a divine act, and in every instance, relieve them of their fear.

The disciples seem to completely ignore their responsibilities, which were to endure and attempt to find inner calm through faith. By the fourth and final crossing, Jesus is totally exasperated and demands to know if his disciples have yet learned anything whatsoever.

Mark's message, an invaluable lesson for the Roman Messianic Jews, is that the disciples still sought a God who rescued them, who removed obstacles. They wanted to remain safe—as children—with a God who acted as an all-powerful, protective parent.

They could not yet fathom a God who not only did not do this, but who actually pushed his followers into dark, nighttime storms. They did not yet have the spiritual maturity from which they could derive inner equilibrium and serenity in the midst of trial. They had not yet discovered an inner place of God.

> *On that day, when evening had come, [Jesus] said to them, "Let us go across to the other side." And leaving the crowd behind, they took [Jesus] with them in the boat, just as he was. Other boats were with him. A great windstorm arose, and the waves beat into the boat, so that the boat was already being swamped. But Jesus was in the stern, asleep on the cushion; and they woke him up and said to him, "Teacher, do you not care that we are perishing?" He woke up and rebuked the wind, and said to the sea, "Peace! Be still!" Then the wind ceased, and there was a dead calm. [Jesus] said to them, "Why are you afraid? Have you still no faith?" And they were filled with great awe and said to one another, "Who then is this, that even the wind and the sea obey him?" (4:35-41)*

"Do you still not perceive or understand? Are your hearts hardened? Do you have eyes, and fail to see? Do you have ears, and fail to hear? And do you not remember?" (8:17-18)

Uncertainty, depression, and anxiety run rampant along this second path. We teeter on the cliff side of chaos. But we must jump off that cliff. Like Jesus' followers, we are called to step out in faith and make a fearful journey through the conflict of opposites for the sake of our souls.

Like the disciples, our frightened hearts call out: "Fix it! Fix me! Show me the strength I was promised. Use that strength on my behalf—please, please!" We remember the first path of Matthew fondly—at least back then we could discern the top of the mountain then, even if the path was rocky and difficult. We pray that someone—or something—will arrive to dispel the fear in our hearts, subdue our panic.

The simple, unadorned maxims of twelve-step programs often seem appropriate to this time. Developed for people caught in dismal circumstances, determined to escape without resorting to old patterns, these clear words provide tools for coping with trial. Note how well the effortless simplicity and beauty of the well-known Serenity Prayer, adopted by Alcoholics Anonymous, captures the essence of Mark and the second path:

> *God, grant me the serenity*
> *to accept the things I cannot change,*
> *the courage to change the things I can,*
> *and the wisdom to know the difference.*

We must describe—encircle—the inner places that hold our chaos and conflicts in the same way that Jesus circled the Sea of Galilee. As our faith grows, so does our courage. We choose to walk directly into that chaos and pray. We will learn the deepest, most important lessons in the tempests of our own stormy seas. And we will emerge ready to engage in proper action—action born not from our ego-self, but from the Christ within.

It is also vital that we not travel alone. We will absolutely require at least one human being to steady us. More are highly recommended. The presence of wise counselors in our life cannot be underestimated, and others who are on the same path that we are, or who have traveled it ahead of us are invaluable. Self-isolation and "go it alone" attitudes come from our fearful selves, resisting being known and changed, and it is important for us to resist them back.

Although the Gospel of Mark doesn't have much joy, it does have a continuing and resounding message of strength and faith. Despite all the differences in the crossing accounts, the core truth remains the same: the Christ is always with us. This truth must constitute the foundation of our daily spiritual practice, as we strive to stay awake and in trust.

Gripping the gunwales of the small boat of our humanity, we cannot forget that we are never alone. Even if we are blinded, whether by avoidance or fear or pain; even if we make mistakes; even if we feel abandoned, tossed to the heavens at one moment and to the depths at the next—we will never be alone.

Teachings about Power
Caesarea Philippi, The Transfiguration, and The Journey to Jerusalem

In Mark's eighth chapter Jesus and his disciples move to the foothills of Caesarea Philippi, recognized today as Israel's northern boundary with Lebanon and Syria. In the first century, well-known natural springs flowed from these mountains into the Sea of Galilee and from there to the Jordan River, where they finally emptied into the Dead Sea. Mark has carefully selected this topography because it evokes the Jewish creation story in Genesis.

That story tells of a dome-like vault protecting the earth from the seas of chaos. A crack in the vault would release a flood and wash the entire world away—and the waters gushing from above would look precisely like flowing springs.

Furthermore, these particular springs were already the source for great seas and rivers that held significant places in a terrifying history for the

Jews. Now Mark presents another of his paradoxes: though fear is ever-present, life cannot exist without water. We will see that this chapter is a metaphorical turning point for the entire gospel.

Jesus asks his followers a daunting question: "Who do you say that I am?" Peter responds: "You are the Messiah." Mark then details a seemingly strange instruction from Jesus to his disciples—that they keep his divinity confidential. But the command does not come from a need for secrecy or any sense of modesty or shame.

Instead, its motive is love and wisdom. Jesus knows that his disciples still do not understand the full path of true discipleship. They lack the maturity to comprehend all the complexities and implications of "Messiah" themselves, and thus were not competent to communicate it to others. His question and Peter's answer are therefore the prelude to a great teaching.

First, Jesus recounts the series of events he knows are imminent—his suffering, rejection, death, and resurrection. Upset, Peter begins to rebuke Jesus for the prediction. Abruptly, Jesus snaps at him: "Get behind me, Satan! For you are setting your mind not on divine things, but on human things." Why is the word "Satan" used? Because Peter's reaction proves that he is still "young" in his faith, and tempted by immature notions about an omnipotent God.

Peter has become accustomed to thinking of the Messiah as a wonder-worker, with the power to banish every difficulty. He assumes that Jesus could—and would—save himself from death. Jesus' response dramatically emphasizes the message from the crossing stories: "If you are only looking for a miracle-working Messiah, then you have not yet understood the nature of your faith.

Jesus then talks about the true path of discipleship. He tells those gathered that if they want to follow him, they will experience great trial and conflict. They cannot avoid, evade, or divert their fate, nor can they count the cost. They can only accept and endure. Finally, he promises them that if they choose to do this, if they follow the path, they will come to know God.

FIVE—CROSSING MARK'S STORMY SEA

These inspired messages were specifically directed to the Messiahnians, who regarded Peter not only as a great hero who died for his faith, but as the founder of their community. This narrative inspired them that they too could be like Peter—whose faith had wavered, had been immature, but who *still* had gone forward and eventually prevailed.

From this very decisive point on, Mark's narrative changes dramatically. The circling ends, and in the same way that the spring waters joined, and rushed straight downhill to become sea and then river, so does the route of Jesus and his disciples. The increase in the size and potential danger of the water corresponds to the increased peril for the travelers.

Every step they take on their journey from the spring to the Sea of Galilee, then down the Jordan River valley and finally into Jerusalem, moves them closer to the moment of Jesus' crucifixion. Mark dramatically juxtaposes these elements of overflowing life and imminent death.

> *Jesus went on with his disciples to the villages of Caesarea Philippi; and on the way he asked his disciples, "Who do people say that I am?" And they answered him, "John the Baptist; and others, Elijah; and still others, one of the prophets." [Jesus] asked them, "But who do you say that I am?" Peter answered him, "You are the Messiah." And [Jesus] sternly ordered them not to tell anyone about him. Then [Jesus] began to teach them that the Son of Man must undergo great suffering, and be rejected by the elders, the chief priests, and the scribes, and be killed, and after three days rise again. He said all this quite openly. And Peter took [Jesus] aside and began to rebuke him. But turning and looking at his disciples, [Jesus] rebuked Peter and said, "Get behind me, Satan! For you are setting your mind not on divine things but on human things." [Jesus] called the crowd with his disciples, and said to them, "If any want to become my followers, let them deny themselves and take up their cross and follow me. For those who want to save their life will lose it, and those who lose their life for my sake, and for the sake of the gospel, will save it. For what will it profit them to gain the whole world and forfeit their life?" (8:27-36)*

RADICAL TRANSFORMATION

Six days after the teaching at Caesarea Philippi, Jesus takes three disciples—Peter, James, and John—to an unnamed high mountain. On that mount, they witness their Messiah suddenly appear even brighter, nobler, more holy and beautiful. Mark's words are that he is "transfigured before them."

Then, as the three look on in amazement, Jesus is joined by the Hebrew icons Moses and Elijah. These represent the two pillars of Judaism, and they are seeming opposites. Moses is the law-giver, who stands for stability and tradition. Elijah is the prophet of compassion and mercy and is much more progressive. Mark uses the vision of 'trans-figuration' to show Jesus the Christ as the joining of these two aspects, thereby gaining the whole.

Although the disciples have actually seen Jesus in his full glory, once again Jesus orders them to conceal their knowledge. Since they still lack understanding that conflict and suffering are essential parts of God, they are not yet matured enough to speak.

> *Six days later, Jesus took with him Peter and James and John, and led them up a high mountain apart, by themselves. And [Jesus] was transfigured before them, and his clothes became dazzling white, such as no one on earth could bleach them. And there appeared to them Elijah with Moses, who were talking with Jesus. Then Peter said to Jesus, "Rabbi, it is good for us to be here; let us make three dwellings, one for you, one for Moses, and one for Elijah." [Peter] did not know what to say, for they were terrified. Then a cloud overshadowed them, and from the cloud there came a voice, "This is my Son, the Beloved; listen to him!" Suddenly when they looked around, they saw no one with them anymore, but only Jesus. As they were coming down the mountain, [Jesus] ordered them to tell no one about what they had seen, until after the Son of Man had risen from the dead. So they kept the matter to themselves, questioning what this rising from the dead could mean. (9:2–10)*

After descending the mountain, Jesus now leads the disciples directly to Jerusalem. This moves them much closer to the painful end of their teacher's physical life. Along the way, Jesus never stops teaching, though he knows they will not fully understand many of the lessons until after they have actually witnessed his death and resurrection.

Over and over again, through story and image and phrase, Mark reiterates the primary tenet: "Walking a spiritual path is not only worthy; it is of greater value than life itself." As they drew closer to Jerusalem, Mark recounts Jesus' language as suddenly filled with dreadful and horrific imagery.

Severed limbs, ravaged flesh, and the fires of hell become pervasive, but these images help prepare the disciples for the intense pain and conflict they will soon feel in their hearts, souls, and minds. Two thousand years later, we can see that the psychological accuracy of these metaphorical descriptions is stunning.

Mark wants to emphasize the depth of commitment needed for the Roman Messianic Jews to survive. In essence, he demands that they must, in their prayers, ask for the very fire in which they will burn. He further insists that they will have to be "salted with fire," a reference found only in Mark's gospel. Why "salted"?

In the first century, salt was more valuable than almost anything else—equal to gold. It could preserve meat and therefore gave protection from starvation and illness. Furthermore, it protected against dehydration in the arid desert. In short, it meant survival. Wars were launched and fought over it. In the Temple, only meat that had been treated with salt was offered. Infants' lips were rubbed with salt to protect against evil. Romans tied salt to the heads of those they executed and specially wished to offer to the gods.

Those who believed that Jesus was the Messiah were very likely to be executed—sacrificed in the arena—and were therefore likely to receive the precious salt. This is perhaps the most powerful paradox stated in Mark's gospel: salting as a sign of sacrificial death and also as a metaphor for the inestimable worth of God's love. When Messiahnians heard "Everyone will be salted with fire," they clearly understood that they were receiving a promise and a blessing that would make their death immensely valuable.

RADICAL TRANSFORMATION

"And if your foot causes you to stumble, cut it off; it is better for you to enter life lame than to have two feet and to be thrown into hell. And if your eye causes you to stumble, tear it out; it is better for you to enter the kingdom of God with one eye than to have two eyes and to be thrown into hell, where their worm never dies, and the fire is never quenched. For everyone will be salted with fire. Salt is good; but if salt has lost its saltiness, how can you season it? Have salt in yourselves, and be at peace with one another." (9:42–50)

The lessons that Jesus teaches in Mark's crossing accounts and at Caesarea Philippi are some of the most challenging in all of the gospels to comprehend and to adapt for our daily lives. They force us to purge our traditional conception of God as a super-parental divine rescuer. These lessons have a clear message: God is certainly capable of rescuing us, but God will not always rescue us, because rescue may stop our growing maturity.

The journey is long and full. It by necessity contains peacefulness, joy and ecstasy, pain, conflict and paradox—all of which we must eventually learn to balance in order to reach a capacity for inner serenity and know our place in God. This is the way of the Christ. And this is also the way of Quadratos.

In this second path, it is as if we were in a tiny boat on a menacing sea in a great storm. The storm is so fierce that we feel completely directionless. We hope that the pattern we are learning and trying to follow is true, but we really haven't a clue. On an emotional level, it is clear to us that we know nothing about anything useful that can save us.

What should we do? We have only two helpful choices. We can perform the one simple task we have: we can row. And we can pray. We can surrender all of our habits and assumptions. We can have faith and not allow the demons in the depths below nor the thunder and lightning above to deter us.

One of the dangers of this path is our desire to choose one opposite over another. We often want to move in the direction of Elijah or Moses—to retreat to the known rules, or to relinquish them entirely and fall into a group hug—precisely why Mark gives us the image of the trans-figuration (literally meaning *"across figure"*).

When challenges arise, we need to realize that our impulse to force a resolution or move in one direction or another is due to our immaturity. Our best course for now is simply to pray and meditate, remain aware of all options, resist definitive movement, and try not to fall back on our old ways.

Faced with pain and conflict and left to our own limited resources, we tend to overuse our intellect. We attempt to *think* our way out of the dilemma. Or, we distract ourselves from our pain by arguing. We can find ourselves arguing with everyone, even with Mystery itself. It is not unusual to hear people who are struggling with this path make derisive comments about God. These are narrow courses driven by our fearful, threatened egos.

However difficult, we must try to ignore that inner "chatter." We must pray to enter our necessary trials more deeply, rather than to be rescued from them. Most importantly, we need to accept and accept and accept some more, even though we often don't understand exactly what is happening or how our experience "fits" into the process.

The second path of Quadratos is about "losing life" to gain it. We are attempting first to learn what that means and second to accept it. Through prayer and proven counsel, we learn to receive our trials as they arrive in our lives and live with them, knowing that we cannot hasten or alleviate the rigors of the path itself.

Every time we attempt to avoid a situation, we only reduce our opportunity to grow, to learn from the journey. Like the immature disciples looking for a God who merely provides, we are, in fact, asking that God become smaller. Fortunately, God is not so paltry. Mystery will not be diminished; nor will it ever abandon us, no matter how childishly we are behaving.

Mark's particular attention to Peter holds two lessons for us. One is the critical practice of self-compassion—absolutely crucial as we make our inventory. Wisdom can travel only through error, difficult though that is. Can we forgive ourselves all our many errors? They do teach us deeply.

The other is a reiteration of the counsel we received in Matthew: find help. However, now we are receiving more specific advice. Peter is a genuine *mentor*. He is someone who has traveled the path, a person who has made the journey successfully and can serve as a trusted spiritual guide, a soul-friend. At this point in our journey, we need someone like this—a living example with whom we can share our travails and whose advice we can trust.

Especially without help, the stresses of this path will cause many of us to make a choice to stop right now and return to what our protective brains and our fear thinks is a safe harbor. But stopping now comes at great cost, for this is the place where we will discover our level of commitment and our true willingness to rely on God's grace.

If we abort the journey at this point and retreat to our old ways, we will gradually and inevitably discover (or others will tell us) that our lives will indeed change, taking on a pattern of increasing narrowness and rigidity. Therefore, although we are tempted to stop, to negotiate—to make bargains to shorten or ease the burden of the inner work that must be done—extend compassion to these inner voices while not heeding them. We want more than a less-than-complete life in the less-than-satisfactory company of a less-than-perfect and mysterious god. We want the "good news."

Facing Conflict
Confrontations in Jerusalem's Temple

After their long trek, the group finally arrives in Jerusalem. Jesus goes directly to the Temple, where a bustling scene of commerce confronts him. People buying and selling animals for sacrifice fill the courtyard. The "holiest" sacrifices are designated the most expensive by the Temple system—even modest offerings bore exorbitant prices.

Jesus, outraged over the injustice forcing humble petitioners into corrupt practice, unhesitatingly begins to overturn tables and pronounces that the Temple is no longer a "house of prayer" but a "den of robbers." Recognizing a direct threat to their authority, the priests and scribes intensify their talk of murdering the charismatic and contentious interloper.

As noted in the preface, I want to reiterate that this section of Mark describes Temple behavior that occurred at an unusually low point in that religion's history. These are absolutely *not* descriptions of the great heart of Judaism at its origins, in subsequent centuries or today.

By the first century CE (and until the Temple was destroyed in 70), Judaism had fallen under the corrupting influence of rigid laws, unforgiving spirit and an oppressive cultic priesthood exacting exorbitant prices for sacrificial animals. There were other parts of Judaism in that century, such as the Essenes and holy sages, who held to a more mystical and compassionate understanding.

However, these mystical groups were not the most visible and influential segments of Judaism—and were not those who came into conflict with Jesus. That segment, those about whom Mark writes, were members of the Temple priesthood who had sold out to the Roman Emperor and were abusing their religious power and authority.

Mark knows that his Christus community is in direct opposition to the Roman Emperor and some Jewish religious leaders. He wants to fortify his audience with the example of the Messiah he shows here—confident, forceful, walking directly into conflict. This is encouragement for the Messiahnians to give them the strength to face their own conflict, regardless of what they might have to endure as a result.

> **Then they came to Jerusalem. And [Jesus] entered the temple and began to drive out those who were selling and those who were buying in the temple, and he overturned the tables of the money changers and the seats of those who sold doves; and he would not allow anyone to carry anything**

> through the temple. He was teaching and saying, "Is it not
> written, 'My house shall be called a house of prayer for all the
> nations'? But you have made it a den of robbers." And when
> the chief priests and the scribes heard it, they kept looking
> for a way to kill him; for they were afraid of him, because the
> whole crowd was spellbound by his teaching. (11:15-18)

The following day Jesus reappears and directly confronts the Temple authorities. They argue, the tension mounting quickly as Jesus emphatically and clearly responds to their inquiries. After the argument, he leaves but then returns to Jerusalem and the Temple once again. This time he speaks in parables, each crafted for Mark's Christus community.

One story told of heartrending conflict and loss endured by "a man who planted a vineyard." Nonetheless the man persists, and the parable closes telling of a "rejected stone" that eventually becomes a "cornerstone." This parable, with its references to planting, building, and a vineyard that will produce new wine, was a powerful message to the Messianic Jews.

"Persist," it says. "Even though you are cast aside, the vines will still be planted, and recognition of the Messiah will yet come. You and your community are the cornerstone of the foundational changes in your faith. Your lives, your sacrifices, are not in vain."

> Again they came to Jerusalem. As he was walking in the
> temple, the chief priests, the scribes, and the elders came to
> him and said, "By what authority are you doing these things?
> Who gave you this authority to do them?" Jesus said to them,
> "I will ask you one question; answer me, and I will tell you by
> what authority I do these things. Did the baptism of John come
> from heaven, or was it of human origin? Answer me." They
> argued with one another, "If we say, 'From heaven,' he will say,
> 'Why then did you not believe him?' But shall we say, 'Of
> human origin'?"—they were afraid of the crowd, for all
> regarded John as truly a prophet. So they answered Jesus,
> "We do not know." And Jesus said to them, "Neither will I tell
> you by what authority I am doing these things." (11:27-33)

> *Then he began to speak to them in parables. "A man planted a vineyard, put a fence around it, dug a pit for the wine press, and built a watchtower; then he leased it to tenants and went to another country. When the season came, he sent a slave to the tenants to collect from them his share of the produce of the vineyard. But they seized him, and beat him, and sent him away empty-handed. And again he sent another slave to them; this one they beat over the head and insulted. Then he sent another, and that one they killed. And so it was with many others; some they beat, and others they killed. He had still one other, a beloved son. Finally he sent him to them, saying, 'They will respect my son.' But those tenants said to one another, 'This is the heir; come, let us kill him, and the inheritance will be ours.' So they seized him, killed him, and threw him out of the vineyard. What then will the owner of the vineyard do? He will come and destroy the tenants and give the vineyard to others. Have you not read this scripture: 'The stone that the builders rejected has become the cornerstone; this was the Lord's doing, and it is amazing in our eyes'?" When they realized that he had told this parable against them, they wanted to arrest him, but they feared the crowd. So they left him and went away. (12:1–12)*

Mark's next chapter brings the conflict with the Temple authorities to a dramatic conclusion. Once again Jesus speaks, this time of destruction and rebirth. His imagery is vivid, powerful. Mark wants the Messiahnians to understand the nature of fundamental change—and to understand that serious conflict is one of the necessary and predictable steps of all transformation.

In the same way that Jesus the Christ died but was resurrected, they needed reassurance that their faith would not be ended by the terrible tribulations they were experiencing in Rome. Their belief in the Christ would survive—continue—even strengthen.

"This is how change works," Mark teaches. "This is the way strong foundations are built. You must clear out the old. There are always extreme struggles as the old beliefs fight back then crumble to make room for the new ones arising." These principles gained even greater impact (and irony) to readers in subsequent decades because only a few years after Mark wrote his gospel, Jerusalem's Temple was leveled in Rome's great assault.

Jesus' final exhortation in this chapter is to "keep awake!" All three synoptic gospels—Matthew, Mark, and Luke—use these words, but each place them at a different point in the account, presumably to call specific attention to the matters of greatest import to each author. Mark locates them directly at the close of the contentious debate with the Temple authorities and ensuing lessons on the nature of deep change—and immediately prior to the Passion account. He does this as a reminder to his audience, telling *them* to remain awake and vigilant because there is no escape from necessary suffering. It is part of their journey.

> *When you hear of wars and rumors of wars, do not be alarmed; this must take place, but the end is still to come. For nation will rise against nation, and kingdom against kingdom; there will be earthquakes in various places; there will be famines. This is but the beginning of the birth pangs. As for yourselves, beware; for they will hand you over to councils; and you will be beaten in synagogues; and you will stand before governors and kings because of me, as a testimony to them. And the good news must first be proclaimed to all nations. When they bring you to trial and hand you over, do not worry beforehand about what you are to say; but say whatever is given you at that time, for it is not you who speak, but the Holy Spirit. Brother will betray brother to death, and a father his child, and children will rise against parents and have them put to death; and you will be hated by all because of my name. But the one who endures to the end will be saved. (13:7–13)*

> *"Truly I tell you, this generation will not pass away until all these things have taken place. Heaven and earth will pass away, but my words will not pass away." (13:30-31)*

FIVE—CROSSING MARK'S STORMY SEA

"And what I say to you I say to all: Keep awake." (13:37)

∽

When we are anxious and spinning out of control, we often search for messages and outer signs to help calm ourselves. And we tend to find them, even if such signs don't objectively exist. Through the centuries, it has been easy for people to read Mark's words about apocalyptic happenings, look around their world, and take his words literally. But we do not need to prepare for external "end times." We are more interested in universal truths, particularly as they relate to Quadratos. We understand that if we transform our inner selves, we will *not* cause or be party to the external events that lead to catastrophe.

In this journey of inner transformation, we can understand that the images in Mark's gospel are invaluable metaphors for the powerful feelings that we undergo in the second path, when death and destruction and collapse dressed in depression and despair surround us.

Our message today echoes Mark's message to believers in Rome long ago: "This is not the end, even though sometimes it feels as though it might be. Inner and outer conflict are to be expected. So are the uncertainties that always arise with conflict.

Try to remember: when deep change occurs, this is what the beginning of something new looks and feels like. Hold on. Be still. Wait! Later, you will be able to recall this moment, and see how unexpectedly the new cornerstone was chosen, and with what deep purpose it was laid."

As we walk this path in faith, our immature ego-self reluctantly begins to crumble. Resistant to change, it fights back just as the Temple authorities did, and it does so with great skill and determination. Do not be surprised. "Keep awake!"

Staying Present
The Passion

Mark's Passion account sharpens the focus of all the lessons he has presented thus far, bringing the main spiritual question of the gospel to a more precise point: How do we have trust in the path we have chosen despite our pain and fear? In keeping with the rest of Mark's gospel, this account of the Passion is the shortest of the four (and remember, it was the first written by about a decade).

Starkly and unsparingly, Mark weaves an emotional fabric of powerful conflict and deep, painful abandonment. Written with the certain knowledge that many of the Christus followers would relate very directly to the feelings it conveyed, he knows that they will not simply recollect the death it describes; they will see their own deaths reflected in every word.

The Last Supper and Gethsemane

Mark's telling of the Last Supper is particularly poignant. Jesus foresees his betrayal by an intimate someone "dipping into the same bowl," and he says so. Rome's Messianic Jews were familiar with this same kind of perfidy. When the centurion knocked on their door, they knew the likelihood was that they had been given away by someone close to them. When they heard the words of the gospel, it must have been as though the Messiah himself was warning them not to be disloyal to each other, and not to abandon the new community of the Son of Man.

After Jesus' meal with his disciples, the group proceeds to the Mount of Olives. There, Jesus tells his followers that even though only one will betray him, all of them will desert him. Peter protests, specifically reiterating the word "desert." As always, Mark chooses his words with extreme care.

We may recall that Matthew, less precise a wordsmith than John and with a different purpose, uses the words "deny," "desert," and "betray" interchangeably in his gospel. Mark, however, is not such a generalist. When he uses each of these words, they have subtly different connotations.

In Mark's gospel, Jesus uses the word "betray" to refer to those who totally give up their belief or who, like Judas, turn someone else over to the authorities. He uses the word "desertion"—which literally means to turn one's face in another direction—to describe those who give in to the impulse to avoid conflict—something that, as Jesus predicts, every single one of the followers will do without exception.

By the time Mark wrote this gospel, it is likely that Peter had already deserted Rome, then returned and been killed for his faith. I believe that Mark is encouraging his audience not to flee as Peter had while simultaneously extending great compassion to them. When he focuses on Jesus' prediction that given the circumstances, inevitably "all" would desert, he is telling the Messiahnians he understands their emotional and physical *need* to flee.

Jesus knows that the combination of young faith and terrible challenges can lead to a lapse in faith, in vigilance. He also knows that desertion, unlike betrayal, will not critically damage the soul—deserters can redeem themselves, turn around again, and return to the path. Mark's choice to emphasize these words of Jesus vividly conveys essential counsel to the Christus followers in Rome.

Mark also chooses the word "denial" in this passage to connote the lowest level of abandonment. He uses "denial" when someone claims "not to know"—even when one actually does—illustrated by Peter's denial of knowing Jesus. This choice of words tells the Christus community that even the most faithful of disciples can have momentary lapses and abandon their faith. But they can also understand their error, repent, and be restored.

Mark knew that before the knock on the door came, the Messiahnians would have ample time to reflect. However, the moment the door opened and the centurion asked his question, there would be time for only one answer. Mark therefore wants his readers to understand that they, like the disciples, have four choices, each one with different spiritual and moral consequences.

His examples and his language are precise. "When you are asked, 'Are you a follower of the Christus?' you can answer yes, or you can deny, or you can desert, or you can betray. Those are your four choices and your *only* choices." Mark implores them to directly examine their beliefs ahead of time, and to do so thoughtfully and deeply for their own sake and for the sake of their community.

When it was evening, [Jesus] came with the twelve. And when they had taken their places and were eating, Jesus said, "Truly I tell you, one of you will betray me, one who is eating with me." They began to be distressed and to say to him one after another, "Surely, not I?" He said to them, "It is one of the twelve, one who is dipping bread into the bowl with me. For the Son of Man goes as it is written of him, but woe to that one by whom the Son of Man is betrayed! It would have been better for that one not to have been born." (14:17–21)

When they had sung the hymn, they went out to the Mount of Olives. And Jesus said to them, "You will all become deserters; for it is written, 'I will strike the shepherd, and the sheep will be scattered.' But after I am raised up, I will go before you to Galilee." Peter said to him, "Even though all become deserters, I will not." Jesus said to him, "Truly I tell you, this day, this very night, before the cock crows twice, you will deny me three times." But [Peter] said vehemently, "Even though I must die with you, I will not deny you." And all of them said the same. (14:26–31)

Jesus then leads the disciples to a section of the Mount called Gethsemane. He takes aside the same three disciples who had accompanied him at the transfiguration: Peter, James, and John. Jesus requests that they stay awake with him as he prays in his time of grief.

Since these were the three who had witnessed the transfiguration, one might assume them to be more mature disciples who will understand and comply with these instructions. However, they do not; instead they sleep.

During their slumber, Mark recounts, the solitary Jesus prays the central message of this gospel: "Dear Father, even though you are omnipotent, please provide me with what you know to be best, even if it isn't what I want (or yet understand)." Furthermore, this passage notes that Jesus is greatly "distressed and agitated" and "throws himself on the ground" to pray. The Greek word used in this text conveys a sense of intense distress.

After his prayer, Jesus wakes the sleeping disciples and remonstrates only with Peter. Once again, Mark is keeping the focus on Peter, and his words are gentle, evidence of his understanding and compassion for the heartrending dichotomies between desire and reality. Indeed, Mark's words from Gethsemane are so apt that Matthew used them also and they have fallen into common parlance: "The spirit indeed is willing, but the flesh is weak."

> *They went to a place called Gethsemane; and [Jesus] said to his disciples, "Sit here while I pray." [Jesus] took with him Peter and James and John, and began to be distressed and agitated. And Jesus said to them, "I am deeply grieved, even to death; remain here, and keep awake." And going a little farther, [Jesus] threw himself on the ground and prayed that, if it were possible, the hour might pass from him. [Jesus] said, "Abba, Father, for you all things are possible; remove this cup from me; yet, not what I want, but what you want." He came and found them sleeping; and he said to Peter, "Simon, are you asleep? Could you not keep awake one hour? Keep awake and pray that you may not come into the time of trial; the spirit indeed is willing, but the flesh is weak." (14:32–38)*

Pilate and the Crucifixion

The scene next moves to the high priest's courtyard after Jesus' arrest. Twice asked by a serving girl and once by a bystander whether he is one of Jesus' followers, Peter denies that he is. Mark's telling of Peter's denials differs slightly from Matthew's account, but the difference is very meaningful. In Matthew, Jesus says that Peter will deny him three times "before the cock crows." In Mark, Jesus says that the thrice-repeated denial would happen "before the cock crows twice."

But wouldn't Peter have remembered Jesus' words when he heard the cock crow the first time? This is a tiny detail; however, it intensifies the impression of Peter's helplessness in the face of his all-too-human fear. Even when reminded by the initial crowing, he was unable to stop himself, unable to change course.

Well aware that Rome's genocide was continuing over a protracted period, Mark knows that no one who betrayed his neighbor or his friend could legitimately use the excuse of surprise. They had plenty of time to consider their answer before the soldier's knock came. Peter's example emphatically drives that reality home.

> *While Peter was below in the courtyard, one of the servant-girls of the high priest came by. When she saw Peter warming himself, she stared at him and said, "You also were with Jesus, the man from Nazareth." But he denied it, saying, "I do not know or understand what you are talking about." And he went out into the forecourt. Then the cock crowed. And the servant-girl, on seeing him, began again to say to the bystanders, "This man is one of them." But again he denied it. Then after a little while the bystanders again said to Peter, "Certainly you are one of them; for you are a Galilean." But [Peter] began to curse, and he swore an oath, "I do not know this man you are talking about." At that moment the cock crowed for the second time. Then Peter remembered that Jesus had said to him, "Before the cock crows twice, you will deny me three times." And he broke down and wept. (14:66–72)*

The Passion account proceeds to Jesus' appearance before Pontius Pilate, where the parallels between Jerusalem and Rome continue. Pilate ignores what he knows to be the truth about Jesus and accepts the judgment of the "crowd," agreeing to Jesus' crucifixion. Nero, by scapegoating the Messianic Jews for the fire in Rome, had also abandoned obvious truth and taken an expedient course that would be politically popular. Mark intensifies the pain of these betrayals, both of which moved beyond personal matters into public catastrophes.

> *Now at the festival [Pilate] used to release a prisoner for them, anyone for whom they asked. Now a man called Barabbas was in prison with the rebels who had committed murder during the insurrection. So the crowd came and began to ask Pilate to do for them according to his custom.*

FIVE—CROSSING MARK'S STORMY SEA

> *Then he answered them, "Do you want me to release for you the King of the Jews?" For he realized that it was out of jealousy that the chief priests had handed [Jesus] over. But the chief priests stirred up the crowd to have [Pilate] release Barabbas for them instead. Pilate spoke to them again, "Then what do you wish me to do with the man you call the King of the Jews?" They shouted back, "'Crucify him!" Pilate asked them, "Why, what evil has he done?" But they shouted all the more, "Crucify him." So Pilate, wishing to satisfy the crowd, released Barabbas for them; and after flogging Jesus, he handed him over to be crucified. (15:6-15)*

After the trial, the scene moves to a courtyard where Mark provides a dramatic image: the soldiers strip Jesus and robe him in purple. This is a message, since purple was the color reserved for royalty (and note that this is completely different from the red robe described in Matthew). A crown of thorns is placed on his head and his is mocked as "King of the Jews."

Mark uses the ugliness and childishness of this scene—and Jesus' complete lack of response to it—as an illustration of the crudeness and brutality of temporal power contrasted with the maturity and dignity of Spirit. And it was abundantly clear that temporal power was vested in the representatives of the Temple and the soldiers who belonged to Pilate and to Rome.

When the time arrives for Jesus the Christ to be led to his greatest physical trial, the crucifixion, the purple robe is removed, and he is described as in "his own clothes." Once again, Mark is precise: spiritual power needs no outward trappings.

> *Then the soldiers led him into the courtyard of the palace (that is, the governor's headquarters); and they called together the whole cohort. And they clothed him in a purple cloak; and after twisting some thorns into a crown, they put it on him. And they began saluting him, "Hail, King of the Jews!" They struck his head with a reed, spat upon him, and knelt down in homage to him. After mocking him, they*

> *stripped him of the purple cloak and put his own clothes on him. Then they led him out to crucify him. (15:16–20)*

Mark's depiction of the crucifixion is very brief. It contains no extra words and few explanations. He does write that Simon of Cyrene, described as the "father of Alexander and Rufus," carried the cross for Jesus. It is possible that Alexander and Rufus were members of Rome's Messianic Jewish community. If true, this mention provides another link to these followers.

Furthermore, if Alexander and Rufus had accepted execution in Rome, their mention here would have provided further inspiration to the Christus believers. In an account with language as sparse as Mark's, their mention would seem to have some significance, but I can only conjecture.

> *They compelled a passer-by, who was coming in from the country, to carry [Jesus'] cross; it was Simon of Cyrene, the father of Alexander and Rufus. (15:21)*

Jesus is led to Golgotha, stripped naked, and crucified with two bandits. Contrary to what has often been thought, the stripping of Jesus was not a *specific* attempt to dishonor him. Nakedness was the norm for Roman executions, but it was especially shameful for all Jews, who considered public nudity a terrible disgrace.

As Jesus hangs on the cross, awaiting death, everyone taunts him: bystanders, the bandits, the chief priests, and the scribes. Finally, at three o'clock, six hours after being nailed to the cross, Jesus cries out the beginning words of Psalm 22: "Eloi, Eloi, lema sabachthani?" which means, "My God, my God, why have you forsaken me?"

Mark's gospel records these as Jesus' only words—and through the millennia they have been subject to myriad interpretations. Many have believed that Mark's Passion shows Jesus betrayed and consumed by feelings of despair, but I believe that this interpretation is neither correct nor supported by the text itself. Furthermore, it is completely inconsistent with Mark's message to Rome's Messianic Jews.

This crucifixion account is both heartrending and heart-filling, an image of Jesus painfully, yet exultantly, moving into the final moments of his human life, fully awake. In the first century, as we noted in our study of Matthew's gospel, it would have been no aberration, nor any great surprise for Jesus—or any Jew—to have recited the words of this particular psalm at the moment of death. Jewish tradition called for pious Jews to die with the words of Psalm 22 on their lips. Reciting the first words would have indicated the same thing as a Christian starting to pray, "Our Father …"

Strengthening my belief in this crucifixion as a moment of triumphant suffering is the nature of Psalm 22 itself, a work that every devout Jew would have known from beginning to end. This psalm does, indeed, begin in lament. However, it continues as a celebration of trust and faith in the midst of agony and even death. If we understand that Jesus was *quoting* from a great and jubilant prayer, a core piece of Hebrew scripture, it makes absolutely no sense to think of him sagging from the cross, bloody, abandoned, and inconsolable.

Psalm 22 ends with these words: ***"To [God], indeed, shall all who sleep in the earth bow down; before him shall bow all who go down to the dust, and I shall live for him. Posterity will serve [God]; future generations will be told about the Lord, and proclaim the Lord's deliverance to a people yet unborn, saying that [God] has done it"*** **(Psalm 22:29–31)**. This is the full picture Mark gives the Roman Christus followers of this defining moment.

In Mark's gospel Jesus the Christ is indeed betrayed, and when he gives a "loud cry and breaths his last," he is certainly bloody and he is certainly alone. Not a single one of the disciples is noted as having been around him when he dies—not even Mary, his mother—although it is mentioned that some women, including Mary of Magdala, watch "from a distance."

Mark gives no indication that Jesus surrenders to bitterness or resentment. On the contrary, Jesus calmly predicts his fate to his disciples, and though he is distressed in Gethsemane, his prayer is clear: he accepts the necessity of his suffering and death if that is God's will for him. The shame and mockery heaped on him by the soldiers and those around the cross do not affect him. He refuses the palliative wine he is offered.

Yet, while there is no bitterness or resentment in this account, there is intense suffering and great sadness. Jesus' final moment is a crying out, a proclamation of being present to pain as Jesus marshals all his energy, all the strength of his belief, in a last, great triumphant outbreath.

We must weep as we read these words. Ever since the teaching at Caesarea Philippi's springs (8:27), Mark's gospel has been focused on lessons that a type of suffering must be endured because such suffering is part of the nature of God—and this crucifixion shows the terrible and moving and unforgettable image of that truth.

After the death, Mark recounts that among the watching strangers and enemies, a centurion upon seeing the serene and stately strength of Jesus, exclaims, "Truly, this man was God's son!" How immensely meaningful these six words are!

When the Messianic Jews went to be sacrificed in Rome, they too would face a centurion. Surrounded by strangers and enemies, shackled and dying, they would also be taunted. Mark called on them to understand that the manner of their death contained the seed of conversion, residing in the power of great spiritual example, and would proclaim the reality of Jesus the Christ that could be carried forward to coming generations.

> *Then they brought Jesus to the place called Golgotha (which means the place of a skull). And they offered him wine mixed with myrrh; but he did not take it. And they crucified him, and divided his clothes among them, casting lots to decide what each should take. It was nine o'clock in the morning when they crucified him. The inscription of the charge against him read, "The King of the Jews." And with him they crucified two bandits, one on his right and one on his left. Those who passed by derided him, shaking their heads and saying, "Aha! You who would destroy the temple and build it in three days, save yourself, and come down from the cross!" In the same way the chief priests, along with the scribes, were also mocking him among themselves and saying, "He saved others; he cannot save himself. Let the Messiah, the King of*

FIVE—CROSSING MARK'S STORMY SEA

Israel, come down from the cross now, so that we may see and believe." Those who were crucified with him also taunted him. When it was noon, darkness came over the whole land until three in the afternoon. At three o'clock Jesus cried out with a loud voice, "Eloi, Eloi, lema sabachthani?" which means, "My God, my God, why have you forsaken me?" When some of the bystanders heard it, they said, "Listen, he is calling for Elijah." And someone ran, filled a sponge with sour wine, put it on a stick, and gave it to him to drink, saying, "Wait, let us see whether Elijah will come to take him down." Then Jesus gave a loud cry and breathed his last. And the curtain of the temple was torn in two, from top to bottom. Now when the centurion, who stood facing him, saw that in this way he breathed his last, he said, "Truly this man was God's Son!" There were also women looking on from a distance; among them were Mary Magdalene, and Mary the mother of James the younger and of Joses, and Salome. (15:22–40)

In this very difficult second spiritual path, we must hold tenaciously to the lessons of Jesus the Christ and the example of Peter that we find in the gospel of Mark. Through the actions of these two figures, more powerfully than through their words, we can gain counsel to help us traverse this chaotic sea.

Aside from Jesus himself, Peter is the primary figure of this gospel, placed in every chapter except those of the crucifixion and resurrection. Why? Because Peter is very much like us. He struggles to remain "awake." He faithfully follows all the steps. He is present, bodily and spiritually, at all of the important moments.

Yet Peter falls asleep at a critical moment. He denies Jesus, despite having been warned and in the face of a vivid reminder—the first cock's crow. He does not stop himself. And then he cries. And then he disappears and is not at the crucifixion. He is nowhere for the remainder of the gospel. Why?

For Mark, Peter represents a living, breathing historical example, one filled with large measures of human weakness and uncertainty. Peter was a great hero of the Messianic faith who ultimately died for his beliefs, but Peter failed—and did so more than once. This is a message that failure and guilt are redeemable, regardless of the number of lapses and even though resolution might take a very long time and be filled with uncertainty.

Once Peter shed his sincere tears of regret, his spiritual and literary purpose was ended as far as Mark was concerned, and he disappeared from the recital. But Peter's usefulness to us as an echo of the second path is immeasurable and unceasing: attentiveness, struggle, repeated failure, and no resolution.

Congruent with the Serenity Prayer, which was quoted earlier in the chapter, Jesus is presented with challenges he "knows he can change." He ascertains this through prayer, and that knowledge makes him decisive and forceful. Over and over, Mark characterizes Jesus' response with the word "immediately." In the Passion account however, Jesus faces trials he knows he cannot, and should not, change.

Therefore, in the Passion with full understanding, Jesus the Christ embodies the deep and true power of surrender. He accepts. He stays centered, calm, and dignified. He does not speak out, for there is nothing to say. His example conveys that there is nothing external that can or should be fought. His only battle is the same as ours in this second path—to stay awake, to stay connected to Mystery, and to use all of our energy to proclaim God's love, even in the midst of pain and conflict.

The Resurrection Announced

Mark's resurrection narrative is a puzzling, even startling, end to a profound gospel. It contains four elements that are completely unique to it, particulars not found in any of the other gospels.

After Jesus' burial, the same women who watched him die "from a distance" go to the tomb to anoint the body. They did this, not because they believed in resurrection, but because they wanted to be certain that Jesus' burial was accomplished in accordance with Jewish law.

When the women arrive at the tomb, they see what Mark describes as a "young man dressed in a white robe." This is the first puzzlement. Although it has been assumed by many that this figure is an angel, Mark does not tell us this.

The young man presents the second surprise when he informs the women that Jesus has "been raised." He goes on to issue instructions to the women, telling them to inform the disciples of a pending meeting with the risen Christ. In the narrative that follows, however, all the way to the end of the gospel itself, we read of no actual sighting. It simply isn't there. Decades later, another ending was added that did contain a sighting but the original gospel has none.

The meeting with the risen Christ that the women are asked to tell the disciples about is located in Galilee. This is the third oddity. A first century reference to Galilee customarily meant the entire region of the Sea of Galilee. Mark is pointedly directing the disciples to find their risen Messiah in the place he has used throughout his gospel as a metaphor for chaos and wilderness.

The fourth enigma is the most interesting of all. The text says that the women fail to fulfill their instructions. Instead, they flee and "say nothing" to anyone. They are clearly frightened. Indeed, "afraid" is what Mark chooses as *the final word he writes* in his gospel to the Messianic Jewish community of Rome.

Christian readers in subsequent years apparently found this ending so unsettling that not only one but two more "satisfactory" endings were added in the second century. Although many have attempted to give a coherent, logical reason for Mark's original closing, in my opinion none offered have been sufficient or logical.

Through the lens of Quadratos, it is clear the original ending is not obscure, nor some kind of odd lapse or digression. Mark's gospel is extremely precise, pointed, accurate, and consistent. The word "afraid" was chosen because it best resonated with the terrified Messianic Jews of Rome to whom Mark wrote.

This word served as a direct challenge to them—an implicit question. It asked: "When the soldiers come to your door, what will your answer be? Will you betray, or desert, or deny? Or will you give witness to the Messiah?"

> *When the sabbath was over, Mary Magdalene, and Mary the mother of James, and Salome bought spices, so that they might go and anoint him. And very early on the first day of the week, when the sun had risen, they went to the tomb. They had been saying to one another, "Who will roll away the stone for us from the entrance to the tomb?" When they looked up, they saw that the stone, which was very large, had already been rolled back. As they entered the tomb, they saw a young man, dressed in a white robe, sitting on the right side; and they were alarmed. But he said to them, "Do not be alarmed; you are looking for Jesus of Nazareth, who was crucified. He has been raised; he is not here. Look, there is the place they laid him. But go, tell his disciples and Peter that he is going ahead of you to Galilee; there you will see him, just as he told you." So they went out and fled from the tomb, for terror and amazement had seized them; and they said nothing to anyone, for they were afraid. (16:1–8)*

On the second path of Quadratos, Mark's original (and heretofore perplexing) ending fits us too. And the fit is precise. It challenges us. Which type of disciple are we?

Will we manage to endure our continuing ego death and also bear witness to it? Will we betray it and give up amid all the temptations and distractions with which we are faced? Will we desert, turn our faces away, and run? If we do, will we return?

Will we accept one (or many) of the possible distractions and deny the path? How long will it take us to recover our direction? Will we ever recover? Or heeding Mark's counsel, will we somehow manage to have trust in our chosen journey and make our way through the uncertainty and confusion?

Our walk through this second path will not be likely to look as unswerving and true as that of Jesus' from the flowing spring down to the city. Eventually, when we are more mature in our journey and as we proceed through further cycles of Quadratos, it may straighten a bit; but now, at this early stage, we are much more like the disciples, like Peter.

Jesus said "all" would desert him—and despite their sincerity they all did. We will probably desert, too, in some way or another—but remember, Peter shows us that desertion is redeemable.

This is a miserably uncomfortable process, but through it we will learn what we "can change" and what we "cannot change." As we paddle across the choppy sea of chaos, sometimes we will fall over the side of the boat and gulp a fair amount of seawater. We will get seasick. But, as long as we keep praying—and rowing—we will not be lost at sea.

Indeed, the Christ promises us that the far shore will grow closer and closer. Awareness of the grace that guides us will begin to dawn, surely and certainly. The storms will quiet and land will appear.

Our boat will slide smoothly onto the sand of a golden beach and right over a rise, just behind the sea grass, the most beautiful and fragrant garden we can possibly imagine awaits. John's glorious garden is preparing our welcome. In the shade of a bending tree, amongst the blossoms, we will find a bench, and we will see our name engraved upon it.

Hold to faith. Let our courage be blessed. We will find rest.

Prayer for The Second Path

Psalm 22

My God, my God, why have you forsaken me?
Why so far from my delivery?

So empty in the anguish of my words?
I call to you in the daytime but you don't answer
And all night long I plead restlessly, uselessly.

I know Your holiness, find it in the memorized praises
Uttered by those who've questioned and struggled with you
Through all the generations
These, my forebears, trusted in you
And through their trusting you touched them Held and delivered them
Trusting they cried out to you and you met them face-to-face
Their confidence was strong and they were not confounded.

But I am not as they.
Utterly alone, I am cast out of the circle.
A worm, a living reproach, scorned and despised, even less than
  despised,
Unheard, unseen, unacknowledged, denied;
And all who encounter me revile me with cynic laughter
Shaking their heads, parting their nattering lips, mocking,
"Let him throw himself at God for his deliverance," they say,
"Since that is who he trusts let the Lord save him."

And they are right:
How not trust You, and what else to trust?

You I entered on leaving the womb
You I drank at my mother's breast
I was cast upon you at birth
And even before birth I swam in you, my heart's darkness
Be not far from me now
When suffering is very near
And there is no help

FIVE—CROSSING MARK'S STORMY SEA

And I am beset all around by threatening powers
The bulls of Bashan gaping their dismal braying
mouths Their ravenous roaring lion mouths
I am poured out like water
My bones' joints are snapped like twigs
My heart melts like wax
Flooding my bowels with searing viscid emotion

My strength is dried up like a potsherd
My tongue cleaves woolly to the roof of my mouth
And I feel my body dissolving into death's dusts
For I am hounded by my isolation
Am cast off and encircled by the assembly of the violent
Who like vicious dogs nip at my hands and feet
I count the bones of my naked body
As the mongrels shift and stare and circle
They divide my clothes among themselves, casting lots for them

So now, in this very place, I call on you
There is no one left

Do not be far from me
Be the center
Of the center
Of the circle
Be the strength of that center
The power of the absence that is the center
Deliver my life from the killing sharpnesses
Deliver my soul from the feverish dogs
Save me from the lion mouths
Answer me with the voice of the ram's horn

And I will seek and form and repeat Your name among my kinsmen
In the midst of everyone I will compose praises with my lips
And those who enter your awesomeness through my words
    will also praise

RADICAL TRANSFORMATION

All the seed of Jacob will glorify you
And live in awe of you
All those who question and struggle
Will dawn with your light
For they will know
You have not scorned the poor and despised
Nor recoiled disgusted from their faces
From them your spark has never been hidden
And when they cried out in their misery

You heard and answered and ennobled them
And it is the astonishment of this that I will praise in the Great Assembly
Making deep vows in the presence of those who know your heart
Know that in you the meek eat and are satisfied
And all who seek and struggle find the tongue to praise
Saying to you:

May your heart live forever
May all the ends of the earth remember and return to you
And all the families of all the nations bow before you
For all that is is your domain
Your flame kindles all that lives and breathes
And you are the motive force of all activity
The yearning of the grasses, the lovers' ardor
And they that rise up, live and eat the fat of the earth will bow before you
Before you will bow all those who lie down, find peace, and enter the dust
For none can keep alive by his own power—you alone light the soul
Distant ages to come shall serve you, shall be related to you in future times
Those people not yet born
Will sing of your uprightness, your evenness, your brightness
To a people not yet born,
That is still yet to come,
That this is how you are.

translation by Norman Fischer

FIVE—CROSSING MARK'S STORMY SEA

EXERCISES FOR THE SECOND PATH

The exercises of Quadratos are cumulative. On the second path, we continue the practices of *creating temenos* and *welcoming the other*. These are present throughout all four paths. They are particularly essential on the second path where we often feel exhausted, conflicted, anxious, needing trust and the experience of every voice. Remember, this is transformation. We are moving through a type of death—and it can be very difficult.

Hold the Tension of the Opposites

Christianity provides a powerful image of the practice of holding the tension of the opposites. The tradition's earliest form of the cross was a simple **+** drawn with four arms of equal length. This form of the cross was known throughout the Middle East for thousands of years *before* the time of Jesus. It was this shape that was venerated during the years these gospels were composed, and it served—with rare exception—as the shape of the baptistry into the seventh century.

When we read Jesus' words "pick up your cross and follow," it was this shape that was most likely being referenced by Mark. Its equal arms formed a symbol known from antiquity to represent the joining of all opposites—female with male, heaven with earth, and especially death with life.

This equidistant shape is also the seed pattern from which ancient labyrinths (beginning about 6,000 BCE) are drawn. Labyrinths, which have a serpentine path into a center and back out, signify a journey of transformation. This cross—and the meanings it represents—are at the very heart of the Quadratos Journey and logo.

When you pray and meditate, visualize the mark **+** in your mind, trace it on your heart and find—or make—such a cross and keep it near you. In prayer and in practice with others, listen and attempt an inner experience of extending respect to all perspectives. This is a deepening and expansion of "The Other" exercise we advanced in the first path.

When we now try to find truth in each and every perspective no matter how opposed we feel initially, if we are sincere, we will inevitably uncover great interior conflicts. Resist every tendency to take one side over another. Understand that paradoxical truth is our objective.

Examine the fact that the tendency to choose any one side at the expense of its opposite is an ego-defense. It serves no purpose except to make us feel better in the moment. The ego-self feels calm after such a choice because it has something definite to latch onto—no uncertainty, no dilemma, no shades of gray, and no anxiety.

But this tendency is extremely harmful almost by definition. Human interaction is complex, and if it is to be approached maturely it can almost never be judged with the kind of simplistic exactitude that soothes the ego. Observe your own inner reactions to each perspective and continue to refrain from choosing specific positions.

When we do this, and accompany it with prayer and spiritual practice, an even greater truth will be revealed that goes still further—an unexpected way that folds the opposites together. But we are not yet there. On this second path our challenge is to patiently *endure* the opposites, listening intently to all sides, choosing none. Holding the tension of opposites, living with our anxiety, and not having any certainties are the requisite trials as we keep to our journey, trusting and believing in a new epiphany.

When we are learning to trust this practice for the first time, our experience is often more one of hope than of knowing an epiphany will come. Stay the course. Pray. Listen to others more experienced on this journey. Keep the mind clear from attempts to "think through" to an answer. Wait!

Ask To Be Deepened

The lyrical poetry of Psalm 22 holds great mystery, grace, and wisdom. It is possible that a time of deepest abandonment can open feelings of peace, trust and even praise within us.

A Buddhist prayer used before meditation recites: "I pray that I may be given the appropriate difficulties and sufferings on this journey so that my heart may become awakened, and my practice of compassion and liberation for all beings may be fulfilled."

Václav Havel, writer and former Czech president, has said: "Hope is not the conviction that something will turn out well, but the certainty that something makes sense, regardless of how it turns out."

Our practice in the second path, in the midst of great concern, pain, and emotional deprivation, is to pray to remain steadfast through these moments, and that we will have the courage to live the answer that arrives from the Christ.

HOW DO WE MOVE THROUGH SUFFERING?
The Core Question of The Gospel of Mark

Good news! The Gospel of Mark opens with the hopeful reassurance that our trials actually represent good news—a further advance of our spiritual journey, along which we will continue if we persevere in our practices.

John the Baptist calls us to "repent our missing the mark": to scrutinize our lives, recognize the core source of our pain, acknowledge appropriate guilt, correct our heart and mind through asking for forgiveness, and then move on.

The storms at sea ask us to remember that we are not alone in the boat. They also tell us to listen for our inner "Rescue me! Fix me!" voice. When we hear it, we can know that this is a temptation to fall into feelings of helplessness and victimization. Mark asks us to respond with our greatest inner strength and determination to keep going without losing compassion for ourselves and our frailties.

The transfiguration advises us that the nature of unity (trans-figure) is the joining of opposites, and that holiness (wholeness) holds both discipline and compassion. We also need to be mindful that we lack understanding, and that we should wait and learn more before we speak, especially about our supposed wisdom.

The teachings on the road to Jerusalem tell us that we are on a deep and mysterious journey of transformation that will often be filled with pain and will seem completely incomprehensible. We will be unable to continue unless we pray to Spirit for help and accept that this is the nature of the second path.

The confrontations in the Temple teach us to take courage and walk toward our inner and outer conflicts. The tension and anxiety we find in conflict are necessary and inevitable as the old ego-self struggles with Spirit.

Jesus' teaching about tribulation cautions us that when we find ourselves wanting to point fingers—externalizing our conflicts onto others—our practice instead should be to focus on the necessary transformation of our own inner lives. In this way our journey continues, and we do not become party to increasing the conflicts of others.

Mark's passion account tells us to look to Peter's example and the example of the Christ. Peter's story shows that we can expect to fall into denial, or even desertion, and resolution may not come quickly. Jesus the Christ gives us an image of suffering as part of God and teaches us that through surrender, we will come to know Spirit more deeply.

The resurrection announced asks us a significant question: What will our response be when our old self is dying, our beliefs, comforting traditions and habitual responses—especially when the cost is turmoil, anger, grief and fear? In the second path, it seems that almost every moment holds this question. The coming third path allows us to look back with the knowledge that a better answer was on the way. But in the intensity of the second path, to which truths will our attitudes and actions give witness?

Chapter 6
BEING IN JOHN'S GLORIOUS GARDEN

PSALM 126

When you bring us out from enclosure
We will be like dreamers
Our heads thrown back with laughter
Our throats vibrating with song
And the others will say,

Yes,
Great happenings
have happened to them
The ones who have struggled
long with their questions

Yes,
Great things would have happened to us
And we would be dizzy with the joy of them
Drunk on water in an arid land,
Our tears—Our joy's seed
We'd go out weeping
And come back singing
Our arms full of sheaves.

translation by Norman Fischer

How Do We Receive Joy?
The Third Path

In one electric, life-changing instant it seems as though everything in us shifts and a blinding new reality enters. Until this point, so much has been struggle. Our toes searched for firm purchase on the mountain path of decision, and we cowered in the battering storms as we were tossed in the treacherous sea of the second path.

Nonetheless, we remained faithful through all difficulties and missteps. We prayed that our yearning, outstretched hand would be met by a firm answering grip that would lead us ashore. However, this is not what we get. We get infinitely more. Yet no step we have taken, nor prayer we have prayed, could have prepared us for the wonder of this moment.

What arrives and opens in us feels like the everlasting embrace of an eternal guardian—or an intimate lover. We are filled with an immediate and unexpected experience of union. It is a feeling that is full, un-reflected, visionary, and totally indescribable. The sensations of this moment will differ for each of us.

Some of us will be aware of a new energy; we may tingle or tremble. Some will feel a deep stillness. A great calm or exuberance may arise. Sight may seem brighter, clearer. Flashes of creativity and new insight may burst into life. Minds may race into full engagement or blissful emptiness. Almost universally we will perceive everything as gift.

With this opening, it is as though we have walked through a gate into the most beautiful springtime garden imaginable. Immeasurable beauty and bounty surround us. Our senses are confounded. Breezes ruffle our hair as we stroll, and birds call out their jubilant songs.

We can feel how our fragile footprints are being overlaid by the Great Spirit, the enfolding of Mystery, the Christ. We have a clear sense that we have entered a new plane of understanding where this largesse is freely available, a gift bestowed on all—not earned by any action and completely unconditional.

This is the third path and The Gospel of John. As the path unfolds through the apostle's metaphor of a garden—specifically, the Garden of Eden—we discover a bounty that feels as though it truly holds everything. We feel as though we have finally arrived at the point we have been headed for—at last! This is the culmination. We have made it.

And in one way that is true. John's gospel is a vision that is simultaneously unitive and illuminative. There is absolutely nothing that can equal its inner experience. This feeling is precisely what poets and mystics try to describe and certainly one of the main reasons people use drugs and alcohol. They are trying to achieve an encounter with this bliss. It is the pinnacle, the apogee and the heart of all.

When we relax and surrender to this epiphany, our attention gradually refocuses. Our perception expands and sharpens. We notice much more than the garden flowers and the warmth of the new embrace. We become aware of the expanding roots, leaves, buds, and blossoms—the foundation and the future.

Time expands. We sense the past and realize that our garden also contains dirt and worms and the sere brown memories of last season's blooms. We feel the rhythm of its unceasing cycles of decay into beauty into decay into beauty. We feel the truth of this cycle stirring as we think of our lives.

As powerful as our bliss feels it is only an instant, and the sense of epiphany is only one part of one path of a full journey, in the same way that blossoms are only one brief season of a garden. The treasure and essence of the third path is much more than a moment. It is an experience of union, of enfolding paradox.

The third path's capacity to hold ambiguity means it can—and does—contain *everything*. It holds joy. It holds conflict. It holds boredom. It holds compassion. It holds cruelty. It holds ecstasy. It holds pain. It holds love. It holds cynicism. It holds hope. It holds misery. It holds striving. It holds hate. It holds peace. In it is every gradation of light and dark, of each day, and every passage of the seasons. It welcomes our full human complexity. It invites, accepts and celebrates each and every aspect of our human enigma.

Therefore, the glorious garden of John's gospel also contains a profound caution—not against the gift, but against the limitations of our understanding. In the third path, our insights are not yet fully mature *although they feel so*. It does not take much reflection to observe that the world is full of people who reached a point of epiphany and immediately rushed out to share their supposed wisdom but created only havoc instead. Wisdom is a much longer journey.

New revelations need space and careful sheltering. Matthew and Mark asked us to continue moving. John asks us now to abide and receive. If we do, we will find that our awareness of complexity and interconnection expands. We will gently move toward a comprehension of our proper place within the whole. When questions about meaning and purpose begin to arise from *that* awareness, we will better understand and then eventually be ready to leave and take up the fourth path.

A critical equilibrium, which is the face of maturity, will reveal itself to us. If we leave too soon, we won't completely absorb our lessons. The young stalks planted by our journey thus far will never grow strong enough to support the blossoms that try to open. New buds filled with promise will wither. Yet if we remain too long, our journey is incomplete, and our inner reformation obstructed.

A glorious garden must be sensitively tended. Too little water, and flowers will shrivel. Too much, and roots will rot. With either extreme, we will find our garden reduced to its soil and we will have to begin again—or be satisfied with plastic flowers.

The core question of this third path is, *How do we receive joy?* In part, our answer is the discovery and exploration of a dynamic harmony. How many times has each of us turned our back on the experience of joy through fear and cynicism? Alternatively, how many times have we clung tightly to joy and watched as it inevitably and remorselessly thinned into illusion?

An even greater tragedy is abandonment of the journey itself through anxiety—arising from our trepidations and the pain of our losses, never understanding how close we came to finding real vitality and peace. Psychology cites the three primary ways we defend ourselves against perceived threat and also against the risks of change. These are sentimentality, cynicism and assertion of power over another. These, too, are among the risks we run on the third path.

At first glance, the directions for this path seem simple. They are basically "relax and enjoy," but for most of us, this may not be so easy. Most of us are better trained for "doing" than for just "being," and when we manage to relax, we don't tend to do so in an attentive way. But beingness and attentiveness are exactly what are needed now.

Surprisingly, "enjoy" may present even more challenges than "relax." Many of us can't even rationalize enjoyment as a reward for the suffering we have endured. We are unaccustomed to feeling worthy. We are used to giving, have been trained in its virtues, but often know little to nothing about receiving.

SIX—BEING IN JOHN'S GLORIOUS GARDEN

However, "enjoy" means we must learn the deep truth of all gifts: a receiver with an open and thankful heart is absolutely essential or the gift does not exist. It disappears. For many of us this comes as entirely new and very difficult information. But it is critically important.

Thanks to the inner "stripping" we have undergone on the previous two paths, we are now in an eternal, unconditional embrace we can actually see and feel. But there is a catch: our enjoyment is needed to complete the relationship. Don't misunderstand. The loving embrace is unconditional. It's ours no matter what, and we don't have to do anything to earn it. But without our enjoyment of that love, we *deprive* Spirit and the universe of our "resounding joy." And in an interconnected universe that joy can reach far indeed.

Simply "enjoying love" may seem a gentle insight compared to the drama and hard-fought struggles of the first and second paths, but for many of us this matter is anything but simple. The experience of union may throw some of us into an acute depression, because we are so certain we don't deserve what we have received.

Our time on the third path requires us to acknowledge our own worthiness. We cannot progress until we learn to put away the inner whips with which we remind ourselves of even our tiniest inadequacies. In this garden, it is our time to embrace the fact that we are loved simply because we are alive, not because of anything we do.

We will luxuriate in the words of this gospel and we will also study its demanding challenges. What were the needs and conditions of the culture two millennia ago that inspired John to such beauty, mysticism, and rigor? We saw the unsettled Messiahnian beginnings in Antioch and empathized with the agonies of the Christus believers in Rome. Now we will visit the teeming complexity of the Aegean port of Ephesus to share in the excitement and promise of its blossoming Christian community.

Birthplace of The Gospel of John
Ephesus on the Aegean Sea, 100 CE

At the end of the first century, Ephesus was a major seaport and the fourth largest city in the Greco-Roman world—after Rome, Alexandria and Great Antioch. Chosen by the Roman Empire as the capital of its Asian provinces, it sat due east of Athens on the Aegean Sea in what is today known as Turkey. Both port and capital city, it boasted a culturally diverse and thriving population. A large portion of its economic wealth, during the first century CE, derived from its 200-year history as Rome's largest and most important slave market.

Ephesus was also very significant in early Christianity, primarily because it most likely provided a haven for some of the greatest icons of the faith. The apostle Paul arrived in Ephesus in the mid-50s CE to teach and did so for about three years. He (or someone who accompanied him) is credited with founding the community there that later came to call itself "Christian."

Stories abound that the apostle John, author of the gospel, took Jesus' mother, Mary, to Ephesus to live out her life after her son's death. Mary of Magdala is also thought to have lived and perhaps taught in the city before moving to Gaul where she died. These figures provided a rich soil of faith and experience in which the Followers of The Way could learn and mature.

It is generally believed that The Gospel of John was written in Ephesus sometime between 95 and 105 CE, though some scholars posit Alexandria as the manuscript's original location. (The cultural dynamics of the two cities were similar in so many respects that this debate regarding location makes little difference to the Quadratos thesis.)

For many years, it was thought likely that both The Gospel of John and the book formally titled *The Revelation to John* (though simply known as *Revelation* by most people) were written by the same author named "John." This was assumed since both were composed at approximately the same time, in almost the same place.

SIX—BEING IN JOHN'S GLORIOUS GARDEN

Today it is believed that that there were two "Johns." Most scholars think John the Apostle wrote the gospel and that a zealous Christian known as John the Seer authored Revelation. Due to his zealotry, the Seer was imprisoned by Emperor Domitian on the Isle of Patmos, near Ephesus. He wrote his book there, from his cell, in about 95 CE.

Although there are two authors, both the Gospel and Revelation source from the same historic period and have similar concerns. They each describe an epiphany and its effects. They both deal with issues of tribalism and diversity. However, though their focus is linked, the two books differ dramatically.

Revelation graphically depicts the inner, even bloody, strife that occurs when the "old temple" is outgrown. A strenuous and vicious fight is waged against transformation by the less mature self, which fears every change and can see no possibilities beyond resistance. Since Revelation is not included in the Sunday Reading Cycle, it is not fully analyzed in this book. A more thorough exposition of the work will have to await a future writing. However, an awareness of Revelation's strife is important on the Third Path of Quadratos. Without its cautions, naivete and denial can arise and easily retard—if not altogether stop—the journey.

The Gospel of John has a different focus. The epiphany we read of is visionary and liberating. John has filled his gospel with meditations that guide us along a profound interior process in order to deepen our epiphany as it arrives. We are led to connect with rather than fight against the differing elements encountered. Sincere effort leads us toward a comprehension of union—necessary for transformation. Then it is possible for our journey of expansion to continue.

John the Apostle is thought to have left Jerusalem for Ephesus years before the Great Temple's destruction. In Ephesus, he joined a community that had been founded by the rich teachings of the apostle Paul and had enjoyed a practice of inclusion for more than a decade. John, it is believed, lived and taught in Ephesus until his death of old age.

As we read his work, it is important that we keep ourselves anchored in history. A fervent evangelist, John seemed to have no interest in accommodating his views to those of his mother tradition, Judaism. He believed that the inclusive path of Jesus the Christ was a step beyond the Judaism of his day and never hesitated to express that view. His job, as he most likely saw it, was to call the diverse people of Ephesus to a radical form of community and to advocate for the Messiah who had come for all.

The Ephesian Christian community matured very differently from those in Rome and Antioch. The culture was unique. The city had a diverse population with many well-traveled citizens, no religious persecution, and highly skilled religious teachers. It is, of course, impossible to tell what the ingredient of the immense slave trade contributed to this complex matrix. Predictably, in Ephesus, in contrast to Rome and Antioch, many non-Jews became followers.

The congregation, therefore, developed to address not just the spiritual needs and beliefs of Messianic Jews, but a wide assortment of pagan believers, as well. Building a coherent Christian community that encompassed this multiplicity of traditions was a vibrant process that required many years—and especially benefited from the wisdom of great inspiration derived from its remarkable teachers.

When The Gospel of John was written, it was seeded in the rich soil of Paul's teaching, which had been nurtured by additional learned teachers and deep practice for almost fifty years. Furthermore, the community had by that time been totally separated from Judaism for ten years—a distinction unique to this gospel. The Ephesians firmly considered themselves members of a separate new faith. They self-identified as "Christians" and their place of worship as the "New Jerusalem."

A multi-tribal community, they did not regard Jesus as the Jewish Messiah who had come only for the Jews. They followed a universal Christ who had come, died, and been resurrected for *all*. Their Messiah would lead them to an inner temple in a new Jeru-Shalom where everyone would find welcome.

Needing a way to form community and confirm members, the new faith had developed a "baptism" ritual. And by the time of John's gospel, this practice had become Christianity's rite of entrance, although actual forms varied throughout the first century with different groups. As noted earlier, one type of baptism as performed by John the Baptist was a version of the Jewish ritual for cleansing and purification today called a *mikvah*.

In the writings of the apostle Paul, we see this Jewish ritual transformed into a process of initiation that joined an individual to the Christ. Gradually, this new Christian rite achieved equal stature with the traditional Jewish ritual of circumcision, and then after the break with Judaism the new rite replaced the Jewish one entirely.

As the Christian tradition of baptism grew, it built on the Jewish rite of washing and went far beyond "cleansing" and required much more commitment than a mere willingness to be dunked in the river. Christians seeking to be baptized—men and women alike—were required to undergo a lengthy period of reflection and practice. It was mandated that baptismal candidates make a commitment to service that involved heavy responsibilities within the faith community.

Only if they fulfilled these criteria were they eligible for the final ritual, which was designed to provide an internal experience of Jesus the Christ's life, death, resurrection and call to service. The process was so complex that it was tantamount to what we would today consider ordination. Indeed, one of the most eminent scripture scholars, Raymond Brown, suggests that John's entire gospel may have been written as a series of reflections for those preparing to be baptized.

Christianity's impact in Ephesus far exceeded changes in the ritual of baptism, however. For millennia, each village, city and region had its own god or goddess, which could never be the god of anyone outside that particular community. And because all religions of the time believed that everything in life was in the hands of these powerful beings, religious beliefs held the gravity of survival practices. It was believed that the sun literally rose each day based on the wishes of the gods.

Therefore, in the law and custom of the time, tribal outsiders were universally regarded not only as unbelievers, but also as people who represented concrete threats to the harmony and existence of the world.

There were unceasing disputes, even battles, over the supremacy of the various deities and the practices followed in the service of each.

It is important that when we think of the quarrels and the eventual rift between Judaism and Christianity, we realize that historically neither religion held the forms we see today. As Judaism developed, it departed markedly from the practices in the region. It became monotheistic, recognizing God as a single God above all other "false gods." Nonetheless, in its organization it remained strongly tribal, defined by bloodlines.

The Torah pronounces that all people come from Yahweh (G–d)—are created in his image—and are therefore to be respected as brothers and sisters. However, Jewish belief in the first century held that Jews had special privilege and that their deity's omnipotence was available only to them. Furthermore, that power could only come through the Temple priests who carefully negotiated with and appealed to Yahweh through elaborate rituals developed over the centuries.

Christianity, by the time of John's gospel—although it had not yet become a formal religion of any kind—had begun to break with this ancient tribal pattern. Ephesus had heard the apostle Paul preach the invitation that women and men, Greek and Jew, free and slave, all share their lives with each other following one God. The new faith wanted everyone to understand and follow its vision. The gospel shouted out the affirmation of this joyous summons: "*All* are one; no one is excluded; join us!"

The Christian approach to social structuring was a stark departure from the long-held practices of the Hebrew tribes, the old Temple, and the traditional strictures of tribalism itself. Historically, all tribes consisted of a core group whose membership evolved primarily through blood or marriage or locale (although other members might be allowed in by agreement of the group). Judaism, for example, granted automatic membership through the blood of a Jewish mother.

Christianity, however, changed the rules of tribe by *actively* inviting everyone. In the Mediterranean region of the time, and in fact most of the world, this was a radical—even blasphemous—concept. But the cultural diversity of Ephesus welcomed these deeply inclusionary beliefs and Christianity quickly grew.

SIX—BEING IN JOHN'S GLORIOUS GARDEN

Using the core teachings of the Hebrew Testament, particularly those in the book of Genesis, John reworks them into a more inclusionary and Christian perspective. He pens new metaphors for the Garden of Eden and for Adam and Eve. Further, his fresh stories transform the old accounts of trial and suffering into tales resonating with the jubilant message that *through Jesus the Christ, Paradise is now recovered for all!*

This reshaped garden of Christianity *welcomes* people rather than casting them out. It doesn't consider them usurpers of the divine; rather, it invites them to share in its bounty and beauty. In this way, John illuminates the new faith for his diverse audience. It is familiar to the Jewish Christ followers who already know these stories but is also comprehensible and welcoming to newcomers.

Unmistakably visionary, John's poetic words also make vast metaphysical pronouncements quite different from common understanding of the Hebrew Testament in the first century. Although that testament holds many passages of immense beauty, and Yahweh certainly extends understanding to his people, the Temple authorities often emphasized passages that recount swift punishment and little mercy. For the priests and their followers, Yahweh's awesomeness primarily derived from the vast power he readily wielded.

In direct contrast, The Gospel of John also proclaims Jesus the Christ as eternal and immensely powerful but leaves out the images of punishment. John's focus is different. He wants to emphasize that the Christ's power and authority originate from a divinity based in wisdom and love—a contrast that must have startled not only his Jewish but also his Greco-Roman audience.

The comportment of Jesus and his "pronouncements" differentiate John from the Gospels of Matthew, Mark, and Luke. In John, a divine Jesus completely in charge of every single event that is recounted, always speaks first, bestows wisdom and miracles, and carries his own cross. He is sure, confident, and serene.

In another departure exclusive to this gospel, Jesus the Christ engages in cordial discourse with a wide assortment of people whom tribal custom of the time would have deemed socially inferior or unacceptable. And though Jesus is clearly respectful and welcoming to these diverse peoples—among them women, Greeks, and a blind man—his presence in the accounts is nonetheless unfailingly powerful and divine. He *stands*, always, with the authority of God and does not hesitate to use that authority to *bestow* truth, mercy, and miracles.

With this royal demeanor not found in the other gospels, Jesus uses language that is assured, emphatic, and not in the least collegial. There are no soft and approachable beginnings to Jesus' sentences. Although Jesus certainly directs events and performs miracles in Matthew, Mark, and Luke, often forcefully, we would not characterize his actions in those accounts as bestowing. By contrast, we can readily do so in John's gospel.

In this gospel, Jesus the Christ graciously, gracefully, and very firmly lays down the core principles on which he wishes believers to focus: union and complexity and compassion. He makes it clear that when he gives this instruction he does so with the full force and authority of God's divine power, which he clearly claims for himself. He further charges that believers have a duty to accept these precepts as immutable truths. Finally, his commands for action are explicit: "Go out and practice these principles in your lives!"

John's gospel is a full-hearted proclamation that all is unified. The diversity and exuberance of the Ephesian Christian community is inextricable from the gospel itself. Each came from the other; each led the other forward. In this exciting synergy, for a few remarkable years Ephesus became the heart of Christianity in precisely the same way Jerusalem had been the heart of Judaism.

Being in the Garden
Approaching John Today

The poetry and depth of John's words represent the third path in its fullest blossoming. John was a mystic. His language resonates with continuous ecstasy and deep peace. Of the four gospels, John's was the last written and is placed last in the Christian Testament.

However, as we have noted, when taught in the ancient church, certain passages were chosen to be used primarily for the Seasons of Lent and Easter, the traditional church periods for reflection on death and new life. This was likely done because this gospel describes the third path—epiphany and rebirth—and because John's gospel and the third path are completely different in form, in tone, and in substance from the other paths.

As we proceed on our spiritual journey, we will discover the succor of John's gospel on an ongoing basis in our inner lives. We will be able to find and feel the many tiny epiphanies that are continually occurring all around us no matter what specific "path" we are focused on.

I am certain that this is in part why the ancient reading cycles, with full inspiration, placed sections of John's gospel within the other gospels. "Behold!" its words cry out, "See the flowers. Smell the air. Appreciate the dirt and the bugs. Be blessed. Know joy. Feel worthy. Share the gift."

Let us move to examine some concepts that will help us to enter into John's gospel—and an experience of the third path—as fully as possible.

Western spirituality has used terms like "enlightenment" and "illumination" to describe what we are calling the third path. These words result from attempts by mystics to express a sense of their own experiences. They *feel* as though light has somehow arisen in them, and so they have turned this feeling into a metaphor.

We are moving from not-seeing to seeing, and it is easy to characterize this in terms of our bodily senses as a movement from the "dark" (where our physical sight is limited) into the relative clarity of "light." But this kind of metaphor is much too small for what we are actually experiencing.

Furthermore, these terms can lead us into difficulty because they imply a sense of switching from a flat, one-sided state into another equally flat state. The third path is not so limited. It is complex. It is neither light nor dark, but rather an enfolding of the two, and of up and down, of right and left, of all opposites into an intricate, and ever-changing harmony. It doesn't proceed in "steps" and "stages" like the other paths tend to do. It isn't linear at all. It is non-sequential, its aspects frequently simultaneous, undifferentiated.

With regard to this third spiritual path, the word "path" itself is almost a contradiction. It arrives as a complete and unitive experience. And once we are on it—*in* it—we don't walk or engage in much activity at all. We stay still and observe. We stay still and feel. We stay still and pray.

In a mature spiritual life, these are the practices that will fill and illuminate everything we do. Here our habit of reflection on ourselves in relation to others begins to deepen and become threaded into the tapestry of our lives.

Another concept that can help us comprehend the nature of this path is an understanding of the word "symbol." Symbol comes from two Greek words, *sum* and *ballein*. *Sum* means "together" and *ballein* is "to throw." Thus, *sumballein*, which became "symbol," is "to throw two or more things together."

When we use or make a symbol, we throw together disparate elements such as word and picture or heart and head. This is important because it is the capacity to deal with paradox, an essential aspect of the truth of union and the third path.

Contrast the meaning of symbol with the Greek word *diabol*, from which *diablo* or "devil" is derived. *Dia* means "across" and again, *bol* derives from ballein, "to throw." *Diaballein* or *diabol* is, therefore, "to throw across."

Using this understanding, we can see that the second spiritual path—which we recently traversed—was a diabolic inner landscape, a tempestuous place of obstacles thrown across our path, where opposites appeared separate, distinct. The temptations of unbalanced ego surfaced continually, and we felt lost as opposites tore at us.

At the third path, in a surprising flash we have been given the capacity to know *sym-bol*. Harmony has replaced our experience of searing trial, and we are resting in a garden instead of battling the stormy seas of *dia-bol*.

SIX—BEING IN JOHN'S GLORIOUS GARDEN

The strain and exhaustion of the second path begin to fade and we move into our springtime garden. Green buds appear on the wizened brown twigs of our soul.

What we feared damaged beyond repair—dead—comes back to life. We look back with a sense of meaning, knowing that the course of events could not have been otherwise and was worth the pain. We begin to relax into our blessings and the self-value they imply. We dare to believe that we hold a blossom within.

As we revel in the harmonious union John has given us, it is important to separate the Quadratos journey from what we may have learned in traditional historical teaching. Much of traditional teaching about John's priceless words has not been remotely consistent with his original, deeply loving and mystical intention. Instead, many readers, teachers, and institutions—over many centuries—have misinterpreted John's priceless and *symbolic* words through the eyes of *diabol*. Indeed, in some cases they continue to do so.

Unfortunately, once the original fourfold reading cycle was abandoned, churchgoing Christians lost the possibility of the full journey of psychological and spiritual transformation in the gospels, and with it the complexity of *symbol*.

The joyous message of John's gospel—of oneness—was crushed into the one-dimensional meanings that conformed to the more linear narratives of Matthew, Mark, and Luke. This is the tragic and inevitable result of an incomplete spiritual journey—and reinforces the importance of restoring the full understanding of Quadratos.

The words of this gospel have been—and sometimes still are—viciously misused and have metamorphosed into weapons for the razor-sharp sword of self-righteousness. Historically, they have all too often been converted into justifications for enslavement and even murder.

While appalling, this is not surprising, for it is precisely what happens if one leaves the third path too quickly or fails to continue on to the lengthy and fully transformative practice of the fourth path. It is the terrible hidden peril of the third path, which we will learn about as we continue.

In this gospel, we will read passages that seem at odds with John's core message and realize, with compassion, that John himself fell victim to the very same shortcomings against which his gospel cautions.

Among the deeply inspired, beauteous, and resonant words lurk an array of strident passages that are clearly angry and much less inspired. Many people today consider John's gospel to be anti-Semitic, because John frequently rails against "the Jews." However, we must remember that John himself was a Jew, as was Jesus.

When John penned his angry words, he was inveighing against a segment of the Pharisees who a decade earlier had penned a curse upon the Messiahnians and urged that they be driven out of the synagogues and entirety of Jewish life. (We might think of this as similar this to those abroad who curse the United States—but actually are referring to those in charge of the U.S. government whose policies they find reprehensible, rather than U.S. citizens in general.) John's harsh words are an historical window into the tremendous pain and trauma of the fight among the ancestral family of Judaism at the end of the first century.

An unfulfilled spiritual journey risks becoming mired in the distortions of *diabol*, and John's discordant words are a precise and terrible mirror of that eventuality. For his own personal and historical reasons, John separated the old Temple authorities and some particular Pharisees from his extraordinary universal vision and made resentful judgments against them in his gospel.

Horrific consequences developed. By the Middle Ages—a period that follows the loss of the three-year reading cycle—John's words against "the Jews," although *not* directed against an entire faith or tribe, began to be especially singled out by those with an anti-Jewish agenda. The accepted church interpretation of John's words became literal, the verses totally stripped of their message of visionary unity and *sym-bol*.

SIX—BEING IN JOHN'S GLORIOUS GARDEN

This simplistic interpretation focused on the surface meanings of John's words and particularly seized on John's flashes of anger and frustration against some Pharisees—on *dia-bol*. This shaped the gospel into a strident tool for an evangelism that focused on Christian self-righteous superiority and dominion over other religions.

Instead of inspiring a dynamic harmony, John's gospel was used to inspire hate, pogroms, and murder. It has produced division within us, within our churches, and between Christianity and other world religions. Those in Christianity who use and promote these interpretations continue to divide us today, far beyond misapprehension, as an ongoing, active tragedy.

It is imperative that we reach for the ancient view of wholeness available to us in this gospel and couple it with our understandings of history and psychology. By doing so, we will understand the necessity for the full four-path spiritual journey.

We will become empowered to restore our richest and most meaningful practices, refreshing them in ways that are useful now in this time. John's rhythmic verses and metaphors carry us into the deep truth of a Oneness beyond categories, beyond words, into the rich paradoxes of *sym-bol* and of Mystery.

So, let us begin our study of the third path starting with the Prologue, which contains some of Christianity's most significant passages. We'll move on to what I term John the Witness (John the Baptist in a new role) and the wedding at Cana, then the teaching stories of Jesus and Nicodemus, the woman at the well, the man born blind, and the raising of Lazarus. Lastly, we will discover John's unique Passion which culminates in his resurrection accounts.

Remember that, unlike Matthew and Mark, John is not distracted by any of the requirements of telling a linear story but remains focused only on the eternal. His words are sure, steady, and beautiful, exuding a confidence that leaps into our hearts. They describe that transcendent and soul-filled place celebrated by prophets and sages, by poems and symphonies, and by every enduring painting and hymn. John's glorious garden is before us. Let us open the gate and enter its bounty.

The Most Crucial Words in Christianity
"The Christ"

The introductory eighteen verses of The Gospel of John, commonly known as the Prologue, contain some of Christianity's most important concepts—ideas with such far-reaching implications that they ask us to devote extra preparation and attention from us.

You may recall that at the beginning of this book, I named five keys as an aid in understanding Quadratos and The Four-Gospel Journey. The first key is the importance of recovering the full name, Jesus *the* Christ, rather than the currently used single name Jesus. The three-word name was the normal expression used by all early believers. Within it is a great truth that the apostle Paul wrote about, one that greatly influenced all of the gospel writers and particularly John.

Paul wrote, in a passage from Colossians that we quoted earlier, that *[the Christ] is the image of the invisible God, the firstborn of all creation; for in [the Christ] all things in heaven and on earth are created, things visible and invisible, whether thrones or dominions or rulers or powers—all things are created through [the Christ] and for [the Christ]. [The Christ] is before all things, and in [the Christ] all things hold together.* **(Col. 1:15–17)**

The apostle Paul, through this and many other influential writings, made it clear that he understood "the Christ" to be an overarching reality existing eternally with Jesus as an individuated embodiment of that reality. This became accepted belief, and it is why the religion is named Christian, rather than Jesusian. It is also why, in the early centuries of Christianity, baptism proclaimed believers as becoming "a Christ," as they rose up out of the water and entered into their new, greater reality.

This truth is proclaimed in its most certain and poetic words in the Prologue of The Gospel of John. The words are very clear. They speak of a reality existing in a time before time—before Genesis. John uses the term "the Word" (*Logos* in Greek) to express the same eternal reality that Paul expressed by "the Christ" (*Christos*).

SIX—BEING IN JOHN'S GLORIOUS GARDEN

In the beginning was the Word, and the Word was with God, and the Word was God. He was in the beginning with God. (1:1-2)

Subsequently, the Prologue tells us that Jesus came to us as a human manifestation of the Christ.

And the Word became flesh and lived among us, and we have seen his glory . . . (1:14)

Why is this distinction between eternal reality and human manifestation so vitally important? If "the Christ" began with Jesus' conception, which has been the increasingly mistaken belief for nearly a thousand years, then it is quite natural for our religion to be focused—as it is—on the personality of Jesus, because his personage would constitute the end-all and be-all—the entire point.

Precisely what words Jesus actually spoke and when he spoke them would assume immense importance. Biographical details would be endlessly fascinating and significant. The quest for new excavations and interpretations would be never-ending. *Which is precisely the focus we see today!*

Yet despite devoted study of that historical personage, people would be filled with confusion that is never satisfied and conflicts that can never be resolved. *Exactly as they are today!*

Why? Because the lifelong spiritual needs (not to mention psychological and emotional needs) of millions of people worldwide who think of themselves as Christian, would be—and are— focused on the biographical details of a brief human history in ancient Palestine that can never be completely known. There will *never* be enough bones or papyrus—or analytical wisdom—to meet those inner needs. Those needs can never be satisfied in this manner.

However, *if* we grasp the depth of the Prologue, we open ourselves to a new possibility. We give ourselves a completely new understanding that *can* address our conflicts and confusions.

Jesus the Christ is a human-divine *unified reality* that presents two faces to us: one that is loving and familiar and another that is vast and mysterious. We can pray to them both just as Christians have for many centuries.

Jesus walks with us in our hearts as the visible, human manifestation of the Christ. We know that when we pray to Jesus our sense of relationship is close and intimate. We can feel that he holds our hand firmly in his.

The Christ, our God, is the other face. The Christ is ineffable Mystery, that we experience in our deepest core, feelings and experiences we cannot contain by ourselves—our greatest pain and our overwhelming joy.

The Christ is boundless, powerful, beyond anything we can know or comprehend with no beginning and no end. It is to the Christ that we turn in our humility. The Christ shares and supports us in everything we ask. Jesus and the Christ are two expressions of a great and creative process which we are invited to enter and make our own.

When we restore the meaning of the great name *Jesus the Christ*, we begin to see how much confusion has resulted by using the two parts of the great name interchangeably. Jesus and the Christ are not the same. They are *not* interchangeable.

Jesus was born. The Christ was not. Jesus died. The Christ did not. Jesus rose. The Christ did not. Jesus went away. The Christ did not and never will. Every prayer we speak and every hymn we sing asks to be heard with this new discrimination from both our hearts and our minds.

Many philosophers and metaphysicians have described our world as separated from the timeless truth of All, as if by a veil through which we can dimly see. Two thousand years ago in the Middle East, Jesus came to "remove the veil" so that we might at last enter into the greater truth of the Christ—and that truth encompasses the reality of all things in the universe.

In each succeeding generation since that time, we have been granted greater access to tools enabling us to widen our understanding and appreciation of Mystery. Today when we ponder God and the process of creation, we have the truth within our hearts, and use religion and philosophy. But we also use psychology, science, sociology, anthropology and many other disciplines. When we use these tools, we are following the instructions in John's Prologue and becoming the *"children of God... born not of... the will of man or woman, but of God."* **(1:13)**

When we seek answers about our faith amidst the confusion and conflict of today, our solution is not to run back to Jesus' biography. That dooms the very promise which Jesus' coming offers. Instead, our focus needs to be on the reality of the Christ, the boundlessness always at work.

St. Paul tells us that the Christ was "the spiritual rock" from which Moses and the Hebrews drank (1 Cor. 10:4). The Christ and Jesus were made visible as one in the first century. The Christ is with us now and will be with us for eternity. If this is the presence that we come to know today, then we can have no fear of tomorrow. Let us hold this vision in our hearts and minds as we enter the majesty of the Prologue's eternal vision.

Beyond Time
The Prologue

The opening passages of the gospels of Matthew, Mark and Luke link history and geography as metaphorical guideposts for their intended audiences. In this way, they become places from which to begin or to continue. The opening of John, however, does not concern itself with such earthbound matters. No mundane human conceptions such as history, place, or time are found in the extraordinary first words of The Gospel of John.

The Prologue is exquisite, mystical poetry. Its serenity and sonorous majesty immediately carries its readers to the time before time, the unfolding of the deepest of mysteries. Echoing the pronouncements and rhythms of Genesis—*"In the beginning when God created the heavens and the earth"* **(Gen. 1:1)**—its words rise far above both personal and didactic discourse.

They recite only the greatest of truths and expound only on the most elevated realms of the heart and soul. Intended to inspire rather than reassure, they pronounce what John clearly *knew*. They are the most expansive context possible for the series of meditations on Jesus the Christ that forms this gospel.

John's Prologue clearly and joyfully proclaims the Christ as the alpha and the omega, an eternal presence with no beginning and no end. These rapturous verses must have echoed profoundly in the Christian hearts of Ephesus—particularly when spoken in their original Aramaic language.

When one says the word "Messiah" in Aramaic it ends with an outbreath. Each time "Messiah" was spoken, there was a sensory re-creation of the single breath from which all and everyone began. Even with the apostle Paul's translation to the Greek word *Christos*, and the loss of this visceral experience, the poetry remains so powerful that we are deeply moved by it two thousand years later.

The Prologue uses "the Word"—*Logos* in Greek—which was a concept promulgated much earlier by a Hellenistic Jew named Philo. Well known to Jews of the time, Philo's *Logos* was a sort of emanation from God that was not really separate from God.

John, who uses several Greek-based ideas in his gospel, chose Philo's *Logos* for his Prologue, overlaying *Logos* onto Paul's concept of Christos—the eternal reality which Paul had titled, expressed, and taught in Ephesus for many years.

John writes that the Word was with God in the beginning, and that later the Word was made flesh in Jesus. Without John's insight, we might think today that "the Christ" and "Jesus" were synonymous, and that "the Christ" came into being only with Jesus' conception.

John's mature vision also clarifies the birth stories of the child Jesus found in the Gospels of Matthew and Luke, helping us see that these are accounts of Jesus' fleshly incarnation as an aspect of the Christ but do not in any way tell of the beginning of the Christ.

SIX—BEING IN JOHN'S GLORIOUS GARDEN

In the beginning was the Word, and the Word was with God, and the Word was God. He was in the beginning with God. All things came into being through him, and without him not one thing came into being. What has come into being in him was life, and the life was the light of all people. The light shines in the darkness, and the darkness did not overcome it. (1:1–5)

He was in the world, and the world came into being through him; yet the world did not know him. He came to what was his own, and his own people did not accept him. But to all who received him, who believed in his name, he gave power to become children of God, who were born, not of blood or of the will of the flesh or of the will of man, but of God. (1:10–13)

And the Word became flesh and lived among us, and we have seen his glory, the glory as of a father's only son, full of grace and truth. ... From his fullness we have all received, grace upon grace. The law indeed was given through Moses; grace and truth came through Jesus Christ. No one has ever seen God. It is God the only Son, who is close to the Father's heart, who has made him known. (1:14, 16–18)

"The Word became flesh." With these words, John identifies Jesus as a commingled reality of spirit and humanity, the exemplar of all aspects of oneness: of heaven and earth, life and death, east and west, light and dark, male and female, height and depth, past and future—all existing eternally.

The sublime meditations of John help us to enter into this understanding, an experience of deep unity, enabling us to join what is outside of time to that which is within time. This is the great gift of the Prologue of The Gospel of John. Through faith and love, it leads us to the truth of the cosmos and shows us that all else is illusion we can ignore.

Although it is possible for us to transform any part of the gospels we find meaningful into a prayer for regular use, the foundation of our deepest belief is expressed in the Prologue. Many have adapted it for their own as a profound personal invocation. One example is the following adapted text which illustrates this beautifully.

> In every beginning is *[the Christ]*, and *[the Christ]* is with God, and *[the Christ]* is God. *[the Christ]* is in the beginning with God. All things come into being through *[the Christ]*, and without *[the Christ]* not one thing comes into being. What comes into being in *[the Christ]* is life, and that life is the radiance of all people, of all creation. The Radiance shines in the darkness, and the darkness does not overcome it.
>
> *[the Christ]* is in the world, and the world comes into being through *[the Christ]*; yet our unawareness does know *[the Christ]*. *[the Christ]* comes to what is *[the Christ]*'s own, and *[the Christ]*'s own people do not accept *[the Christ]*. But to all who receive *[the Christ]*, who believe in *[the Christ]*'s name, *[the Christ]* gives power to become sons and daughters of God, who are born, not of blood or the will of the flesh or of the will of man and woman, but of God.
>
> And *[the Christ]* becomes flesh and lives among us, and we see *[the Christ]*'s glory, the glory as of the Creator's only offspring, full of grace and truth. From *[the Christ]*'s fullness we have all received, grace upon grace. The law indeed was given through Moses; grace and truth come through Jesus the Christ. No one has ever seen the Creator. It is the Creator's only offspring—*[the Christ]*—who is close to the Creator's heart, who makes the Creator known.

To open a more image-filled, intuitive prayer for your personal use that still illuminates the essence of the experience, try making other changes. Substitute "Love," "Breath," "Wisdom" or "Compassion" in all the places that *[the Christ]* appears above. Slowly read each altered text, noticing the tiny cues that the body and the soul give you. Which image best speaks to your heart? Which best helps you capture a sense of Oneness and Mystery? Pray with the adaptation that forges the best inner connection for you.

SIX—BEING IN JOHN'S GLORIOUS GARDEN

Much of John's Prologue, and indeed his entire gospel, is preoccupied with the concept of illusion. Scholars believe that this may well have become part of John's work due to his almost certain familiarity with the Greek philosopher Plato. Plato wrote that our everyday minds live in what he characterized as a shadowy cave of veiled sight.

If we are deep in a cave, we cannot see light directly; all we see is its reflection on the floor and walls. While we may believe that the reflection is the source of light, our belief is illusion. Similarly, the experiences we have in unopened hearts and minds feel as though they are "really real," but they are not. We are living in some manner of illusion. What we think we "know" is just inference rather than direct experience.

Some have held that when John writes, "The Word was in the world," he implies that spirit and matter are separate, with spirit holding a higher value than matter. In this text however, "world" does not mean the physical place we occupy. John understood that if we do not enter into transformation with the Christ—if we do not learn the experience of spirit and matter as one—then we are caught in "the world" and are unaware that something more exists.

Therefore, whenever we read the word "world" in this text, it is important for us to understand that it is this limited, illusory, Greek conception that is intended by John. As we join and journey with the Christ, our small, shadowed, illusory "worlds" fall away. We gain increasing revelation of the full and unlimited nature of God, and hence increasing awareness of genuine reality. John does not condemn the body or physical matter; he condemns only our *illusion* that body and matter are separate from spirit and heaven. All are one, without separation, in John's glorious garden.

Yet the habits of acting as though things *are* separate—a perspective of dualism rather than unity—are pervasive and well rooted, which nourishes the misconception that opposites are conflicting realities. Dualism accepts no middle ground.

Dualism tells us that things or people are either one thing or another with no degrees of difference or nuance. It celebrates or denigrates extremes of behavior such as asceticism on the one hand or material success on the other. Acting from these rigid and unrealistic attitudes limits our humanity.

When we are faced with them, whether inside ourselves, or reflected in the behavior of another, most of us feel confusion and anger. We are seeing the face of *dia-bol* in action. If we wish change, we begin by addressing this in ourselves. We will need prayer and discernment with each and every habitual and unreflective attitude we hold.

Sym-bol, the truth of unity, requires that our re-reexaminations be far reaching. Let us look at a famous line from the Prologue that holds another of our fondest presumptions so often quoted: **The light shines in the darkness, and the darkness did not overcome it. (1:5)**

This line is commonly and completely misinterpreted. However, if it was properly understood it could start all of us on a profoundly transformative path—or at least lead us to question much of what we have been taught.

The misunderstanding occurred gradually and perhaps in some ways, inevitably. Although we know that Israel is in the Middle East, in our desire to see Jesus in our own lives we sometimes forget everything that is implied by the fact that Jesus' home was located in Asia.

This means that Jesus' personal worldview had at least as much resonance, if not more, with the philosophies of Asia as with those of Greece and Rome. This is particularly true with respect to language. The native language of Jesus and the first evangelists was Aramaic.

John attempted to convey his understanding and experience of an Aramaic Messiah to the very diverse Ephesian population. Following Paul's earlier example, he wrote in Greek, the predominant language of Ephesus, and as we have noted he also used many widely circulated Greek ideas.

The Aramaic worldview was entirely different from the Greek one, forcing John to translate whole cultures as well as words. Aramaic is a poetic, image-based language filled with metaphors of the earth, of nature and agriculture.

SIX—BEING IN JOHN'S GLORIOUS GARDEN

By contrast, first-century Greek was more conceptual. It focused more on comparative values based on thought, and its metaphors naturally inclined to the more cerebral and metaphysical. Unfortunately, the inevitable dichotomy of culture and language that John encountered when he translated Aramaic poetry into Greek concepts led to much of the tragic narrowing and the misinterpretations from which this gospel still suffers today.

Our understanding of the well-known last line of the first stanza of the Prologue, *"The light shines in the darkness, and the darkness did not overcome it,"* is perhaps one of the most lamentable results. In Aramaic, each and every segment of the night and day has a singular word that paints a particular picture of that time, shaded by the balance between light and dark. *No* segment is either wholly dark or wholly light. Each "night word" contains an aspect of light and every "day word" contains darkness and shadow. A sense of wholeness is implicit in all of the descriptors.

Therefore, when we read "The light shines in the darkness, and the darkness did not overcome it" with the original and more Aramaic interpretation, we understand the line very differently. It is clear that light is *not overcome* by the dark. Light and dark *coexist*. *John's line is not about light banishing darkness; rather, it acknowledges and honors the reality that light and dark always play together in infinite variations.*

This is the sense of reality that John fully understood and, we must presume, intended. We can clearly see how far common belief has retreated from this early truth. John probably never imagined the limited interpretation that would ensue from his words. If he had, he might have written this instead: *The light shines in the darkness, and the darkness does not overcome it, as light and dark play together in harmony and shadows form.*

Instead, today in places of worship, we hear again and again that God is light (and only light), and that light reigns over the dark. This same perception is pervasive throughout every aspect of our culture: good guys wear white hats; bad guys wear black ones. Spiritual maturity is often described as en*light*ened.

Correspondingly, in many places of the world, people with darker skin are perceived with fear and suspicion. Difficult emotions are often characterized as "dark" and felt to be dangerous.

We frequently feel it necessary to shun not only these feelings, but these people, to conceal them, enslave them and even kill them. We have, in effect, demonized the entirety of the dark. In doing so, we have diminished—even cut off—parts of ourselves, of each other, and of our world.

Vestiges of the earlier, fuller, more Aramaic understanding remained and were expressed in Christianity for a long time. The builders of Chartres Cathedral, the first example of Gothic architecture, surely grasped the depth of John's poetry. They built a cathedral specifically designed so that neither light nor dark overtook the other. Instead, a dynamic interplay between them allowed light to pour from the vividly colored windows into the cathedral's shadowy darkness, where the two met to form new shades of color.

Unfortunately, by the eighteenth century the rhythms and understandings of the four-gospel reading cycle had been lost for a very long time. Chartres Cathedral was remodeled, although perhaps "defaced" would be the more appropriate word according to the standards of John's text.

An overzealous bishop replaced about ten percent of the colored windows with uncolored opaque glass. This made the space brighter, which was his objective, but dramatically altered the balance of light and dark in one part of the Cathedral. Nonetheless, it is still possible for visitors today to experience the earlier, more shadowed effect.

But the terrible error persists. By now, almost everyone believes without question the misinterpretation of John's poetic, unifying line. For centuries upon centuries, Christians have been erroneously taught in word, prayer and song that light is holy, and its greatest purpose is to wipe out the evil dark.

Therefore, places of worship have quite naturally enshrined this interpretation through architecture that is over-illuminated by sun or electricity. These gleaming edifices are making a philosophical statement,

SIX—BEING IN JOHN'S GLORIOUS GARDEN

which is their intention. However, in the physical proclamation of the superiority of light over the dark, they are also unknowingly rejecting the genuine wholeness of light and dark in harmony. And we are lulled into a false and shallow comfort, flattened and *dia-bolic*.

The prayers we pray, the hymns we sing, and the daily language we speak have not gone unscathed. A one-sidedness of language that raises up *only* light and purity as "holy" feeds and increases our instinctual fear of the dark. Because our eyes don't work as well in the dark after the sun sets, we fall headlong into the unexpected. We naturally retreat to a place of light—imagined or real—forgetting in the process that much of our spiritual work asks us to come to terms with our instinctual nature.

How often do we vainly attempt to shun these "dark" aspects? In so doing, we ignore what we know: that when we cut off psychological or emotional aspects of ourselves, they do anything but disappear or rest quietly, benignly neglected. Even if they sometimes operate under our conscious "radar," they grow anxious, stronger, more needing of attention and understanding. They move out of balance and find ways to slip into our lives and collectively into the world.

The more we try to focus only on the bright and sunny aspects of our existence, the more the hidden and unknown in us will call out. The dark, our unease and the foreign are holy also, and The Gospel of John specifically calls us to the task of recognizing them, loving them, and giving them welcome as part of our wholeness.

The third path's proclamation of wholeness—the vision wherein all opposites are unified—is not only a spiritual condition for which we yearn. Psychology tells us that unless we are able to perceive ourselves in this entirety, we will continually "split off " the aspects of ourselves that we have not accepted or integrated, stunting the creativity and vitality that make us human. In extreme cases, this can even put us in danger.

On a communal level, even if we believe that we have erased racism from our conscious minds, we need to bring much deeper discernment to this question. Our habits of language, our lives, and every aspect of our cultures have been embedded in racism for a very long time and run deep indeed.

Let us be thoughtful and welcome both *words* and *images* of darkness in all their manifestations—whatever that may mean for each of us. Only in this way may find a course that leads out of the divisions of fear, racism and war that continue to tear our bruised souls and the world apart.

Transforming John the Baptizer
John the Witness

This gospel shows John the Baptist in a different role. Here he is John the Witness, though his importance is in no way lessened. Although in this gospel, John performs baptisms (mikvahs), he does not baptize Jesus. Instead, John's main purpose in this text is to serve as a witness to revelation. He identifies Jesus as divine and illustrates his presence as the "Lamb of God," referencing Exodus and Isaiah. This shift in John's function matches the development of Christianity's baptism ritual in Ephesus, reinforcing its internal and transformative nature.

> ***The next day he saw Jesus coming toward him and declared, "Here is the Lamb of God who takes away the sin of the world! This is he of whom I said, 'After me comes a man who ranks ahead of me because he was before me.' I myself did not know him; but I came baptizing with water for this reason, that he might be revealed to Israel." And John testified, "I saw the Spirit descending from heaven like a dove, and it remained on him. I myself did not know him, but the one who sent me to baptize with water said to me, 'He on whom you see the Spirit descend and remain is the one who baptizes with the Holy Spirit.' And I myself have seen and have testified that this is the Son of God." (1:29-34)***

An Ancient Story Retold
The Wedding Feast at Cana

The story of the wedding feast at Cana concludes the opening section. Once again, John skillfully and sensitively recovers Hebrew narratives, bringing them forward and restating them in persuasive Christian terms.

SIX—BEING IN JOHN'S GLORIOUS GARDEN

Messianic Jews identified with the stories and found increased promises in them, while non-Jews felt the warm welcome of new traditions full of openness, celebration, and meaningful ritual.

John's account of the wedding feast evokes Adam and Eve in the Garden of Eden—the second chapter of Genesis. This echo functions much as his Prologue does which calls forth the memory of the first chapter and the seven-day creation, when God speaks and the world comes into being.

Although not obvious to us today, to the Ephesians a story about a wedding implicitly referenced Genesis. In the first century, weddings were always held outdoors in gardens or courtyards—never in public buildings. Therefore, the first words, "On the third day there was a wedding," automatically meant "garden," which in turn recalled the story of Adam and Eve.

Genesis described that Adam and Eve's life in the Garden of Eden was blissful and completely carefree. Yet that untroubled state could not last. The pair's innocent delight had been coupled with a grant of self-will.

An irresistible inner longing called them to exercise the free choice they had been given. Assisted by the intervention of a snake (the ancient symbol of transformation and rebirth), they chose to try to become more connected with God—more "like gods"—and ate the fruit of knowledge.

When they ate, their carefree life vanished. In effect, they began the process of growing up. Their decision gained them a more mature relationship with God, but it also had hard consequences. The heaviest price that God exacted for their temerity was ejection from the garden. Paradise, their child-like world of beauty and abundance, was lost forever.

By using a wedding (and garden) metaphor, John wants to communicate to the Christians in Ephesus that through the power of Jesus the Christ paradise is regained. And he expands the story so that Adam and Eve become Everyman and Everywoman and the account transforms into a vital and present experience.

In this account, it is Jesus and Mary, his Mother, who exemplify the great promise of Genesis—a deeper connection with God. However, John has made a significant switch. Instead of receiving punishment for wishing to become more closely connected as Adam and Eve did, at Cana they celebrate!

Remember that there were similar "updates" in the Gospels of Matthew and Mark in the story of Jesus' baptism, when the heavens tear and the voice of God speaks. Instead of the voice pronouncing floods or destruction or punishment, as had often been the case in traditional belief, the voice in the Christian gospels instead confers blessing. John's account of Cana's wedding feast similarly reforms the story in attitude, metaphor, and meaning.

Cana's wedding echoes Adam and Eve in its focus on Mary and Jesus. Throughout, Jesus doesn't refer to Mary by name but only as "woman." This is a literary device that John uses to clearly designate her as Everywoman—as Eve, the first woman—just as Jesus parallels Adam.

However, by *naming* the Messiah and his mother at this wedding, John makes a vastly important change in his "update" of Genesis. These figures are perfect and completely incorruptible. Therefore, they aren't like Adam and Eve, after all.

The occupants of this *new* garden are not mere humans who, through the effrontery of their actions lost their purity and were punished by God. John is making a powerful and inspiring argument for the promise of the new faith: its garden is all-powerful, all-encompassing, and will last forever.

Further in the wedding story, Jesus orders that huge vessels made of stone (an "incorruptible" material) be filled with water, presumably for use in the traditional Jewish mealtime washing ritual. However, once again John converts a well-known Hebrew ritual into something larger and more expansive. In this case, the water meant for cleansing is transformed into the joyous wine of a wedding—a celebration of symbol, of two becoming one, of unity in the Christ.

SIX—BEING IN JOHN'S GLORIOUS GARDEN

On the third day there was a wedding in Cana of Galilee, and the mother of Jesus was there. Jesus and his disciples had also been invited to the wedding. When the wine gave out, the mother of Jesus said to him, "They have no wine." And Jesus said to her, "Woman, what concern is that to you and to me? My hour has not yet come." His mother said to the servants, "Do whatever he tells you." Now standing there were six stone water jars for the Jewish rites of purification, each holding twenty or thirty gallons. Jesus said to them, "Fill the jars with water." And they filled them up to the brim. He said to them, "Now draw some out, and take it to the chief steward." So they took it. When the steward tasted the water that had become wine, and did not know where it came from (though the servants who had drawn the water knew), the steward called the bridegroom and said to him, "Everyone serves the good wine first, and then the inferior wine after the guests have become drunk. But you have kept the good wine until now." Jesus did this, the first of his signs, in Cana of Galilee, and revealed his glory; and his disciples believed in him. (2:1-11)

John could not have given us more perfect allegories for the third path. In Matthew and Mark, we strove mightily, and like the Baptist we declared the coming of change in our souls. Now suddenly it has arrived. The wedding day is here!

While not really unexpected, its jubilant feelings are unfamiliar; we have a sense of being caught unaware, as though Cana's water were suddenly, remarkably, converted into wine. We have been engrossed in survival—abruptly we are now filled with the elixir of celebration. We feel so completely refreshed and different that we wonder if our cells have changed, if somehow, we have been transubstantiated.

In her spiritual classic, *The Interior Castle*, the sixteenth-century abbess Teresa of Avila described the feeling with precision (writing in the third person):

> *Unexpectedly—while she is praying aloud, for instance, and not thinking about interior things—she seems to suddenly burst into sweet flame. It is as if a powerful fragrance had engulfed her and spread through all her senses, though this is a phenomenon that utterly transcends the sensual.*[6]

Four centuries later, Thomas Merton described the feeling in *No Man Is An Island*:

> *For if we continue in our prayer, we "remember" Him, that is to say, we become conscious, once again, of Who He really is. And we see that He has found us. When this consciousness is the work of grace, it is always fresh and new. It is more than the recovery of a past experience. It is a new experience, and it makes us new men. This newness is the "delight" and the "exercise" which are the living evidence of contact with the Spirit of the Lord. It makes us "swoon" in our spirit in a passage from death to life. Thus are our eyes opened. We see all things in a new light. And we realize that this is a new beginning.*[7]

In John's gospel, his metaphors of the wedding and the Garden of Eden are apt. As we move into the third path, we feel deeply accompanied—and somehow safer. Our personal, interior experience blooms with new beginnings, fresh vitality, and a sense of purpose. At this moment, we feel that the pieces have come together and all taints have been removed. The vision we hold seems whole and incorruptible.

Possibility surrounds us like the expanding, colorful images we see when we look through a kaleidoscope. Yet on some level we know that the glorious feelings of the wedding celebration must be temporary. We understand that our absolutely pure and true vision will require patience and practice if we want it to develop into a mature marriage that deepens with our lives. And yet today we celebrate—fully, even ecstatically. As we should.

---

[6] Teresa of Avila, *The Interior Castle*, translated and with an introduction by Mirabai Starr (New York: Riverhead Books, 2003), p. 171.
[7] Thomas Merton, *No Man Is An Island* (New York: Harcourt, Brace, 1955), p. 231.

SIX—BEING IN JOHN'S GLORIOUS GARDEN

Unlocking the Door
The Great Teaching Discourses

The next ten chapters of John are known as the great teaching discourses. In them, the writer employs a natural and persuasive evangelism designed for the melting-pot city of Ephesus. The stories reference the beliefs prevalent among the local tribes and build upon the principles set forth in his first chapter.

Each story offers up reflections of a specific truth as though John was turning a diamond and examining the glistening brilliance of a particular facet. Further, he does this with a lyrical pacing so the rhythm of the stories helps the reader move gently into increasingly fresh and deepened perspectives.

We will study four of these stories, which early Christianity appears to have used as final meditations and reflections before baptism. Today all four are read on the Sundays of Lent in churches which use the three-year reading cycle. (The Roman Catholic cycle leaves out the Nicodemus story).

All four share the same structure. They begin with a question representing a specific danger of separation, of *dia-bol*. The central figures in each story initially appear trapped by their normal, logical, ego-based thought processes. It is as though they are locked in a dim windowless room. As each conversation progresses, we see that Jesus offers a "key" that, if accepted, will unlock the door and allow egress to a place with light, clear understanding and the truth of limitless union.

Each story also breaks a solemn convention of first-century Judaism. Even conversing with a "Messiah for all tribes" verged on heresy for a Pharisee like Nicodemus. And Jesus' conversation with a Samaritan woman (likely a priestess) breaks both tribal and gender taboos.

When Jesus mixes a healing poultice for a blind man on the Sabbath, he shatters the commandment not to work on the Jewish day of rest. Finally, in the last tale he violates ancient custom when he orders a tomb unsealed and commands others to touch a dead body.

Each discourse, each story, has the same design. Finally, the stories combine to form an overall progression and the full lesson. In the first, Nicodemus the Pharisee makes little progress and departs from his encounter with Jesus as an unchanged man. Each story repeats the same pattern of question and answer (but with a different questioner in a slightly different setting) and with each story, comprehension slowly increases.

Step by step, John shows a growing acceptance of paradox. By the time of the last story, the gifts of wisdom offered by Jesus are fully received, and a significant new truth is absorbed. Let us turn to the four discourses and observe the process of inner "unlocking."

Impenetrable Barrier
Nicodemus a Teacher of Israel

Nicodemus, a Jewish Pharisee, comes to query Jesus about his purported divinity and the principles he proclaims. This is the only place in all of the gospels in which Jesus is portrayed in genuine conversation with a Pharisee, rather than in a disputatious power struggle.

It is especially remarkable because Nicodemus is no lowly questioner; he is clearly identified as a "leader of the Jews" and a "teacher of Israel." John uses this story to examine what he sees as the overarching challenge to new believers: being solely wedded to tradition and therefore closed to new belief and revelation.

As with so much in John, a duality instantly emerges when the sense of honest inquiry in the conversation is juxtaposed against the detail that Nicodemus comes to Jesus "by night." Nicodemus certainly does not want anyone to see him talking with Jesus, deemed by some Pharisees as a dubious teacher at best and at worst, a blasphemer.

However, maybe this isn't stealth at all. Recall that in Judaism, just past sunset marks the time when day begins and God's action starts anew. By setting the conversation at night, John may have been raising the possibility that the Pharisee himself is considering a new path, filled with questions as a potential new believer yet beset with inner turmoil, a poignant dilemma that must verge on sacrilege for Nicodemus.

SIX—BEING IN JOHN'S GLORIOUS GARDEN

Nicodemus' central question is whether or not Jesus is just another teacher among many or truly the Messiah. Although the miracles Jesus performs seems to verify his divinity, Nicodemus finds the teachings confusing.

They are in conflict with what he has *always* been taught: that the Messiah would come only through devout obedience to every precept of Mosaic law, that he would arrive only for the Jews, and that Jews are Jews because they are born to Jewish mothers.

Most importantly, Nicodemus believes these things because Mosaic law says they are true, rendering any contradiction of them false. "How could a different truth be possible?" Nicodemus asks. How could a Jew be a Christian? How could the Messiah not be exclusively for the Jews? Similarly, how could a Savior come for everyone? How could something new grow? How could some kind of rebirth be possible?

Nicodemus is trying to understand the same issues that were almost certainly dwelling within the hearts of many citizens of Ephesus, no matter what tribe they came from, whether they were already converted or prospective believers. Jesus responds that the ties of "flesh" and bloodline though real are spiritually meaningless. The real birth is a new birth through Spirit "from above."

These words are the first words directly spoken by Jesus in John's gospel about transcending the strictures of tribe, and they give Ephesus a revolutionary new commandment: "The new faith calls you to go beyond your old teachings and discover a new and wider and more vital teaching." Still, Nicodemus questions.

> *Now there was a Pharisee named Nicodemus, a leader of the Jews. He came to Jesus by night and said to him, "Rabbi, we know that you are a teacher who has come from God; for no one can do these signs that you do apart from the presence of God." Jesus answered him, "Very truly, I tell you, no one can see the kingdom of God without being born from above." Nicodemus said to him, "How can anyone be born*

after having grown old? Can one enter a second time into the mother's womb and be born?" Jesus answered, "Very truly, I tell you, no one can enter the kingdom of God without being born of water and Spirit. What is born of the flesh is flesh, and what is born of the Spirit is spirit. Do not be astonished that I said to you, 'You must be born from above.' The wind blows where it chooses, and you hear the sound of it, but you do not know where it comes from or where it goes. So it is with everyone who is born of the Spirit." Nicodemus said to him, "How can these things be?" Jesus answered him, "Are you a teacher of Israel, and yet you do not understand these things?" (3:1-10)

In the face of Nicodemus' continued disbelief Jesus gives a fuller response, its primary text quoted below. The Ephesians, who had years of background in Paul's teaching, and who understood the Prologue as the great pronouncement of Jesus the Christ, surely grasped the intention of John's words, which are an open, expansive, and compelling vision:

"If you can understand the totality that I represent, then the illusion in which you live will be dispelled and you will enter into the fullest comprehension of God. In *that* presence, separation of any kind is meaningless. Through this awareness is the true saving of your soul."

Tragically, in the long centuries of misunderstanding that have followed those early, joyous years in Ephesus, much of John's gospel has been seen in a narrower and more literal sense. The great Prologue has been read as a mere announcement of Jesus' birth, and the gospel itself as one of four accounts of Jesus' life. Words from the story of Nicodemus—specifically, the passage "God so loved the world" found in 3:16–18—have been equally viewed through this literal interpretation.

These words have become a statement of a Christian duty to salvation in its most narrow and divisive sense. They have been applied to the entire world, and—worse—used as an implicit right authorizing condemnation of non-Christians. At their most innocent levels of misuse, these three verses have been at the forefront of rejection and self-righteous condescension.

At their worst, they have been the justification for so-called "holy" wars and the slaughter of Jews, Muslims, indigenous peoples and other non-Christians.

Yet the entire story of Nicodemus is about *overturning* narrow vision and tribalism, and John's consistent use of the word "world" as a place of immature understanding confirms this. Therefore, we read in John's words that God cares so much about trying to remedy our being stuck and unaware that he continually sends Jesus the Christ to help us be more open and mature. His promise is that if by The Christ we can transcend our limitations, we can rejoin God in timeless eternal life.

Therefore, it is the greatest tragedy that these particular words have been so misused—when their specific intention was precisely the opposite. These words are intended by a loving Jesus to offer the greatest awareness and reward to an obstinate "teacher" who is stuck in yesterday's truth, and Jesus offers his wisdom while refraining from even the smallest emotional force to persuade him.

> *[Jesus said,] "For God so loved the world that he gave his only Son, so that everyone who believes in him may not perish but may have eternal life. Indeed, God did not send the Son into the world to condemn the world, but in order that the world might be saved through him. Those who believe in him are not condemned; but those who do not believe are condemned already, because they have not believed in the name of the only Son of God." (3:16–18)*

Ask and Be Filled
The Woman at The Well

In the story of the woman at the well, Jesus asks a woman of Samaria to give him a drink of water. Until this point in the text, Jesus has limited himself to conversations and contacts within his customary levels of class and tribe. Now he crosses well-drawn boundaries.

When he speaks to the woman at the well, he not only breaks gender taboos, but also tribal proscriptions, because he is a Jew and she is a Samarian. Note that John again uses only the word "woman" when he refers to her, which in the Greek style is a designation for Everywoman.

Their discourse is genuine and thoughtful. Jesus regards the woman's inquiries with as much seriousness as he does those of Nicodemus, the "teacher of Israel." This behavior on Jesus' part would have been regarded as completely radical.

Jews of the time were particularly forbidden to step outside tribal boundaries, and absolutely no one spoke to women as equals, publicly or privately. With what appears to us today to be an uncomplicated story, John explicitly and conspicuously elevates the status of women, as he does in other instances in his gospel.

Jesus the Christ's simple request for a drink would also have been fraught with drama and meaning for John's readers. His clear request to "serve me," addressed to the non-Jewish Everywoman, would have been clearly understood as an allegorical and universal call to worship.

Jesus, the Jewish Messiah, was inviting *all* to serve—women and men and people of all tribes. The use of water in the request, the essence of all life from which everything ushers forth, added to the power of this deeply symbolic act.

Water takes on further meaning here. The first story of the Hebrew book of Genesis spoke of "a wind from God [sweeping] over the face of the waters" (1:2). John echoes Genesis yet again, and we read the words of Jesus sweeping over the story of Jacob, which John uses as shorthand to refer to all the patriarchs of Judaism. Jacob merely provided a simple well for his people that satisfied their bodily needs. By contrast, Jesus offers "living water."

Examine the layers of meaning: Jacob's well was only for *his* people, while Jesus' water is offered to all who were willing to take the initiative of asking for new understanding. John emphasizes that the water for Jacob's tribe was merely water from the temporal "world" and therefore limited in power.

SIX—BEING IN JOHN'S GLORIOUS GARDEN

John's implicit instruction to Ephesus is, "You are now filled with the living water of Jesus the Christ. This 'living water' is for more than mere life, more than the body. It is sustenance for life everlasting. And it is for all of you—women and men from every background."

> *He left Judea and started back to Galilee. But he had to go through Samaria. So he came to a Samaritan city called Sychar, near the plot of ground that Jacob had given to his son Joseph. Jacob's well was there, and Jesus, tired out by his journey, was sitting by the well. It was about noon. A Samaritan woman came to draw water, and Jesus said to her, "Give me a drink." (His disciples had gone to the city to buy food.) The Samaritan woman said to him, "How is it that you, a Jew, ask a drink of me, a woman of Samaria?" (Jews do not share things in common with Samaritans.) Jesus answered her, "If you knew the gift of God, and who it is that is saying to you, 'Give me a drink,' you would have asked him, and he would have given you living water." The woman said to him, "Sir, you have no bucket, and the well is deep. Where do you get that living water? Are you greater than our ancestor Jacob, who gave us the well, and with his sons and his flocks drank from it?" Jesus said to her, "Everyone who drinks of this water will be thirsty again, but those who drink of the water that I will give them will never be thirsty. The water that I will give will become in them a spring of water gushing up to eternal life." (4:3-14)*

Jesus' next words to the woman are not lengthy, but to the readers of Ephesus they were packed with significant implications. With clear reference to Jerusalem's Great Temple, Jesus predicts that new places of worship will arise; the old acknowledged mountains and temples will not remain the sole sources of spiritual power.

Jesus then says that the time has come to worship in "spirit and truth." These words are a specific reference to the dual prophets: Elijah as a Hebrew representation of mercy and compassion (spirit) and Moses as that of the law and discipline (truth). Once again, John transforms Hebrew traditions renouncing old metaphorical separations.

John is saying that in Jesus the Christ, Moses and Elijah are remade into an undivided spiritual principle, a union of apparent paradox, in which the two elements constantly negotiate with each other. In the Christ, "spirit and truth," mercy and discipline, compassion and wisdom are fluid parts of an indivisible whole.

The chapter closes with the words that "many Samaritans" accept Jesus' teachings. This indicates that some transition to new understanding is being made—and spread to others. This is a further step from the case of Nicodemus, who is unable to accept the new revelation at all.

> *Jesus said to her, "Woman, believe me, the hour is coming when you will worship the Father neither on this mountain nor in Jerusalem. You worship what you do not know; we worship what we know, for salvation is from the Jews. But the hour is coming, and is now here, when the true worshipers will worship the Father in spirit and truth, for the Father seeks such as these to worship him. God is spirit, and those who worship him must worship in spirit and truth." (4:21-24)*
>
> *Many Samaritans from that city believed in him because of the woman's testimony. (4:39)*

Who Truly Sees, and Who Does Not?
The Man Born Blind

In the next story, Jesus sees a man blind from birth and gives him sight by mixing spittle with mud and then smearing the paste over the man's eyes. The man is subsequently questioned by the religious authorities about the cure. This story includes the same basic elements as those of Nicodemus and the woman at the well: references to the water that brings new life and understanding, the limitations of old beliefs and tribalism, and a questioning of Jesus' divinity.

However, in this story the focus—its particular facet of the diamond—lies in an emotional dilemma faced by believers. When voices outside the new Christian community question their faith and their decisions, how should they best sort out their complicated feelings?

SIX—BEING IN JOHN'S GLORIOUS GARDEN

Remember, John is not literal. He gives no details of the man, nor does he name him. Instead, John once again uses his subject to represent Adam or Everyone. And in John's overall metaphor, "sight" always denotes "inner sight."

The account simply relates that Jesus applies the crude, elemental substance of mud to the man's eyes enabling him to "see." John is therefore teaching the lesson that when anyone gains sight, she or he can then realize a wider truth from that which they have been taught since birth. We can "see" the reality of the Christ.

John uses other figures in this story to represent community and inner voices to which the Ephesians could relate. These Pharisees stand for close-minded obstruction and judgment. The man's parents, who do not speak actual words of condemnation, typify those who were unconscious, unaware, not searching and hence not open to revelation. They in effect, represent those who are progenitors, responsible for continuing their own blindness. Inclusion of these characters enabled the Ephesians to view themselves and engage in self-scrutiny without the sting of a pointed finger.

Within John's metaphor of inner sight, he further uses the parents to directly carry the message of revelation. "Don't be unconscious," John urges. "Ask yourself the deep questions. In what ways are you blind from birth? What parts of you cannot see? What will it require for you to receive sight?"

With great wisdom and subtlety, John is calling attention to the reality that, as beautiful as epiphany may be, stepping out of tribalism and the traditions of centuries will present enormous emotional, spiritual, and cultural challenges.

This story offers practical counsel that addresses the confused feelings of the newly converted Christians whose friends and families had not followed their path and were naturally full of uncertainties. "Of course, they are unable to comprehend," John is saying. "They haven't had your experience. How can you expect them to see what you see? And when they reject your experience and fall into self-righteousness, they are *twice* blinded. It is natural for them to assault you with questions and doubts."

Then, in closing, the blind man says, "I believe," showing that he has accepted the "new" understanding—and demonstrating a further movement toward acceptance than had been made in the previous story.

> *They brought to the Pharisees the man who had formerly been blind. Now it was a sabbath day when Jesus made the mud and opened his eyes. Then the Pharisees also began to ask him how he had received his sight. He said to them, "He put mud on my eyes. Then I washed, and now I see." Some of the Pharisees said, "This man is not from God, for he does not observe the sabbath." But others said, "How can a man who is a sinner perform such signs?" And they were divided. So they said again to the blind man, "What do you say about him? It was your eyes he opened." He said, "He is a prophet." The Jews did not believe that he had been blind and had received his sight until they called the parents of the man who had received his sight and asked them, "Is this your son, who you say was born blind? How then does he now see?" His parents answered, "We know that this is our son, and that he was born blind; but we do not know how it is that now he sees, nor do we know who opened his eyes. Ask him; he is of age. He will speak for himself." (9:13–21)*
>
> *He said, "Lord, I believe." And he worshiped him. (9:38)*

The story does not end with the blind man's statement of belief. John goes on to amplify the theme of "blindness," his metaphor for lack of spiritual maturity. When challenged by these Pharisees, Jesus responds that if they were merely "blind" (that is, ignorant of truth), they would be free of sin. (The word means "to miss the mark.") However, since they stubbornly refuse to acknowledge their ignorance, accepting the illusions of the "world" and persisting in claiming to "see," they do indeed sin.

In the progression of the stories leading to increased comprehension and acceptance of truth, this picture of the Pharisees is a vivid image of the opposite position—self-satisfaction and the rejection of continual growth. John knows it is critical that the new believers of Ephesus grasp this principle. In the midst of their ecstatic self-transformation, they— like all new believers—will find it very easy to slip into a belief that their learning is over and their position is right—and from there, the perils of self-righteousness are a mere hairsbreadth away.

> *Jesus said, "I came into this world for judgment so that those who do not see may see, and those who do see may become blind." Some of the Pharisees near him heard this and said to him, "Surely we are not blind, are we?" Jesus said to them, "If you were blind, you would not have sin. But now that you say, 'We see,' your sin remains." (9:39-41)*

Allow the Tears to Fall
The Raising of Lazarus

The story of Lazarus' raising is generally considered one of the consummate biblical proofs of Jesus' divinity. And though John includes details that emphasize the miraculous nature of Jesus' actions, there are other, deeper messages in this account revealed through its dialogue.

Mary and Martha are sisters whose brother, Lazarus, is very ill. They ask Jesus for help. Giving no reason, he refuses. Lazarus subsequently dies, and four days later Jesus goes to meet Mary, who is still grieving deeply. John recounts that Jesus the Christ is "greatly disturbed in spirit and deeply moved," and he weeps.

At Lazarus' tomb Jesus is "again greatly disturbed." He commands that the stone be removed from the tomb. Lazarus emerges still in burial bandages. Jesus instructs that he be "unbound" and freed.

We have made note of the fact that in John's gospel Jesus is never less than a divine presence—he is the initiator of every action, the ultimate *bestower* of everything good, in full control of all events, and apparently unaffected by any requests or entreaties. Yet here, John shows Jesus in great emotional distress.

In this passage, Jesus the Christ weeps—only one of two instances in any of the gospels where he does. What precipitates the divine tears? Why is Lazarus raised? Because Jesus the Christ's heart is open, and when he meets with Mary and goes to the tomb, confronted in each case by genuine grief in the face of genuine loss, he needs to respond. *Compassion* is the divine impetus to restore life.

Jesus firmly states, "Unbind him and let him go." The story of Lazarus is an analogy for the Ephesians about their new Christian revelation. It told them it is good—even necessary—for the old ways, the old dogma, to die so that resurrected life could appear. It told them their grief was appropriate and all right. It told them that through feelings of compassion, an epiphany would burst through their hearts into reality, and that that same compassion would guide them into a free, "unbound" new life.

> *When Mary came where Jesus was and saw him, she knelt at his feet and said to him, "Lord, if you had been here, my brother would not have died." When Jesus saw her weeping, and the Jews who came with her also weeping, he was greatly disturbed in spirit and deeply moved. He said, "Where have you laid him?" They said to him, "Lord, come and see." Jesus began to weep. So the Jews said, "See how he loved him!" But some of them said, "Could not he who opened the eyes of the blind man have kept this man from dying?" Then Jesus, again greatly disturbed, came to the tomb. It was a cave, and a stone was lying against it.*
>
> *Jesus said, "Take away the stone." Martha, the sister of the dead man, said to him, "Lord, already there is a stench because he has been dead four days." Jesus said to her, "Did I not tell you that if you believed, you would see the glory of God?" So they took away the stone. And Jesus looked upward and said, "Father, I thank you for having heard me. I knew that you always hear me, but I have said this for the sake of the crowd standing here, so that they may believe that you sent me." When he had said this, he cried with a loud voice, "Lazarus, come out!" The dead man came out, his hands and*

SIX—BEING IN JOHN'S GLORIOUS GARDEN

feet bound with strips of cloth, and his face wrapped in a cloth. Jesus said to them, "Unbind him, and let him go." Many of the Jews therefore, who had come with Mary and had seen what Jesus did, believed in him. (11:32–45)

John's gospel focuses on the challenges of paradox and the truth of union, and these matters are at the center of all his teaching discourses. In our earlier paths, we were asked to overcome obstacles, but on this path we are invited to sit and peacefully ponder each encounter as we are led on an expedition through reality and illusion.

Each of John's stories presents us with a contradiction of the great unitive vision. Reflection on these, and on corresponding instances in our own lives, will give us the opportunity to observe the main psychological work of the third path. Our untransformed ego-self-will persistently try to spring traps, tempting us to perceive our world and ourselves as a series of divisions instead of an indivisible whole.

Our immature ego will keep asking us to separate things and to make either/or judgments. It will try to force everything into black or white. This provides an opportunity for us to study the beauty and subtleties of the many shades of gray—while we also practice patience.

Nicodemus' struggle reminds us that at the moment when the glorious, undifferentiated vision arises within us, the Nicodemus aspect inside us will feel uncomfortable. We all share some of Nicodemus' characteristics. We have a well-worn way with which we are accustomed to looking at the world and approaching new things.

Many of us also have at least a touch of *dia-bol*. We rush to find an appropriate category for every new experience. In this story, we see that Nicodemus was obviously drawn to Jesus, but his questions could not be satisfied through logic alone, which made him uncomfortable.

When we feel likewise drawn and desire fully rational answers, we will simply have to withstand our discomfort and understand that we may not be able to get them. Our path asks us—just for a moment—to suspend our deductive minds. This is a new reality. We need to remain awhile and let it soak in. Patience, patience.

The story of the woman at the well was placed after the story of Nicodemus for a reason. Intellectually, Nicodemus knew everything; yet in a deeper sense he knew nothing. The woman at the well had none of Nicodemus' kind of knowledge. She was a woman (though perhaps a priestess) and she was from Samaria, a region at that time deemed unsophisticated, inhabited by "hicks."

Yet Jesus selected her to receive two great acknowledgments: the call to service, and knowledge of the difference between the old well water and the new "living water." Accepting Jesus' statements from her heart, and not challenging him from her rational mind, she therefore understood their meaning immediately. She made no philosophical inquiries at all and had a question only about her worthiness as a non-Jew.

The lesson of this story is a call to a practical form of self-examination, asking us to think about how we understand events. How do we move beyond the ways we typically think about ourselves and our past experiences? If we reflect on the self-definitions we use—as the woman did—it is likely that the limitations we have been holding about others and ourselves will be revealed and fall away.

If we reflect on the self-definitions we use—as the woman did—it is likely that the limitations we have been holding about others and ourselves will be revealed and fall away.

Those limitations are, once again, driven by the less mature ego. With its self-protective instincts, it would have us live out of our narrowest, fear-driven natures rather than our most expansive. This diminishes not only our creativity and vitality but also that of others. Our work here is to identify and become aware of our narrowness.

Where are all the places within us that the tendrils of fear and division have reached, and how deeply? How are we less open than we might be?

What parts of our garden are being watered from the old well rather than from our unceasing supply of living water?

The third path also places us in a new context with respect to others and our actions towards them. The story of the man born blind affords us the opportunity to examine the sources of feelings we carry and how we deal with them in a social, or even a communal, setting. It tells us that we cannot expect those who have not had a like experience to understand or appreciate our "new sight."

At the same time, we are neophytes and are thus unable to see ahead clearly ourselves. When we look backward, our new vision has increased our clarity—but does not easily predict what lies ahead.

If we think we know exactly what is going on and what we should do and how others should behave, the consistent advice of the third path is
… Do nothing except meditate and pray. Sit still. Rest in the garden and reflect. Close your eyes and use your inner sight. Watch the vision unfold around you.

The story of Lazarus serves us as a reminder: his dead corpse is like our old ways of thinking and feeling, the self we are leaving—bound up, stinking, and keeping our emotions blocked, as though hidden behind a rock in a dark cave. Let us use this image of Lazarus to energize ourselves, to release the trapped and limited places inside us.

We long to act from our inner truth but often feel unable to do so, because fear or a sense of emptiness stops us. Each time we pretend, each time we act from someplace false, our soul registers a small inner betrayal. Now is the time to grieve for those accumulated betrayals—our lost truths—and shed our long-held genuine tears. Our weeping is critical—a component that will help to release new sources of vitality we will need for our journey. Our bindings fall away and we gain energy for our real freedom.

A Truth Greater Than Suffering: The Passion
No Great Drama—Entering Jerusalem

By the time The Gospel of John was written, Jerusalem had become a desolate and deserted city. It had been largely abandoned after its destruction by the Romans in 70 CE. However, its significance was not gone. It continued as a symbol—one of the most powerful in Talmudic and biblical lore. It was King David's great accomplishment.

Jerusalem represented the historical, emotional, and spiritual center of the Hebrew faith, and was the location of the First and Second temples. It was where the heads of the twelve tribes had met. Jerusalem was the promise of a place where the diversity of the Hebrew people could find creativity and harmony.

Part of this derives from the name itself. As you may recall, Jeru-Shalom would translate as City of Peace. However, the peace of shalom is complex, differing greatly from our normal English sense of the word. Shalom comes from a root word that means "wholeness," thus in the Hebraic sense it has a connotation of joining of opposites. That is the reason *shalom* is used as a greeting when meeting as well as leaving someone—times that contain both beginning and end, coming and going. *Shalom* makes the unity of opposites implicit.

Therefore, John takes full advantage of Jeru-Shalom, its deep meaning and its iconic status. It is his preeminent symbol for an inner reality of "communion," a place where all tribes, not just Jews, could live in dynamic harmony.

He carries the concept further, in support of his deeper theology, and makes Jerusalem a place in which opposites can *reconcile* and a new vitality reign. This gave the Ephesians an image of genuine community as they struggled to define themselves and move forward into the challenges that faced them as a diverse group of new Christians.

In the Gospels of Matthew, Mark, and Luke, Jesus took long journeys throughout Israel and the surrounding region, all of which ended in Jerusalem. However, John's gospel is located almost entirely in Jerusalem and its Temple. The city itself is a thematic focal point. Many of the lessons are taught there, and others (such as that of Lazarus) take place only a few miles outside the city.

In this gospel, Jesus' entrance into Jerusalem is not the climax to a lengthy and arduous journey, and although assembled crowds do shout acclaim, there are no accounts of the journey or preparations, or instructions for entry. A mere three verses describe the entry, and one of them contains the small notation that Jesus finds his own donkey and sits himself down upon it. John's focus is clearly elsewhere.

> *The next day the great crowd that had come to the festival heard that Jesus was coming to Jerusalem. So they took branches of palm trees and went out to meet him, shouting, "Hosanna! Blessed is the one who comes in the name of the Lord—the King of Israel!" Jesus found a young donkey and sat on it; as it is written: "Do not be afraid, daughter of Zion. Look, your king is coming, sitting on a donkey's colt!" (12:12-15)*

Stripped, Selfless, and In Service
The Last Gathering

Subsequent to his understated arrival into Jerusalem, which occurs just before the Feast of Passover, Jesus gathers with his disciples for John's version of the Last Supper. This account is entirely different from those found in the other gospels.

John's depiction gently and affectionately shows that Jesus and his followers are devoted to each other. He doesn't focus on the meal; there is no bread, no passing of a cup—indeed, no description of food whatsoever. Only four verses into the chapter, Jesus rises and begins a poignant, intimate ritual, washing the feet of each and every one of the disciples. Peter objects vehemently, but Jesus insists that they would all understand "later."

Throughout John's gospel, there are continual references to water—the transformed water at Cana, the "living waters" of the well, the pool in which the blind man is instructed to wash, and Jesus' tears. An essential component of any garden (and therefore a seamless accompaniment to John's other core metaphor), water is also the basic requirement for life on earth. It is present at birth, and its absence leads to death. Because of its necessity and the vitality it brings, water is a component of many sacred rituals. Now, in John, it is used during a tender and intimate ceremony of foot washing.

The Christian ritual of baptism uses water to express the elements of death and rebirth. In the early church, deacons performing baptism were instructed to grasp the initiate around the chest from the back, lowering the individual under the water in such a way that a "startle response" was triggered, thereby providing an experience of near death.

Arising, the person was then blessed and announced to the community as moving forward into new life with Jesus the Christ. In the early part of this chapter, I mentioned the scholarly belief that John's entire gospel may have been written as requisite contemplations and teachings in preparation for a Christian's entrance into baptism.

Remember that each gospel writer uses the intensity of the Passion to emphasize and make specific the answers to the spiritual question offered by his text. John's core question is: How do we receive joy? The Passion moves this question to the specific: How do we move from our old beliefs into the new? How do we resurrect into new balance and move forward in the Christ?

When we know that the words of this gospel were originally used for baptism and understand that the Passion was a graphic representation of this final and all-important question. John's use of water symbolism at this juncture becomes an even more delicate, startling and powerful image.

The recitation of the foot washing is simple and quietly paced, yet John's words touch upon all of his major themes: baptism, communion and service. Jesus rises from the table and removes his robe, leaving only his loin cloth, which he covers with nothing more than a towel.

Jesus the Christ, God on earth, who has heretofore moved through this gospel as nothing less than a divine presence, strips down and presents himself to his disciples in a way that would have been appropriate only for a husband with his spouse, or a servant before his master. And then Jesus washes their feet—*their* feet! There could have been no more perfect exemplar of both the intimacy and selflessness of Spirit in service, and it reinforces the dialogue between Jesus and Peter that follows.

Peter strenuously objects to his feet being washed by Jesus. Jesus tells Peter quite firmly, that if he is unwilling to receive the gift he is being offered, he can no longer continue as a disciple. Peter capitulates and agrees to the washing, even finding enthusiasm for the prospect.

John is sending a twofold message to Ephesus about the genuine nature of union and intimacy. As Jesus washes feet, he shows *humility in giving*. As a chastened Peter accepts his bounty with sincere gratitude, an example of *humility in receiving* is provided. John knew that the abilities to discern, understand, offer, and accept genuine relationships could prove critical to the Christian community.

Jesus also singles out one of the disciples from the rest, noting that he is "not clean." John identifies this "one" as Judas, the betrayer. What does Jesus mean by "not clean"? The meaning becomes clear if we recall the new process of Christian baptism, which was a ritual washing designed to provide *an internal experience of Jesus' death and resurrection leading to rebirth.*

According to The Gospel of Matthew, which was written before John's gospel, and was almost certainly known to John and John's readers, Judas falls into despair after betraying Jesus. Judas commits suicide, and therefore does not live through the physical experience of Jesus' death and arising. Judas, therefore, *does not complete his journey*. He does not live through Jesus' death into resurrection—and in John's mystical understanding, Jesus the Christ is aware of this result to come, and knows that Judas is therefore not "clean."

In words that ring with authority, Jesus lastly commands those present that they continue the foot washing with all others as a ceremony of union, intimacy and humble service. Now known as *"the mandatum"* (a Latin word meaning *command*), this ritual was earnestly embraced for a period of approximately one hundred years.

Every time Christian followers met, when the bread was broken and the wine from the cup was poured, those present also washed each other's feet. Today, in many Christian churches, the ritual is still performed—but generally only once a year, at Easter. In this gospel, the mandatum also introduces the themes that John pursues in the next chapters.

> *Now before the festival of the Passover, Jesus knew that his hour had come to depart from this world and go to the Father. Having loved his own who were in the world, he loved them to the end. The devil had already put it into the heart of Judas son of Simon Iscariot to betray him. And during supper Jesus, knowing that the Father had given all things into his hands, and that he had come from God and was going to God, got up from the table, took off his outer robe, and tied a towel around himself. Then he poured water into a basin and began to wash the disciples' feet and to wipe them with the towel that was tied around him. He came to Simon Peter, who said to him, "Lord, are you going to wash my feet?" Jesus answered, "You do not know now what I am doing, but later you will understand." Peter said to him, "You will never wash my feet." Jesus answered, "Unless I wash you, you have no share with me." Simon Peter said to him, "Lord, not my feet only but also my hands and my head!" Jesus said to him, "One who has bathed does not need to wash, except for the feet, but is entirely clean. And you are clean, though not all of you." For he knew who was to betray him; for this reason he said, "Not all of you are clean." After he had washed their feet, had put on his robe, and had returned to the table, he said to them, "Do you know what I have done to you? You call me Teacher and Lord—and you are right, for that is what I am. So if I, your Lord and Teacher, have washed your feet, you also ought to wash one another's feet. For I have set you an example, that you also should do as I have done to you." (13:1–15)*

SIX—BEING IN JOHN'S GLORIOUS GARDEN

Held in the Arms of Love
The Discourse on Intimacy and Union

Following the foot washing, John delivers four entire chapters best described as mystical poetry. In Christian scholarship, this narrative is variously known as "the discourse on intimacy and union" or "the eucharistic discourse." In three of the four chapters, Jesus addresses his disciples. Jesus' words in the last chapter of the discourse—words that are particularly elevated—are addressed directly to God the "Father," in the form of a prayer.

The lengthy verses of the discourse, which are among John's most significant passages, are deeply inspirational. They resonated with the disciples, and through them, with all of Ephesus. They announce an eternal truth—a message that comes from "before the foundation of the world."

They tell of a loving, personal, and intimate God who addresses followers by the title "friend." This would have been an astonishing change to many of the new Christians. Tribal gods had not been friends; Greek gods of the time were distant and whimsical, and the Hebrew god described by the Temple authorities was one who sat in judgment. Proximity was unexpected, even startling.

In these chapters we again find the same beautiful, poetic prose that began this gospel, and much of the vocabulary duplicates John's core metaphors: "world" and "see" are frequently inserted to represent the secular world of illusion and divine sight.

However, the text is set in a long, elegant discourse on intimacy from Jesus to his disciples at the final meal. Jesus speaks about their sense of fear and isolation, and early in the recitation he proclaims that an Advocate will be sent who will not only accompany them, but hold them in the arms of eternal love.

Within the verses we can discover another of John's garden metaphors—a vineyard, with words that, interestingly, refer to Jesus himself being pruned of branches that "bear no fruit." Jesus goes on to talk of friendship and to use dramatic images of childbirth to illustrate the pain and division experienced by those who are without faith and beset by illusion.

Over and over again, he uses words that could be treasured by the Christians in Ephesus as new wisdom to ponder and reinforcement of their inner certainty. The final words of Jesus' prayer at the end of the meal (and of the discourse) are another lyrical promise of eternal accompaniment:

> *"I made your name known to them, and I will make it known, so that the love with which you have loved me may be in them, and I in them.'" (17:26)*

> *"And I will ask the Father, and he will give you another Advocate, to be with you forever. This is the Spirit of truth, whom the world cannot receive, because it neither sees him nor knows him. You know him, because he abides with you, and he will be in you." (14:16–17)*

> *"I am the true vine, and my Father is the vinegrower. He removes every branch in me that bears no fruit. Every branch that bears fruit he prunes to make it bear more fruit." (15:1–2)*

> *"This is my commandment, that you love one another as I have loved you. No one has greater love than this, to lay down one's life for one's friends." (15:12–13)*

> *"You are my friends if you do what I command you. I do not call you servants any longer, because the servant does not know what the master is doing; but I have called you friends, because I have made known to you everything that I have heard from my Father. You did not choose me but I chose you." (15:14–16)*

> *"Very truly, I tell you, you will weep and mourn, but the world will rejoice; you will have pain, but your pain will turn into joy. When a woman is in labor, she has pain, because her hour has come. But when her child is born, she no longer remembers the anguish because of the joy of having brought a human being into the world." (16:20–21)*

> *"The hour is coming, indeed it has come, when you will be scattered, each one to his home, and you will leave me alone. Yet I am not alone because the Father is with me. I have said*

SIX—BEING IN JOHN'S GLORIOUS GARDEN

this to you, so that in me you may have peace. In the world you face persecution. But take courage; I have conquered the world!" (16:32–33)

"As you, Father, are in me and I am in you, may they also be in us, so that the world may believe that you have sent me. The glory that you have given me I have given them, so that they may be one, as we are one, I in them and you in me, that they may become completely one, so that the world may know that you have sent me and have loved them even as you have loved me. Father, I desire that those also, whom you have given me, may be with me where I am, to see my glory, which you have given me because you loved me before the foundation of the world. Righteous Father, the world does not know you, but I know you; and these know that you have sent me. I made your name known to them, and I will make it known, so that the love with which you have loved me may be in them, and I in them." (17:21b–26)

As we read the passages from this first part of John's Passion and contemplate them, our most difficult challenge is to pause. Our desire is to race ahead. Even reading these words may seem slow, even redundant. We know that the heart of the Passion is next, and it seems that the very best lessons are surely there. Yet waiting is one of the great lessons of John.

Every bit of the bountiful spring garden in which we are now resting is worthy of our attention. As we quietly sit in this third path of our Journey of Quadratos, we aren't climbing mountains, nor are we enduring stormy seas. The angst in our lives has calmed somewhat. Of course, we still must pay careful attention—but instead of tensing for danger, we are more able to be focused on discerning complexities and details as they reveal themselves.

Jesus' entry into Jerusalem is not presented as very important to us; but Jerusalem itself looms large—indeed, it is vital. It represents the place where the twelve tribes met: Jeru-Shalom, where diversity sought the complex harmony of ever-changing opposites. Once again John asks us: What is the true picture of our inner and outer complexity?

This question must be followed by: How can we be known in our fullest, richest reality? These are the natural queries that begin to arise as we rest in awareness of union, and they will gradually increase as the close of the third path draws nearer. And these flowering buds will then lead us into the primary challenge of the fourth path: How are *we* Jeru-Shalom?

We observe with wonder that everything is one—undivided, unbroken, and unswervingly whole. At the same time, everything is unique and individual. Both realities are limitless, yet our entire journey is in vain if we attempt to comprehend this truth (or believe we have done so) with any separated part of ourselves—with only our intellect or our emotions or our senses or our spirit. We must continue to sit meditating upon the wondrous garden, and—as Jesus did—meet each aspect as it arises with as much of ourselves as we are able.

If we can summon our *full* presence, we will discover that each encounter reveals a unique meaning, showing us its interplay with the whole, and we will gain a sense of undivided comprehension. This is John's assurance to us from across the centuries. If we do not take the time to receive this full pattern, then we will stand no chance of its fulfillment in the fourth path. Be in peace and patience. There are no shortcuts here.

John also gives us the opportunity to wrestle with some of our deepest feelings about self-worth—those feelings that can divide us from spiritual development and the richest relationship with God. Can we feel our own difficulty with unworthiness in the poignant imagery of Jesus' final meeting with his disciples? Can we open to its intimacy and sensuality? Can we begin to sense a new set of inner questions?

How would *we* feel if Jesus the Christ, clad only in a towel, were on his knees before us and wanted to wash our feet? Would we be able to receive that extraordinary gift with a whole heart? Or would we, like Peter, resist?

Jesus the Christ is firm with Peter, and his admonition applies to us as well. We cannot be on the journey unless we are able to receive. We must be able to participate in both sides of a relationship—giving *and* receiving.

SIX—BEING IN JOHN'S GLORIOUS GARDEN

This is not easy, since we are so often raised to believe that thinking of ourselves is "selfish" and negative. Indeed, most of the third path is devoted to the practice of receiving, of just being still, and becoming aware of what is offered by the Great Mystery all around us.

Jesus' demeanor in the foot washing could scarcely be more humble, and we understand that we are called to a similar humility. However, it is equally important to realize that there was nothing weak about Jesus' humility.

To the contrary. Jesus understands to his core that he is *accompanied* on his journey—that he will never be alone or bereft. He therefore walks forward in confidence, clarity, and command. Humility does not imply that we must be soft or timid or weak. Humility derives from the most profound strength.

The sensuality of the foot washing opens up another issue in this gospel that is both important and—unsurprisingly—paradoxical. John's gospel is extremely "earthy": Jesus asks for a drink of water; he mixes spit with mud for the blind man's poultice; he weeps; he strips to a towel; he washes feet; he carries his own cross; he cooks breakfast on the shore. Indeed, his physical presence is probably stronger here than in any of the other gospels.

Yet, as noted earlier, John's gospel has often been accused of elevating spirit over body. And it does. In the Prologue and in Jesus' discourse with Nicodemus, John uses the word "flesh" synonymously with "world." And we know by now that "world" is pejorative in John's lexicon. "Flesh" is therefore clearly relegated to the territory of illusion and is certainly not equal to "spirit."

However, John has told us that he believes in divine, timeless wholeness wherein spirit and matter are unified. Where do we find the answer to this apparent paradox, and to the several inconsistencies created by it in the gospel? In the same place that accounts for John's stridency about the Pharisees: in the personal disharmonies of the man himself. And we should treat this paradox in the same way—by focusing on what are clearly the more compelling and inspired elements of John's great verses.

When we properly focus on John's inspiration, we should include rather than dismiss the elements of earthiness and sensuality. Indeed, we need to give them our close attention. With his earthy and physical language, John proclaims unity despite himself.

We are in physical bodies, just as Jesus the Christ came to a physical earth in a physical body. Our physical senses give us our information about the world. In fact, as we sit in the garden and allow ourselves to become open to the fullness of God's bounty, what do we notice?

As our senses sharpen, we pick up the buzzing of the bees and the rustling of the wind through the leaves. We become aware of the remarkable artistry in the veining of every leaf and bird feather. Inevitably at some point, we sense the musculature beneath our own thin skin that miraculously holds us at 98.6 degrees in both snow and blistering sun. We wiggle our toes and stretch our arms and enjoy the sun or perhaps the taste of a raindrop on our tongue. This is God's gift of sensuality awakening—becoming more sensitive and appreciative.

Our reflection is twofold: first, wholehearted enjoyment; second, sensory epiphany—thoughts about the ways in which we have rejected and neglected our bodies and our sensuous selves in the past. For many of us, this has had significant personal, family, and even community impacts. Now it is time to examine the fullness of the physical natures we have been given by God, without fear or self-rejection.

The beautiful, meditative discourses on intimacy and union poetically restate all of John's great themes. They speak of new birth. They wash us with words of care and loving kindness. When we read them, we can—and should—find vast and resonant reassurance in their eloquence: all is connected and all is well.

Within the verses however, we will also sense the coming of new challenge and more growth—note the sharp metaphorical pruning shears in the vineyard. As much as John wants us to keep our focus in the garden, he cannot avoid reminding us that there is further walking ahead and the trimming is not done.

Inner Strength and Calm
In the Garden and Courtyard

In chapter eighteen, as John moves to Jesus' arrest, he sets this account within his primary metaphor: a literal garden. There is no reference to the Mount of Olives or to Gethsemane, the place of "pressing" and agonized heart of which we read in Matthew and Mark. John's story is as dramatic in what it does *not* say as it is in what it *does* say.

Jesus' arrival with the disciples at the garden is followed by the almost simultaneous arrival of Judas and a detachment of soldiers accompanied by police sent from the chief priests and Pharisees. Jesus walks forward and inquires as to their mission. Although he knows what they have come to do, once again Jesus initiates the action and offers himself. Shocked, the group falls back. They had expected a powerless victim. Instead, they are met with unexpected strength and calm.

In the face of their bewilderment—and in an echo of the Hebrew Testament's "I Am"—Jesus twice proclaims, "I am he." The apparent strength of the soldiers pales against the real strength of Jesus the Christ as he meets his oppressors.

This is John's lesson to Ephesus: the soldiers are merely of "this world"—crippled by illusory, dichotomized thinking. It is evident that they have no real power. Not a one of them lays a hand on him. Even so, Peter rushes to defend Jesus, and in doing so cuts off the right ear of the high priest's slave. Jesus firmly directs Peter to put his sword away.

Then, in this garden, free from agony and indecision, he rhetorically asks, ***"Am I not to drink the cup that the Father has given me?"*** There has been no prayer, no questioning, and seemingly little or no sense of inner turmoil.

> *After Jesus had spoken these words, he went out with his disciples across the Kidron valley to a place where there was a garden, which he and his disciples entered. Now Judas, who betrayed him, also knew the place, because Jesus often met there with his disciples. So Judas brought a detachment of soldiers together with police from the chief priests and the*

> *Pharisees, and they came there with lanterns and torches and weapons. Then Jesus, knowing all that was to happen to him, came forward and asked them, "Whom are you looking for?" They answered, "Jesus of Nazareth." Jesus replied, "I am he." Judas, who betrayed him, was standing with them. When Jesus said to them, "I am he," they stepped back and fell to the ground. Again he asked them, "Whom are you looking for?" And they said, "Jesus of Nazareth." Jesus answered, "I told you that I am he. So if you are looking for me, let these men go." This was to fulfill the word that he had spoken, "I did not lose a single one of those whom you gave me." Then Simon Peter, who had a sword, drew it, struck the high priest's slave, and cut off his right ear. The slave's name was Malchus. Jesus said to Peter, "Put your sword back into its sheath. Am I not to drink the cup that the Father has given me?" (18:1–11)*

John's Passion account next moves to the courtyard of Annas, a former high priest and the father-in-law of Caiaphas, the current high priest. Remember from the story of the wedding at Cana that "courtyard" is a garden metaphor? John is therefore moving the tale from one garden into another. The confrontation in Annas' courtyard is a more complex account than the arrest scene however, and it replaces the stories of Jesus' trial before the high priest that are found in all of the other gospels.

Two disciples—Peter and an unnamed man—follow the officers who arrested Jesus. However, a woman acting as guard stops Peter at the gate. (Note that John once again records a woman in a nontraditional foreground role.) The unnamed disciple is able to get Peter through the gate, after which the guard inquires of Peter whether or not he follows Jesus. Peter denies that he does.

The pair continue into the courtyard, where Annas, Jesus, the soldiers, and others are gathered, warming themselves around a charcoal fire. Despite the story line of Jesus' inquisition, in this second gathering the real focus is on Peter and on discipleship.

SIX—BEING IN JOHN'S GLORIOUS GARDEN

Annas begins his interrogation, asking only about Jesus' relationships with "his disciples and his teaching." Jesus responds that he has nothing to hide and suggests that Annas inquire of "those who [have] heard what I said." Though present, neither Peter nor the unnamed disciple speak. Annas continues. Jesus, completely composed, rebukes Annas for his questions.

A soldier slaps Jesus for his effrontery, but that does not deter him. Jesus is then sent on to Caiaphas. The disciples remain in the courtyard around the fire. While they were waiting, Peter twice more denies his discipleship, and the other disciple never speaks, not a single word.

This was John's perfectly inspired mirror for the Ephesian Christian community. During Annas' questioning, everyone is present around the charcoal fire: leaders of the old faith traditions, their minions, the enforcers of secular power, disciples of the "new way," and Jesus the Christ. The new and the old, the temporal and divine worlds, John's "truth" and "illusion"—all stand together, speaking and not speaking.

Special attention should be drawn to the figure of "another disciple," who is not named and who appears only here. There has been much conjecture about his purpose and which disciple he is, especially since there is another figure identified as the "unnamed disciple" who is also designated as "loved" by Jesus, who appears at the foot washing, the crucifixion, and the resurrection. It is our belief that "another disciple" is *not* the "unnamed" disciple.

John is scrupulous about naming and not-naming in his gospel and I think that John intends the figure here in Annas' courtyard to serve as an "everyman," or in this case, as "every disciple"—a representative of those especially committed Christians on whom the future of the faith rests.

The "other disciple" remains silent—in this account. It is clear that he is still connected to the old order, for he "is known to the high priest." He has influence sufficient to get Peter through the gate into the group who are solely people connected to the high priest plus soldiers and slaves. (Remember that Peter, once inside, disavows Jesus when questioned.)

I believe that the "other disciple" may represent those Christians in Ephesus who were engaged and moving forward yet remained internally caught by the shaming voices of the old Temple and some of the Pharisees. In essence, they were on the fence. John wants them to realize how damaging their silence and dual allegiance might be.

Peter denies Jesus thrice, but we see his actions in a very different way than in the other gospels. The denials all come in the context of the preceding discourse on intimacy, which speaks about willingness to lay down one's life for a friend. Peter's first denial is necessary so that he might stay close to Jesus—as are the second and third denials.

Peter is, in effect in enemy territory. As he asserts at the final meal, Peter is determined to show his willingness to follow his lord anywhere and lay down his life for him. In these efforts, however, he continues to display his spiritual immaturity, slicing off an ear and denying his path—even though Jesus' fate was foreordained and unstoppable by him.

Yet in this gospel Peter's errors are clearly shown within the context of love and friendship. After the triple betrayal, the scene ends abruptly with no statement of remorse at all. The primary issues for the Christians of Ephesus were the dangers of acting from spiritual immaturity and the need to examine their motives before they act.

> *The soldiers, their officer, and the Jewish police arrested Jesus and bound him. First, they took him to Annas, who was the father-in-law of Caiaphas, the high priest that year. Caiaphas was the one who had advised the Jews that it was better to have one person die for the people. Simon Peter and another disciple followed Jesus. Since that disciple was known to the high priest, he went with Jesus into the courtyard of the high priest, but Peter was standing outside at the gate. So, the other disciple, who was known to the high priest, went out, spoke to the woman who guarded the gate, and brought Peter in. The woman said to Peter, "You are not also one of this man's disciples, are you?" He said, "I am not." Now the slaves and the police had made a charcoal*

fire because it was cold, and they were standing around it and warming themselves. Peter also was standing with them and warming himself. Then the high priest questioned Jesus about his disciples and about his teaching. Jesus answered, "I have spoken openly to the world; I have always taught in synagogues and in the temple, where all the Jews come together. I have said nothing in secret. Why do you ask me? Ask those who heard what I said to them; they know what I said." When he had said this, one of the police standing nearby struck Jesus on the face, saying, "Is that how you answer the high priest?" Jesus answered, "If I have spoken wrongly, testify to the wrong. But if I have spoken rightly, why do you strike me?" Then Annas sent him bound to Caiaphas the high priest. Now Simon Peter was standing and warming himself. They asked him, "You are not also one of his disciples, are you?" He denied it and said, "I am not." One of the slaves of the high priest, a relative of the man whose ear Peter had cut off, asked, "Did I not see you in the garden with him?" Again Peter denied it, and at that moment the cock crowed. (18:12–27)

Facing Off at High Noon
Pilate and Jesus Meet

After the encounter with Annas and Caiaphas, Jesus is sent to Pilate's headquarters. The Temple authorities who have been questioning him refuse to enter however, because it is the day before Passover. The Jewish leaders have ritually cleansed themselves (specifically of yeast according to ritual requirements), and since Pilate is a gentile, in meeting with him they risk coming into contact with "unclean" elements, which would prevent them from partaking of the Passover meal. After conversation outside with the priests, Pilate ascertains this and has Jesus brought inside for questioning, which means that in John's gospel, there are no priests present during Jesus' meeting with Pilate.

All alone, Jesus, representing truth incarnate, faces off against Pontius Pilate, embodiment of the temporal world of illusion and of Rome's power.

In their exchange, Jesus confidently proclaims his timeless sovereignty and Pilate, locked into the world of illusion, totally fails to comprehend him. This encounter is a stark statement of John's two opposing principles, and it stands in marked contrast to all of the other gospels.

In Matthew, Mark, and Luke, Jesus remains mute; he refuses to answer Pilate. In The Gospel of John, however, Jesus the Christ is never hesitant, never silent. He always demonstrates the full force of greater truth. Pilate, remaining trapped in his ignorance and self-righteousness, has Jesus removed for flogging.

Although mocked and struck in the face, Jesus never wavers. He is impervious to every assault, every question, insult, and blow. This is the human-divine model John wants to present to his audience—the picture of one who is confident, even loving, in the face of all trials.

> *Then they took Jesus from Caiaphas to Pilate's headquarters. It was early in the morning. They themselves did not enter the headquarters, so as to avoid ritual defilement and to be able to eat the Passover. (18:28)*

> *Pilate entered the headquarters again, summoned Jesus, and asked him, "Are you the King of the Jews?" Jesus answered, "Do you ask this on your own, or did others tell you about me?" Pilate replied, "I am not a Jew, am I? Your own nation and the chief priests have handed you over to me. What have you done?" Jesus answered, "My kingdom is not from this world. If my kingdom were from this world, my followers would be fighting to keep me from being handed over to the Jews. But as it is, my kingdom is not from here." Pilate asked him, "So you are a king?" Jesus answered, "You say that I am a king. For this I was born, and for this I came into the world, to testify to the truth. Everyone who belongs to the truth listens to my voice." Pilate asked him, "What is truth?" (18:33–38)*

> *Then Pilate took Jesus and had him flogged. And the soldiers wove a crown of thorns and put it on his head, and they*

dressed him in a purple robe. They kept coming up to him, saying, "Hail, King of the Jews!" and striking him on the face. (19:1–3)

[Pilate] entered his headquarters again and asked Jesus, "Where are you from?" But Jesus gave him no answer. Pilate therefore said to him, "Do you refuse to speak to me? Do you not know that I have power to release you, and power to crucify you?" Jesus answered him, "You would have no power over me unless it had been given you from above; therefore the one who handed me over to you is guilty of a greater sin." (19:9–11)

Critical Distinctions
The Counting of the Days

Over and above the dissimilarity of the events themselves, one of the most striking differences in John's Passion is the timing of the events. In the Gospels of Matthew, Mark, and Luke, the Last Supper is the Jewish sacred meal of Passover. Indeed, most Christians today believe that Passover is *the* definitive date for the final meal. But in John's gospel, that last gathering is not held within Passover—an immensely significant fact.

In The Gospel of John, the ritual of foot washing and the meeting with Annas occurs on the evening of Preparation Day—the day before Passover. (Remember that Hebrew days begin at sundown, not midnight.) The subsequent meeting with Pilate and the crucifixion itself happens during the daylight hours of Preparation Day, again *before* Passover begins.

Not only does this change of timing allow John to (again) reframe Hebrew tradition, but it also provides an intensely different and dramatic backdrop for the entire Passion. To get some sense of the context that John is trying to set up, it is helpful to read an excerpt from the Hebrew book of Exodus describing Preparation Day:

> *The Lord said to Moses and Aaron in the land of Egypt: This month shall mark for you the beginning of the months; it shall be the first month of the year for you. Tell the whole congregation of Israel that on the tenth of this month they are to take a lamb for each family, a lamb for each household. If a household is too small for a whole lamb, it shall join its closest neighbor in obtaining one; the lamb shall be divided in proportion to the number of people who eat of it. Your lamb shall be without blemish, a year-old male; you may take it from the sheep or from the goats. You shall keep it until the fourteenth day of this month; then the whole assembled congregation of Israel shall slaughter it at twilight. (Exod. 12:1–6)*

These verses, recounting sacred rituals practiced for centuries, would have been familiar to all of John's Jewish readers. Passover, one of the holiest of Hebrew holidays, requires that ten nights after the new moon and three nights before the Passover meal, every house is to choose and "keep" an unblemished male lamb for three days. And "keep" doesn't mean simply that the animal is set aside; "keep" means that the youngling actually lives within the household, honored and cared for. Imagine the tangled emotions of the family as the day of death for this little creature approaches.

In the days of the Great Temple, animals were frequently sacrificed for many rituals and reasons. On regular days, the animal was delivered to the Temple, the priest took the animal from the bearer, slaughtered it, removed a portion of the meat as payment, and burned the remainder.

On Preparation Day, however, the head of the house was required to personally bear the lamb to the Temple for sacrifice. There, the priest handed the ritual knife to the householder, who had to slit the lamb's throat himself and then drain its blood into a large bowl that was given to the priest. The priest emptied the bowl, filled with the lamb's blood, over the Temple's high altar. The bloodless carcass was then taken back home, where it was prepared and then eaten during the Passover meal.

SIX—BEING IN JOHN'S GLORIOUS GARDEN

It has been estimated that ten thousand lambs were slain at the Great Temple on each Preparation Day in the first century. It is likely that blood was flowing down the Temple's steps and running through the streets of Jerusalem by noon on that day. The city must have been filled with the sight and stench of butchery. This may even have been an intentional part of the ritual, serving as a graphic reminder of the massacre visited upon the firstborn in Egypt on that same day some twelve hundred years earlier.

It is on this day of bloody slaughter, and of the memorial of bloody slaughter, that John places Pilate's judgment and Jesus' crucifixion. Lest there be any confusion about the clear parallel he is drawing, John notes Pilate issuing his judgment "about noon," the time of the height of the ritual carnage, and it is pronounced from the "Gabbatha." This is a term that appears only in this gospel and refers, in Aramaic (though John calls it Hebrew—the languages are closely related), to a high stone platform—a clear reference to the ancient Temple mount.

The analogy is clear, and with it John's inspiration once more focuses on the larger point, perhaps overturning actual history a bit. Passover memorializes the liberation of the Jewish people. First-century Jews expected the Messiah to come for them—and to be another warrior-liberator, like Moses, freeing them from the heavy yoke of Roman rule.

John wants to be very clear that Jesus is indeed the Messiah; however, his definition is quite different. First, the arms of John's Messiah are wide open in active invitation to all of humanity, not only Jews. More importantly, he is not a warrior-liberator figure at all. Instead, this Savior is "one who serves."

Therefore, in John's Passion Jesus does *not* celebrate the Passover meal; rather, he washes feet and *actively chooses* the role of the lamb. He is intimate and servant—and is even willing to be a physical sacrifice. John is telling Ephesus to look beyond the events of history. John's statement is that Jesus' life is not *taken* from him by either Jewish or Roman authorities. Instead, Jesus offers his physical body so that through his resurrection all may come to know that death is simply an illusion.

> *When Pilate heard these words, he brought Jesus outside and sat on the judge's bench at a place called The Stone Pavement, or in Hebrew Gabbatha. Now it was the day of Preparation for the Passover; and it was about noon. (19:13-14)*

A Peaceful and Willing Death
The Crucifixion

Following Pilate's sentencing, John says only that Jesus goes to Golgotha, and that he personally carries the cross on which he will be crucified. There is no mention of suffering, no exhaustion, no agony. Indeed, reading the passage, one might well assume that the cross was very light.

As noted about the timing of the judgment, during those same hours Jewish fathers and heads of households would have been taking their lambs to the Temple for slaughter before returning home to have the meat prepared for the Passover meal. They would have been standing in long lines, clutching their male lambs, as they waited to mount to the altar, their arms tired from holding the squirming bodies. The air would have been filled with bleating, and with the sights and smells of death.

In contrast to this noisy, bloody, chaotic mess, Jesus the Christ, the Lamb of God, walks calmly, willingly, and triumphantly amidst the sight and stench of death. Throughout John's Passion, only a majestic and serene Jesus the Christ is recounted—a figure completely present to every moment of his human life, supremely at one, even at ease, with its events—again, startlingly different from the Passion accounts in the other three gospels.

When Jesus reaches Golgotha, the Place of the Skull, John simply states with no adjectives, no elaboration, that Jesus is crucified. John adds only that Jesus is between "two others." Even in this physical description, John places Jesus in the center of two—a position of *sym-bol*, of joining, of the union that is the omnipresent theme of this gospel.

> *Then [Pilate] handed [Jesus] over to [the Temple authorities] to be crucified. So they took Jesus; and carrying the cross by*

*himself, he went out to what is called **The Place of the Skull**, which in Hebrew is called **Golgotha**. There they crucified him, and with him two others, one on either side, with Jesus between them. (19:16–18)*

Watching the crucifixion close to the cross, is a small group that includes Mary the mother of Jesus, Mary Magdalene, Mary the wife of Clopas, and "the disciple whom [Jesus] loved," who is possibly John himself, the author of this gospel. This differs from the narratives in Matthew, Mark and Luke which mentions no disciples being present at the cross, and describes the women as viewing the death from quite a distance.

Jesus on the cross speaks only a few words—some to his mother and to the "disciple whom he loved." His words had nothing to do with death. He didn't recite Psalm 22, as noted in Matthew and Mark. Instead, Jesus explicitly joined the disciple and his mother, announcing him as Mary's new "son." And oral tradition holds that John took Mary into his household, first in and around Jerusalem and then later in Ephesus.

From John's perspective, however, these words gave divine instruction to Ephesus that, in the Christian faith, families could be formed by ways other than by blood, which had been the accepted practice for generations beyond number. Tribal and familial bonds could be loosened, and families could be formed by love and by intention and by commitment.

Once again in complete control of events though near death, Jesus says, "I am thirsty." John notes that this was "in order to fulfill the scripture." John is referring to Psalm 69, King David's prayer for deliverance from his enemies, wherein he was given poison to eat and vinegar to drink. Jesus on the cross drinks wine from a sponge held by a "hyssop" branch, a shrub whose branches were used for sprinkling both blood and water during Jewish rituals.

In Matthew and Mark's gospels, wine was put to Jesus' lips but he did not drink. In Luke, no wine was offered. In John's gospel, water transformed into wine celebrated the union of marriage at Cana, and now wine marks the reunion that would soon occur with the resurrection. By drinking voluntarily, Jesus "fulfills" the ancient Hebrew prophecy. In the psalm,

David prayed for deliverance. On the cross, Jesus symbolically "drinks" the illusions of the world, transforming them into illuminating truths through his life, death and resurrection.

His earthly purpose completed, Jesus speaks three words "It is finished"— then bows his head and dies. I feel certain of two things. First, that until the final moment, Jesus' head is upright and unbowed. Second and most important, Jesus the Christ is in complete control of this event. I believe that he chooses the precise moment of his death— that his earthly life is in no sense taken from him.

Indeed, in Roman Catholic translations, this text reads: "Then bows his head and delivers over *the* spirit." No less a scholar than Raymond Brown, pre-eminent in the study of John, argues that "*the*" is the correct translation and that this moment is a statement of resurrection and a prefiguration of Pentecost. Through his death, Jesus the Christ breathes out and delivers the spirit to all. In the context of Quadratos and the third path, this divine breath of Spirit shatters all illusions and awakens the human/divine union within all.

Therefore, we can see that although this end is astonishing in its outward circumstances, it is deeply metaphysical and completely consistent with the themes of this gospel. What did Ephesus take from John's writing? We have no way to know, but certainly any person praying these words as preparation for baptism could not have failed to be both challenged and uplifted by Jesus' message and demeanor in this scene.

> ***Meanwhile, standing near the cross of Jesus were his mother, and his mother's sister, Mary the wife of Clopas, and Mary Magdalene. When Jesus saw his mother and the disciple whom he loved standing beside her, he said to his mother, "Woman, here is your son." Then he said to the disciple, "Here is your mother." And from that hour the disciple took her into his own home. After this, when Jesus knew that all was now finished, he said (in order to fulfill the scripture), "I am thirsty." A jar full of sour wine was standing there. So they put a sponge full of the wine on a branch of hyssop and***

SIX—BEING IN JOHN'S GLORIOUS GARDEN

held it to his mouth. When Jesus had received the wine, he said, "It is finished." Then he bowed his head and gave up his spirit. (19:25b–30)

After the crucifixion, in another part of the account unique to John, soldiers come to break the bones of those crucified so that their deaths would be hastened. John recounts that when they come, they didn't break Jesus' legs because "he was already dead." There was a prohibition against breaking any of the bones of the sacrificial lamb, so this detail completes John's analogy with the Passover lamb.

Then a soldier pierces Jesus' side with his spear. Blood and water issues forth. What an amazing—even shocking—image! Let us consider all of the elements this dramatic vision provides to the Ephesians. In it, they could see combined the familiar old blood rituals of sacrifice, the earthy realities of human birth in which blood and water issue forth from the mother, the "living waters" of Christianity, and the waters of baptism, which contains the experience of death and resurrection. All the intimacies of life and death were poignantly offered in this single, sudden event.

Then the soldiers came and broke the legs of the first and of the other who had been crucified with him. But when they came to Jesus and saw that he was already dead, they did not break his legs. Instead, one of the soldiers pierced his side with a spear, and at once blood and water came out. (19:32–34)

Return to the Garden
The Burial

The passages about Jesus' burial contain more references that are obscure to most contemporary readers but that were extremely significant to John's audience. Joseph of Arimathea and Nicodemus ask to take Jesus' body so that they could bury him properly—an affront to Jewish authority and tradition. First, men never prepared bodies—only women—and certainly not men of high position. (Nicodemus was a Pharisee and Joseph had sufficient stature to speak with Pilate.) Second, handling a dead body made a person ritually unclean.

The fact that Joseph and Nicodemus are willing to defile themselves just hours before the Passover meal breaks another taboo. Furthermore, Nicodemus himself brings the traditional myrrh and aloes for embalming—and a huge and expensive quantity of them—making it quite clear that neither he nor Joseph expect Jesus will rise.

Unsurprisingly, John once again sets his story in a garden—this time holding a new tomb near Golgotha. As we've learned, the Garden of Eden metaphor figures prominently in this gospel, but as a general metaphor gardens represent places of perpetual death and resurrection. Living things die, or appear to, just as living things are reborn, or seem to be. The entire process is a dynamic interaction of opposites. The future of its dying is held by the living plant, and the fallow ground holds the seeds and power of rebirth. Together those aspects of life and death echo the same eternal reality, so John provides yet another image that is a powerful preparation prayer for the baptism ritual.

> *After these things, Joseph of Arimathea, who was a disciple of Jesus, though a secret one because of his fear of the Jews, asked Pilate to let him take away the body of Jesus. Pilate gave him permission; so he came and removed his body. Nicodemus, who had at first come to Jesus by night, also came, bringing a mixture of myrrh and aloes, weighing about a hundred pounds. They took the body of Jesus and wrapped it with the spices in linen cloths, according to the burial custom of the Jews. Now there was a garden in the place where he was crucified, and in the garden there was a new tomb in which no one had ever been laid. And so, because it was the Jewish day of Preparation, and the tomb was nearby, they laid Jesus there. (19:38-42)*

As we know, John's gospel is read in pieces in the lectionary, wisely interspersed throughout the other gospels. Because of this, in the Sunday reading cycle we get morsels of visionary joy and ecstasy spread out as intermittent illuminations. When we move through the gospel from beginning to end in Quadratos' third path, we get the full measure of John's wisdom.

SIX—BEING IN JOHN'S GLORIOUS GARDEN

Once again, in two settings of his garden metaphor that inherently offer a context of change and complexity, John teaches lessons about spiritual immaturity. In the first, the calm of Jesus is contrasted with the zeal of Peter and his drawn sword. This is a picture of us in the third path. We want to jump ahead, and right *now!* But we can easily miss the mark, because we are not yet ready.

In the courtyard scene, we are given more complexity on which to reflect. Both Peter and the unnamed disciple have confused allegiances. Those of the unnamed disciple are clear to us—we may still have lingering attachments to people, places, and attitudes that seem expedient but are actually detriments to our transformation.

Peter's misalignment is more subtle. Peter is creditably following his loyalty to his friend and teacher, Jesus—but in doing so, he is being disloyal to the principles of his faith and spiritual practice which are more rigorous. This is a trap for us also, equally subtle. If we genuinely examine our motives, how often are we attracted to the teacher rather than the teaching, the surface rather than the substance?

In the rest of the Passion account, the focus is on Jesus as a spiritual model. Throughout, Jesus maintains his demeanor of humility and inner strength. Removing his clothing, Jesus the Christ shows an astounding level of intimacy as he washes the feet of his disciples. Then subsequently, with Annas and Pilate who seek to harm him, he is not subservient at all. Not arrogant, he is forthright—even forceful—in every instance.

Although Jesus is largely silent in other gospels, John shows him freely responding to the questions he is asked by these powerful men as an equal, without rancor or resentment. This illustrates the wholeness of the third path. The antagonists represent many of our inner voices which in these scenes, we see as ever-present, yet balanced with our deepest spiritual nature. Asking and answering, we are able to make an assessment of what is real and what is illusion.

Jesus' calm, strength, and confidence are our model. Secure in the knowledge that he is not alone and capable of seeing through the illusions of the temporal world, he is always cognizant of his true purpose. When the decision goes against him, he accepts it as part of his destiny and raises no objections, refusing to be a victim in any way whatsoever. The Romans may have sentenced him, but he gives himself freely to the crucifixion—even carrying his own cross—because he understands the truthful odyssey of his earthly life.

This is the attitude we must pray to claim as our own, knowing it to be critical in the latter part of the third path. We will not always find fairness. Illusion will win out many times, in many places, and in many ways. It did with Jesus; it did for the Ephesians, and it has thousands of times in the millennia since then.

We must continue our reflection until we can discern this difference and avoid the trap of resentment and victimhood. Then we will be able to move forward into the fourth path. However, if we find ourselves unwilling to carry our own cross, that is a definite sign that we have reverted to the second—or even—the first path.

As a bit of an aside, but an important one, notice that through John's symbolism, Jesus' confrontation with Pilate personifies the battle between two great opposing forces: Jesus the Christ as the representative of what is divine and real and of God, and Pontius Pilate as that of the temporal "world" of illusion.

This scene, which took place at high noon, has a lot of the same dramatic tension as the famous showdown at the OK Corral. Notably, no Jews— not even the Temple authorities John finds so obnoxious—witness the two powers squaring off, which is further evidence that John does not blame the Jews for Jesus' death.

Jesus' instruction that Mary form a new family with "the disciple whom [Jesus] loved" mirrors our own progression. Mary symbolizes our progenitor, our parent, our culture. She gave us birth and transferred much of value to us—as well as possibly some beliefs we have had to overcome, such as tribalism, categories about ourselves and the world, and other limited, untrue, and unproductive judgments.

SIX—BEING IN JOHN'S GLORIOUS GARDEN

The beloved disciple, on the other hand, is making a journey like ours. He has been following a difficult path, and he will soon see through death and the torn veil and find the truth of unity. Mary and the disciple, the old and new, will form a family; blood and water will flow together. Likewise, our old assumptions and resentments will die and new possibilities will flower, when we, too, are able to join that which has been separate, or that which we have believed to be separate.

Jesus, after drinking the bitter wine, declares, "It is finished." He exemplifies the desire—heart, mind, body, and soul—to drink of the world's bitterness with loving embrace and thus for it to be transmuted. This is what we wish to learn.

When the undivided reality of everything—emotion, mind, spirit and flesh—becomes our reference point, it is then possible for even the most excruciating experiences to open into a calm acceptance and transcendence. This awareness has been reported often, for example, by hospice workers and chaplains in war zones.

There is a caution here—revealed perhaps through the words of John's own gospel and maybe suffered by the writer himself: a dynamic balance is the key to the third path. It is possible to become spiritually over-exalted. This is not uncommon for mystics, sometimes even for their followers.

They often come to see the mind and spiritual planes as most important, and their emotions or their physical body as obstructions to their spiritual growth. This can lead them to fall out of balance with their humanity and to denigrate emotions or physicality.

Earlier we discussed John's possible discomfort with "the flesh." Psychologically the lack of pain in the crucifixion account could reflect such discomfort. Over-exaltation is not unusual, to be sure.

Extremes in diet, emotional or sexual repression and self-mutilation are among the many ways a lack of balance asserts itself. When these behaviors are present, we can be certain that at least in those parts of our lives, our journey has stopped, even regressed.

It is just as possible to lose balance in the other direction. When exposed to the vision of union, some feel an ego-response of desperate unworthiness. John recognized this voice of unworthiness and acknowledged it in the encounter between Jesus and the reluctant Peter about footwashing. I believe that John was concerned primarily with the euphoria of Ephesus, and the possibility of a plunge in the other direction—down into unworthiness—remained a mere mention.

We, however, need to be aware that this plunge is a real risk. We can slide right out of feeling elevated—or never feel any rising at all—and fall into deep despondency, even depression. Again, such a response is an indication that our journey has halted and needs help.

The Passion tells us to open our hearts and souls in joy, to receive all that is before us, and to expand far beyond our intellect and our ever-yammering ego-self. If we can do this, our openness will change how we meet the world and how the world meets us. We need to sit in the garden, sing in the garden, paint in the garden, contemplate in the garden, pray in the garden.

At some point, it is possible that we will become engaged so deeply that our toes will become roots and our embrace will be as solid as the trunk of an oak tree. We won't be "in" the garden anymore. We will BE the garden.

Touching Eternity
The Resurrection Accounts

John's gospel has three appearances of the resurrected Jesus in the original text (and another was added later for a total of four). In their original forms, Matthew's gospel has only one appearance; and Mark has no appearance at all, only an announcement. And we will see that Luke recounts two appearances of Jesus after the crucifixion. Why are there more appearance accounts in John than the other gospels?

The main reason lies in the nature of the gospel itself. John uses very specific teaching methods. We compared John's approach at the beginning

SIX—BEING IN JOHN'S GLORIOUS GARDEN

of the gospel to the slow turning and examination of the carefully cut facets of a diamond. Now at the gospel's close we can see the pattern of infinite glimmers within that diamond, especially those that reach far below its surface. The remarkable structure of this gospel is a multidimensional journey through spirals that simultaneously ascend and descend.

The Gospel of John is structured masterfully. It begins with the poetic pronouncement of exalted themes and divine truths in the Prologue, and leads the reader to the poignant recounting of the crucifixion of a single human body and its resurrection as the proof of those truths.

The resurrection accounts use the same dramatic arc—beginning from the immense, then progressing to the particular. In them, John begins with the clearly divine, and inevitably overwhelming event of the resurrection and brings the revelation of its exalted truths straight back down to human, everyday life.

In every section of the appearances, John provides meditations that focus on a particular principle. First, he asserts a truth; then he either expands it, or he exhorts against failure to understand it.

John illustrates his points either through several stories, each focusing on a figure with distinctive characteristics and a dilemma, or through the use of differing and vivid metaphorical locations. Sometimes he employs both techniques, which we see with clarity in the resurrection accounts.

These four accounts summarize, reinforce, and complete John's core messages. The gospel is like a great symphony, with its melodies brought together in the resurrection accounts like an inspirational and resolved climax.

The Prologue presents all of the truths with which John is concerned, and the balance of the gospel elucidates them. Likewise, the first appearance account reiterates John's primary message, and the subsequent ones comment on that message or, more accurately, contain important caveats.

Increasing the richness, all the elements of the first appearance—the setting, the participants, their actions, the tone, the words themselves—

echo the Prologue's themes, but this time in a pragmatic, comprehensible human context. Indeed, these concluding chapters stand in clear contrast to the central part of the gospel, which consists of lengthy discourses and lengthy sentences. These chapters are simple and direct, the sentences short and commanding.

Recall that in our discussion of the Prologue, we examined John's use of a Platonic metaphor—Plato's shadowy cave of veiled sight—to refer to the illusion of the "world" versus the reality of divine truth. Note two things in the following chapters: the setting of each appearance and the use of the words "see and believe." John is moving his inspirational principles into the realm of lived reality—and he wants to be sure no reader misses the connections he is making.

The Way of Heart
The First Appearance of Jesus the Christ Resurrected

Jesus' death falls on a Friday afternoon, just before Sabbath (or "Shabbat," the "day of rest" at the end of the Jewish week, beginning at sundown Friday and continuing until sundown Saturday). In that peaceful time of dark before dawn, "on the first day of the week"—that is, early Sunday morning—Mary of Magdala arrives at Jesus' tomb and sees that the stone has been removed from the entrance.

Consistent with his other updates of Jewish tradition for his Ephesian audience, John eliminated the references to Shabbat, using instead the more secular phrase, "first day of the week." All of the other gospels describe the resurrection as having occurred on the day after Shabbat.

This may seem like an insignificant change in language. However, it is actually not so small. By not referencing everything to Jewish tradition, John validated developing Christian practice, thus setting the stage for the eventual adoption of Sunday as the Christian feast day and "day of rest."

Keep in mind that another two hundred years would pass before Christianity was fully acknowledged and legalized by secular authorities and Sunday could officially become a non-workday. Until then, Christians

SIX—BEING IN JOHN'S GLORIOUS GARDEN

followed the custom of the Messianic Jews. Saturday was their traditional Sabbath and their rest day. Then they met in the first hours of Sunday morning in remembrance of Jesus' resurrection, and went to work for the rest of the day.

In the early morning of the first day, as John tells it, Mary of Magdala races to tell Simon Peter and "the other disciple" that Jesus' body has been removed from the tomb. At a run, they follow her back, and upon arrival at the tomb, each of the men enters and confirms it empty. John notes that the wrapping linens are "lying there," implying that Jesus' body has been stolen and defiled. The men "see and believe" that the body has been taken and, assuming theft, they return to their homes.

Mary remains, grief-stricken and weeping. She looks in the tomb just as the men had, but she experiences an entirely different vision. She sees angels who ask why she weeps. She responds with her sense of deep loss—her "Lord" has been "taken away."

From behind her, she hears the question repeated. Turning, Mary sees someone she thinks is "the gardener." She begs him to tell her where Jesus' body has gone. The gardener then calls out, "Mary!" Suddenly recognizing him as Jesus, Mary responds, "Rabbouni!" ("My teacher").

Throughout the gospel, Jesus has used only a kind of philosophical address, for example, calling his mother "woman"—one of the ways in which John emphasizes that his intention is in the nature of a meditation on themes rather than a narrative about specific individuals.

The single exception was Lazarus, whom Jesus summoned from his tomb by name—until now. Suddenly, in this poignant moment of grief at his own tomb, an engaged, risen Jesus speaks directly and uncharacteristically. "Mary!" he calls out, startling her.

This encounter at Jesus' tomb, unlike the after-death scenes found in any of the other gospels, occurs with only one witness, Mary of Magdala. Further, the other three gospels make no mention of a garden in the burial scene or the two angels, nor the actual appearance of Jesus at the tomb itself.

John clearly has allegorical intentions in mind. Beginning with the Prologue and continuing throughout the gospel, he has determinedly worked to provide a new Garden of Eden metaphor for Christianity. In this first resurrection account, through the construction of extraordinary symmetries, he perfects his task.

Centuries prior, the Great Temple of Jerusalem was specifically constructed and sited so that everyone who entered it would have an inner and symbolic reentry into the Garden of Eden. Its main gate faced east to the rising sun—the same direction as the entrance to the ancient garden of Hebrew scripture.

By continuing into the heart of the Temple, one reached the Holy of Holies, the Inner Sanctuary, where images of palm trees and flowers covered the walls. Two immense sculptures of cherubim (angels)—a reminder of the two angels who guarded the entrance to Paradise—arched over the heart of the room. They protected the Ark of the Covenant, the most sacred relic of the faith, containing Moses' tablets and pieces of manna from the arid desert where the Jews had suffered for so long.

John's Jewish readers are now offered a consummate vision of a new garden. Here at Golgotha, exquisitely timed just before the sun rose in the east, John has matched his gospel image with all the historical Jewish symbols. Grief-stricken Mary, in a fresh, living garden, symbolic of Eden, looked into the opened tomb and beheld two angels centered over an empty space.

John has constructed a metaphorical Holy of Holies. Observe however, the vast difference between the two settings: the new one is outdoors, freely reached, expansive—while the old one was in a closed-up, guarded room deep within the Great Temple. And the new holiness, seen between the angels, is not a relic, a "mere" object. Instead, it is the site of a mysterious, divine event—Jesus' resurrection—whose truth is the gateway to all of the promises of the Christian faith.

Mary's silent, lonely weeping deepens the Eden allegory. In Eden, first was only Adam. Then one became two in partnership. Here in this garden of resurrection, we also see a solitary figure—weeping for her lost teacher and companion. Her tears of grief summon the resurrected Jesus to be in relationship with her, through faith, forever.

SIX—BEING IN JOHN'S GLORIOUS GARDEN

John is using Mary's tears to reiterate and complete a point he has made many times before: the journey to wholeness cannot be accomplished through intellect alone. The path to the Christian inner sanctuary—its Holy of Holies—requires that the heart be opened and joined to intellect and spirit.

The simplicity of Jesus' appearance to Mary is also significant. He comes quietly, almost seeming to glide into the scene. Neither his entrance nor his manner is extraordinary. There are no radiating beams of light, no sounding trumpets. This is a quiet and intimate setting, although it is very emotional. Its peacefulness holds the most astonishing revelation of Christianity: Jesus died; yet Jesus lives.

John is communicating that the most trustworthy path is based on direct experience. His words are an implicit caution against relying solely on the received knowledge of history or traditions or writings, and their tone provides assurance that truth proceeds quietly and steadily.

Great attention was paid to naming in Genesis. John echoes and modifies that emphasis here. In Genesis, "the man gave names" to the creatures of the earth, thereby acknowledging their unique nature and assigning them their role. Upon expulsion from the garden as they went into trial, he named the woman Eve, which means "mother of all."

We find no less significance in John's retelling. In this peaceful, heart-filled scene, Jesus. appearing as a gardener, addresses Mary directly by her given name. "Mary!" Jesus calls. The sudden calling of Mary's true name in this garden is a repeated and larger version of his earlier direct address to Lazarus, whom he told to "come out" of his tomb.

John's dramatic moment here says, in effect, "Mary, your tears have shown that your heart has truly opened to me. Therefore, I know that you are able to understand this moment and the path before you, which is the path into Paradise. We have been bound together now, in union, by the revelation of my rising. I will be your eternal companion."

And this "naming in the garden" is carried forward into Christian baptism, which in the first centuries included all those gathered, proclaiming the new one's name on arising from the waters.

Another level of meaning, almost certainly more obvious to the original audience than to readers today, can be found in the name Mary itself. Mary is *Miryam* in Hebrew, rabbinically translated as "bitterness" (from the root *merum*). Presumably, John's readers would have made the connection readily, but he makes certain of it by having Mary weep, both here and in the previous account of Lazarus.

Although some texts offer up to seventy possible sources and translations, the interpretation of the name Mary as "bitterness" seems most logical because all the Marys weep. Mary, Lazarus' sister, weeps (but the other sister, Martha, does not). Jesus himself weeps in response. Mary of Magdala weeps profusely at the tomb, crying for help. However, in every instance the tears of loss shed by the Marys evoke compassion, and are turned to tears of joy through Jesus' intervention.

> *Early on the first day of the week, while it was still dark, Mary Magdalene came to the tomb and saw that the stone had been removed from the tomb. So she ran and went to Simon Peter and the other disciple, the one whom Jesus loved, and said to them, "They have taken the Lord out of the tomb, and we do not know where they have laid him." Then Peter and the other disciple set out and went toward the tomb. The two were running together, but the other disciple outran Peter and reached the tomb first. He bent down to look in and saw the linen wrappings lying there, but he did not go in. Then Simon Peter came, following him, and went into the tomb. He saw the linen wrappings lying there, and the cloth that had been on Jesus' head, not lying with the linen wrappings but rolled up in a place by itself. Then the other disciple, who reached the tomb first, also went in, and he saw and believed; for as yet they did not understand the scripture, that he must rise from the dead. Then the disciples returned to their homes. But Mary stood weeping outside the tomb. As she wept, she bent over to look into the tomb; and she saw two angels in white, sitting where the body of Jesus had been lying, one at the head and the other at the feet. They said to her, "Woman, why are you weeping?" She said to them, "They have taken away my Lord,*

and I do not know where they have laid him." When she had said this, she turned around and saw Jesus standing there, but she did not know that it was Jesus. Jesus said to her, "Woman, why are you weeping? Whom are you looking for?" Supposing him to be the gardener, she said to him, "Sir, if you have carried him away, tell me where you have laid him, and I will take him away." Jesus said to her, "Mary!" She turned and said to him in Hebrew, "Rabbouni!" (which means Teacher). (20:1–16)

When we read this appearance story two millennia later, we do not share the connections with the Temple that John's readers did. Yet the spiritual wealth available to us is nonetheless abundant. Although all of John's major themes can be found in the appearance of the resurrected Jesus the Christ to Mary of Magdala in the garden, there are three that are of particular importance for us in the third path.

The first is how we may come to "see and believe"—or not. The second is hearing the sound of our true name. The third is having the patience to know bitterness—to endure the difficulties that are a necessary part of spiritual growth.

Brought by Mary, Peter and the other disciple look into the tomb. They believe they see an empty tomb. That is after all, what they expected to see. Before their eyes is a pile of unwrapped linen—no body and no rational explanation. They return home.

Mary then looks again into the tomb—but brings more of herself to the experience. She looks with her heart not simply her mind. She sees cherubim. And afterward as she grieves, the resurrected Jesus the Christ joins her.

We face the same choice many times daily. Our lives will largely flow from our expectations. The more we are able to be present in our fullest selves to any moment or situation in our lives, the more likely we are to see angels rather than emptiness—and to know how deeply we are accompanied.

For some of us, this will not be terribly difficult. It is our natural inclination. For others of us, it will be a rigorous task. And for all of us, the process of opening at an emotional level will present challenges, chief among which are addressed by the second and third appearance accounts.

Onerous or not, this third path moves primarily, though not exclusively, through our hearts. There is no possible way to comprehend wholeness with intellect only—or for that matter, with body only. Heart is where we are able to feel the range and reach of the All, and allow its entry into us for the work of transformation, so that we may joyously proclaim, "Rabbouni!"

If we are not fully present—not open to possibility—we will be unlikely to hear our "true name" when it is called. When the full experience of deep new vision arrives, it somehow creates in us a refreshed, even a new, sense of identity. We feel more aligned with the deepest, most powerful and authentic ways in which we can know ourselves. We move our focus from the beautiful blossoms of John's garden and gain comprehension of the roots. We feel anchored, centered.

Traditions and rituals throughout the world acknowledge the opening of this extraordinary and very personal inner awareness. In all cultures, at birth or shortly thereafter a name is chosen for each new life. Many of the world's rituals allow people to take a new name when they cross to some designated level of awareness or commitment including the ritual of Christian baptism.

In most religious communities, a name change was once mandatory. Now either a new name is selected or the old is reaffirmed. The pope of the Roman Catholic Church, for example, chooses a highly symbolic new name after he is elected. These rituals are designed to recognize, honor, and assist with what is acknowledged as a core change.

Understanding "bitterness," exemplified by the name Mary, is complex, a bit unexpected, and often difficult to manage. It is also an unavoidable element of full transformation. It is no accident that throughout the centuries, one of the names for Mary, the mother of Jesus, has been *Mater Dolorosa*, Mother of Sorrows—and that many images of great art depict her weeping.

SIX—BEING IN JOHN'S GLORIOUS GARDEN

We encountered suffering in our first and certainly our second paths, and had to move through it. But now it is time to deepen that reality and transcend mere endurance. Whole *does not mean idyllic*. No life is lived without the reality of pain.

When pain arises in our lives, we are confronted with choices—and again, the degree to which we hold ourselves present to each moment will largely determine what we decide. We may bring only our small ego-self and respond from the categories of *dia-bol*. If we do, then gradually we will end up with an embittered heart.

If instead we can stay open, as Mary does after Lazarus' death—even though she is surely disappointed that Jesus has not come soon enough to save her brother—then our pain can transform into compassion. If we can grieve without losing our faith, as Mary of Magdala does, then we will be rewarded with divine awareness. A compassionate heart carries both the reality of pain and the hope of joy. It moves us forward.

These elements are the fullness of the extraordinary and uplifting feelings of the third path—not their contradiction. The garden overflowing with flowers is simultaneously a picture of death and decay.

At the joyous moment of a baby's birth, in the ecstasy of new life, the baby cries. Grief and sorrow can be profound and enriching, just as the cello and bass are the deep tones that keep a symphony from flying off into sentimentality.

In the Locked House
The Second Appearance of Jesus the Christ Resurrected

The second appearance of Jesus the Christ resurrected, as down-to-earth as the first, narrows its thematic focus to the letting go of anger and resentment. It is essentially cautionary. The story opens with the disciples in a house that is "locked for fear of the Jewish authorities."

This is John's shorthand to Ephesians for their trepidations and uncertainties about moving forward despite the pressure they feel from the authorities of the old religion. They could "lock the doors" of their lives and their attitudes, says John, or they could choose another, more positive course.

Jesus appears before them. After a greeting in the name of "peace," repeated twice, he commands the disciples to receive "the Holy Spirit," which he confers by breathing upon them. This is an echo (once again) of Genesis, where it is said that God "breathed into [Adam's] nostrils the breath of life; and the man became a living being" (Gen. 2:7).

John is emphasizing that joining with Spirit needn't be a complicated ritual involving sacrifices in a temple. It is a simple, natural, and regular practice—as easy, yet profound, as breathing.

The resurrected Jesus then proceeds to talk to the disciples about their responsibilities now that they have received the infusion of Spirit. The Oxford New Revised Standard Version (NRSV), which is used throughout this book, translates the two Greek verbs in this passage as "forgive" and "retain."

These translations are technically correct and theoretically possible. However, they are more congruent with the practice of priests granting (or denying) forgiveness than with the consistent message of John's gospel, which is the release of pain from one's heart and life. The original Greek words have great subtlety, and other possible translations make more sense.

The first verb in the verse is *aphiemi*, which means "to send away, cancel, or release." The second is *krateo*, which means "to hold, hold fast, or keep." Using these definitions, we might translate Jesus' words as: "Receive the Holy Spirit. If you send away sins from another, they are sent away from them; if you hold onto them, they are held fast."

These words are about the work of the Holy Spirit within the heart of each individual and that individual's responsibilities. John is pointing out both a promise and a caution to his readers.

In a more expanded version, we might restate this verse as: "If, *within yourself*, you are able to unlock your heart's doors and send away your feelings of judgment over differences with others and over being wronged, then *your* heart will be freed. If, however, you do not choose to release *yourself*, then the trespasses you hold against others will remain alive, held fast *within you* and in the world."

John's specific inclusion of Jesus' words about forgiveness in his gospel to Ephesus is a practical mandate. He is promoting amity and shalom in a diverse Christian community and city.

The more commonly accepted interpretation of this passage is that Jesus is conferring the privilege and responsibility of forgiveness specifically on his disciples—and, by extension, on the priesthood. This makes much less sense to me. I find this perception not only contradictory within the gospel, but also contrary to John's clear intention of fostering harmony in Ephesus' Christian community.

> *When it was evening on that day, the first day of the week, and the doors of the house where the disciples had met were locked for fear of the Jews, Jesus came and stood among them and said, "Peace be with you." After he said this, he showed them his hands and his side. Then the disciples rejoiced when they saw the Lord. Jesus said to them again, "Peace be with you. As the Father has sent me, so I send you." When he had said this, he breathed on them and said to them, "Receive the Holy Spirit. If you forgive the sins of any, they are forgiven them; if you retain the sins of any, they are retained." (20:19-23)*

What cautions might we, in today's world, take for ourselves in this second appearance? One is the challenge of balance. Jesus, in his human body, "showed" his hands and side. One of the critical dangers of the third path is that in our attempts to remain in ecstasy, we may fail to find a productive way to sustain matter and spirit together. There is a notable risk that we will try to supersede our wounds by moving out of our bodies into some ethereal place that is "only spiritual." Conversely, we may risk "over-embodying" our wounds by moving from acceptance into indulgence.

What does this mean? It means that our human journey is exactly that—human. Our human experience is embodied, and our journey can proceed only through acceptance of that reality. "Human" (and "humility") derives from *humus*, earth. This reminds us that we are made of the same elements as the soil.

Many teachers assert that we are not bodies being spiritual, but rather spirit, or spiritual beings, having the experience of a body. This is a difference without a distinction. We are both matter *and* spirit, human *and* divine. We do ourselves no service in our quest for spiritual maturity when we try to supersede our bodies or, in fact, when we separate ourselves in any way, rather than bending our efforts to encourage the harmony of our complexity.

The opposite extreme—over-embodying—presents an equal challenge. Quadratos tells us that all is whole, and all is well, and gives us a path of acceptance on which we can walk. As we inhabit the third path, we can peacefully observe and become conscious of how many "inner tribes" make up our individual harmony.

However, we must remain cognizant that many of the behaviors we carry are ones we developed as adaptations in our earlier, less mature stages in the "locked house." "All is well" does not in any way mean that all the behaviors within us are good or productive.

We still need to assess what serves our mature life, and what does not. If we use the third-path revelation as an excuse for indulgence, we will find ourselves merely circling through the rooms of our personality, instead of moving through the door of transformation.

So, what does Jesus in the second appearance tell us about how to open that door? First, the disciples "rejoice." This parallels Mary of Magdala's tears of joy. The disciples move into the realm of their feelings, giving us guidance to the path we also must follow.

Jesus next pronounces, "Peace be with you." We, too, must strive for peace—to maintain a peaceful, open, and willing inner diversity. Then Jesus exhales the Holy Spirit into the disciples who gratefully accept it.

SIX—BEING IN JOHN'S GLORIOUS GARDEN

This sense of personal advocacy, of companionship and perpetual memory, is the essential understanding of the Holy Spirit we must grasp and accept in the third path. We need to inhale it fully, breathing deeply, contemplating, meditating, and praying.

This is the perfume of the garden of our lives. When we have it, we will know we are no longer alone. We will never be paralyzed by fear again, and the door to the house will swing open.

The final words of the second appearance are like a fresh breeze rushing in through the door, displacing the old, stale air inside. Jesus commanded his disciples to "send away" their sins and judgments, to free themselves from the narrow vision of one-sidedness, lest they cause suffering within themselves and the world.

This understanding varies considerably from what has been widely accepted as the meaning of these verses, and it is crucial that we understand this in the third path. In this time of new revelation, the danger of imbalance continues its threat. Gravitating toward partial truths, for example, prevents genuine forgiveness. We can move to forgiveness only from a steadied center that balances both our intellect and our emotions.

This is best accomplished through a learned practice of compassion. Without it, we may rely too heavily on our intellect, fall into judgment and cynicism, and fail to access the leavening of the heart. If, on the other hand, we tip the other way and place too much emphasis on our emotions, we can easily fall into sentimentality and fantasy, losing the necessary guidance of our reason. Only in our attempts at balance will the door stay open, so that the breath of the Holy Spirit coming through the portal may enliven our compassion.

Further complicating matters, our culture's understanding of the word "forgiveness" has become distorted in a way that makes the conventional translation of John's verses very misleading. Forgiveness does not mean that we sit in judgment of others and then condescend to be "understanding" of what we deem to be their failings or their sins against us.

This is false forgiveness and will keep us locked in self-righteousness, breathing fetid air. Genuine forgiveness allows us to move to a posture outside the need for judgment and requires us to, instead, release judgment *within ourselves*. The "sins" we forgive are actually the attitudes we hold within our *own* hearts. This resurrection appearance helps us to compassionately understand the actions of others anew—as their emanations of fear, loneliness, or loss.

With Thomas in the "Shut" House
The Third Appearance of Jesus the Christ Resurrected

A week later, Jesus visits the disciples, and again they are described as in a house, although this time it isn't locked—merely "shut." This time, the disciple Thomas is present. In Greek, Thomas is Didymus, which means "twin." John uses this name to explore the voices of faith and doubt—internal and external—which inevitably buffet and challenge believers.

As Christianity exploded in size in the early decades, many problems and opinions naturally arose. Who would claim authority and marshal support? When and how were ritual circumcision and ritual cleansing going to be converted to the new rite of Christian baptism? What size table was needed for all the new members, men and women, to sit and converse? Which accounts of Jesus were most correct? Which teachings could be trusted?

Even if these matters could somehow be settled, there were pragmatic challenges in day-to-day dealings with diversity. How could people and their practices be harmonized into a coherent and loving whole? How could an individual transform inner conflicts into resolute faith? John offers the image of Thomas to address these specific dilemmas.

Thomas is, in effect, John's "straight man." He questions everything, always requires literal proof, and is now memorialized in the expression "doubting Thomas." True to his nature, Thomas is completely unable to believe in the resurrection based on the story told him by the other disciples.

SIX—BEING IN JOHN'S GLORIOUS GARDEN

He needs specific, concrete evidence and says so. "(I need to) put my fingers in the mark of the nails and my hand in his side," says Thomas. Without comment or criticism, Jesus offers Thomas the chance to verify the injuries—and Thomas' skepticism vanishes.

As we noted when we discussed the teaching discourses, John is always working on many levels—turning his allegorical diamond. Doubt is scarcely the sole issue in this appearance, albeit the primary one.

In all four appearances, Jesus appears in human form, but in both the second and third appearances, John notes that he appears with the holes of the crucifixion still in his body. The resurrected body is not miraculously made undamaged, a detail found only in John's gospel. John is proclaiming to Ephesus that resurrection occurs in a regular human life and that faith is not flawless. It has doubts and it has wounds, neither of which need be hidden.

Additionally, John uses a profoundly inspirational choice of words in the third appearance account. The holes in Jesus' body are referred to not as wounds, but as "marks." John is clear that Jesus *chose* his crucifixion. Therefore, Jesus could not have been "wounded," but he was certainly "marked"—and he did not flinch or hesitate to show those marks.

This is a distinction of great value to the Ephesian Christians building a community among diverse people. The group's ability to receive each other's differences as marks of glory rather than pejorative tribalistic damage or "wounds," enables the individual members of the group to avoid roles of victimhood by more freely expressing vulnerability and compassion for self and others.

Jesus' final words in this appearance ring out as a challenge. Though tolerant of Thomas' need for proof, Jesus also calls Thomas to task. He questions the depth of Thomas' belief, wondering if he has become satisfied only because his doubting intellect has been assuaged. Note that John once more distinctly uses the verb "see."

Jesus' last words in this account are "Blessed are those who have not seen and yet have come to believe." They are a deep caution and support for belief that honors the truth of the heart as well as the head—transcending the limitations of physical sight (recall Plato's cave) and the deceptions of the divided and divisive intellect.

This is critical for the Ephesians—and for all Christians who would come after them, who would be generations removed from the historical events recounted by the gospel. Does your faith require physical evidence or intellectual proof? Or is the Christ alive for you in your heart, and in the midst of your life?

> *But Thomas (who was called the Twin), one of the twelve, was not with them when Jesus came. So the other disciples told him, "We have seen the Lord." But he said to them, "Unless I see the mark of the nails in his hands, and put my finger in the mark of the nails and my hand in his side, I will not believe." A week later his disciples were again in the house, and Thomas was with them. Although the doors were shut, Jesus came and stood among them and said, "Peace be with you." Then he said to Thomas, "Put your finger here and see my hands. Reach out your hand and put it in my side. Do not doubt but believe." Thomas answered him, "My Lord and my God!" Jesus said to him, "Have you believed because you have seen me? Blessed are those who have not seen and yet have come to believe." Now Jesus did many other signs in the presence of his disciples, which are not written in this book. But these are written so that you may come to believe that Jesus is the Messiah, the Son of God, and that through believing you may have live in his name. (20:24–31)*

The third appearance, with its story of Thomas, was the original ending of The Gospel of John. Many of us may find it the one to which we most closely relate. Why? For one thing, like us, Thomas wasn't there. He wasn't at the crucifixion, the burial, or the first resurrection appearance.

Furthermore, he is profoundly a man for our times. He's rational, a "show me" guy, just like most of us have been trained to be. He is the mirror of our human dilemma, and his struggle to live the principles of the Prologue, of Jesus the Christ, is ours.

Since Thomas is a disciple, we have to assume that something in his heart is touched by some words or evidence or actions of Jesus the Christ. And despite Jesus' explicit promise that he will return ("I go and prepare a place for you(.) I will come again and will take you to myself, so that where I am, there you may be also." 14:3) Thomas remains doubtful enough to hamper his belief. He insists on direct sensory experience. He cannot trust the truth of his own inner call, much less the words of anyone else.

Thomas the Twin personifies John's "world" of illusion in its most intimate guise. Thomas had initially opened his heart. He is neither a Pharisee like Nicodemus, nor an outsider, but a genuine disciple. He longs for belief.

In the house with the other disciples, he faced a door which, though not completely barred or "locked" by fear was shut. Thomas, instinctually protective of the illusions so carefully crafted by his intellect—and unable to transcend them—kept it closed. This is a predicament many of us recognize all too well.

What does John tell us about Thomas, and what more can we intuit, and how is this of value to us in the third path? Presumably, Thomas overcame his self-protective doubt when he became a disciple. Yet his subsequent actions tell us that he likely neglected to build an inner practice to support his decision. Perhaps he lacked friends on whom he could rely or failed to extend his trust to them.

Rather, he indulges his questioning intellect, falling back into the comfortable, rational understanding with which he is familiar. He does not persist in or expand the ecstasy that had initially compelled him, and hence he is spiritually immature and unprepared to accept the truth of the resurrection when it arrives. If we follow Thomas' path, and fail to take the positive and expansive steps available to us, we too will find the door closed and the fresh air of transformation unavailable when it comes.

Faith requires real commitment. The eyes that read only words cannot see past the veil. Does this mean we should push all doubt aside? Absolutely not. Doubt is faith's true companion. Does this mean faith can, or should, be discovered only on the level of our feelings? Again, absolutely not.

In the garden, the whole flower is treasured—root, stem, and blossom—with each part distinct, yet all are necessary to nature's plan. Further, the separate elements of soil, light, air, and water are all needed if the blossom is to reach its greatest beauty and have the vigor to fend off its predators.

Complexity is strength. Our intellect needs the vitality of our emotions, and our vulnerable emotions require gentle guardianship by our intellect. Faith needs doubt to test itself. It raises the questions that fertilize faith, keeping it flexible and invigorated.

We should ask, which is the richest soil in which we can plant ourselves? What spiritual tradition or practice calls our heart to discipleship? Jesus' counsel to Thomas' doubt can give us perfect direction. When he enters, Jesus speaks, and then repeats, an instruction for balance and harmony: "Peace be with you." That should be our core instruction to ourselves, the daily condition for which we strive, as well as that toward which we journey—inner and outer peace.

Jesus offers the marks on his side and his hands to Thomas without hesitation. John's use of "marks" rather than "wounds" is as significant to us today as it was to the Ephesians. Each of us has been marked by our lives. We can choose to identify the signs of these profound passages as "wounds"—signs of our past (and sometimes present) suffering at the hands of others.

We can use these signs to derive sympathy and attention and a sense of importance. Alternatively, we can choose to acknowledge them as the "marks" that identify our singular humanity—significant and necessary parts of our journey. We can hide our "marks," or we can offer them up to others, when appropriate, so that those pathfinders can use them as trail signs while making their own way through the wilderness.

SIX—BEING IN JOHN'S GLORIOUS GARDEN

There is a special lesson for us in the way Jesus offers Thomas the "proof" required by demanding intellect. Jesus does so gently, without explanation, recrimination, or harangue. This is a very tough lesson for most of us, and its difficulty relates directly to how well we are "rooted" in our own particular garden.

Another vocabulary might refer to this as how well we are "centered." Can we merely be present to the need of another without extracting our own self-importance from the encounter? Are we able to give without needing to receive—esteem or attention or inner self-elevation—at the expense of another?

If we can answer yes, the further question is—are we yet able to be as gentle with ourselves as we are with others? When we contemplate this example of Jesus, we may find we need to sit in the garden in seasons other than spring. We may require the darker days of autumn and winter, where the deepest self-honesty, pain, and even failure abide, before we gain the full measure of this lesson. Our love for ourselves is often the hardest to come by, yet the most necessary for our journey. Without it, we have no roots and our garden will fail.

Toward the end of the gospel, and with great tenderness, Jesus asks Thomas his central question. He asks him to examine the source of his belief. Was its source faith or evidence? This question fills every aspect of our lives, no matter what tradition we are in—or even if we are in no spiritual tradition whatsoever. What "system" do we believe in, and how do we arrive at our belief?

What is the framework for our life on earth, our relationships with others, and our view of death? In the deepest places of ourselves that we can discover, do we feel isolated or accompanied? Are we able to hold a vision of unity that connects our inner aspects to each other, or (to use other words) connects us to ourselves, and then to others, and finally to All?

Are our steps taken in trust, even without understanding? Or do we fear life—and death? These questions are crystallized in the one question Jesus asks Thomas, "Have you believed because you have seen me?" And they are at the deepest core of our questioning and self-discovery in Quadratos' third path.

The final words of Jesus in this gospel are the blessing, the challenge and the promise of this third path. These original final words present a very personal affirmation, entreaty and hope. They ask us to "see" with faith's eyes, to "come to believe" in Mystery and the promise of life.

This is why our time in the garden must be sheltered. It takes time to know the fullness of the truths whose disclosure began with our ecstatic entry through the garden gate. Yet we must now leave so that we can garden alongside the one who appeared as a gardener.

John has scrupulously revealed the complex and wondrous nature of union to us. Through poetry, dialogue and story, that revelation has expanded and deepened our feelings of epiphany. John has encouraged—even insisted—that we allow their full meanings to unfold in our lives and that we bring our full selves to the experience. Now, as we come to the end of this path, we begin to sense why we cannot remain here, why we need to move on to the fourth path.

The deep inner comprehension we have is clear to us only so long as we sit, unmoving, in the garden. But that immobility will inevitably lead only to stagnation or retreat. Therefore, we must continue on despite the fact that our safety disappears the moment we step into our regular lives. We do not yet know how to walk the path of truth, but we will find our guide in The Gospel of Luke.

On the Beach
The Fourth and Final Appearance of Jesus the Christ Resurrected

Most scholars believe the account of the fourth appearance of Jesus the Christ resurrected was added later and was written by a different author. Compared with the rest of John's gospel, the allusions and writing style of this account have an uncharacteristic awkwardness. It also introduces an entirely new metaphor—fishing.

It seems unlikely that just at the close of his inspired magnum opus John would have abandoned the metaphors he spent so much effort building. It

SIX—BEING IN JOHN'S GLORIOUS GARDEN

is much more logical that he closed his gospel with the blessing and entreaty to Ephesus and future generations found at the end of the third appearance. Regardless of its authorship, however, the fourth account is both interesting and useful to our discussion.

The fourth appearance has its own message, complete with a different vitality from the others. Unlike the earlier parts of John, which transpired mainly in the city of Jerusalem, this account begins elsewhere. We join the resurrected Jesus and seven of his disciples on the beach of the Sea of Tiberias, which was the Roman name for the Sea of Galilee.

As in the first account with Mary of Magdala in the garden, the location is open and expansive, matching the message of its words. The setting also holds a subtler meaning: in Christianity, old superstitions have been dispelled by a greater power. Rather than the fearsome place of Jewish experience that we read of in the Gospel of Mark, *this* sea is the backdrop for physical and spiritual nourishment.

Much of this account centers on a lengthy series of actions that revolve around fishing and hold clearly metaphorical meanings, primarily reiterative of John's earlier themes. However, the end of the narrative is another matter. Not only is its theme consistent with the rest of John's gospel, but it also serves Quadratos admirably and carries us forward into The Gospel of Luke very nicely. Therefore, I will happily examine its words without any concerns about their authorship.

As noted, the physical setting is spacious and unobstructed—and so are the images presented. In the first appearance, Jesus shows himself to Mary as a simple gardener. Here, equally unadorned, he stands on the beach serving breakfast to his disciples. Repeating the earlier image of Annas' courtyard, mention is made that the meal is cooked over a charcoal fire.

After the repast, there is a measured—almost ritual—exchange between Jesus and Peter. Using his personal name, "Simon son of John," Jesus asks Peter three times, "Do you love me?" Three times—the equal number of times Peter had earlier denied Jesus in Annas' cold courtyard—Peter replies, "Yes ... I love you."

Jesus responds to Peter twice with a direct instruction about humility and service: "Feed my lambs...Tend my sheep." The third time, however, Jesus gives a lengthy teaching to Peter in a lyrical passage that is the primary message of this account.

Its wise and lovely words counsel that the presumptuous autonomy of youth passes, and is replaced in maturity by stretching "out your hands, [when] ... someone else will fasten a belt around you and take you where you do not wish to go." When we read these words in this gospel's context of their direct juxtaposition to Peter's thrice-made denial, and then when we recall Peter's subsequent story, a kind of tragically glorious beauty opens for us.

After his experiences with the resurrected Jesus, Peter stays awhile in Jerusalem and then moves on to Rome, only to encounter the slaughter of the Messiahnians. He hastily leaves the city, but receives a vision of the Christ as he flees, which causes him to return to Rome and die a martyr's death. Peter was indeed taken by his faith "where he did not wish to go"—yet despite his clear fears and misgivings, he made the choice to follow.

The complexity of this passage is wonderful. The first image of outstretched hands—open, seeking, willing—describes a mature soul not closed and settled in its ways. The deeper implication of the story is twofold: first, without the element of "asking," of willingness, there is no maturity; second, unless one asks, nothing will come.

The next words of this chapter are the more commonly noted. They form a powerful picture, rich with meaning. "Someone else will fasten a belt around you," Jesus begins in his words to Peter.

In first-century Israel, all men wore a large belt—about four inches wide—that cinched the tunic, an undergarment, in at the waist. It also provided a way to tuck the tunic up, still covering the loins and protecting modesty (hence "girding one's loins"), when needed for less encumbered movement. The image of "belt," therefore, brings Jesus' instruction directly and explicitly into daily life.

SIX—BEING IN JOHN'S GLORIOUS GARDEN

This "belt" that "will come" also refers directly to one of the best-known passages of the Hebrew scriptures. Found in the book of Isaiah, the lyrical verse addresses the qualities of the Messiah and the positive transformations his coming will cause within the community. The specifically relevant section of the lengthy and beautiful passage follows. Note how many of John's other important words are also present.

> *He shall not judge by what his eyes see, or decide by what his ears hear; but with righteousness he shall judge the poor, and decide with equity for the meek of the earth; he shall strike the earth with the rod of his mouth, and with the breath of his lips he shall kill the wicked. Righteousness shall be the belt around his waist, and faithfulness the belt around his loins. The wolf shall live with lamb, the leopard shall lie down with the kid, the calf and the lion and the fatling together, and a little child shall lead them. (Isaiah 11:3b–6)*

Of course, many Christian Ephesians would have been familiar with the entire passage. In reading John's gospel, they would have instantly connected various words—"see," "breath," "lamb," and "belt"—with that earlier beloved text. They would have understood that the Jewish heritage of their Christian faith was long and honored. They would have seen that Jesus has come to earth to carry that heritage forward in a new way. And with these final words of this gospel, both they and centuries of readers after them will know that the new Jeru-Shalom is a living reality.

> *When they had gone ashore, they saw a charcoal fire there, with fish on it, and bread. Jesus said to them, "Bring some of the fish that you have just caught." So Simon Peter went aboard and hauled the net ashore, full of large fish, a hundred fifty-three of them; and though there were so many, the net was not torn. Jesus said to them, "Come and have breakfast." Now none of the disciples dared to ask him, "Who are you?" because they knew it was the Lord. Jesus came and took the bread and gave it to them, and did the same with the fish. This was now the third time that Jesus appeared to the disciples after he was raised from the dead. When they had finished breakfast, Jesus said to Simon Peter, "Simon son of John, do*

you love me more than these?" He said to him, "Yes, Lord; you know that I love you." Jesus said to him, "Feed my lambs." A second time he said to him, "Simon son of John, do you love me?" He said to him, "Yes, Lord; you know that I love you." Jesus said to him, "Tend my sheep." He said to him the third time, "Simon son of John, do you love me?" Peter felt hurt because he said to him the third time, "Do you love me?" And he said to him, "Lord, you know everything; you know that I love you." Jesus said to him, "Feed my sheep. Very truly, I tell you, when you were younger, you used to fasten your own belt and to go wherever you wished. But when you grow old, you will stretch out your hands, and someone else will fasten a belt around you and take you where you do not wish to go." (21:9-18)

Regardless of any questions about authorship, this final teaching of John's gospel is both timely and joyous. We are at the close of the third path, and despite all of our work and revelation, at this point on our Journey of Quadratos we remain immature and uncertain. Our arms are filled with young blossoms. We have a vision, some concepts, some ideas, even some deeper, budding sensibilities—but no real practice or maturity.

The possibility of falling back into fear and division is still a strong and constant threat. We must remain open and allow ourselves to be guided, according to John's verse, as if "by a belt," whether or not the places we are taken are where we wish to go, or even if we feel we have outgrown them.

As we move from the third to the fourth path, it is The Gospel of Luke that first opens to receive our fragrant bouquet and then unfolds to gird us in a sturdy belt. Words of inspiration and experience will guide us surely as we walk its roads, and wisdom greater than ours will take us where we need to go. If we are patient and true, we will continue to deepen. Eventually, we will come to a day of the greatest shalom and sense of purpose we have ever known—and on that day, we will smile as we gather our provisions and herald the day of beginning once again.

Prayer as We Leave The Third Path

Psalm 122

Joy drenched me when you said
Come inside my house

Now our feet stand within your gates, Jeru-salem
Planted upon your wholeness

Jeru-salem,
Place where each is welcome
All belong

For this is the place
Toward which people ascend

Giving thanks with their mouths
Singing the thousand names of the nameless
And here stand the upright chairs of David's justice
Pray for the peace of Jeru-salem
Pray that all who love her will be well

May there be peace within her walls
Plenty in her palaces
For the sake of all that lives and
is Let me speak these heart words:
Peace, peace,
Peace for Jeru-salem

And for your sake
From inside your house
I pledge myself to seek the good

translation by Norman Fischer

EXERCISES FOR THE THIRD PATH

As we noted earlier, the exercises for Quadratos are cumulative, each path building upon the next. The first path asked us to begin the practices of *creating temenos* and *welcoming the other*. In this way, we can begin to create safety and listen to the voices we are not accustomed to hearing.

The second path asked us to practice *holding opposites in tension and accepting that deepening often results from difficulty*.

The exercises for the third path build on these, though they, like the earlier exercises, are completely worthwhile standing on their own. They come to us as we leave behind our exhaustion from the strain of opposites and arrive in an epiphany.

Receive the Epiphany

For most of us, the epiphany of the third path arrives as gift. The experience is so exalted—obviously much larger than our small selves— that we feel it cannot come from any source other than from beyond— from Spirit, from God. Even those who struggle with the gift due to a sense of inadequacy feel the power of its source.

Our practice now is that which all the contemplatives and mystics speak of as a practice of *being*. This is not an experience we can summon, although it requires our fullest intention, and we can certainly encourage it. And then our work is to relax and understand that this is not a goal-oriented quest. We need to melt and receive the blossoming awareness into our bodies, minds, and hearts. The "doing" is simple.

Go outside, preferably to a garden or place of nature. (If that isn't possible, seat yourself facing a window with a view of a tree, flowers or some nature aspect.) Sit comfortably, and for a period of no less than fifteen minutes, calmly and quietly notice your surroundings. Place your attention on as many details as you are able. Do this daily. Vary the times of day you sit. Observe the changes, daily, weekly, by season—in the outside and in yourself.

Expand Awareness of "Dia-bol"

The gift arrives in us so that we may gradually grow into a wider, more paradoxical and whole interior vision (remember: symbol—*sumballein*, "to throw two or more things together").

However, in order to accomplish this work, the energy of the gift must first help us to deconstruct and cleanse the vestiges of our former beliefs and attitudes. This can take time, and involves our participation in a great deal of prayer and meditation as well as inner scrutiny. This is, therefore, our "stage two" exercise.

As we observe the beauty of the divine whole, if we are honest and faithful, inevitably we will also be able to discern many aspects and voices within ourselves. We will see and hear those that still move stiffly and speak with the judgmental divisions of black and white.

Gradually, we will develop the capacity to identify our own Nicodemus voice that has unreflectively accepted a belief because mother or father or the government or a book or some other authority figure said it was so.

As we wind our way through the third path, our practice is to continue our discovery of exactly how pervasive dualism is in our life via the keeping of a "John's Journal." Maintain your journal in writing or, if it is easier for you, through an audio or video recording. In your journal, chronicle when you "catch" yourself in dualistic thinking or preconception. Make an entry every day.

If an actual experience hasn't occurred, try to find one—in a hymnal, prayer, poem, or journal article. Or try to imagine one—with a friend, a family member, in business matters, at church, in politics—anything at all in your life.

Think of your "normal" response, and honestly assess its degree of dualism. If it lacks the fluidity of John's great vision, meditate until you are able to discern a more creative solution, and enter that into your journal. Consider this little book a spiritual awareness manual.

HOW DO WE RECEIVE JOY?
The Core Question of The Gospel of John

The exalted language of the prologue proclaims a vision of the Christ and creation beyond time and announces the unity of all in All. This is the base on which our very being rests.

Cana's wedding feast reminds us that our call in the third path is the full enjoyment of the wedding celebration. We are in an epiphany, after all. Yet we should not confuse this with the ongoing work of the marriage itself. That portion of the journey will open, and soon.

The great teaching discourses—the stories of Nicodemus, the woman at the well, the man born blind, and the raising of Lazarus— tell us that our inner fears and yesterday's beliefs and teachings can easily put a stop to our journey. The third path asks us to recognize new wider teachings and quell the power of unreflectively held traditions, if we are to throw off our bindings and move into more vital life.

Jerusalem is Jeru-Shalom, a metaphor for our spiritual home where opposites are joined and our infinitely complex natures can find an original expression in harmony with ourselves and others.

The ritual of foot washing and the discourse on intimacy and union bring us face to face with our deepest issues of unworthiness, challenging us to reflect on what is really required for a relationship of intimacy—for communion. They also bring our burgeoning sensuality to the fore and force our acknowledgment of its equal partnership with our emotional and spiritual nature.

The gathering in the garden, the courtyard and the meeting with Pilate give a prescription for how we may mediate the voices of old and new as they arise within us. We need to be particularly mindful of the ways in which we are still learning and attached to outmoded and unproductive ideas, behaviors or people.

SIX—BEING IN JOHN'S GLORIOUS GARDEN

Jesus' calm embrace of his crucifixion and death teaches us that when we are on a genuine journey and allow things to unfold within a context of wholeness, pain can open into an experience of deep meaning, serenity and transcendence.

The first resurrection appearance of Jesus the Christ tells us to be alert for the sound of our true name when it is called. Will we hear it? And when we do, what charge or mission does it convey?

The second and third appearances of Jesus the Christ are lessons to us about maintaining our spiritual balance. Are we able to free our hearts from judgment and blame of others? Are we able to see and sustain a balance between matter and spirit? Between doubt and faith?

The fourth appearance of Jesus the Christ asks us how we will move forward into the fourth path and beyond. Will we be able to stay open? Will we remember that we will always need to receive appropriate guidance as we continue our journey?

Chapter 7
WALKING LUKE'S ROAD OF RICHES

COLEMAN'S BED [8]

*Make a nesting now, a place to which
the birds can come, think of Kevin's
prayerful palm holding the blackbird's egg
and be the one, looking out from this place
who warms interior forms into light.
Feel the way the cliff at your back
gives shelter to your outward view
and then bring in from those horizons
all discordant elements that seek a home.*

*Be taught now, among the trees and rocks,
how the discarded is woven into shelter,
learn the way things hidden and unspoken
slowly proclaim their voice in the world.
Find that far inward symmetry
to all outward appearances, apprentice
yourself to yourself, begin to welcome back
all you sent away, be a new annunciation,
make yourself a door through which
to be hospitable, even to the stranger in you.*

*See with every turning day,
how each season makes a child
of you again, wants you to become
a seeker after rainfall and birdsong,
watch how it weathers you to a testing
in the tried and true, tells you
with each falling leaf, to leave and slip away,
even from the branch that held you,
to go when you need to, to be courageous,
to be like a last word you'd want to say
before you leave the world.*

---

[8] This poem references two sixth-century Irish saints. St. Coleman, a bishop, was known for his talent as bard and poet. St. Kevin, a charismatic teacher and animal lover, was so dedicated to his own spiritual growth that he, among others, inspired the Irish monastic movement.

Above all, be alone with it all,
a hiving off, a corner of silence
amidst the noise, refuse to talk,
even to yourself, and stay in this place
until the current of the story
is strong enough to float you out.

Ghost then, to where others
in this place have come before,
under the hazel, by the ruined chapel,
below the cave where Coleman slept,
become the source that makes
the river flow, and then the sea
beyond. Live in this place
as you were meant to and then,
surprised by your abilities,
become the ancestor of it all,
the quiet, robust and blessed Saint
that your future happiness
will always remember.

David Whyte

How Do We Mature In Service?
The Fourth Path

The fourth path makes it possible for all our childhood dreams—and our adult hopes and aspirations—to become realities. Is your desire to find, give, and receive love? Know true friendship? Be a person of respect to yourself and others? Learn how to live with both strength and equanimity despite the travails that life gives you? Be at peace when you contemplate your life—and death?

These are the riches promised—and delivered—by the fourth path of Quadratos. One would think everyone on the planet would be lining up to walk down this road.

Instead, the fourth path is largely neglected and often even omitted as a formal part of most spiritual and psychological processes. Unsurprisingly, it is misunderstood by the very people who most require its wisdom.

There is a widespread belief among teachers of religion, spirituality, and psychology that once revelation has been experienced, a transformed life will *naturally* follow. After all, once we have that precious epiphany we know that God is love, and God loves us, and All is One. Or, in psychological terms, we gain the insight that frees us of the burdens of unearned shame, and the larger pattern of our life is revealed.

It is assumed that with such knowledge, a person's greatest trials are over and that given a bit of gentle shepherding, everything will somehow automatically proceed in a positive direction. All it will take is simply thinking about our new understandings, coupled perhaps with a bit of reading and talking and some meditating.

We will simply become "self-aware," "self-actualized," "spirit-filled," a "true Christian," etc. The vocabulary varies, but the unrealistic expectations at this juncture are consistent. They are also always wrong and very often tragic.

The problem is that no fundamental change actually occurred in the third path. We had a *moment*. Much was revealed. But that moment has thus far served only one purpose. It has made us more conscious. We have become aware that it is possible for our feelings, our thoughts, and our attitudes—even our daily lives—to change.

However, our egos are still in an immature state. They are struggling to evolve through fragile new understandings, but they are completely unequipped to help us deal successfully with our fourth-path challenges. Old patterns are still controlling many of our core emotions and exerting powerful influences on our behavior.

Nonetheless, filled with new energy and excitement about our fresh insights, we confidently stride out of the safety of the third path's garden and into what we are certain will be our renewed and joyous life. But the realities of the fourth path—real life—come charging straight at us the minute we take our first steps.

If we are lucky, that onslaught will merely take the form of a minor crisis. More often though, what we experience will be closer to some sort of crushing opposition in our lives. To meet this opposition constructively will require a mature, seasoned response and a practical application of the principles of paradoxical union that were revealed to us in the third path. Unfortunately, we haven't yet reached the level in our journey that will enable us to muster a response of that order.

Our still young ego-self has only *tasted* a new way; it hasn't yet transformed itself into maturity, or even had a chance to practice being mature. So, what happens when our crisis hits? The ego-self tries to address the problem, to protect itself in the best way it knows how. Its first and most compelling instinct is to get rid of anxiety as quickly as possible, because it assumes anxiety is a threat.

And at this point, the ego knows how to accomplish this only by a return to its earlier, more accustomed pattern—that is, making a judgement or taking action, usually by selecting one of the available opposites. In our discussion of the third path, we called this *dia-bol*, choosing half of the union over the other—light over dark, up over down, left over right, masculine over feminine, rote over original, or vice versa.

The most common model is our choice of whatever we perceive is right over wrong. If our "old ways" used to externalize our problems and point fingers at others, this will be what our ego will likely turn to now when it looks for solutions. If we used to abandon unity and our own self by internalizing our fear and going into depression, that same avoidance will call out to us again. *Dia-bol's* lengthy list of possible ways to elude anxiety is almost endless.

This presents us with a new emotional dilemma. We learned in the third path that we need to resist these divisions, yet we have no real idea exactly how to do so. If they are not consciously on the Journey of Quadratos, most people give in to their confusion and discomfort at this point and retreat backward.

SEVEN—WALKING LUKE'S ROAD OF RICHES

The quandary proves too much for them, and they choose a familiar behavior from the second path—or even the first. And after their ego makes some choice of avoidance, it then covers the decision up with a denial system. Psychology calls this "rationalizing."

The ensuing untruths created by the cover-ups and the denials proliferate. In fact, the reason many of us feel we live in an unsatisfactory world is largely a result of the number of people engaging in this continual avoidance and denial behavior over and over and over again. All those untruths add up.

If, however, we make a decision to walk ahead on the fourth path, the crises we meet cannot be covered up. Why? Because transparency and learning to confront our dilemmas directly are part and parcel of the process of maturing.

As we stand in the courage of our journey—remaining steadfast in the times of our inner discomfort, praying, and using Luke's gospel— we begin to fully engage the fourth path. Although, when we stepped ahead in faith and the path opened in crisis, we learn that that powerful onslaught might actually serve a purpose.

Any over-exaltation or arrogance we might have had from our time in the third path needs to be tempered now. "Go slowly" is the very first counsel we receive from Luke. We are asked to shelter our revelation, newly birthed, so that Spirit can nestle deeply, making her home in us comfortable and her course to our inner selves wide and unobstructed.

In this way, the messages of Spirit can live side by side with those of the ever-chattering, control-driven intellect and receive equal attention. We discover that when Mystery is our in-breath, our ego-self will find it easier to quiet and be more patient.

The time does come, however, when Luke firmly instructs us to step out of shelter and grow active in the building of our new lives. This is how we find the answer to the fourth path's core question: How do we mature in service? As we move outward, our journey becomes a tumultuous and passionate adventure in discovering how to recognize and seize our strengths and navigate our relationships.

At times, we undergo rigorous testing. Occasionally, this feels as perilous as crossing a deep chasm on a tightrope with no net beneath us. At other times, the gospel counsels us in a slower and more repetitious fashion. But the lessons are always available for us to use according to our unique needs and rhythms.

We have setbacks, of course, and our increased awareness causes these to be more painful than before. Yet thanks to our third path epiphanies, we are happily sensitized to surpassing bliss. Therefore, no matter what difficulties we encounter we find many more experiences of joy than we have ever known to be possible.

Gradually, as we walk this path we learn how to express our singular and completely original life in a way that serves us—and others. With the help of Matthew and Mark we kept moving—even when scraped by sharp rocks from our past. Now Luke suggests that we recover some of those "sharp edges"—re-examine them, understand and accept them as valuable and even beautiful foundational pieces of our history.

We find ways in which we can build a place of homestead for our genuine life that shelters the full family of our inner self. The unruly child in us has a place to play, and the quiet child, a place to dream. The adult has space for joy, exercise, passion, action, thought, anger, challenge, and the expression of beauty.

The sage of all seasons has space for prayer and making amends and service. Even the rebellious teenager is welcomed. As we honor and commit to protect the infinity of our richness, we recognize that this multitude is, indeed, the solid basis on which our inner peace is built.

Self-acceptance of our originality—and our comfort with it—readily moves outward. We feel less overwhelmed and threatened by diversity of all kinds. We begin to discern previously unseen variances. As we do so, we see the opportunities within them. The outside world becomes a kaleidoscope of flashing possibilities that open to us in ways we could not have previously imagined—in friendships, jobs, and varieties of networks at all levels.

Simultaneously, the path of true service simultaneously begins to open in our lives. Having become more compassionate with ourselves, we naturally carry that into relationships with others. The ways in which we respect each other, act, negotiate, join, separate, and perform service change dramatically. We help our neighbors whenever we can. We invite them to visit and help *us*—although many of us find that reciprocity very difficult.

However, we have come to understand that genuine service, like real relationships, must move in two directions. Gradually, the practice of respect and compassion in our interactions fills our lives with the pragmatic truth that we cannot deprive others of even the smallest freedom and still insist on our own.

It is these lessons that hold the seeds of real solutions to our present-day dilemmas—in communities and institutions (including our churches), in countries, and between nations.

Birthplace of The Gospel of Luke
Great Antioch and the Roman Empire, Mid-80s CE

The precise location of origin is not certain with this gospel, but it is highly likely that we find ourselves once again in the city of Great Antioch on the Orontes. Scholarship indicates that Luke probably wrote from the same city where Matthew had written his gospel a decade or so earlier.

Remember that in Matthew's time Messianic Jews were still part of Judaism, and his gospel concerned itself with the pain of these Jews whose center—the Great Temple and the priestly lineage—had been lost. Luke, believed to have been a companion of Paul and a seasoned follower, almost certainly knew Matthew's gospel well; indeed, he had likely preached from it.

Matthew's gospel addressed a single community, as did those of Mark and John. Luke, however—writing later than Matthew and Mark (though before John), as Christianity was evolving and spreading—directed his message to multiple groups throughout the Mediterranean region.

These communities, only beginning to call themselves Christians, had endured a series of dramatic events in the previous decade, and despite their deep faith and fervor, they found themselves troubled by high levels of pain and resentment.

To understand this fully, we need to briefly review some history. Nero had executed the Jewish Christus followers of Rome twenty years earlier, although persecution had not extended to Christus believers throughout the rest of the empire at that time.

Then in 70 CE, Vespasian leveled the Great Temple of Jerusalem and massacred all its priests, throwing Judaism into total disarray. In the steps that religion took to survive, a process began that still resonates in the lives of Christians and Jews.

The slaughter resulted in a complete lack of religious authority. The Pharisees, educated teachers of Jewish religious law but previously not officially connected to the Temple, stepped into the vacuum. By the mid-80s CE, the time of Luke's gospel, their role had significantly increased.

In many Jewish communities, their voices rose to roles of clear leadership. In others, they represented merely one of many voices struggling to advise how best to move forward in the face of great loss. Eventually, the Pharisees became the primary voice of the Jewish community, reunifying the people in the absence of the Temple and its priests—but not before Luke begins to write.

When the Temple stood, all important rituals were hosted there, and only priests officiated at them. After the Temple fell, all rituals were forced to change dramatically. The Pharisees helped to rebuild a new Judaism that centered on home and synagogue life, with larger roles for the family and the rabbi.

As one example, Seder—the Feast of Passover—had always been a family meal accompanied by an informal retelling of the Jews' coming out of Egypt. Indeed, it was this simple evening meal that Jesus shared with his disciples before the crucifixion.

Now it became more formal. Special, ritual ingredients were designated, as was the sequence of the service and the manner of the retelling. Beginning in the 80s, remaining teachers and sages (largely the Pharisees) started to write down and systematize these changes, making it certain that their faith would survive with its solemnity and resonance intact despite the loss of its hierarchy.

Some of the Pharisees took a further step. Their objective was surely the health and survival of their ancient faith and tribe, and we must assume they believed that wisdom and necessity guided their actions. Nonetheless, the results of the harsh decision they made are with us yet today.

These Pharisees, and we are not certain of their numeric strength, advocated for the removal from Judaism of all variant sects who believed that the Messiah had already come. Chief among these were the Followers of The Way (the Christus sect), who maintained that the Messiah had arrived for the salvation of all people—not just Jews.

These Christus followers persisted in talking about their beliefs to anyone who would listen, complicating what the Pharisees were working so hard to rebuild. To them, the upstarts presented a severe problem, for every convert to Christus belief represented a direct threat to their efforts to sustain Judaism.

The Followers of The Way did not leave their religious home quietly or even voluntarily. Some Pharisees' reactions were draconian. They argued for forcible removal and shunning of the sect, even going so far as having funerals for these individuals and sitting shiva, a seven-day ritual for grieving the dead.

Communities with strong pharisaical influence followed these recommendations. Jewish families and synagogue communities were confused and filled with pain by this rending, whether or not they cooperated with the formal ejections.

Worse still, these Pharisees wrote a formal curse, making the banishment unmistakably clear. And they further recommended that it be added to the close of every Shabbat service. Its words entreated God to bring his wrath down on anyone who believed that the Messiah had come.

Anyone who failed to recite this curse aloud at the end of the service was deemed suspect, which further fractured trust. The family of Abraham was rent asunder by these spiritually shattering events and filled with pain, anger, bitterness, resentment, and self-pity. It was amidst this upheaval that The Gospel of Luke was born.

Reluctantly but surely, Luke's audience is coming to understand that they are being severed from Judaism. They proudly call themselves Followers of The Way, or of the Christus, but are relatively inexperienced as religious communities. They have faith and strength—and no small amount of zealotry. They carry pain, and it is likely that some of them have a touch of arrogance attached to their lingering resentments.

They have also migrated all over the Mediterranean basin. This has presented them with persecution from another quarter. The Roman government is more than nervous about the Christus followers—it is terror-stricken.

The Roman Empire had skillfully used the ancient tribal antipathies of the Mediterranean world first to conquer and then to maintain dominance. The mutual distrust of the people it ruled was the primary way in which the empire ensured the stability of its far-flung realms.

However, as we discussed in John's gospel, the egalitarian principles of Christianity overturned many tribal beliefs and customs that led to conflict. Christian beliefs therefore threatened the entire structure of the Roman Empire. Rome's fear of this message led it to oppress the Christus communities—and the persecution steadily increased.

Although some scholars believe that The Gospel of Luke was written to a high Roman official in defense of Christianity, others think it was a teaching written in Antioch designed to be distributed among these burgeoning communities across the Mediterranean world. Because of its style and its content, the latter view seems more likely—this gospel is a clear "how to" manual.

How were the nascent Followers of The Way to move forward in the face of being cursed by some Pharisees, abandoned by most of their Jewish friends, and oppressed by the Roman Empire? How could they deal with the hurt and resentments that threatened to poison their lives and divide their families?

Should they verbally dispute and defend themselves against each hurt? Should they take up arms and fight? Should they hold to traditional practices? Did the Christ ask them to develop new and original ways? And if yes, what precisely were those new ways in actual practice in their lives?

The Gospel of Luke gives answers to these questions based on the teachings of Jesus, which were radical for their time. Luke draws a stark spiritual line, using his gospel to focus on spiritual maturation. He instructs the Followers of The Way to stringently challenge themselves, speak their truth boldly, yet maintain inner equanimity and avoid self-righteousness.

Faced with opposition on all sides, the course Jesus teaches in Luke's gospel is for the Christus believers to "be" peace, rather than taking up arms or trying to effect change through anger. This gospel is filled with instructions about growing into the capacity for mature relationships and compassion and generosity without boundaries. The transcendent and enduring parables of the Good Samaritan and the Prodigal Son are found only in The Gospel of Luke.

Luke knows these are the pragmatic lessons that will help the zealous new believers to not only survive, but to grow beyond their zealotry. Luke invites the emerging faith into a great adventure of Spirit—a journey of healing, examination, and transformation. He challenges Christianity to cross into unknown lands and thrive, despite social and communal bitterness and legal persecution.

Walking the Road
Approaching Luke Today

As we each walk through the fourth path and The Gospel of Luke, we are tugged in every direction. From the first huge setback most of us hit, to our time of quiet shelter, through our continuing trials—and errors—we are often unsure of our bearings and only know we are committed to carry on.

Gradually, profoundly, and perhaps with a bit of surprise, we realize that our struggles have not been just for our own sake at all. The true questions appear: Whom does the grace we have received serve? How may we bring this grace to everyday life, relationships, and family? When our personal or communal values are challenged, what do we do? What is the proper use of our new strength and courage?

True answers to these questions do not come quickly or easily. Indeed, they will require us to enflesh the way of Jesus the Christ. We will have to be compassionate and fearless—perhaps even act unconventionally in the face of misunderstanding and direct opposition.

Since the Journey of Quadratos is about a maturing spiritual transformation, it now becomes very clear why the early church put The Gospel of Luke fourth in the reading sequence. This is a series of teachings specifically designed to expand on the basic truths of the other gospels and to establish a discipline that moves them into everyday life.

This gospel is also a much fuller story of Jesus' life, from his conception through his death and resurrection. Unlike any of the other gospels, it tells of Jesus' childhood, describing how he "grew in grace and truth." It is, in itself, an account of spiritual maturation.

If we are able to continue in this path—or like the apostle Peter, recover and come back to the path—we discover new moral realizations and a shining courage. As we will learn as we study this gospel, Luke employs the word "heart" throughout as an integrated image of mind/body/spirit. We learn that we can act from our hearts in this expanded sense and when we do, we are freed in a radical way.

We experience the power that comes with speaking and acting from the divine in us *joined* to our inner truth. Not only do we discover that others receive us differently, but our fears diminish and even disappear. We no longer carry the fear of failure—being thought badly of—or being shunned, or betrayed, or the fear of loss; nor are we burdened by the contrary fear of success.

SEVEN—WALKING LUKE'S ROAD OF RICHES

Luke knows that epiphany is of no value in isolation; for that reason, teaching the myriad ways of mature service is his goal. He accomplishes this largely through the structure of his gospel. Almost every important event takes place "on the road," on the land between destinations. This is precisely the same way we mature in the process of our lives—in between experiences and places.

Although Luke is supportive of his readers' fervent beliefs, he is well aware that no one bursts fully formed—wholly integrated—into a mature spiritual life. His use of "road" is, therefore, a precise metaphor for this lengthy and often frustrating time of inner exploration and outer practice.

Though the words seem paradoxical, as we become comfortable with an unceasing process of growth the road eventually reaches its destination within us. We learn to relax and accept our place as part of the continuous process and pattern of Mystery—which will never cast us out—and absorb the strength that knowledge gives us. As we do, we increasingly act to accept our responsibilities as part of the whole.

In this way, we genuinely help transform the world, since most of the horrors created by humankind that occur only in the complicity of our silence or non-action. Our burdens therefore increase—but likewise our joys and relationships, as well as our opportunities for action and empowerment and service.

Additionally, we can surmise while reading The Gospel of Luke, that the author studied other gospels and texts and learned well from them. We believe, for example, that Luke was a disciple of Paul. We will see that their words frequently share a zealous, ardent style.

This zeal likely suited the enthusiasm of Luke's readers. We can also find many places where Luke repeats large sections almost verbatim from The Gospel of Matthew; but as we will see, the "almost" is significant, because Luke brings these accounts to different conclusions than Matthew does in every single instance.

Although Luke predates John (so he could not have read that gospel), he uses one similar technique, often reframing Jewish tradition, making

Christianity the more open and charitable option. Also, similar to John, Luke's resentment against the particular Pharisees who were persecuting Messianic Jews sometimes overwhelms him.

The resulting strident tones, such as a curse or berating text derived from Matthew, sit in odd contradiction to sublime teachings about openness and generosity. These inconsistencies, like those in John's gospel, serve as examples of human struggles in the midst of deep inspiration.

We will examine the gospel in three sections: its opening stories (including the angel Gabriel's appearance to Zechariah and Mary), the nativity, and the account of Jesus in the Temple as a young boy; the middle section containing "the lessons;" and finally, the Passion and the resurrection accounts.

As we read, observe how the straightforward language is perfectly suited to this pragmatic phase of our journey. Note how Luke's almost circuitous style of storytelling holds the rhythm of walking the path, footfall upon footfall, again and again.

This is exactly how we will learn to put these lessons firmly into our lives—with practice and more practice, building habits upon which we can call even in crisis. The first three paths of Quadratos are the (relatively) fast ones. Luke's road holds the greatest riches, but it is also the road of patience and persistence.

A Valuable Mirror
The Acts of the Apostles

The original second half of The Gospel of Luke is known as "The Acts of the Apostles," or what some contemporary authors refer to as "The Book of Mission." Originally, Luke and Acts were considered a single body of work—the longest in the Christian Testament. Acts tells of the apostles Peter and Paul and their lives of service and reflects many of the same themes found in Luke.

It does not appear that Acts was read as a gospel text in any of the ancient Sunday cycles, nor is it found in the contemporary Sunday sequences.

However, Acts does have a place of distinction. Some of its passages are read *before* the gospel text over the Sundays of the Easter Season.

Since it is not in the Sunday cycle, Acts has not been included in this book for study. However, the original intent of both of these volumes—Luke and Acts—was that they work together seamlessly. They have a strikingly similar thematic sequence and development, and can be of great value to us.

I suggest that you read the two volumes side by side if you wish to add additional richness to your journey. For example, read the first two chapters of Luke and then read the first two chapters of Acts. I believe you will discover that they mirror each other, and that what happens with Jesus in Luke happens with Peter and Paul in Acts.

By using the two volumes, you will observe a picture of maturation that moves back and forth between being a disciple and an apostle, learning and serving—the same roles that are true for all Followers of the Way of the Christ.

The Salutation—To the "Lover of God"
The Gospel of Luke: The Opening Stories

Luke's opening salutation to "most excellent Theophilus" has caused great conjecture among scholars. Theophilus translates as "lover of God." However, the words "most excellent" suggest that Luke may have been addressing a wealthy, well-educated Roman official, inviting speculation that this gospel is an apologia for Christianity. In contrast, it has also been proposed that the intention was a generic salutation to *all* "lovers of God."

Despite the controversy, The Gospel of Luke is not a letter at all. It is clearly a book—speaking to the challenges of the early Christians and the great opposition they were facing—and its style differs startlingly from the other gospels. This is no document of great pronouncements.

Rather, though interspersed with zealotry, it is almost chatty. By recounting stories that hold contradictions—and particularly the contravening of convention—Luke encourages his readers to wrestle with ambiguity and to elevate their moral sense.

> *Since many have undertaken to set down an orderly account of the events that have been fulfilled among us, just as they were handed on to us by those who from the beginning were eyewitnesses and servants of the word, I too decided, after investigating everything carefully from the very first, to write an orderly account for you, most excellent Theophilus, so that you may know the truth concerning the things about which you have been instructed. (1:1-4)*

Willingness and Silence
Zechariah and Elizabeth and Mary

Immediately after saluting Theophilus, Luke tells the story of Zechariah and Elizabeth, descended from priestly and royal lineage, and thus "elevated" in Jewish society. Despite this status however, their community assumes they are sinners because they are childless—a clear indication of God's disfavor.

In the Semitic culture of the day, Elizabeth's barrenness is certainly a matter of the deepest shame for the couple. And we can be certain that in their village, tongues wagged and gossip raged to discover their presumed sins. But in fact, Zechariah and Elizabeth are upright and blameless—only childless.

One day while Zechariah serves at Temple, the angel Gabriel comes to him promising that a child, a son, will finally be his, and that the boy will grow up to be very important in Jewish history. Zechariah, though he must have been delighted with the news, is terrified of the angel and reacts with doubt to the prophecy.

Gabriel responds to Zechariah's lack of belief with immediate punishment. He renders the new father mute and thus incapable of sharing the news of his great gift. Elizabeth, for her part, goes into seclusion for five months as soon as she becomes aware of her conception.

SEVEN—WALKING LUKE'S ROAD OF RICHES

The dearth of community support suffered by Zechariah and Elizabeth mirrors the predicament of the Christus communities. They, too, had been faithful followers of a holy journey and had received the announcement of a great birth—a grace to be made visible in their lives. But Judaism, their historical family, had been unable to understand or appreciate that experience. Instead, many in their faith family had responded with curses and shunning.

This is an extremely pointed story—particularly with which to open the gospel. Luke is telling his readers to temper their zeal. "Stop and think," he counsels. "No matter what joy is in your heart, be silent for a time. Gather wisdom before you speak."

Both Zechariah and Elizabeth exemplify the virtues of husbanding an experience and allowing it to grow and mature before it is offered up publicly. Luke knows that euphoria needs time to settle. Resentment from others—which may fester and cannot quickly be overcome—is to be expected. The wise course requires patience.

> *In the days of King Herod of Judea, there was a priest named Zechariah, who belonged to the priestly order of Abijah. His wife was a descendant of Aaron, and her name was Elizabeth. Both of them were righteous before God, living blamelessly according to all the commandments and regulations of the Lord. But they had no children, because Elizabeth was barren, and both were getting on in years. Once when he was serving as priest before God and his section was on duty, he was chosen by lot, according to the custom of the priesthood, to enter the sanctuary of the Lord and offer incense. Now at the time of the incense offering, the whole assembly of the people was praying outside. Then there appeared to him an angel of the Lord, standing at the right side of the altar of incense. When Zechariah saw him, he was terrified; and fear overwhelmed him. But the angel said to him, "Do not be afraid, Zechariah, for your prayer has been heard. Your wife Elizabeth will bear you a son, and you will name him John. You will have joy and gladness, and many will rejoice at his birth, for he will be great in the sight of the Lord. He must never drink wine or strong drink; even before his birth he*

will be filled with the Holy Spirit. He will turn many of the people of Israel to the Lord their God. With the spirit and power of Elijah he will go before him, to turn the hearts of parents to their children, and the disobedient to the wisdom of the righteous, to make ready a people prepared for the Lord." Zechariah said to the angel, "How will I know that this is so? For I am an old man, and my wife is getting on in years." The angel replied, "I am Gabriel. I stand in the presence of God, and I have been sent to speak to you and to bring you this good news. But now, because you did not believe my words, which will be fulfilled in their time, you will become mute, unable to speak, until the day these things occur."

Meanwhile the people were waiting for Zechariah, and wondered at his delay in the sanctuary. When he did come out, he could not speak to them, and they realized that he had seen a vision in the sanctuary. He kept motioning to them and remained unable to speak.

When his time of service was ended, he went to his home. After those days his wife Elizabeth conceived, and for five months she remained in seclusion. She said, "This is what the Lord has done for me when he looked favorably on me and took away the disgrace I have endured among my people." (1:5-25)

The name of the angel Gabriel is extremely significant in Luke's gospel. Nowhere else in the four gospels is an angel identified by name. Gabriel means "God is my strength" in Hebrew, and derives from the traditional Jewish belief that there are four angels who always surround us. Rafael stands behind and represents healing; Oriel stands in front of us and represents illumination or knowledge; Michael is at our right hand and stands for mercy; and Gabriel—power and judgment—is at our left.

Therefore, when Luke invokes the name Gabriel in these deeply cautionary accounts, he emphasizes to the Christus community that the *power* of the Jewish faith has not abandoned them even if the Jewish *community* seemingly has. They can rest assured that they carry God's strength with them into their new lives, and thus they will be protected.

SEVEN—WALKING LUKE'S ROAD OF RICHES

In the same chapter, the angel Gabriel next appears to Mary and tells her that she will give birth to a son she should name Jesus. Mary does not understand how this could be true, because she remains a virgin.

Though she questions Gabriel, she is not frightened, and unlike Zechariah she does not challenge the prophecy. Her response appears to be more an expression of curiosity; she is completely accepting of the prediction, despite her lack of understanding. She wonders how events will unfold, but fully accepts their happening.

Still, she chooses not to speak of the impending birth. She joins Elizabeth in seclusion for three months until her baby is viable, afterward returning home. Luke uses the opportunity to strongly reiterate his point: "Even for a gift as great as the birth of the Messiah," he seems to say, "my advice is to stay silent and allow time for the seed to mature before you speak or act."

In Matthew's gospel, it is Joseph who receives the prediction about Jesus' birth from an unnamed angel. In fact, the entire birth narrative revolves around Joseph and his predicament and his actions. In Luke's gospel however, Joseph receives only a mention. Everything here—the announcement and as we will see, the subsequent nativity story—focuses on Mary.

> *In the sixth month the angel Gabriel was sent by God to a town in Galilee called Nazareth, to a virgin engaged to a man whose name was Joseph, of the house of David. The virgin's name was Mary. And he came to her and said, "Greetings, favored one! The Lord is with you." But she was much perplexed by his words and pondered what sort of greeting this might be. The angel said to her, "Do not be afraid, Mary, for you have found favor with God. And now, you will conceive in your womb and bear a son, and you will name him Jesus. He will be great, and will be called the Son of the Most High, and the Lord God will give to him the throne of his ancestor David. He will reign over the house of Jacob forever, and of his kingdom there will be no end." Mary said to the angel, "How can this be, since I am a virgin?" The angel said to her, "The*

> *Holy Spirit will come upon you, and the power of the Most High will overshadow you; therefore the child to be born will be holy; he will be called Son of God. And now, your relative Elizabeth in her old age has also conceived a son; and this is the sixth month for her who was said to be barren. For nothing will be impossible with God." Then Mary said, "Here am I, the servant of the Lord; let it be with me according to your word." Then the angel departed from her. (1:26-38)*

Mary goes to visit Elizabeth in her seclusion-place in Judea. When greeted, Mary responds to Elizabeth in verses that form a hymn of praise commonly called the Canticle of Mary. The words are lovely, but the most interesting part about them spiritually and psychologically, is their grammatical tense.

They speak of a future time, of circumstances that many are hoping will come to pass—yet they are written in declarative present and past tense, as though the events they describe have already taken place, giving the beauteous prose the voice of one who walks in the equanimity of total faith, seeing the future as already inevitable and perfected.

The way this hymn is written makes it the prayer and practice of one who holds a clear, positive vision of the future. Anyone who reads and prays these words is challenged to find an inner spiritual level that matches their serenity, which is clearly Luke's intention. Luke hopes that his audience will be able to use Mary and her prayer as a model from which to derive an unshakeable strength.

> *In those days Mary set out and went with haste to a Judean town in the hill country, where she entered the house of Zechariah and greeted Elizabeth. (1:39-40)*
>
> *And Mary said,*
> *"My soul magnifies the Lord,*
> *and my spirit rejoices in God my Savior,*
> *For he has looked with favor on the lowliness of his servant.*
> *Surely, from now on all generations will call me blessed;*
> *For the Mighty One has done great things for me,*
> *and holy is his name.*

*His mercy is for those who fear him
from generation to generation.
He has shown strength with his arm;
He has scattered the proud in the thoughts of their hearts.
He has brought down the powerful from their thrones,
And lifted up the lowly;
He has filled the hungry with good things,
And sent the rich away empty.
He has helped his servant Israel,
In remembrance of his mercy,
According to the promise he made to our ancestors,
To Abraham and to his descendants forever." (1:46–55)*

Welcome the Unfamiliar
The Nativity Account

The nativity story is distinctive in Luke's gospel. The author uses it to illustrate another profound spiritual practice. In Luke's account, Joseph and Mary live in Nazareth in times that were both civilly and religiously oppressive. Authorities order them to Bethlehem for "census taking."

Unlike the nativity found in Matthew's gospel, where a star announces Jesus' birth and where the illustrious Magi follow that star and are adoring witnesses who pay homage, here we find no comfortable home birth. In Luke's account, Mary and Joseph are forced to leave home and travel when Mary is near to term. They don't even have the shelter of an inn.

Instead, Jesus is born in a stable, a rough room that houses animals, likely open, attached to a house or another open building. His tiny body rests in a manger, a feedbox. The environment as described could not have been more raw, instinctual, uncomfortable—or unconventional.

Yet the manger as birthplace was an apt metaphor for Luke's readers. They, too, had been cast out of their original home, and hospitality in their new environment was meager. But Luke challenges them to transcend their bitterness and resentment. He asks them to see that their uncomfortable new circumstances are the perfect, powerful, and perhaps even *destined* way that the Christ can be born in them.

Luke tells of an angel that announces Jesus' birth to shepherds in the nighttime fields. But when he writes of shepherds, he certainly does not mean those passive fellows leaning on their crooks or carrying a lamb that we see today in crèche scenes at Christmastime.

In the first century shepherds were outcasts, people who had few skills, no resources, and little family. Feared, they lived lives of near starvation, isolated from regular society. Our present equivalent might be the marginalized long-term homeless. Fairly or unfairly, they were considered to be an unstable element, potentially thieving and dangerous. In this scene they represent an extremely uncouth presence.

Yet—in a detail recounted only in Luke's gospel—the angel who announces Jesus' birth came to these lowly and unwanted people not just to accept them, but to honor them and rejoice with them. Notably, they are also the only witnesses of Jesus' birth. As for Mary, although she is clearly the central figure in the scene, she remains silent throughout as she had during her pregnancy, holding her experience "in her heart."

Even though the births in the gospels of Matthew and Luke differ so greatly, spiritually and psychologically both are profoundly true. Matthew is writing to Messianic Jews still in their "home" faith. Luke writes to Christus believers who felt as though they had been cast out onto a lonely road and were surrounded by predators.

Matthew's charge is to hold trust and courage and to "begin anew" no matter what. Luke reminds his readers that their seeming exile offers the perfect conditions for the Christ's birth in them. He encourages them to be curious about the place in which they now find themselves—this rough home on the road—and to rejoice in their blessings, knowing that their future is bright.

In Luke, the baby Jesus is twice referred to as "wrapped in bands of cloth"—swaddled—held secure with strips of fabric binding his arms and legs. This is a great metaphor for the newly "birthed" communities who are equally held securely by the divine truths of their faith. Luke is teaching about the need to focus on basics.

SEVEN—WALKING LUKE'S ROAD OF RICHES

It is not a time for wandering about or reckless speech. It is the time for protecting the infant Christians as they grow in faith, in effect "traveling away" from their original home. Once again, Luke's counsel is to ponder and move out slowly.

> *In those days a decree went out from Emperor Augustus that all the world should be registered. This was the first registration and was taken while Quirinius was governor of Syria. All went to their own towns to be registered. Joseph also went from the town of Nazareth in Galilee to Judea, to the city of David called Bethlehem, because he was descended from the house and family of David. He went to be registered with Mary, to whom he was engaged and who was expecting a child. While they were there, the time came for her to deliver her child. And she gave birth to her firstborn son and wrapped him in bands of cloth, and laid him in a manger, because there was no place for them in the inn. In that region there were shepherds living in the fields, keeping watch over their flock by night. Then an angel of the Lord stood before them, and the glory of the Lord shone around them, and they were terrified. But the angel said to them, "Do not be afraid; for see—I am bringing you good news of great joy for all the people: to you is born this day in the city of David a Savior, who is the Messiah, the Lord. This will be a sign for you: you will find a child wrapped in bands of cloth and lying in a manger." And suddenly there was with the angel a multitude of the heavenly host, praising God and saying, "Glory to God in the highest heaven, and on earth peace among those whom he favors!" When the angels had left them and gone into heaven, the shepherds said to one another, "Let us go now to Bethlehem and see this thing that has taken place, which the Lord has made known to us." So they went with haste and found Mary and Joseph, and the child lying in the manger. When they saw this, they made known what had been told them about this child; and all who heard it were amazed at what the shepherds told them. But Mary treasured all these words and pondered them in her heart. (2:1–19)*

A Quality of Heart
The Boy Jesus in the Temple

The sole place in the entire gospels to tell of Jesus in his childhood follows. Luke recounts that in the year Jesus is twelve years old, Joseph and Mary, accompanied by many other faithful Jews, take him on their annual expedition to Jerusalem to celebrate Passover. On their return, Jesus somehow manages to stay behind.

His parents, assuming he is with others in the crowd, are completely unaware he is missing. When they realize he is gone, they hurry back to the city in search of him. They find Jesus in the Temple, intently questioning the teachers there.

This account is particularly fascinating as a demonstration of Luke's ability to delicately balance sensitive emotional realities, because Luke uses it as a metaphor for the young Christus community. We know this because a literal reading is clearly not fruitful—a twelve-year-old, not yet bar mitzvahed, would have been deemed too young to have been allowed to converse in the Temple.

When queried by Joseph and Mary about why he went to the Temple, Jesus respectfully refers to it as "my Father's house." And there he was, on the cusp of adulthood. Luke says little more, only that he subsequently *matures* in age and spiritual understanding.

Luke's message is that the Christus followers, who began in Judaism, should honor their early foundation. However, they need to realize that their genuine strength and maturity is to be found in the present—in a departure from their home faith.

Luke again counsels patience when he refers to Mary watching her son's maturation. He takes note that every stage is important. None can be skipped. This chapter reiterates Luke's earlier advice to ponder and reflect, and still using Mary as the focus, says that she "treasured these things in her heart."

Luke not only uses the word "heart" twice as many times in this gospel as do any of the other gospel writers, but he uses it differently. In Matthew and Mark, Jesus speaks about the quality of "heart" in those who follow or do not follow. John recognizes that strong emotion is necessary to balance intellect, but he does not use the word heart for this—he employs the word "grief" to express this principle. Luke, however, prefers the word "heart," perhaps because of its well-established Jewish antecedents.

However—in Luke's account—although "heart" is used, and used a great deal, Jesus does not speak the word himself. Instead, Luke uses it to exemplify the character and attitudes of Jesus' followers: twice with respect to Mary; with John at the river; in chapters six, eighteen, and twenty-one; and finally, in the first resurrection appearance. What is the purpose of this frequent and singular reference?

"Heart" as Luke applies it, is certainly connected to the emphasis on Mary in the nativity, and very likely is also intended to connect to earlier Hebraic traditions. In Hebrew teachings, "heart" implies a unitive aspect of one's humanity that is greater than mere emotion—encompassing body, feelings, will, intuition, and thought—everything but soul.

Consider these words from Deuteronomy: ***"You shall love the Lord your God with all your heart, and with all your soul, and with all your might. Keep these words that I am commanding you today in your heart."*** **(6:5-6)** These are part of the verses put in mezuzahs on the doorposts of Jewish houses and are also part of the daily liturgy.

Luke wants his audience to understand that the road to spiritual maturity winds through compassion—a path of the feminine, the intuitive, and leads to the integrated heart in this fully unitive sense. The early appearance of the iconic angel Gabriel, and now the metaphor of heart, both resonate as Luke brings forth these well-understood Jewish truths to powerfully amplify his message.

> ***When they had finished everything required by the law of the Lord, they returned to Galilee, to their own town of Nazareth. The child grew and became strong, filled with wisdom; and the favor of God was upon him. Now every***

year his parents went to Jerusalem for the festival of the Passover. And when he was twelve years old, they went up as usual for the festival. When the festival was ended and they started to return, the boy Jesus stayed behind in Jerusalem, but his parents did not know it. Assuming that he was in the group of travelers, they went a day's journey. Then they started to look for him among their relatives and friends. When they did not find him, they returned to Jerusalem to search for him. After three days they found him in the temple, sitting among the teachers, listening to them and asking them questions. And all who heard him were amazed at his understanding and his answers. When his parents saw him they were astonished; and his mother said to him, "Child, why have you treated us like this? Look, your father and I have been searching for you in great anxiety." He said to them, "Why were you searching for me? Did you not know that I must be in my Father's house?" But they did not understand what he said to them.

Then he went down with them and came to Nazareth, and was obedient to them. His mother treasured all these things in her heart.

And Jesus increased in wisdom and in years, and in divine and human favor. (2:39–52)

The fourth path is one of maturing practice, and it is long, steady, seemingly repetitive. The first lesson is, "Be silent!" and it is carried by the announcement stories of Zechariah, Elizabeth, and Mary. In varying ways, they tell us to welcome new experience, but to abide before we speak to others or act on that experience, so that the appropriate discernment can be developed.

This appears similar to the practice of the third path, where we were told to sit in the garden and reflect on our revelation. Yet this advice differs in its intention. In the third path, our waiting allowed us to become aware of the gifts we had received—revelation and the reality of union.

Now the reason for our delay is so that we will have the time and opportunity to gradually develop an *integrated response* to events in our lives—particularly to crises. Studies have shown that a quick and instinctive first response is good when taking multiple-choice tests. It is almost certainly not a productive way to address almost any other problem, however—whether the problem is with children, a relationship, work, one's community, or the discernment of inner truth.

Certainly there can be emergencies that overturn this rule; but generally time should be taken to evaluate options. Meditation takes time, as does the discovery of a proper and loving course. Yet even if we do not devote ourselves to any deep discernment whatsoever, long human experience shows that the habit of keeping silent for a time before speaking will yield great benefits in our lives. "Hush!"

Luke's stories go on to tell us that when we do contemplate and pray, we should have faith in what we discover in that inner process. Real transformations take place at a very basic inner level. It is simultaneously terrifically delicate and intensely dynamic. Will we be able to coax our ego-self away from its determined role as the holder of rigid boundaries into a new future that is more flexible and more consonant with the divine reality of *sym-bol*?

Our threatened ego-selves resisted change in the second path, but that was nothing compared to what happens now. Look at Zechariah. When change appeared wearing the face of the angel Gabriel, he was "terrified; and fear overwhelmed him." We have begun to comprehend that the greater responsibilities of our new lives may well give us much greater trepidation.

When we feel increased anxieties, rigidity, or judgment, we can be certain these are all signals of our immature ego resisting transformation. Eventually, though, our fears will dissipate. Beginning our day with a time of contemplation will help immensely.

In meditation, we can review the gifts in our life. We can be thoughtful about our dilemmas. We can ask for help from God in these challenges. We can even request a deeper bond with the frightened aspects of ourselves and actually "speak" with them, assuring them that they needn't fear— that greater safety and connection, which will comfort them too, is the goal.

Even though most of us won't find ourselves in small gossipy towns when our lives genuinely change, we will also need to be prepared for opposition that comes from without. Often the fiercest criticisms will be heard from our closest family and friends. Be neither surprised by this nor resentful.

Every change we make asks them to make adjustments also. Life asks them to alter their picture of us in many ways, their expectations, and their ways of relating to us. This is difficult for them. Be compassionate. Our new lives will be easier if we follow the example of Mary, who went to join Elizabeth, and seek out people who are likewise on a spiritual or transformative journey.

Those with similar experiences of transformation will be able to share with us and support us in our efforts. The best recommendation is to meet our own and others' resistance with a reflective—even playful—curiosity, holding our attitudes as lightly and flexibly as we can: "I wonder how all this will turn out—how unexpected circumstances will intervene to use this situation for the best?"

The Canticle of Mary expresses the future design of the Great Mystery as perfect. It shows us that we are already a part of a wondrous and beautiful plan. Many scientists of today have constructed mathematical formulas concluding that there is no such thing as linear time—that present, past, and future are mathematically one. Mary's Canticle held that exalted insight almost two millennia ago and still offers it to us today.

As we walk through our daily lives on the hard ground of what we call "reality" this may seem like the most arrant nonsense or some sort of silly crystal-gazing, yet many well-respected physicists and mathematicians with advanced degrees from major institutions would disagree. Before you mock too heartily, remember that there was a time when Galileo was imprisoned for expounding the theory of a round Earth when everyone else thought the world was flat. If we believe in the power of holding a positive vision of the future, and if we can hold Mary's insight as a clear mental picture on our journey, our belief cannot fail to help us walk with an unshakeable equanimity through trying days.

Why? Because holding a positive system of belief is an extremely pragmatic approach psychologically and spiritually. We tend to act in the direction of our expectations, therefore a sincere faith that things will be well inspires us to behave in a manner that creates positive effects in ourselves and others. Consequently things do improve. Physiologically, many parts of our brains and our bodies are outside our conscious control and do what *they* deem best for the individual as a whole system, often based on survival needs.

Even on a more conscious level, when we hold a belief that "things" are improving, on a core level our behavior will be more expansive and relaxed. We will tend to engage in activities that invest in a future that we feel is growing and beneficent.

That behavior will lead in turn, to responses from others that will generally tend to be positive and expansive. And with positive behavior that pattern continues. Conversely, if we believe that "things" are getting worse, then despite our best efforts to be benevolent, our core behavior will tend to be contracted, because this is an appropriate survival response. Our unavoidable negativity will then generate corresponding negativity and encourage more contraction in others.

Holding a positive vision does not mean being unrealistic or denying our full personality in any way whatsoever, as is conveyed by the shepherds and the manger at Jesus' birth. These visitors to the divine event and its rough location stand for the rudest, crudest, most hidden and instinctual aspects we each carry within ourselves.

In earlier paths we made their acquaintance and identified their sources, but now we must invite them into our home and make a place for them at the birth of our new self and in our ensuing life—no matter how uncomfortable we may find that job.

This welcome is not a passive task, for Luke shows that the angels went out to the shepherds. In the same way, the aspects of ourselves that we think of as our "highest" must seek out those we think of as our "lowest" or "ugliest," so that the two may come together in the fertile beginnings of what psychologists call "integration."

This is difficult and gradual, and the work is far more than mere acceptance. Acceptance all too readily becomes resignation. This task asks that we truly love and rejoice in those "lowly" aspects and fully join with them. Only in this way can we ensure that we have all the parts of us available when we need them for appropriate action—that no part of us has been cut off or repressed.

So how do we perform this joining? Some of us might find ourselves guided by a psychotherapist, a spiritual director, or a master teacher. But what if we don't have, or don't choose to make use of, these resources? What do we do?

Probably the best basic process for self-remedy is described by the fourth step of twelve-step recovery programs: "Make a searching and fearless moral inventory." Take as long as is necessary to *write it all down*. Not only should both strengths and weaknesses be revealed, but they should be shared with a trusted friend or counselor.

Though we suggested this in the second path, keep in mind that we have reached a different phase of growth, one with new understandings and a different purpose. It is time to do this again. We need to find our angels and send them out to join our shepherds. The angels need the deep grounding bass of the instinctual self, and the shepherds need the soprano tones of hope. Together they can sound a holy chorus.

Luke used the account of the young Jesus in the Temple to "reframe" Jesus' early years in order to mirror and support the experience of his audience. We can likewise use this story to understand that our lives hold many elements. As we grow, much of our history will remain valuable—even essential—while other parts will need to be discarded.

Transformation will require some shedding—but of what? What do we need to preserve, and what do we need to leave behind in order to move forward—and what is the proper timing? We examined our history in the second path and looked for the tentacles of division in the third, but now our chore is more complicated. We must continue those tasks while learning to convert our discoveries into productive behaviors that will endure.

SEVEN—WALKING LUKE'S ROAD OF RICHES

There are myriad dilemmas in this process of deciding on and implementing change. Many people have been raised in a particular faith and cherish their tradition as an unwavering and nourishing certainty throughout their lives, while others have an early experience of religion that is abusive and later decide to leave their tradition for a different faith or for none at all.

Family is equally complicated: a family of birth can be wonderful and supportive—but it can also be terrible and hurtful. Marriages and partnerships offer continual testing, as do careers and employment.

A mature life must make difficult decisions about change regardless of society's expectations, and must do so on a fairly regular basis. Only discernments made from the most patient waiting, respectful dialogue, attentive prayer, and the considered work of our fullest selves can tell us whether in a particular instance, we should stay where we are or cast a part of our lives aside.

Some of us resist any movement whatsoever because it is too frightening, too foreign. Others of us find ourselves drawn to change merely for the sake of change—longing for an idyllic (and nonexistent) "other" person or place or condition.

Another risk is the danger of moving to the rigidly opposite position of whatever wounded us, without understanding that this is only a new title for a wound that is still alive and well, and sadly unaddressed. As examples of this, think of children of alcoholics who despite no problem with alcohol, become inflexible and unforgiving teetotalers; or those who, injured by marriage, swear off committed relationships permanently.

Enormous change in beliefs and circumstances we value greatly requires—and deserves—enormous examination. If we do decide to move in a different direction, how do we take our leave and when? How do we prepare ourselves for the inevitable process of grief that always follows loss? What will our responsibilities be if our choices initiate grief or pain or damage within others?

All of these issues are closely tied to Luke's expansive use of the word "heart." When the angel Gabriel came to Mary with news of momentous change, she received his message with her *heart* and was not terrified as Zechariah had been. Luke's Hebraic "heart" calls us to experience the world not only from the rational and linear perspectives, but also from the nonrational and nonlinear, counting them as co-equal.

Throughout the gospel, Luke uses the word "heart" to mean mind, body, and feelings all together. The pulsing heart is also an apt metaphor for the movement of our lives in the fourth path of the Quadratos journey. We move inward in contemplation then outward in action. Depending on our personality type, some of us may move in the opposite direction. Nonetheless, the rhythm of alternating movement remains the same.

This is a pattern we will find in this gospel. It is one to put into place in our lives. Gradually, as we become conversant with it we will find it becomes a comfortable and natural practice. From the place of heart, we move deeper and further.

Right Action, Accountability and Risk-Taking
Speak and Act in Truth: John Son of Zechariah

Luke begins chapter three with a recitation of names that would have evoked a sordid history of temporal and spiritual corruption to his contemporaries: Tiberius, Pontius Pilate, Herod, Philip, and the high priests Annas and Caiaphas. As he moves on into references from the book of Isaiah that plead for repentance and forgiveness, John enters the narrative.

In this gospel, John is identified by his first name, and as the son of Zechariah (who is a priest). He is the child of whose birth we read earlier. He is also the same John identified as John the Baptist in the Gospels of Matthew and Mark and simply as "John" in The Gospel of John.

In each gospel, John performs mikvahs, or Jewish baptisms at the River Jordan. In each, his appearance also announces the arrival of a particular spiritual practice. In Matthew, John urges the new journey out from the place of the old Temple. In Mark, his call is to endure the trial of "repentance" in the wilderness, which we can now recognize as the second path of Quadratos.

In The Gospel of John, he points to, and proclaims, the great visionary reality of Jesus the Christ, the glorious epiphany of the third path. In Luke, John calls the assembled crowd to accountability for their actions as they begin the long walk to full maturity.

In all four gospels John quotes from Isaiah, concluding his words in the other three with, "Prepare the way of the Lord, make his path straight." In Luke, however, John speaks an additional five lyrical lines of joyous prophecy assuring all present that:

> *Every valley shall be filled,*
> *and every mountain and hill shall be made low,*
> *and the crooked shall be made straight,*
> *and the rough ways made smooth;*
> *and all flesh shall see the salvation of God. (3:5–6)*

John's next words address "the crowd." This time, unlike in Matthew's gospel, there is no distinction made between the crowd and the Pharisees and Sadducees. No one escapes his scathing judgment. John rails against every last person present as part of the "brood of vipers" whom he challenges to "bear fruits worthy of repentance."

What does this mean? Luke means, in these words he attributes to John, that the message of Jesus the Christ requires that *everyone* make a genuine correction of their conscience and a change in their behavior, or else they are not genuinely maturing. Merely asking for forgiveness does not suffice.

When the crowd requests specific advice, John's response focuses on actual practice rather than ideology. He calls his listeners to lives of scrupulous honesty, moderation, and sharing. He gives clear examples to each group present. He speaks with such maturity and strength that he prompts queries as to whether he himself is the Messiah.

Yet he claims no personal power, declaring himself merely a vessel for a higher divinity. This was a pointed lesson to teachers and evangelists of the new faith to maintain perspective and not misinterpret the adulation that inevitably arises in the relationship of teacher and student.

This instruction makes Luke's gospel very, very different from Matthew's. In that gospel, John separates out those he perceived as the historic villains, pointing his literary finger at them as the "vipers." Luke does not make that separation. His John gave a charge to every single person present at the River Jordan, and the overall message is not literary.

Rather, his concern is the evidence of lives changed through the practice of charity and justice. As far as Luke is concerned, if one fails to "bear fruits" from one's faith—from grace received—then one is morally equivalent to a "viper" whose poison will kill that very grace.

His moral judgment is directed to the practice of the person, rather than to that person's status or tradition. Luke attempts to encourage his audience to think of people as individuals rather than as categories. Additionally, he directs his words not only to the Christus believers, but also to the Jewish community as a plea against the influence of certain Pharisees.

> *In the fifteenth year of the reign of Emperor Tiberius, when Pontius Pilate was governor of Judea, and Herod was ruler of Galilee, and his brother Philip ruler of the region of Ituraea and Trachonitis, and Lysanias ruler of Abilene, during the high priesthood of Annas and Caiaphas, the word of God came to John son of Zechariah in the wilderness. He went into all the region around the Jordan, proclaiming a baptism of repentance for the forgiveness of sins, as it is written in the book of the words of the prophet Isaiah,*
>
> *"The voice of one crying out in the wilderness:*
> *'Prepare the way of the Lord, make his paths straight. Every valley shall be filled,*

SEVEN—WALKING LUKE'S ROAD OF RICHES

and every mountain and hill shall be made low,
and the crooked shall be made straight,
and the rough ways made smooth;
and all flesh shall see the salvation of God.'"

John said to the crowds that came out to be baptized by him, "You brood of vipers! Who warned you to flee from the wrath to come? Bear fruits worthy of repentance. Do not begin to say to yourselves, 'We have Abraham as our ancestor'; for I tell you, God is able from these stones to raise up children to Abraham. Even now the ax is lying at the root of the trees; every tree therefore that does not bear good fruit is cut down and thrown into the fire." And the crowds asked him, "What then should we do?" In reply he said to them, "Whoever has two coats must share with anyone who has none; and whoever has food must do likewise." Even tax collectors came to be baptized, and they asked him, "Teacher, what should we do?" He said to them, "Collect no more than the amount prescribed for you." Soldiers also asked him, "And we, what should we do?" He said to them, "Do not extort money from anyone by threats or false accusation, and be satisfied with your wages. As the people were filled with expectation, and all were questioning in their hearts concerning John, whether he might be the Messiah, John answered all of them by saying, "I baptize you with water; but one who is more powerful than I is coming; I am not worthy to untie the thong of his sandals. He will baptize you with the Holy Spirit and fire. His winnowing fork is in his hand, to clear his threshing floor and to gather the wheat into his granary; but the chaff he will burn with unquenchable fire." (3:1-17)

The scenes of John son of Zechariah at the river provide a prologue to the concrete actions offered up and reiterated throughout this gospel. And these are the deeds that will call us out of our silence and contemplation. Using John as an example, one of the primary steps is our obligation to step out from the crowd and speak and act truthfully and compassionately despite our fear.

John used the word "crowd" to emphasize the groupthink and moral paralysis that Luke scorns, and likewise John referred to the roots of the trees that bear the "good fruit." This is an important reminder to us that our actions in the fourth path must flow from whole and integrated attitudes, not just from our intellect or our emotion.

If they originate from our separated self, then our actions will likely be contaminated by fear. Although they may have the appearance of wisdom or of charity, false motives will inevitably lie just beneath their surface. They will be a retreat from our journey.

In the third path, we came to understand the *nature* of union. Now in the fourth, it becomes our work to learn how to *act* on that truth—and to act against its opposite. What does this mean? The principle means that we will act and speak from our fullest individual truth, using as much of our integrated self as we can muster, and that we will not shrink from speaking and acting because we are fearful.

But it also means that we will reject the pull of the group. We won't laugh at derogatory jokes, even when everyone else does. When they are made, we might even choose to quietly say something that asserts our contrary truth. When we read media stories, we will think through *both* sides of issues and ask ourselves in what ways both sides are right and in what ways both sides are wrong.

We will query ourselves about how each issue both affects and effects short-term and long-term values that matter to us. After we have done so, we will determine what our genuine opinion is. If we feel strongly and contrarily, we will perhaps find a way to take effective action—action that goes beyond ego-based rhetoric and disparaging others.

Keep Your Path Straight
The Temptations

The devil's attempted seduction of Jesus by three temptations is found only in the gospels of Matthew and Luke. A cursory reading might count them as the same stories, but they are actually subtly nuanced for the unique experience of the communities to whom they are directed.

Matthew's gospel was written in the aftermath of the annihilation of the Temple and the massacre of all its priests. In his version Jesus spends forty days in the desert and the tempter appears at the end of that period.

Luke, however, depicts the tempter taunting Jesus continuously throughout his exile and making the three climactic appearances at the end. This is the emotional experience of the late-first-century Christus followers to whom Luke was writing. They feel constantly bereft, and surely intermittently angry as they struggle with Roman oppression and the process of being cast out of their Jewish home—conditions likely to continue for generations.

It is meaningful that Luke notes Jesus is "about thirty years old," has been baptized, and is "full of the Holy Spirit." The average life expectancy for a man in Palestine at that time was mid to late thirties. In these stories, then, Jesus would have been considered well past the prime of his life. He is a seasoned elder teaching people much younger than he.

The tempter was a metaphor for the short-term, expedient course. He leaves temporarily, "until an opportune time." Due to his age, Jesus represents human as well as divine wisdom. He had actually experienced temptations and uncertainty and was therefore pragmatically credible as well as inspiring for first-century Christus followers.

In the first temptation, the devil taunts Jesus to show his power by making a loaf of bread out of stone. Significantly, Luke uses the singular, "stone," although in Matthew, the word is the plural, "stones." Luke refers to a single stone, thereby conjuring the image of a foundation's cornerstone newly laid, while Matthew, speaking to another audience, evokes the many stones of the former Temple and creates an image of them fallen, lost, and useless.

Here the temptation lies in the insubstantiality of short-term gratification represented by bread to be consumed versus the rewards of long-term effort symbolized by the stone as part of a foundation of faith. "This is the first stone you are putting down," Luke is saying. "This is about your commitment to the work of faith. Spirit will sustain you."

Luke's depiction of the second temptation is also similar to that of Matthew, but there are two differences. This temptation is placed second by Luke instead of Matthew's third, probably because Luke's readers would find it the greater temptation. In it, the devil shows Jesus "all the kingdoms" and offers power and "all this authority" over them if he will only worship the tempter.

This is a poignant message to the Christians, who would certainly have been strongly drawn by the opportunity to set themselves above their persecutors. By expanding the temptation with "all this authority"—meaning control over religious and temporal realms (words not found in Matthew)—Luke heightens the message of enticement for the oppressed Christus believers. He understood that any form of self-righteousness, no matter how desirable it felt, would only have increased strife in the community, ultimately leading to increased persecution of the heavily outnumbered group.

In the last temptation, which places Jesus on the pinnacle of the Temple and dares him to throw himself down, the tempter mocks Jesus with the words "[God] … will command his angels concerning you, to protect you." Luke quotes from Psalm 91, which is devoted entirely to words about rescue and safety.

In contrast, the word "protect" does not appear anywhere in Matthew's text. Luke understood the deep longing for personal protection in the hearts of his readers, especially since the tempter challenged Jesus to doubt God's protection and act stupidly.

This reference to Psalm 91, the word "protect," and the dramatic image of Jesus perched precariously atop the symbol of Judaism could scarcely be a more direct message. "Do not be rash in your actions," Luke counsels. "Your position feels frightening, but testing God is only arrogance—not a true path of faith. Faith is a steady journey of living and growing in truth. Do not be tempted. Do not let the frightened part of yourself determine the course you take."

SEVEN—WALKING LUKE'S ROAD OF RICHES

> *Jesus, full of the Holy Spirit, returned from the Jordan and was led by the Spirit in the wilderness, where for forty days he was tempted by the devil. He ate nothing at all during those days, and when they were over, he was famished. The devil said to him, "If you are the Son of God, command this stone to become a loaf of bread." Jesus answered him, "It is written, 'One does not live by bread alone.'" Then the devil led him up and showed him in an instant all the kingdoms of the world. And the devil said to him, "To you I will give their glory and all this authority; for it has been given over to me, and I give it to anyone I please. If you, then, will worship me, it will all be yours." Jesus answered him, "It is written, 'Worship the Lord your God, and serve only him.'" Then the devil took him to Jerusalem, and placed him on the pinnacle of the temple, saying to him, "If you are the Son of God, throw yourself down from here, for it is written, 'He will command his angels concerning you, to protect you,' and 'On their hands they will bear you up, so that you will not dash your foot against a stone.'" Jesus answered him, "It is said, 'Do not put the Lord your God to the test.'" When the devil had finished every test, he departed from him until an opportune time. (4:1–13)*

After Jesus struggled with the devil, he leaves the desert and returns to the region of Galilee where he travels from place to place preaching and performing miracles.

In one notable story, Jesus goes to a synagogue in Nazareth, and in the midst of his family and neighbors reads a portion of a scroll from Isaiah.

The scroll's text proclaims an anointing and the bringing of good news to the poor, captive, blind, oppressed, and others.

Those assembled congratulate Jesus, and he perceives their unspoken desire for him to perform miracles for them—"the things we have heard you did at Capernaum." Jesus not only demurs but chides the crowd.

He recounts the ancient story of Elijah, who though the land was filled with people in desperate need of miracles, had refused, granting only a single miracle—and that one for a gentile. Reproached, the Nazarene congregation becomes enraged and arise en masse, driving Jesus out of the town and toward a cliff over which they plan to hurl him. But Luke recounts "he passes through" their midst "and goes on his way."

Through this wonderful story, Luke illustrates the resistance of the old social and religious frameworks to a new message that encourages the inclusion of all—even "gentiles." "Expect anger," Luke is saying, "and do not be surprised if it comes in groups that threaten your life.

Remember this example of Jesus in Nazareth. He proclaims his truth—a universal love that supplants tribalism—and when people rise against him, he does not back down; nor does he argue or dispute. Filled with the power of the Spirit, he simply ignores the rage directed against him and walks away, going about his business."

> *Then Jesus, filled with the power of the Spirit, returned to Galilee, and a report about him spread through all the surrounding country. He began to teach in their synagogues and was praised by everyone. When he came to Nazareth, where he had been brought up, he went to the synagogue on the sabbath day, as was his custom. He stood up to read, and the scroll of the prophet Isaiah was given to him. He unrolled the scroll and found the place where it was written:*
>
> *"The Spirit of the Lord is upon me,*
> *because he has anointed me*
> *to bring good news to the poor.*
> *He has sent me to proclaim release to the captives*
> *and recovery of sight to the blind,*
> *to let the oppressed go free,*
> *to proclaim the year of the Lord's favor."*
>
> *And he rolled up the scroll, gave it back to the attendant, and sat down. The eyes of all in the synagogue were fixed on him. Then he began to say to them, "Today this scripture has been fulfilled in your hearing." All spoke well of him and were amazed at the gracious words that came*

from his mouth. They said, "Is not this Joseph's son?" He said to them, "Doubtless you will quote to me this proverb, 'Doctor, cure yourself!' And you will say, 'Do here also in your hometown the things that we have heard you did at Capernaum.'" And he said, "Truly I tell you, no prophet is accepted in the prophet's hometown. But the truth is, there were many widows in Israel in the time of Elijah, when the heaven was shut up three years and six months, and there was a severe famine over all the land; yet Elijah was sent to none of them except to a widow at Zarephath in Sidon. There were also many lepers in Israel in the time of the prophet Elisha, and none of them was cleansed except Naaman the Syrian." When they heard this, all in the synagogue were filled with rage. They got up, drove him out of the town, and led him to the brow of the hill on which their town was built, so that they might hurl him off the cliff. But he passed through the midst of them and went on his way. (4:14–30)

Gifts of Response-ability
The Beatitudes

At every turn, in ways large and small, Luke's gospel cultivates the development of a maturing practice of faith. Luke shows Jesus departing to pray in advance of every significant action. In the sixth chapter, Jesus returns from his prayer and calls all the disciples together. From the group he designates twelve as apostles. For the remainder of the gospel Luke uniquely distinguishes between the words "apostle" and "disciple," although both words are often applied to the same person.

When "apostle" is used, it means "one who is sent out." "Disciple," however, is always applied in the context of "learner," and is always used when Jesus is teaching. The lesson Luke wishes to give to the emerging Christian communities is clear: the opportunity for apostleship comes with maturity, and yet discipleship—even for apostles—never ends. The spiritual journey will always require "continuing education" in how to offer wisdom appropriately and with compassion.

> *Now during those days he went out to the mountain to pray; and he spent the night in prayer to God. And when day came, he called his disciples and chose twelve of them, whom he also named apostles: Simon, whom he named Peter, and his brother Andrew, and James, and John, and Philip, and Bartholomew, and Matthew, and Thomas, and James son of Alphaeus, and Simon, who was called the Zealot, and Judas son of James, and Judas Iscariot, who became a traitor. (6:12-16)*

The Beatitudes of The Gospel of Luke could scarcely be more different than those in Matthew's gospel. In Matthew, Jesus appears as the typical Jewish teacher, seated, while in Luke we find him standing. In Matthew, the Beatitudes are pronounced from high atop a mountain, while here we are "on a level place."

Matthew speaks of an audience drawn from the provinces of Israel, so we may assume it was primarily Jewish. Luke's audience specifically includes people from outlying provinces—therefore, many gentiles. In Matthew, the sermon is designed as a profound teaching. In Luke, it is more. People come both to "hear him and to be healed." The most significant differences, however, are found in the tone of the Beatitudes themselves and the text that follows them.

Matthew's Beatitudes are solemn pronouncements that ring with the sound of a rich, deep bell. Luke's are personal promises. They are insistent, filled with active, colorful verbs, the personal pronoun "you," and the word "now." They also do not hesitate to predict the direst calamity if one fails to meet the responsibilities of revelation.

Following the recitation of the Beatitudes, there is a rhythmic, repetitive text similar to that found at the same point in Matthew. But Luke offers only two short stanzas and uses much more direct language.

In the first, Jesus recites a code of conduct for his followers that commences with "Love your enemies." In the second, he raises a higher challenge, demanding that the good conduct be extended to everyone and be performed for its own sake: After all, "If you love those who love you, what credit is that to you?"

SEVEN—WALKING LUKE'S ROAD OF RICHES

Luke knows that if the communities can find themselves able to act on this new rule, they will also be breaking the ancient proscriptions of tribe. They will therefore be strengthening all of their relationships and going a long way toward ensuring that they can withstand the challenges ahead of them.

He knows that if they fail to do this, it is likely they will fall back into the old internecine tribal rivalries and even eventually into warfare. This could weaken their ability to meet oppressors with equanimity and might spell the end of faith, for an individual—or even a group. Consequently, his Beatitudes are far more than an elevated code of niceties; they are practical rules for a maturing spiritual life.

> *He came down with them and stood on a level place, with a great crowd of his disciples and a great multitude of people from all Judea, Jerusalem, and the coast of Tyre and Sidon. They had come to hear him and to be healed of their diseases; and those who were troubled with unclean spirits were cured. And all in the crowd were trying to touch him, for power came out from him and healed all of them. Then he looked up at his disciples and said:*
>
> *"Blessed are you who are poor, for yours is the kingdom of God. Blessed are you who are hungry now, for you will be filled. Blessed are you who weep now, for you will laugh. Blessed are you when people hate you, and when they exclude you, revile you, and defame you on account of the Son of Man. Rejoice in that day and leap for joy, for surely your reward is great in heaven; for that is what their ancestors did to the prophets.*
>
> *But woe to you who are rich, for you have received your consolation. Woe to you who are full now, for you will be hungry. Woe to you who are laughing now, for you will mourn and weep. Woe to you when all speak well of you, for that is what their ancestors did to the false prophets.*
>
> *But I say to you that listen, love your enemies, do good to those who hate you, bless those who curse you, pray for those who abuse you. If anyone strikes you on the cheek, offer the other also; and from anyone who takes away your coat do not withhold even your shirt. Give to everyone who begs from you;*

and if anyone takes away your goods, do not ask for them again. Do to others as you would have them do to you. If you love those who love you, what credit is that to you? For even sinners love those who love them. If you do good to those who do good to you, what credit is that to you? For even sinners do the same. If you lend to those from whom you hope to receive, what credit is that to you? Even sinners lend to sinners, to receive as much again. But love your enemies, do good, and lend, expecting nothing in return. Your reward will be great, and you will be children of the Most High; for he is kind to the ungrateful and the wicked. Be merciful, just as your Father is merciful." (6:17–36)

The concluding words of the sermon make reference to the same metaphor as the first temptation and liken faith to building a foundation from stone. More importantly, they constitute a forceful and direct challenge to Luke's readers regarding taking action. They ask why anyone would profess belief and then fail to follow the specific prescription that Jesus the Christ has laid down. With concern and urgency, Jesus delivers a rousing and emphatic finish to his Sermon on the Plain:

"Why do you call me 'Lord, Lord,' and do not do what I tell you? I will show you what someone is like who comes to me, hears my words, and acts on them. That one is like a man building a house, who dug deeply and laid the foundation on rock; when a flood arose, the river burst against that house but could not shake it, because it had been well built. But the one who hears and does not act is like a man who built a house on the ground without a foundation. When the river burst against it, immediately it fell, and great was the ruin of that house." (6:46–49)

When we reflect on the temptations and what they signify for our travel through the fourth path, we see that the first temptation is unsparing. The devil taunts us with challenges such as, "Turn this stone into a loaf of bread," "Seize the sensation of the moment," "Forget the lengthy challenge," or "It's only once; what does it matter?"

But our soul registers each bruise and wound to its self-respect and dignity—and our ego welcomes every opportunity to regress back to its former protective and self-centered ways. If we are truly on the spiritual Journey of Quadratos, we cannot take the expedient course. When this temptation appears, it is time to call our steady friends into service: prayer, reflection, and counselors.

Sometimes choices will seem unclear, in part because the world is complicated, and in part because the tricky ego-self is always on the lookout for ways to retreat back to safety. So, we need to be vigilant and query whether the option we are being offered is genuine and congruent with our journey. The lesson of Jesus the Christ would have us reject anything on which we cannot build further, and in love.

The second temptation speaks to one of our most pernicious challenges. When we are either alight with new zeal or consumed with doubt, the devil offers us "all the kingdoms." This leads us into attempts to get others to join our point of view. We tell ourselves our intentions are only the best. As Luke says, our efforts at persuasion usually begin "in an instant."

Our zeal takes many shapes—we find ourselves displaying hyper-enthusiasm, exploiting affinity, feigning friendship, withdrawing friendship, telling partial truths, sometimes even shaming people. If we prevail, the response we get gives us inner affirmation, confirming our position or reassuring our doubt.

However, lurking beneath our behavior are fear and a desire to control others. Why else would we need the confirmation or the reassurance? Giving in to this temptation leads us to denigrate a point of view that differs from ours and leads us into self- righteousness.

Quadratos calls us to identify our own intimate pattern of exerting control and then to be vigilant in resisting this temptation. Our mature course is to effect change by the example of our lives, rather than by overzealousness or by setting ourselves above others as "experts," no matter how well-intended we think we are.

The third temptation leads us to examine our deep desire to be protected from the consequences of our actions. The further we move into the fourth path, the more we are required to act in truth with clarity and compassion. When we do this, no matter how compassionate we try to be, the repercussions of our change can run the gamut from uncomfortable to agonizing. We are tempted to avoid this discomfort. We can especially wish for protection from the consequences of truth- telling.

Think of how difficult scrupulous veracity can be in a relationship. Think of how high the cost can be of telling political truth—of civil disobedience. As a result we often remain silent, "dance around" the truth, or take action and then retreat into resentment or anger when the consequences arrive. We have watched these behaviors in friends, parents, ministers, political activists, and ourselves. We know we have fallen off the path by choosing avoidance of pain or its consequences, however small, instead of honesty.

All three lessons of the temptations coalesce in the story of Jesus speaking in Nazareth. Jesus was in his hometown being celebrated by family and neighbors until he perceived their desire for him to do "magic tricks" for them. He refused, reproaching them for their shallow attitude, and in return they tried to kill him. He left without comment.

Toned down just a bit (but not all that much), this could be the story of innumerable family gatherings, corporate meetings, academic colloquia, and international assemblies throughout history. A noted person speaks wisdom which is not the common belief and is either not heard or is misunderstood and rejected and/or reviled.

At all levels, families and organizations are usually—and naturally—resistant to new insight. Should we therefore deny our wholeness and never say anything? Of course not. And if (and when) we are rejected, what should we do? As difficult as it may seem, we must bend every effort not to dispute or fight or allow the enmity of others to affect us, but rather simply go on our way.

Luke's definitions and flexible application of the terms "disciple" and "apostle" echo the unceasing cycles of the Quadratos pattern. We are in a lifelong condition of inquiry—of trying to remain curious and flexible as we test ourselves in the world, and the world tests us back. We are always disciple and apostle, these roles bowing to each other in a perpetually challenging minuet of learning and service.

It often seems as though just when we feel that we have achieved a bit of inner equanimity, a fresh challenge arrives sending us on a quick little side trip into arrogance or complacency or self-righteousness. In order to mend our lapse, self-honesty forces us right back into discipleship.

We pray and ask for help once again, often feeling as though our knees can bend no lower and our nose is scraping dirt. Indeed, the condition of apostleship often *leads* us back to discipleship, which then *leads* on out to the apostle's field to share our experience, as the steps of God's dance lead us deeper into Spirit and service.

Another outgrowth of the synergistic association between disciple and apostle is the leveling out of the teacher-student relationship. The more we learn, the more we are able to discern both the strengths and the frailties of those we esteem. When this is understood and welcomed, it can result in growing collegiality and even friendship.

If, however, the teacher or the student has an immature ego that requires either elevation or devaluation, then the relationship will likely falter and eventually be destroyed, often acrimoniously. If this occurs, it will be another opportunity for us to follow Jesus' example and go on our way compassionately, without resentment or rancor.

Luke's Beatitudes are startlingly different from those in Matthew's gospel, and our interpretation of them through the lens of Quadratos is dramatically different from the common conception. Why? Because we view them as guides to living along the fourth path, flowing directly from the revelations of the third path. The epiphanies we received in John's garden came with increased responsibilities—with the need for more reflective responses to ourselves and to others.

These are called out in the Beatitudes—one by one. The "blessed" and the "woe" phrases state the overarching principles, and the text that follows is the amplification of those principles. In strictly psychological terms, the increased awareness of the third path brought new burdens to the maturing ego.

The "blesseds" describe what the ego needs either to give or to let go of, while the "woes" speak about the psychological and spiritual poverty of the reverse course. If the "blesseds" and "woes" go out of balance, they inevitably surface and play out in our lives, resulting in corresponding spiritual consequences—both positive and negative.

Therefore, in Quadratos the Beatitudes are *not* pronouncements about our moods or socioeconomic status, as is commonly thought. They are messages about inner attitudes. Rereading them and reflecting on them from the perspective of Quadratos is illuminating and absorbing the deeper interpretation which follows is of critical importance.

In this radical and far-reaching understanding, being "poor" has nothing whatsoever to do with material goods. You are blessed if you can understand that the revelation you received in the third path came to you in your state of humble *spiritual* poverty and was not in any way from yourself. In this way you will remain a servant of what you have received.

Accordingly, if you are "hungry," your hunger is to feed not only yourself, but others from the grace and spirit you have received. You "weep" because the beauty and truth of epiphany have reached your heart, the essence of your being, and moved you deeply.

Being "hated, excluded, reviled, and defamed" repeats Luke's teaching that deep resistance is a natural reaction to new behaviors and we need to expect its arrival both within and without. It is not in any way a rationalization for being antisocial.

Corresponding to the positive promises offered in the Beatitudes are equal cautions, each preceded by "Woe to." If we are "rich," that means we have converted our revelation into a "feel-good" experience, into immediate gratification, and already "received [our] consolation." If we are "full," we have selfishly taken all the gratification of the experience for ourselves and not extended it to others in any way.

If we are "laughing now," then our revelation stayed in the shallow realm of mere titillation and never reached the deeper, expanded realms of wholeness. And if "all speak well" of us, then we can be certain we have failed to speak out, or to speak our truth, and we are therefore not meeting the responsibilities of the gift we have been given.

In the first stanza immediately after the verses of the Beatitudes, Jesus provides directives for loving action which are familiar to many of us. When we focus them on our inner lives, we see that they are asking us to review our behavior when we feel personally challenged—psychologically, emotionally, even spiritually.

How can we respond to perceived threats from a more encompassing, gracious, and integrated position? At first, this will require us to pause and reflect—often for days. Practice will enable us to accomplish this more quickly and easily.

The second directive contains the well-known words, "Do to others as you would have them do to you." The actual practice of this instruction has a subtlety often overlooked. Most people assume this means we should extend to others the behavior that we think is best, whatever that is. Nothing could be further from the truth intended by these words.

The words call for us to behave as we would have others *do to us*. And what each of us would most like is to be met on our own terms, in our own language, at our own present stage of understanding and development. None of us wants to be bullied or condescended to or lied to or shamed or shunned.

We don't want assumptions made about us. So, this was Jesus' directive to us. We are to meet others on *their own ground of being—not ours*. We are to grant them the same human dignity we would wish them to extend to us.

Each of the "blesseds" and the "woes" in Luke's Beatitudes are grounded in the soundest psychology. They are paired, and they quite clearly inform us that if we do not mature into the expanded understanding and practice offered by the fourth-path "blesseds," we will most certainly contract back into the misery of the "woes." If we want to think in terms of having a carrot and a stick for our journey, we may look forward to joy, and the "woes" surely qualify as the stick.

Remember the horrors of the immature ego we knew in Matthew when we felt as though we were the perpetual victims of an unfeeling, uncaring world where things were tumbling down all around us? Or in Mark, when they were gray, mysterious and unfathomable? Those are the woes.

And we will return to them—all of us will, repeatedly—as we cycle back through the Quadratos process, but we will probably never love them and will always want to shorten our stay. It is well worth our energy to reach for the understanding of the "blesseds."

Even though Luke gives radical counsel for his time, he is no radical. His advice—based on history, experience, and, as we have noted, psychology—is always very practical. He deeply respects Jewish tradition, and constantly counsels self-reflection and a measured pace. Across millennia, he wants us to succeed in our journey.

He asks us to pay attention and follow through, and writes: otherwise, "Why do you call me 'Lord'?" Spiritual transformation is tough. We face threat and challenge from within and without. We need a "well-built foundation," but through our work of the first three paths, the first sturdy stones have already been laid.

Compassion without Boundaries
The Good Samaritan

Luke concludes this chapter with the famous and transcendent story of the Good Samaritan, which appears in no other gospel. The parable opens with a moving restatement of the core Judaic verses of Deuteronomy — the same verses referred to earlier as the spiritual sense that underlies Luke's use of the word "heart" throughout this gospel: "You shall love the Lord your God with all your heart, and with all your soul, and with all your strength, and with all your mind; and your neighbor as yourself."

Queried, "Who is my neighbor?" Jesus answers with a story about a man who had been beaten and left for dead on the road. Both a priest and a Levite, a member of the priestly tribe, pass the injured man by without tending to him. Jewish teachings held that if the priests had touched him, they would have become "unclean" and would thus have been forbidden to perform any ritual.

However, a passing Samaritan, an outcast from Jewish society, sees the beaten man, and stops. He bandages the man's wounds, and places him on his own donkey. They journey to an inn, whereupon the Samaritan pays the innkeeper for his care.

This poignant story offers a revolutionary teaching. The behavior it shows—and held up as expected of Christians—moves well beyond the limitations of ritual or bureaucratic law to the benefit of all people. This was not only timely for the burgeoning Christian communities but essential.

As with the Beatitudes, Luke recognized that this principle of helping others despite their background of birth had the potential to both spread and hold Christianity together, because it supersedes the centuries-old squabbles of class and tribe.

If the fights could end, then larger and more powerful social and economic groups could form, and greater strength would follow. As always, Jesus' message is both divine and practical: act in love and respond to those in need regardless of origins. Luke writes every word of his gospel accordingly.

> *Just then a lawyer stood up to test Jesus. "Teacher," he said, "what must I do to inherit eternal life?" [Jesus] said to him, "What is written in the law? What do you read there?" He answered, "You shall love the Lord your God with all your heart, and with all your soul, and with all your strength, and with all your mind; and your neighbor as yourself." And [Jesus] said to him, "You have given the right answer; do this, and you will live." But wanting to justify himself, he asked Jesus, "And who is my neighbor?" Jesus replied, "A man was going down from Jerusalem to Jericho, and fell into the hands of robbers, who stripped him, beat him, and went away, leaving him half dead. Now by chance a priest was going down that road; and when he saw him, he passed by on the other side. So likewise a*

> *Levite, when he came to the place and saw him, passed by on the other side. But a Samaritan while traveling came near him; and when he saw him, he was moved with pity. He went to him and bandaged his wounds, having poured oil and wine on them. Then he put him on his own animal, brought him to an inn, and took care of him. The next day he took out two denarii, gave them to the innkeeper, and said, 'Take care of him; and when I come back, I will repay you whatever more you spend.' Which of these three, do you think, was a neighbor to the man who fell into the hands of the robbers?" He said, "The one who showed him mercy." Jesus said to him, "Go and do likewise." (Luke 10:25–37)*

Ask for What You Want
Bread at Midnight

After Jesus teaches his disciples the words we know as the Lord's Prayer, he goes on with a pointed and beautiful lesson unique to this gospel. He proposes to the disciples that if they were to go to a friend's home in the middle of the night asking for food to feed a newly arrived guest, the friend would help them, even if the friend is grumpy and only half awake. Why? Not from friendship, but from respect for the perseverance of the request.

This teaching is then followed by the well-known words also found in Matthew's gospel that begin, "Ask, and it will be given you." Luke was taking the opportunity to insert an advanced principle about persistence that he knew his readers badly needed.

The teaching—dramatically set in the middle of the night, so no one would miss the point—emphasizes the need to maintain inner stability and steadfastly ask for what one wants, though the moment or circumstances may not be opportune. Note that the request was for three loaves of bread—far above what would have been required until morning.

The principle is to ask for what one *wants* rather than to ask based on need or subsistence. This parable illustrates the combined lessons of having a keen sense of self-worth, of persistence, and of holding a clear vision for the future—an invaluable combination for moving forward successfully.

And [Jesus] said to them, "Suppose one of you has a friend, and you go to him at midnight and say to him, 'Friend, lend me three loaves of bread; for a friend of mine has arrived, and I have nothing to set before him.' And he answers from within, 'Do not bother me; the door has already been locked, and my children are with me in bed; I cannot get up and give you anything.' I tell you, even though he will not get up and give him anything because he is his friend, at least because of his persistence he will get up and give him whatever he needs. "So I say to you, Ask, and it will be given you; search, and you will find; knock, and the door will be opened for you. For everyone who asks receives, and everyone who searches finds, and for everyone who knocks, the door will be opened." (11:5-10)

Risk and Celebration
Two Stories and the Prodigal Son

Jesus tells a series of three stories to challenge the general thinking of the Pharisees and those whose hearts still follow the pharisaical teachings. At this point in the first century, the Pharisees—still held by their grief and anxiety—were philosophically the people promoting "holding on" and "gathering what is left," rather than moving ahead. Any story that teaches about seeking that which has wandered away is quite pointedly directed at challenging the Pharisees' beliefs.

The first two stories tell of losing and then finding first sheep and then coins. These accounts build to the third story, which is the well-known tale of the Prodigal Son. It, like that of the Good Samaritan, appears only in Luke's gospel. In this third parable, a father has two sons. The younger son leaves home and his traditional obligations, taking his share of the inheritance early in order to explore the larger world.

After squandering everything on this quest, he returns home. Rejoicing at his homecoming, his father holds a great reunion celebration for him. Highly resentful of this welcome, the elder brother refers to the younger as "your son" when he complains to the father about the injustice of honoring the wastrel—effectively disowning his filial relationship. The father refuses to accept the older son's attitude, saying that he was "always with him," and reiterating the need to celebrate what "has come to life."

Through these parables, Luke provides differing ways to consider the cost of holding tightly to material things or to ideologies. He points out the great value in putting material things at risk and going into a wilderness, into darkness or unfamiliar territory, precisely as the first-century Christus followers were doing. In the first two stories, the material possession—the sheep or the coin—is recovered.

In the third, however, although the goods or the inheritance disappears, the much more valuable asset, which is the relationship of father and son is restored. Unfortunately, the embittered older son, by disowning his brother, denies himself all the possibilities represented by this relationship—exploration, wholeness, and joy. In all three parables, Luke's point is that by focusing on the element of heart, the element that is genuinely important—the result is great happiness, rejoicing, and celebration.

> *Now all the tax collectors and sinners were coming near to listen to him. And the Pharisees and the scribes were grumbling and saying, "This fellow welcomes sinners and eats with them." So he told them this parable: "Which one of you, having a hundred sheep and losing one of them, does not leave the ninety-nine in the wilderness and go after the one that is lost until he finds it? When he has found it, he lays it on his shoulders and rejoices. And when he comes home, he calls together his friends and neighbors, saying to them, 'Rejoice with me, for I have found my sheep that was lost.' Just so, I tell you, there will be more joy in heaven over one sinner who repents than over ninety-nine righteous persons who need no repentance. Or what woman having ten silver coins, if she loses one of them, does not light a lamp, sweep the house, and search carefully until she finds it? When she has found it, she calls together her friends and neighbors, saying, 'Rejoice with me, for I have found the coin that I had lost.' Just so, I tell you, there is joy in the presence of the angels of God over one sinner who repents." (15:1–10)*

SEVEN—WALKING LUKE'S ROAD OF RICHES

Then Jesus said, "There was a man who had two sons. The younger of them said to his father, 'Father, give me the share of the property that will belong to me.' So he divided his property between them. A few days later the younger son gathered all he had and traveled to a distant country, and there he squandered his property in dissolute living. When he had spent everything, a severe famine took place throughout that country, and he began to be in need. So he went and hired himself out to one of the citizens of that country, who sent him to his fields to feed the pigs. He would gladly have filled himself with the pods that the pigs were eating; and no one gave him anything. But when he came to himself he said, 'How many of my father's hired hands have bread enough and to spare, but here I am dying of hunger! I will get up and go to my father, and I will say to him, "Father, I have sinned against heaven and before you; I am no longer worthy to be called your son; treat me like one of your hired hands."' So he set off and went to his father. But while he was still far off, his father saw him and was filled with compassion; he ran and put his arms around him and kissed him. Then the son said to him, 'Father, I have sinned against heaven and before you; I am no longer worthy to be called your son.' But the father said to his slaves, 'Quickly, bring out a robe—the best one—and put it on him; put a ring on his finger and sandals on his feet. And get the fatted calf and kill it, and let us eat and celebrate; for this son of mine was dead and is alive again; he was lost and is found!' And they began to celebrate. Now his elder son was in the field; and when he came and approached the house, he heard music and dancing. He called one of the slaves and asked what was going on. He replied, 'Your brother has come, and your father has killed the fatted calf, because he has got him back safe and sound.' Then he became angry and refused to go in. His father came out and began to plead with him. But he answered his father, 'Listen! For all these years I have been working like a slave for you, and I have never disobeyed your command; yet you have never given me even a young goat so that I might celebrate with my friends. But when this son of yours came back, who has devoured your property with prostitutes, you killed the fatted calf for him!' Then the father said to him, 'Son, you are always with me, and all that is mine is yours. But we had to celebrate and rejoice, because this brother of yours was dead and has come to life; he was lost and has been found.'" (15:11–32)

Where Is Happiness?
Jesus' Answer

It is difficult days for Luke's readers, and they are trying to persevere. Oppression from Rome is increasing. This first meant the loss of good jobs, then the loss of any jobs, and eventually the loss of their homes—and all because they are Christians following a new way.

Because these circumstances are not what the new believers had expected from the arrival of the Messiah, Luke crafts an answer to the Pharisees as a message to the Christians that the new kingdom is not a domain, but is instead found "among you"—in the ways individuals relate to each other in community. This would have substantial impact on the Christus group, helping them to find equanimity in their times together and in worship.

> *Once Jesus was asked by the Pharisees when the kingdom of God was coming, and he answered, "The kingdom of God is not coming with things that can be observed; nor will they say, 'Look, here it is!' or 'There it is!' For, in fact, the kingdom of God is among you." (17:20–21)*

Luke provides the story of the Good Samaritan as a clear explication of the responsibilities of Christian duty: love God as ourselves, and minister to our neighbor without hesitation or hierarchy. In the parable, both the priest and the Levite are unthinking, unreflective—blindly following rules passed on to them by their religion and caste. The Samaritan responds with a more engaged and flexible humanity.

Daily, we are challenged in the same way. Outstretched hands and starving children greet us on the sidewalk and in our mailbox. Less dramatically, our friends ask us for time or assistance—even a loan. How do we respond?

The actions of the Samaritan present us with what may be our most difficult challenge to date. He does not hesitate to act. He does not suffer from a lack of compassion, nor does he act from inappropriate guilt or shame. In each instance, based on specific circumstances and our abilities to either give or receive, so must we determine first *whether* to respond— and then how to do so appropriately.

If we act, we need to be certain that our motives derive from our inner wholeness. If they do not, our actions will come from the fractional self of the immature ego—from some outer "should," "have to," or groupthink—and the result will be self-aggrandizement rather than actual compassion.

Knocking at midnight aptly symbolizes the fourth path. Sometimes it seems that that is all we do. We knock on our stubborn habits. We knock on our recalcitrant and fearful egos. We knock at the hearts of those around us and hope for their patience as we make our slow progress. And it often seems that our requests are inconvenient and even embarrassing.

We feel self-conscious and awkward with others. Sometimes our knocking needs to be done at the door of Spirit, and we are just too tired to pray—after all, it is midnight. But knock we must. We need to persevere, and it is important—for our dreams, for our good and whole lives—that we ask for all three loaves. Knocking and asking is the boring repetition from which the richness of our life emerges and rises.

The three stories, which include the Prodigal Son, encourage us to take the risks needed on the fourth path to test ourselves. We know we are at home with and within our God, so we have at some level a deep surety and no risk at all. Yet there will always be parts of us that still feel frissons of fear now and again. A lot of what we are undergoing is new and unexplored, and we need a bit of help and some prodding.

Our actions can seem wildly unwise or unnecessary to others who are outside the process, but this is precisely how we grow. We grasp in ever wider and deeper ways that our capacity for joy and celebration is in some measure directly linked to our corresponding willingness to expand ourselves. As we progress, the change is like the difference between seeing the night sky through a city window and experiencing it from the top of a high mountain. There is simply no comparison.

When we express our truths, others may find our opinions difficult to digest—may consider them unnecessary, even foolhardy. Therefore, truth-telling plays an essential role not only in the story of the Prodigal Son, but throughout Luke's gospel. One of the most formidable demands of the fourth path, reiterated by the third temptation (asking to be protected from consequences), requires speaking and acting truthfully.

It is so much easier to remain silent, yet every justice we desire to see tomorrow is made from the injustice we refuse to act on today. And this is true in our marriages, our jobs, our churches, or our countries. Recognizing the necessity to "speak up" is very simple, but doing so often causes conflict; therefore, opening our mouths can feel like a very weighty decision. Nonetheless, we are not relieved of our obligation to do so. And with practice, it does get easier.

Our ego's difficulty with conflict makes this fourth-path requirement of truth-telling very complicated. Psychologically, the initial impulse of an immature ego—the impulse we encounter in the first path—is to avoid conflict altogether. As we move into the second path, we find that our ego, lacking other tools and desiring to protect us, comes into contact with conflict, either gingerly as though from behind the safety of a fence built of avoidance, or brutishly seeking to force a quick resolution that reduces one's discomfort.

In the third path as we discover the truth of opposites, our experience of conflict seems to lessen. We avoid direct engagement and instead focus on our conscious observation of conflict. In the garden of John, we are resting, learning, and marshalling our forces.

Now, however, in the fourth path we become able to engage conflict productively. Our egos likewise gain the ability to wait in the wings. It is time for truth-telling and truth-acting—with compassion and love—to take center stage. This is a very long process, but also probably one of the most worthwhile goals of the spiritual journey.

To achieve the capacity *to speak and act as our genuine selves with others, in an attitude of compassion and love, and with confidence*—now *that* is truly a cause for rejoicing!

Finally, our delight all comes together—literally—in Jesus' definition of happiness. Community is the great tree that bears the fruit of all our work, and we shall know it by its fecundity and the harvest it offers to us and to all generations. We dance around the sturdy trunk we have helped to grow and continue to feed. Happiness is, indeed, "among us."

Yearning, Acceptance, and Love
The Passion and Resurrection: Entering Jerusalem

Remember that each gospel has differing details of Jesus' final entry into Jerusalem. Luke employs a vivid allegory and has Jesus arriving on "a colt that has never been ridden." We can readily see how well the fresh, energy-filled Christians could relate to these words. By contrast, fulfilling other narrative purposes and sometimes prophecy, in Matthew Jesus enters on "a donkey and a colt that was its foal," in Mark he rides an "untamed colt," and in John a "donkey's colt."

As Jesus and his disciples enter the city in Luke's account, the disciples shout praise to God as they announce Jesus' arrival, while the crowd throws their cloaks onto the road before him. The Pharisees object, offended by the great tumult, but Jesus asserts that "the stones would shout out" if his followers did not.

Only in this gospel do the disciples themselves raise their voices in joyful acclamation rather than the surrounding crowd. With this description of Jesus' entry, Luke depicts the new truth with full confidence and inspiration, directly confronting the old establishment. This is a portrait of that great day in history which shows the beginnings of an immensely vibrant and unstoppable movement—and the picture is still vivid centuries later.

Although hailed as "king," Jesus enters the city weeping—scarcely the demeanor of a traditional king. And in the midst of the celebration, he laments that Jerusalem has not understood "the things that make for peace." With this image, Luke characterizes the deeply revolutionary heart of the new faith and brings forward the major theme of peace. This scene and its words are found only in Luke.

Jesus goes on to predict that Jerusalem's blindness will create only tragedy, clearly foretelling the destruction of the Great Temple and the subsequent large-scale abandonment of the city by the Jews. Luke astutely seizes upon the reality that at the time he wrote—approximately fifteen years after the Temple's destruction—Jerusalem had never recovered and remained desolate.

> *When he had come near Bethphage and Bethany, at the place called the Mount of Olives, he sent two of the disciples, saying, "Go into the village ahead of you, and as you enter it you will find tied there a colt that has never been ridden. Untie it and bring it here. If anyone asks you, 'Why are you untying it?' just say this, 'The Lord needs it.'" So those who were sent departed and found it as he had told them. As they were untying the colt, its owners asked them, "Why are you untying the colt?" They said, "The Lord needs it." Then they brought it to Jesus; and after throwing their cloaks on the colt, they set Jesus on it. As he rode along, people kept spreading their cloaks on the road. As he was now approaching the path down from the Mount of Olives, the whole multitude of the disciples began to praise God joyfully with a loud voice for all the deeds of power that they had seen, saying, "Blessed is the king who comes in the name of the Lord! Peace in heaven, and glory in the highest heaven!" Some of the Pharisees in the crowd said to him, "Teacher, order your disciples to stop." He answered, "I tell you, if these*

were silent, the stones would shout out." As he came near and saw the city, he wept over it, saying, "If you, even you, had only recognized on this day the things that make for peace! But now they are hidden from your eyes. Indeed, the days will come upon you, when your enemies will set up ramparts around you and surround you, and hem you in on every side. They will crush you to the ground, you and your children within you, and they will not leave within you one stone upon another; because you did not recognize the time of your visitation from God." (19:29-44)

Leading as A Servant
The Last Supper

The Last Supper in this gospel is the Passover dinner. Despite the setting of a meal, Luke mentions only wine and bread which Jesus directs to be divided among his followers, identified here as apostles. This designation sets the context of the meal as service. There are explicitly two cups of wine—one early on, and then another "after supper." Once the second glass has been drunk, Jesus announces that one of those present will betray him.

Dismayed, the apostles begin to discuss among themselves who the culprit might be, and then in anger they debate who will later come to be considered the "greatest" among them. Stepping in, Jesus excoriates the authority of the old ways.

Jesus further says that while all of them have gone through trials with him, the criterion for a true leader was not suffering, but service, citing himself as the exemplar. Luke's description of Jesus' reaction to the squabble is entirely different from other accounts, and by it he is clearly establishing a standard for Christian leadership.

If we again recall that each Passion account serves to sharpen the core question addressed by the individual gospel, then the telling of the Last Supper here assumes even greater meaning. The question of Luke's gospel is: *How do we mature in service?* As the gospel moves through its lessons, the question crystallizes. It becomes: *How do we develop an original life that continues to grow and offers itself to the greater good?* This is the context to which the entire Passion is devoted.

Luke even designates the sequence of the cups drunk at the supper to emphasize service. Although there are traditionally a series of cups drunk during the Passover ritual, the gospels of Matthew and Mark mention only one cup at the meal. Luke's account differs, referring to two cups and naming, quite specifically, "the cup after supper."

At the Passover meal, this is the final cup, also known as the Cup of Elijah, or the Cup of Compassion. It is named thus because Elijah was noted for feeding a Sidonian woman—that is, a non-Jew—during a major famine (1 Kings 17:8–16). Luke deliberately refers to that cup in order to evoke for the apostles someone of great faith who, like the Good Samaritan, broke the rules of tribe to act in service. This is the cup from which Jesus pours "the new covenant in my blood."

Luke's unique version of Jesus' words to Peter about his betrayal follows. Even though Jesus has prayed that Peter's faith would remain steadfast, Jesus informs Peter that he will still inevitably deny his Lord before the cock crows. Jesus also knows that Peter will repent his action and specifically asks that when he does so, he use his new understanding to "strengthen your brothers."

Peter, shocked, and at that moment still unaware of his capacity for perfidy, assures Jesus that he will never hurt him—that he will accompany him "to prison and to death." Both of these small variations, found only in this gospel, are directed to Luke's audience, communities who needed to strengthen each other, and who are possibly facing prison and even death.

Finally, the theme of lawlessness arises, as it does in several places in this gospel. This is a matter quite specific to Luke's audience who are being unfairly persecuted for their "illegal" religious faith.

Jesus instructs his disciples to go out as mendicants and spread his word. Then, in a clear reference to the branding of Christians as "lawless," Luke inserts an ironic exchange regarding the purchase of a sword to fulfill the prophecies of Jesus' rebellion.

SEVEN—WALKING LUKE'S ROAD OF RICHES

The zealous apostles offer "two swords," but Jesus calmly quells their ardor. Luke wants to impress upon his audience that the world will always form its own opinions, often false. It is fruitless to fight against such false allegations, for fighting only amplifies them. Rather, the proper course—the course Jesus himself followed in Nazareth—is to simply continue calmly on one's own way.

> *When the hour came, he took his place at the table, and the apostles with him. He said to them, "I have eagerly desired to eat this Passover with you before I suffer; for I tell you, I will not eat it until it is fulfilled in the kingdom of God." Then he took a cup, and after giving thanks he said, "Take this and divide it among yourselves; for I tell you that from now on I will not drink of the fruit of the vine until the kingdom of God comes." Then he took a loaf of bread, and when he had given thanks, he broke it and gave it to them, saying, "This is my body, which is given for you. Do this in remembrance of me." And he did the same with the cup after supper, saying, "This cup that is poured out for you is the new covenant in my blood. But see, the one who betrays me is with me, and his hand is on the table. For the Son of Man is going as it has been determined, but woe to that one by whom he is betrayed!" Then they began to ask one another, which one of them it could be who would do this. A dispute also arose among them as to which one of them was to be regarded as the greatest. But [Jesus] said to them, "The kings of the Gentiles lord it over them; and those in authority over them are called benefactors. But not so with you; rather the greatest among you must become like the youngest, and the leader like one who serves. For who is greater, the one who is at the table or the one who serves? Is it not the one at the table? But I am among you as one who serves. You are those who have stood by me in my trials; and I confer on you, just as my Father has conferred on me, a kingdom, so that you may eat and drink at my table in my kingdom, and you will sit on thrones judging the twelve tribes of Israel. Simon, Simon, listen! Satan has demanded to sift all of you like wheat, but I have prayed for*

you that your own faith may not fail; and you, when once you have turned back, strengthen your brothers." And he said to him, "Lord, I am ready to go with you to prison and to death!" Jesus said, "I tell you, Peter, the cock will not crow this day, until you have denied three times that you know me." He said to them, "When I sent you out without a purse, bag, or sandals, did you lack anything?" They said, "No, not a thing." He said to them, "But now, the one who has a purse must take it, and likewise a bag. And the one who has no sword must sell his cloak and buy one. For I tell you, this scripture must be fulfilled in me, 'And he was counted among the lawless'; and indeed what is written about me is being fulfilled." They said, "Lord, look, here are two swords." He replied, "It is enough." (22:14–38)

Staying Present and in Truth
The Arrest

After the Passover meal, Jesus retires to the Mount of Olives. Everyone from the dinner (minus Judas) follows. Jesus requests that all of them stay apart from him while he prays, which he does once. Note that at this point, Luke designates them as disciples, therefore learners.

By contrast, in the accounts of both Matthew and Mark, Jesus selects three disciples from the larger group, admonishes them to stay awake, and withdraws three times. In John's gospel, the group leave their final meal and go to an unnamed garden where—without prayer—Jesus is immediately arrested.

Although it seems odd that Jesus the Christ would need succor while praying, Luke also provides an angel, who appears to Jesus on the Mount and gives him strength. This element, not found in many of the earliest documents, is presumed to have been added sometime later. The prayer was so earnest that Luke describes Jesus' sweat as being "like great drops of blood falling down on the ground." This detail again emphasizes Luke's focus on passion in the pursuit of Spirit.

Rejoining his disciples and finding them asleep, Jesus inquires why they have not also taken advantage of this opportunity for prayer. Suddenly, Judas arrives on the mountain with a crowd that includes the chief priests, officers of the Temple police and the elders.

In this scene, Luke gives an image of the "old" Jerusalem arriving to snuff out the new. Judas approaches to kiss Jesus, but before he can do so Jesus speaks. This is an allegory Luke's audience understands all too well. They, too, had no need to await the kiss of betrayal. They were aware that they needed to be prepared for the trials that awaited them.

Jesus is taken to the high priest's house, and a crowd which includes Peter, gathers outside. Contrasting with Jesus' acute receptivity to his fate, when Peter is questioned about knowing his teacher, he chooses to lie—in effect, to be "asleep" to his spiritual path. Three times he denies knowing Jesus. When the Lord looks into his eyes, Peter—overcome with contrition—suddenly "remembers" and awakens to the responsibilities of his discipleship. Luke knew how easy it would be for his readers to also "fall asleep" to *their* faith—especially if the slumber maintained their place in the community, their jobs, or their homes.

> *He came out and went, as was his custom, to the Mount of Olives; and the disciples followed him. When he reached the place, he said to them, "Pray that you may not come into the time of trial." Then he withdrew from them about a stone's throw, knelt down, and prayed, "Father, if you are willing, remove this cup from me; yet, not my will but yours be done." Then an angel from heaven appeared to him and gave him strength. In his anguish he prayed more earnestly, and his sweat became like great drops of blood falling down on the ground. When he got up from prayer, he came to the disciples and found them sleeping because of grief, and he said to them, "Why are you sleeping? Get up and pray that you may not come into the time of trial." While he was still speaking, suddenly a crowd came, and the one called Judas, one of the twelve, was leading them. He approached Jesus to kiss him; but Jesus said to him, "Judas, is it with a kiss that you are betraying the Son of Man?"*

> *When those who were around him saw what was coming, they asked, "Lord, should we strike with the sword?" Then one of them struck the slave of the high priest and cut off his right ear. But Jesus said, "No more of this!" And he touched his ear and healed him. Then Jesus said to the chief priests, the officers of the temple police, and the elders who had come for him, "Have you come out with swords and clubs as if I were a bandit? When I was with you day after day in the temple, you did not lay hands on me. But this is your hour, and the power of darkness!" Then they seized him and led him away, bringing him into the high priest's house. But Peter was following at a distance. When they had kindled a fire in the middle of the courtyard and sat down together, Peter sat among them. Then a servant-girl, seeing him in the firelight, stared at him and said, "This man also was with him." But he denied it, saying, "Woman, I do not know him." A little later someone else, on seeing him, said, "You also are one of them." But Peter said, "Man, I am not!" Then about an hour later still another kept insisting, "Surely this man also was with him; for he is a Galilean." But Peter said, "Man, I do not know what you are talking about!" At that moment, while he was still speaking, the cock crowed. The Lord turned and looked at Peter. Then Peter remembered the word of the Lord, how he had said to him, "Before the cock crows today, you will deny me three times." And he went out and wept bitterly. (22:39–62)*

Jesus is taken to the high priest's house, and a crowd, which includes Peter, gathers outside. Contrasting with Jesus' acute receptivity to his fate, when Peter is questioned about knowing his teacher, he chooses to lie—in effect, to be "asleep" to his spiritual path. Three times he denies knowing Jesus.

When the Lord looks into his eyes, Peter—overcome with contrition—suddenly "remembers" and awakens to the responsibilities of his discipleship. Luke knew how easy it would be for his readers to also "fall asleep" to their faith—especially if the slumber maintained their place in the community, their jobs, or their homes.

SEVEN—WALKING LUKE'S ROAD OF RICHES

Pilate, not wanting to anger the populace, realizes that he could shift any fury directed at him by sending Jesus to Herod, head of the Roman government in Galilee. Initially, this pleases Herod, who considers Jesus simply another magician to perform tricks for him. When Jesus refuses this role even when mocked, Herod sends him right back to Pilate, draped in an "elegant robe." (The other gospels note a variety of colors.)

Luke reports that Herod and Pilate became good friends afterward. We can assume they were unified in their desire to silence the obstreperous prophet; and from a deeper perspective we can see that they had joined forces in a battle to keep a threatening new reality at bay.

> *Now the men who were holding Jesus began to mock him and beat him; they also blindfolded him and kept asking him, "Prophesy! Who is it that struck you?" They kept heaping many other insults on him. When day came, the assembly of the elders of the people, both chief priests and scribes, gathered together, and they brought him to their council. They said, "If you are the Messiah, tell us." He replied, "If I tell you, you will not believe; and if I question you, you will not answer. But from now on the Son of Man will be seated at the right hand of the power of God." All of them asked, "Are you, then, the Son of God?" He said to them, "You say that I am." Then they said, "What further testimony do we need? We have heard it ourselves from his own lips!" (22:63–71)*

> *Then the assembly rose as a body and brought Jesus before Pilate. They began to accuse him, saying, "We found this man perverting our nation, forbidding us to pay taxes to the emperor, and saying that he himself is the Messiah, a king." Then Pilate asked him, "Are you the king of the Jews?" He answered, "You say so." Then Pilate said to the chief priests and the crowds, "I find no basis for an accusation against this man." But they were insistent and said, "He stirs up the people by teaching throughout all Judea, from Galilee where he began even to this place." When Pilate heard this, he*

> *asked whether the man was a Galilean. And when he learned that he was under Herod's jurisdiction, he sent him off to Herod, who was himself in Jerusalem at that time. When Herod saw Jesus, he was very glad, for he had been wanting to see him for a long time, because he had heard about him and was hoping to see him perform some sign. He questioned him at some length, but Jesus gave him no answer. The chief priests and the scribes stood by, vehemently accusing him. Even Herod with his soldiers treated him with contempt and mocked him; then he put an elegant robe on him, and sent him back to Pilate. That same day Herod and Pilate became friends with each other; before this they had been enemies. (23:1–12)*

The Green Wood Will Turn Dry
To Golgotha

Once more, Luke provides a significant passage not found in the other gospels. Dramatically depicting the journey to the crucifixion, Luke recounts Jesus' address to the "daughters of Jerusalem," which speaks of frightening times to come and refers to natural cycles. Many have considered this an apocalyptic message.

However, natural cycles inevitably blossom into new life and hope, despite their times of dwindling into barrenness and the dark. Luke's message is therefore not one of despair at all.

Instead, he is entreating once again: "Don't be in denial. Prepare. Terrible adversity *is* coming. However, in God's good time, events will turn, as they always do, because we are all within a never-ending pattern, and that pattern leads to glory."

Indeed, in the ensuing generation the bad times did come, as the Romans set about hunting down Christians and massacring them whenever and wherever they found them. But the circle indeed turned, when the Roman Empire crumbled while Christianity thrived.

SEVEN—WALKING LUKE'S ROAD OF RICHES

As they led him away, they seized a man, Simon of Cyrene, who was coming from the country, and they laid the cross on him, and made him carry it behind Jesus. A great number of the people followed him, and among them were women who were beating their breasts and wailing for him. But Jesus turned to them and said, "Daughters of Jerusalem, do not weep for me, but weep for yourselves and for your children. For the days are surely coming when they will say, 'Blessed are the barren, and the wombs that never bore, and the breasts that never nursed.' Then they will begin to say to the mountains, 'Fall on us'; and to the hills, 'Cover us.' For if they do this when the wood is green, what will happen when it is dry?" (23:26–31)

A Choice of Perspective
The Crucifixion

Jesus walks to Golgotha with two fellow prisoners Luke identifies as "criminals," a precise and resonant word for his audience, many of whom were being charged with crimes against the Roman Empire. In contrast, Matthew and Mark call the two "bandits," and John simply states there are "two others, one on each side."

Jesus' prayer: "Father, forgive them; for they do not know what they are doing," is placed quite abruptly, in the midst of the crucifixion, with no preparation. In context, these simple words are dramatic and rather radical. They contravene traditional tribal law which held that if there was injury, the proper response is injury in return as in the adage, "An eye for an eye and a tooth for a tooth."

Also, this heartfelt prayer is not found in any of the earliest documents. Therefore, it may have been added later. Regardless of when the prayer appeared in this gospel, its words are certainly consonant with Luke's message. Presenting a new social doctrine, they offer a powerful challenge for Christians dying at the hands of the Romans.

As the three hung on their crosses, onlookers cast lots for Jesus' clothes and scoff. And—in an echo of the third temptation—challenge Jesus to use his powers to save himself. The two criminals speak also, and Luke clearly intends for them to represent two competing voices within the Christian community.

The first is frightened and self-pitying, longing for a miracle-worker to rescue him. The other accepts the justice of his sentence, speaks of his faith in Jesus' kingdom to come, and rebukes the first criminal. And though the second criminal is scarcely an equivalent in moral probity, his attitude does bring to mind the kind of peaceful acceptance that Zechariah and Elizabeth displayed about their unexpected childbirth.

This is the attitude that Luke seeks to engender in his audience regardless of their station, circumstances, or tribulations. He implores them to be strong and faithful, and in turn promises that for their efforts Paradise can be theirs.

> *Two others also, who were criminals, were led away to be put to death with him. When they came to the place that is called The Skull, they crucified Jesus there with the criminals, one on his right and one on his left. Then Jesus said, "Father, forgive them; for they do not know what they are doing." And they cast lots to divide his clothing. And the people stood by, watching; but the leaders scoffed at him, saying, "He saved others; let him save himself if he is the Messiah of God, his chosen one!" The soldiers also mocked him, coming up and offering him sour wine, and saying, "If you are the King of the Jews, save yourself!" There was also an inscription over him, "This is the King of the Jews." One of the criminals who were hanged there kept deriding him and saying, "Are you not the Messiah? Save yourself and us!" But the other rebuked him, saying, "Do you not fear God, since you are under the same sentence of condemnation? And we indeed have been condemned justly, for we are getting what we deserve for our deeds, but this man has done nothing wrong." Then he said, "Jesus, remember me when you come into your kingdom." He replied, "Truly I tell you, today you will be with me in Paradise." (23:32–43)*

SEVEN—WALKING LUKE'S ROAD OF RICHES

Jesus' death in Luke's gospel occurs at 3:00 p.m. (or 15:00), after a period of darkness lasting for three hours. Luke also tells us that the curtain of the Temple is torn in two. At the final moment, Jesus loudly and clearly commends his spirit into his Father's hands, and then he dies.

That is *all* Luke describes. No other emphasis or detail is provided. There is no mention of Jesus' reciting Psalm 22. The watching Centurion refers to Jesus only as an innocent "man" rather than an innocent "Son of God."

As a result, when we read this account it is as though each spare, scant sentence has a deep breath between it, and every single word falls directly into our hearts—as though they were written about a beloved friend of ours who died horribly on a recent afternoon—a death in which God took a great interest. This surely must have been Luke's intention, having authored an entire gospel filled with this same closeness and intimacy. It is an extraordinary account, remarkable for its simplicity and power.

> *It was now about noon, and darkness came over the whole land until three in the afternoon, while the sun's light failed; and the curtain of the temple was torn in two. Then Jesus, crying with a loud voice, said, "Father, into your hands I commend my spirit." Having said this, he breathed his last. When the centurion saw what had taken place, he praised God and said, "Certainly this man was innocent." And when all the crowds who had gathered there for this spectacle saw what had taken place, they returned home, beating their breasts. But all his acquaintances, including the women who had followed him from Galilee, stood at a distance, watching these things. (23:44–49)*

I do not exaggerate when I talk of the practical guide to mature spiritual practice that is held within The Gospel of Luke—and much of it is contained in the Passion account. As Jesus the Christ enters Jerusalem on the unridden colt, we are given an amazingly full metaphor for the new lives we are birthing as we leave John's garden.

These lives are fresh. They are original—unique, challenging, young, and powerful. Because, like that colt, they have not yet been ridden, and they are difficult to control.

We are becoming whole. Though we remain part of a larger human community, in our inner lives there is a sense in which we have become our own community. We are laying down our covering cloaks, and we want to shout out our joy. We promise to honor the truth of Jeru-Shalom, where all the tribes can meet and honor their conflicts in peace.

This is a reflection of our inmost selves as well as the outer behavior we will strive for. We will speak our truth but will not demand that others do the same. We can only feel compassion for those who still clutch their cloaks.

John's gospel shows us a Jesus who washes his disciples' feet at the final meal. Luke's Jesus makes the simple statement that now carries that action forward and suffuses our lives: "I am among you as one who serves."

Mandating service, he dismisses being merely "at the table." In other words, faithful followership is not enough. We gained a follower's understandings in the third path. Now, however, we must move forward and become active in the performance of those principles.

Peter's actions are a good reflection for us. We can progress only through taking action. Inevitably, we make mistakes. We can readily get caught up in trying to do things the "right way"—whether those things are a role in our personal lives, a job, or a spiritual journey.

The lesson here is that the point is to stay in humble service to others, even if we get some of the details wrong. Even if we err, it is likely that we are still on the right track—or, like Peter, will be able to return to it.

Jesus also couples his teaching with important comments about being perceived as lawless. This is a great truth. When we act in accordance with our new lives, at times we may—and probably will—be misunderstood. Some people will think we are acting for our own purposes, or for some unknown, sinister reason.

Most people are not accustomed to those who act with genuine selflessness or real self-confidence. Both motivations can inspire suspicion and mistrust. Luke counsels us not to worry about it, but to stay in faith and proceed anyway. We will have "everything [we] need," by which Luke means everything we need *on the level of Spirit*. Remember, that is what sustains us.

As our awareness increases, our prayerful exertions usually do too, although they most likely will not give us the ability to sweat "like blood." Nonetheless, as we gain access to the fullness of our emotional lives, we will often find ourselves overwhelmed by the urge to shout out our joy.

Furthermore, our greater levels of emotional sensitivity and self-awareness will enable us to anticipate Judas' proverbial kiss much sooner than we could previously—whether it arrives as danger, gift, or possible solution. Put simply, we will just "see things coming." This ability, if joined with courage and determination, can assist us to walk further on a proactive path toward the "good fruit" John the son of Zechariah asks of us.

We will begin to operate in a more capable, subtle, and confident manner as we practice and hone our fresh skills. *The most powerful weapons in the universe are truth and love.* Over time, no army, no power, can stand against these two. Yet the old and closed will always resist the new and open.

We will each be judged and charged with inspiring people against the status quo, just as Jesus is charged by the chief priests. And what a wonderful charge that is! Though Herod meant the "elegant robe" as mockery, it became a badge of honor and beauty. We, too, can wear the badge of our journey with pride in the name of Jesus the Christ and our genuine lives.

Jesus' lack of response to the criminal who ridicules him demonstrates a practice of deep compassion—what psychologists term "compassionate autonomy." He isn't lured into the trap of entering the grievances and denial system that mask another's unaddressed, walled-off pain. He understands that there is no real relationship possible with that man. Instead, he meets the criminal (and the others present who scoff) with clarity and understanding. He asks that they be forgiven, because they "know not."

However, a genuine relationship is possible with the criminal who shows greater understanding. Jesus therefore reaches out to him in what is known as "compassionate joining." These are the skills we need to learn and put into practice on an everyday basis. Who are the people we come into contact with who have enough ego-maturity to sustain real friendship? And which would simply pull us into their unfinished emotional problems (and might therefore be kept on a more casual level)?

True compassion does not do for others what they are unwilling to do for themselves. Doing so holds the implicit belief that another person is incapable, or is "less than" we are, and the interaction is robbed of human dignity.

Nor does genuine compassion let us escape into a path of "easy forgiveness." Luke's profound wisdom is that when we are able to put these principles into effect in our lives, we will be filled with a new kind of calm. We will not avoid pain—but pain will cease to be self-inflicted agony.

Jesus' words on the cross are the exemplar of what is, for most of us, life's longest journey: the understanding of the practice of forgiveness. Jesus does not say, "I forgive them." Jesus prays that forgiveness may come from God, the Source of All, moving through him and out to those who are breaking his body. The practice of forgiveness is a long road.

We are responsible only to walk, step by step, breath by breath, removing the poison of hate and enmity toward another human from our own hearts. *That* is the forgiveness for which we strive—an inner cleansing of our own souls. It is not within our power, nor is it our right, to "forgive" or condone or make right any action performed by another. That is solely God's prerogative.

There will be many instances that call us to inner cleansing, to forgiveness. Can we start down the long road? Can we pray Jesus' words? Can we pray ... ***to pray*** Jesus' words?

Jesus' final declaration is a reminder about perspective, and an invaluable frequent prayer: "Into your hands I commend my Spirit." This statement returns to our consciousness the reality that, although we strive to do our piece, we are part of a whole, and it is truly not about us.

Expect the Unexpected
The Resurrected Jesus

Luke's resurrection accounts compare to those of Matthew and Mark like macaroni and cheese compares to *coq au vin*. As in the rest of his gospel, Luke is plain and simple in telling of the risen Christ, but that does not mean the food is any less nourishing—not at all. It is only a matter of style, and a very appropriate one at that.

A group of women that includes the two Marys go to the tomb and find Jesus' body missing. "Suddenly two men in dazzling clothes stand beside them" and proceed to announce the resurrection. The women rush to tell the apostles the news. No one believes the women, although Peter does return to the tomb to check, and he verifies that the winding cloths are indeed empty. That said, Luke sees no reason to elaborate further.

Instead, he switches the narrative away from the tomb and back to the most frequent location for all the lessons of this gospel—the road just between or just outside a place. This time, we are presented with two of Jesus' followers—not apostles—walking to a village named Emmaus, seven miles from Jerusalem.

As they walk along, the risen Jesus joins them, but they are unable to recognize him. The two told the stranger how sorrowful they are about Jesus' death, and with wonder they share the story about the disappearance of his body. The stranger forcefully chides them, reminding them of the resurrection prophecies contained in Jewish scripture.

As they near Emmaus, due to the lateness of the hour, the two invite the stranger to stay with them. He agrees. As they sit at table, the stranger blesses the bread, breaks it, and hands it to the two, whereupon their true sight is restored and they recognize Jesus.

Then he abruptly vanishes. Afterwards the two recall that earlier their "hearts [had] burned" strongly when the stranger had talked of scripture. They set out immediately to return to Jerusalem and share their story with the apostles. When they get back, they hear about another sighting of the risen Jesus. And though the gospel mentions that Simon witnessed an appearance, there are no details given.

While the group of apostles share their experiences, the risen Jesus appears among them a third time. Still forgoing fanfare, Luke describes a very ordinary scene complete with food—which Jesus consumes also, contributing to the proof of his corporeal rising. Once again, Jesus gives his followers a lesson in scripture and "opens their minds." Assuring those assembled that they are "witnesses," he tells them to wait and "stay in the city" until they have "been clothed with power from on high," thereby echoing the opening words of the gospel.

In those days, the Jewish hope was for a great, dramatic and mighty warrior Messiah who would suddenly come and—in a climactic moment—rescue them from all of their travails, smash their oppressors beneath his heel, and raise the Jewish people up forever and ever. Luke's resurrection accounts are completely antithetical to this desire. In a sense, this gospel is a corrective for unrealistic expectations.

Both appearances are very simple scenes where everything occurs in rhythms of ordinary life—at the normal pace of walking, eating, and talking. Jesus always appears in human flesh, and Luke places emphasis on that fact. And yet, everything that happens is divine, extraordinary, and imbued with genuine complexity. Luke is instructing the Christians to expect the unexpected, but to watch for it *within their normal* lives.

Additionally, in both accounts Jesus appears to more than one person, suggesting that the Christus followers search for their experience of the resurrection—the living reign of God—within community. Luke consistently advocates patience, particularly when allotting time for wisdom and strength to mature. He began the gospel with Mary's retreat into silence as she awaits Jesus' birth. Now, nearing the gospel's close he instructs the apostles to resist teaching until they have gained more inner strength.

In these two examples, Luke covers an immense territory. Addressing both the birth of a new spiritual life and the outward expressions of that life, he speaks equally to the female and the male aspects of his audience. As well, he addresses the individual and the community. And in each of these, he continues to counsel as he always has: "Abide, be patient; have realistic expectations. This is a process, not an overnight miracle."

SEVEN—WALKING LUKE'S ROAD OF RICHES

But on the first day of the week, at early dawn, they came to the tomb, taking the spices that they had prepared. They found the stone rolled away from the tomb, but when they went in, they did not find the body. While they were perplexed about this, suddenly two men in dazzling clothes stood beside them. The women were terrified and bowed their faces to the ground, but the men said to them, "Why do you look for the living among the dead? He is not here, but has risen. Remember how he told you, while he was still in Galilee, that the Son of Man must be handed over to sinners, and be crucified, and on the third day rise again." Then they remembered his words, and returning from the tomb, they told all this to the eleven and to all the rest. Now it was Mary Magdalene, Joanna, Mary the mother of James, and the other women with them who told this to the apostles. But these words seemed to them an idle tale, and they did not believe them. But Peter got up and ran to the tomb; stooping and looking in, he saw the linen cloths by themselves; then he went home, amazed at what had happened. (24:1–12)

Now on that same day two of them were going to a village called Emmaus, about seven miles from Jerusalem, and talking with each other about all these things that had happened. While they were talking and discussing, Jesus himself came near and went with them, but their eyes were kept from recognizing him. And he said to them, "What are you discussing with each other while you walk along?" They stood still, looking sad. Then one of them, whose name was Cleopas, answered him, "Are you the only stranger in Jerusalem who does not know the things that have taken place there in these days?" He asked them, "What things?" They replied, "The things about Jesus of Nazareth, who was a prophet mighty in deed and word before God and all the people, and how our chief priests and leaders handed him over to be condemned to death and crucified him. But we had hoped that he was the one to redeem Israel. Yes, and besides all this, it is now the third day since these things took place.

Moreover, some women of our group astounded us. They were at the tomb early this morning, and when they did not find his body there, they came back and told us that they had indeed seen a vision of angels who said that he was alive. Some of those who were with us went to the tomb and found it just as the women had said; but they did not see him."

Then he said to them, "Oh, how foolish you are, and how slow of heart to believe all that the prophets have declared! Was it not necessary that the Messiah should suffer these things and then enter into his glory?" Then beginning with Moses and all the prophets, he interpreted to them the things about himself in all the scriptures. As they came near the village to which they were going, he walked ahead as if he were going on. But they urged him strongly, saying, "Stay with us, because it is almost evening and the day is now nearly over." So he went in to stay with them. When he was at the table with them, he took bread, blessed and broke it, and gave it to them. Then their eyes were opened, and they recognized him; and he vanished from their sight. They said to each other, "Were not our hearts burning within us while he was talking to us on the road, while he was opening the scriptures to us?" That same hour they got up and returned to Jerusalem; and they found the eleven and their companions gathered together. They were saying, "The Lord has risen indeed, and he has appeared to Simon!" Then they told what had happened on the road, and how he had been made known to them in the breaking of the bread. (24:13–35)

While they were talking about this, Jesus himself stood among them and said to them, "Peace be with you." They were startled and terrified, and thought that they were seeing a ghost. He said to them, "Why are you frightened, and why do doubts arise in your hearts? Look at my hands and my feet; see that it is I myself. Touch me and see; for a ghost does not have flesh and bones as you see that I have." And when he had said this, he showed them his hands and his feet. While in their joy they were disbelieving and still wondering, he said to

SEVEN—WALKING LUKE'S ROAD OF RICHES

them, "Have you anything here to eat?" They gave him a piece of broiled fish, and he took it and ate in their presence. Then he said to them, "These are my words that I spoke to you while I was still with you—that everything written about me in the law of Moses, the prophets, and the psalms must be fulfilled." Then he opened their minds to understand the scriptures, and he said to them, "Thus it is written, that the Messiah is to suffer and to rise from the dead on the third day, and that repentance and forgiveness of sins is to be proclaimed in his name to all nations, beginning from Jerusalem. You are witnesses of these things. And see, I am sending upon you what my Father promised; so stay here in the city until you have been clothed with power from on high." Then he led them out as far as Bethany, and, lifting up his hands, he blessed them. While he was blessing them, he withdrew from them and was carried up into heaven. And they worshiped him, and returned to Jerusalem with great joy; and they were continually in the temple blessing God. (24:36–53)

We are not so different from the first-century Christians. There isn't one among us who hasn't longed for a quick solution or a flash of insight or some heavenly intercession that would solve our besetting problem or cure a crisis. That is one of the reasons the lessons of Luke are vitally important to us today. Think of all the major careers in politics, in business, and—yes—in religion that have been won and lost by the precise manipulation of our feelings in this vulnerable area.

How many times have we agreed to something or voted for someone because a quick answer was implied or promised? Or abandoned the person or the positions when we didn't receive the surety we longed for, no matter how facile? On a more intimate level, think of the daily relationships that have suffered because we speak too quickly—or failed to speak when truth is needed.

The resurrection stories teach us about our ability to renew our vitality and stay present to the divine in our lives. When we find ourselves simply walking through our days, will we still feel the burning in our hearts? Will we come back together, break bread, and share our stories with others?

Will we have eyes to be present to the miraculous throughout the day—to stay with wonder and curiosity and a positive attitude—to anticipate the unexpected ways that things can work out? And will we open ourselves to the new kindling of the first path when the beautiful home we have made in the fourth path turns once again to ashes and and a new cycle asks to be recognized?

In our personal relationships, will we understand that a genuine friend shares only when asked—and with mindfulness of the place where our companion is on his or her journey? We will continually meet others who are in different places of understanding than we are, and we need to take this into account when we consider how we think about their words and actions and when we communicate. Judgment and condemnation will have to be suspended, even at times abandoned.

We may even need to meet them in a different path of worship or faith. It is both test and testament of our compassion and our commitment to the journey when we are able to greet all persons with the same degree of love and honor and respect with which we would meet the Christ. This is another of the many lessons on the road to Emmaus.

When Luke speaks of not going out to share God's word until one is "clothed with the power from on high," it is this power—the power of love, compassion and respectful understanding—to which he refers. It is a type of power that has been sadly misunderstood for a very long time in the Christian church and amongst many spiritual traditions. Now we must begin anew. We must endeavor to refashion evangelism and speech with each other and with all others, especially those who are not like us.

And then we can abide in Jeru-Shalom with uplifting joy.

SEVEN—WALKING LUKE'S ROAD OF RICHES

Prayers for The Fourth Path

Psalm 131

You know that my heart is not haughty
Nor my eyes lofty
Neither have I reached for things
Too great and too wonderful for me
But I have calmed and settled my heart
And it is contented
Like a child surfeited on a mother's breast
Like a suckling child is my heart
Let those who question and struggle
Wait quiet like this for you
From this day forth
And always

                                translation by Norman Fischer

Psalm 133

How good
How pleasant
When we abide intimate together
Like warm oil on the head
Trickling down the cheek
Aaron's cheek
And trickling down the neck onto the collar
Like the dew of Mount Hermon
The dew that runs down the mountains of Zion
Where you called forth the blessing
For life, life always

                                  translation by Norman Fischer

EXERCISES FOR THE FOURTH PATH

The exercises of Quadratos are cumulative. By the time we have reached this point, we are ready to begin a series of practices that we hope will become everyday values rather than exercises. Like the lessons within The Gospel of Luke, they support our discovery of the greatest riches of a revitalized life—and the longer we use them, the wealthier our spirits become. Because they are lengthy and ongoing, I have detailed them in a separate chapter which follows, titled "Eight Essential and Continuing Practices."

HOW DO WE MATURE IN SERVICE?
The Core Question of The Gospel of Luke

The Gospel of Luke is a map, guiding the maturation of the spiritual journey into a practice of genuine forgiveness and compassion. From this place of integration, and the joining of heart and mind, we gain the ability to act from love despite tension and conflict.

Zechariah and Elizabeth and Mary teach us to receive the unexpected with equanimity and curiosity, remaining open to possibility. We must be silent for a time and ponder the changes that have come, allowing the opportunity for integration to find its way within us and take root.

The Canticle of Mary blesses us with the model of holding a unified vision of the future. When we put the power of this positive expectation into our lives, they will improve.

The nativity account counsels patience and openness to the unexpected. As we walk the fourth path, our traditional "home" will often disappear. We, too, may need to seek a manger or build a fresh place for the birth of our "child," the new energy of our lives. And we must welcome and offer love to each and every part of ourselves—even the most unformed, awkward, fearful and hidden aspects.

The story of the boy Jesus in the temple reminds us that growth is a process of change. Some of our history is valuable, while some needs to be shed. Some new things are productive; others are not. Patience and discernment of our motives are the focus of our reflection.

John, son of Zechariah, at the river tells us to step up and out from the crowd, engage in acts of generosity and justice and accept responsibility for speaking and acting on our own truth, without concerns about whether our truth will be heard, accepted, or effective. John also cautions against the danger that our greater empowerment may turn into a need for adulation.

The temptations ask us to carefully discern whether we are acting truly or whether when we speak and act, we are actually seeking power for ourselves, power over others, or protection from the consequences of our actions.

The Beatitudes sing out simultaneous promise and strong caution. First, they offer the beauty and blessedness of the fourth path. Then they throw up dire warnings: they promise that if we fail to shelter our new life and act too soon, we will revert to immature behavior—and the consequences will be painful.

The parable of the good Samaritan is a teaching about the importance of responding to human need with care and compassion and without regard to the strictures of societal boundaries or inner unworthiness.

When we are told to knock at the door, we are being counseled to be persistent and proactive in our lives—even if it is difficult or inconvenient. It is wise for us to keep a vision of what is self-worthy and appropriate for our future and ask for that vision to be fulfilled—to ask for "three loaves" not merely two slices for a sandwich.

The prodigal son and other stories of losing and finding remind us that lives lived without risk and exploration are not only dull; they are spiritually empty. The challenges of risk are a necessary tool for our growth. When we push ourselves toward change regardless of the seeming result, we find inner growth and should celebrate.

Luke's passion account speaks to us about the practice of compassion and genuine forgiveness. It does not let us escape into a path of "easy forgiveness," which deprives relationships of dignity. It tells us that genuine forgiveness removes the emotional pain that keeps us in bondage.

The resurrection accounts ask us to have fresh eyes and openness of spirit so that we may always recognize Mystery in our lives when it appears. They also ask us to have the patience to wait for a maturing of heart and mind before we try to carry this message to others, so that when we finally speak we will meet people at *their* place on the journey—and not where we might like them to be. Only in this way can we extend the respect, freedom and safety to others that we desire for ourselves.

Chapter 8

EIGHT ESSENTIAL AND CONTINUING PRACTICES

From the perspective of the fourth path, we ask for practical approaches that help us continue our Journey of Quadratos. We want to be deepened but are not always certain how to accomplish this, particularly at a time when many of our spiritual traditions lag behind. This chapter offers eight essential practices, the basis for all of which can be found throughout the Journey of Quadratos and particularly along the fourth path.

These practices, which have been expanded and placed in a contemporary expression, can be used by individuals as well as groups and communities. They are followed by suggested readings. (Full citations are in the bibliography in the rear.)

While the exercises appear to be focused mainly on individual practice, all have much broader implications. As we realized in the fourth path, this is true of every action we take. The last four exercises move well beyond our personal sphere. The final two are especially powerful in their potential for far-reaching impact.

In this chapter we use Luke as our model, moving from lofty to modest and perhaps back to lofty. Nonetheless, these eight are core exercises, and their practice will keep us maturing in every aspect of our lives. And as our mind and heart flourish, we will help to create a wiser and more compassionate practice of Christianity—and therefore a safer and more harmonious world.

Practice I—Speak Truth and Unity

The deepest level of communication is not communication, but communion . . . We are already one, but we imagine that we are not.

Thomas Merton

The first path frequently brings us face to face with the consequences of fear and untruth in our lives. In the second path we find ourselves caught between opposites. Then in the third path we receive an experience of union that dispels those illusions. Now, in our practice of the fourth path we attempt to learn the practice and actual behaviors of a new way of being and deeper ways of loving.

At the same time, we prepare ourselves to venture onto a new first path and then another and another. If we wish to live ever more consciously within the circle of the four paths, we will continually seek awareness of unreflective thoughts, attitudes and actions that might pull us backward. One of the greatest of these rests in the habits of our speech.

We are responsible for what issues forth from our mouths. And words have immense power. That is why when addressing matters of importance, we should strive to bring forth those deeply reflected, long-held-in-the- belly truths (Elizabeth and Mary again, yes!) rather than the sentence that hurriedly pops out.

We desire our speech to be genuine. We want the opinion we are expressing to be truly our own and not a rehashed version that actually belongs to some authority figure we have allowed to assume too much power in our lives. Spirit calls us to be accountable for our words, asking for the courageous expression of our truth even at the risk of loss of esteem or liberty.

Yet, at the same time we are called to compassion and unity. We are asked to *never* relinquish our truth, but simultaneously never to negate the truth of another—and to do our best to speak in terms of ourselves and with kindness. Particularly in the early years of fourth-path practice, this can sometimes seem a difficult tightrope on which to balance. It often doesn't seem fair, or even possible, to meet all of these requirements.

However, this is one of our greatest challenges and the most important of all the eight practices. That is why we have placed it first. It is foundational. It is threaded throughout every aspect of our lives, particularly filling our families and our workplaces. It is habitual and relational, and change is difficult. Although we can bring our awareness to the problem, we are likely to need help.

One step is to listen patiently and carefully to those more adept than we are. Another is to enlist ourselves in a more formal practice, such as that of *contemplative dialogue* (for which I have listed the website below). However, this is such a vital and problematic issue that I believe it is also a completely appropriate matter for a buddy system. Two friends can commit to helping each other be mindful of compassionate and appropriate speech, as can a small group.

The third path teaches us that the truth of reality is oneness. The human family, and every experience of that family, is part of a whole. This means that *no one and no thing* can ever truly be "other." Therefore, when we use absolutist language—language that is either/or, or language that is separatist in any way, we are expressing an untruth. This clearly has huge implications for our relationships, communities, and spiritual traditions—not to mention politics.

In practice, is this difficult? Of course it is! We not only struggle with ourselves, we struggle with the English language, which is built on categories and specificity. English has many more words than any other language on earth, and though it strives to find the perfect word for everything, it often lacks subtlety.

For example, psychology tells us that every human emotion is a complex combination of feelings: joy contains sadness for example, and laughter is poignant. Yet the English words carry no hint of the undertones—merely the single, dominant aspect. Correspondingly, light can have no dark within it, nor the converse; though in the twenty-four hours of the day, the variations are literally infinite.

We must work constantly to be mindful of our language and to creatively overcome its limitations, stretching to move away from words that separate and reaching for those that unite—even creating new metaphors when possible.

In the paucity of our language, how can we continually describe the reality Merton refers to when he writes, "We are already one, and only imagine we are not"? How do we accomplish the circular reality of wholeness and communion in the linear limitation of our language?

The process must necessarily begin with monitoring our thoughts. This can be a stretch, because it is likely we have not been in the habit of giving them such careful scrutiny. The difficulty is increased by the fact that our culture has become so separated that even words heretofore perfectly innocent—left, right, liberal, conservative—have taken on absolutist and pejorative qualities.

Even our hymnals and prayer books focus on "I" instead of "we." However, if we wish to walk a fourth path of love and compassion, we will be mindful and self-vigilant and refrain from terms such as these—even if we have to sing the song a little differently than everyone else.

Is this about political correctness of any kind? No. Our aim is much deeper. There is no language that is free from a philosophy or worldview. English has millennia of accretions attached to it plus some relatively recent distortions.

Some of them are not a problem, but many of them are. When we take charge of our speech, we are taking responsibility for helping to heal the error of dualistic thought and the painful divisions that it perpetuates.

Let us therefore bend our every effort to speak in the language of "we," "us," and "our"—knowing that eventually, the new Jeru-Shalom will be built upon the words of our honest and respectful and loving wrestling with each other.

Readings

Bernardo Olivera — *How Far to Follow? The Martyrs of Atlas*
Steven Wirth — *The Path of Contemplative Dialogue: Engaging the Collective Spirit,* available at www.contemplativedialogue.org

Practice II—Open and Engage the Truths of Beauty

I asked the earth, I asked the sea and the deeps, among the living animals, the things that creep. I asked the winds that blow, I asked the heavens, the sun, the moon, the stars, and to all things that stand at the door of my flesh . . . My question was the gaze I turned to them. Their answer was their beauty.

St. Augustine

EIGHT—EIGHT ESSENTIAL AND CONTINUING PRACTICES

Most of us are busy and distracted with many demands on our time, energy, and emotions. Few of us are fortunate enough to live in the country, or to have a museum next door. Yet almost nothing integrates and refreshes and brings us more deeply into our soul-work than the experience of beauty.

Beauty has three levels—the appreciative, the collaborative, and the creative. All are satisfying and important, and all will yield riches as fourth-path practices.

Regularly opening ourselves to the appreciation of beauty is invaluable. This does not mean we should trot down to the local Art Museum, unless that experience lifts our soul. Each of us is different. What this does mean is that we should regularly seek out the places that open us to wonder and awe, to a feeling of the holy, of being alive and connected to All.

Once we find them, we need to release ourselves and revel in sight, touch, sound and smell: the entire sensory and tactile experience of beauty. It may be wiggling our toes in a white-sanded beach, being swarmed by a litter of kissing puppies, stunned by the sight of a deep canyon crevice, inhaling the fragrance of a perfect yellow rose—or, yes, contemplating a painting in a museum.

In order to expand our experience, we also use our imagination. We select an episode or a feeling from our lives or our work or our relationships—something from our larger world. We bring that truth into our encounter with beauty in any way that seems appropriate to us. Then we combine the aspect of our life with the art, or the beach, or the puppies.

We just hold it there for a while. Do they relate in any way? Amplify each other? Diminish each other? Spark the thought of something or someone else? Then we try bringing in another aspect of our lives.

We tend to think that comprehending wholeness is a part of the third path, but appreciating beauty can be a dynamic experience that enlarges our understanding of almost anything. It is able to bring a sense of rightness, wonder, and the holy to all parts of our journey.

The *collaborative* experience of beauty can be a bit more difficult to accomplish but is wonderfully rewarding. It is exactly as it sounds—the shared experience of beauty or even better, of beauty-*making*. This might include making music, singing, dancing, working in a garden, or taking a nature walk with others.

Some of us are fortunate or intentional enough to collaborate with others on a journey similar to our own, and then we can expand our experience through the sharing of its contemplative aspects through chanting, or via other creative group projects.

Collaborative efforts have the potential to combine all three forms of beauty: to create, to share, and to appreciate. When this is achieved a special kind of richness opens, because the fourth-path gift of relationship and friendship based in equality that moves in both directions is added to the element of creativity.

The *creative* experience of beauty is by far, one of the most valuable practices on our work of the fourth path. To create means to bring forth something that has not existed before. It is a birthing—by definition, a holy activity. It is unique and wonderfully mysterious.

In the arena of creative expression, we recommend practices that engage the body because of their capacity to overcome the chatter of the ego-self, as well as more unity between mind, heart and body. This is particularly profound—and profoundly important—on the fourth path.

There are many avenues to explore. It is important, however, that we make a commitment to opening the deep well of the nonverbal aspect of ourselves, and becoming accustomed to the reverberation of its sonorous echo in the other areas of our lives. Nonverbal creative work specifically engages the physical and the sensuous—and does so in a very direct way.

We can, of course, do this through drawing or painting whether or not we have training. Without training, simple colored pencils, markers, or tempera paints are probably the most available and satisfying media to use. A *large* brush used on a *large* piece of paper or canvas can be especially gratifying, particularly with brilliantly pigmented tempera colors or broad-tipped markers. Graffiti artists might be on to something!

And it is quite primal and centering to work with a big piece of clay. Many of the new varieties of clay are available in vivid colors and don't dry out quickly. A favorite of Quadratos communities is collage—randomly choosing and cutting out images from magazines and gluing them to a large page, and later contemplating what can be seen in the pattern of the choices made. To these possibilities, we add the creativity of making gardens, and dances, and music.

Whatever the medium, the creative process is the same—and it replicates the process of Quadratos. First, we begin—an admittedly difficult step. We do it anyway. We make the space, take the time, spend as many blank minutes as necessary just sitting.

It is difficult to begin from nothing and go to something. There is typically time spent wrestling with the material. Then more time spent in what feels like vain efforts. (They are *not*. We should not stop.)

Eventually, *something* comes. A feeling emerges from some mysterious place that is akin to being lifted by wings. Time seems to stop, but our hands continue on. We have accessed a deep and holy region—and we have discovered why artists create. In each specific creative task, we will progress from Matthew through Mark to John.

Additionally, as we engage in *regular* creative work with image (or music or dance)—as we practice what we have learned and start to make it a part of our genuine and original new lives, our efforts move us further—into deep encounter with the fourth path. There, we reap other benefits.

Imagery moves easily in all directions, through the full spectrum of human experience. Images can be emotional, physical, intellectual, and spiritual. They can attract, repel, uplift, and horrify. They can be filled with tension or calm, be erotic or mundane.

If in our creative work we stretch to experience and appreciate all of the sides within and around us, we will expand. Our ability to understand and fluidly move through the paradoxical nature of Spirit will inevitably grow. Eventually, so too as will our capacity to share this experience, as it becomes more familiar.

Regardless of what type of creative practice we eventually choose (and maybe we will choose more than one), consider keeping photographs, or record our efforts. In this way, we will be able to remain present to our entire Quadratos journey.

A periodic review will display all our paths before us. We will see the trepidation, the progress, and the joy. We will see Matthew and Mark and John and Luke arrayed before us. We will see the great truths that have moved through us and lead us forward.

Readings

Seena B. Frost	*SoulCollage Evolving: An Intuitive Collage Process for Self-Discovery and Community*
Thomas Moore	*Original Self: Living with Paradox and Originality*
John O'Donohue	*Beauty: The Invisible Embrace*
Lindsay Whiting	*Living into Art: Journeys through Collage*

Practice III–Find the Quiet Center

The path to the center is never straight but always clear.

Gernot Candolini

Meditation and prayer have been strongly recommended throughout the entire Journey of Quadratos, and our need for them will never cease. In the fourth path, we come to understand their practice to be as regular and necessary as our breath.

Historically, across spiritual traditions there have been two major forms of meditation. These have grown from two worship traditions—seen variously as both contradictory and complementary.

In Christianity, they are called by Greek names. One is called "apophatic worship," which derives from the Greek word *aphonais*, meaning "to say no." Its underlying principle is that God is beyond all earthly symbols and human efforts at understanding; therefore, a meditator should attempt to transcend or remove all concepts and "empty oneself."

EIGHT—EIGHT ESSENTIAL AND CONTINUING PRACTICES

When an image or thought arises, it is to be gently dismissed. The meditator's continuing effort is toward achieving what Buddhists call Nirvana—a completely serene, yet connected awareness of the whole, of God.

The second form is called "kataphatic worship" (also spelled "cataphatic"), which comes from the Greek *kata*, which means "down into" or "down with" combined with *phasis*, which is Greek for an utterance which expresses feelings rather than propositions. Kataphatic worship affirms the knowledge of God using expressions of wonder and glory.

Its meditation form usually focuses on an image, although it can also use words or a story or even music. The practice is to focus on the image, move into it, then through it, and eventually find stillness. Some proponents of this type of meditation have claimed that it is more integrated with "real life" than apophatic meditation.

Apophatic meditation can be an active form of prayer employing a mantra and breathing, or it can be a silent contemplation such as that used in centering prayer, which was most notably shaped by Father Thomas Keating (now deceased). This prayer is typically practiced as twenty to thirty minutes or more of quiet sitting.

Another well-known apophatic form is a Society of Friends meeting, which is one hour of silent contemplation. Yet it is possible for such a meeting to suddenly become kataphatic, because if Spirit so moves them members may arise and speak aloud about any subject they wish, and the group will then respectfully meditate upon that subject. Likewise, centering prayer has expanded and developed a hybrid called "imaged centering prayer" introducing kataphatic elements.

Methods of kataphatic prayer range along a continuum from the more traditional gazing upon an icon for an extended period to modern dance. In between are practices such as labyrinth walks and pilgrimage, chanting, brush drawing, collage, working with paint or clay, and ritual.

Sunday worship services are essentially kataphatic prayer forms that use image, senses, and body posture to engage participants and move them into a quiet center. Older rituals made this more apparent because they had greater use of music, incense, costume, and color than we are familiar with today. Nonetheless, present-day religious ritual is still intended to serve this purpose.

Lectio divina is a kataphatic practice directly related to Quadratos, which is found mentioned in documents dating from 220 CE. The words mean "sacred reading". In its earliest form, *lectio divina* was practiced in monasteries. A monk would read a scripture passage aloud, and those assembled would meditate on the passage for an extended period. It likely grew from the ancient Jewish tradition of elders gathering in the Temple to hear, to chant, and then to verbally wrestle with each other about a text from the Torah.

In the sixth century, St. Benedict strongly supported the practice in his writings leading to its wider spread. In the twelfth century, a French Carthusian monk, Guigo II, set the simple reading into a formal four-step process he called a "ladder." This system was used extensively until the fifteenth century when it all but disappeared, only reappearing again following the reforms of the Second Vatican Council in the 1960s.

Today, *lectio divina* is used far beyond monasteries. In his book *Sacred Reading*, Michael Casey describes *lectio divina* as "a means of descending to the level of the heart and of finding God." In its simplest form, this is done by a slow recitation of selected scripture repeated and punctuated with periods of silence. A deep rhythm is developed—as much of silence as of the words—and the listeners are, without effort, moved beyond the questioning mind into a deeper, more peaceful space and ultimately closer to God.

In the formal four-stage process, the beginning is *lectio* (reading), when the listener makes a concerted, repeated study of the words of the selected text. The second stage is *meditatio* (meditation), wherein one asks oneself how the passage affects one's life.

Oratio (reflection/prayer) flows from the text and the meditation and may result in an inner question about what step to take or a prayer of thanks or praise. The final step is *contemplatio* or *actio* (contemplation or action), when one fully enters the prayer experience in awareness, in gratitude, in praise, or perhaps in a discernment for change or action. These stages exactly match up with the Quadratos sequence.

If we wish to consciously combine Quadratos with *lectio divina*, we can use either the preceding or upcoming Sunday gospel reading from the three-year lectionary as our text. In this way, all four gospels are contemplated over a three-year time span in the sequence of Quadratos.

It is even better if this is done in a group. Then there is a community of support that will provide a fresh well of sustaining grace—regardless of which of the four paths is most present in our personal life. If we belong to a church community that doesn't follow the three-year Sunday cycle, we can still follow the Quadratos *lectio* by praying the gospels of Matthew, Mark, and Luke in the sequence and stopping during Lent and Easter every year to pray The Gospel of John.

Another kataphatic method that mirrors the four paths is a labyrinth walk, a form of walking meditation. As our feet cross the threshold, we are seeking growth and change (Matthew). Walking the circuitous path to the center, we note our many exhaustions and anxieties (Mark).

As we rest in the center, contemplating the steps we have taken and those still to come as they are displayed before us, we pray for communion (John). Retracing our path to the beginning, imbued with new understanding we pray to carry out the truths of the blessings we have received (Luke). Labyrinths can now be found in many faith communities and can readily be purchased in portable forms.

Regardless of how we choose to find the quiet center, time and experience have shown that both apophatic and kataphatic approaches are immensely valuable. They lead us to our primary objective: a place where we can rest beneath our mind's chatter, gain perspective, and connect with Spirit.

We may have an individual preference for one form over another based on what we were taught or what we personally find easiest. Because each form has virtues, it is good to experiment; even someone who is very knowledgeable in one form might benefit by stretching to learn the other; the less familiar style may render unexpected richness.

It might even be worthwhile to combine the two styles. Increasingly modern practice is showing us, and encouraging, a great deal of overlap. It may well be that the differences between the two styles are fairly illusory and arbitrary. In the end, the point of meditation is our experience of the reverent stillness, not how we get to it.

I need to add a note regarding both forms of meditation. Meditators typically speak of the "quiet" center (with quiet being today thought of as more a characteristic of apophatic meditation than kataphatic), and modern practice generally posits that meditation is done with the body held still. However, physical "quietness" and body "stillness" are not requisites through the course of ancient practice. Far from it!

I encourage you to free yourself from these current misconceptions. Wholeness is our objective, and wholeness is not a disembodied experience.

Historically, walking, rocking the body, and dance were completely acceptable expressions of prayer and meditation in both "methods." Many people use yoga practice as a form of meditation that incorporates bodily experience, and there are several other movement-based disciplines that provide deeply spiritual experiences to their practitioners.

Remember our discussion in The Gospel of John: spirit is not superior to body, though sadly, many religious and spiritual traditions seem to consider it so. *After* you have mastered the fundamental principles of the form you have chosen, please practice its expression in whatever way works best for you.

Readings

Lauren Artress	*Walking a Sacred Path: Rediscovering the Labyrinth as a Spiritual Practice*
Cynthia Bourgeault	*Chanting the Psalms: A Practical Guide with Instructional CD*
Michael Casey	*Sacred Reading: The Ancient Art of Lectio Divina*
Ana Hernandez	*The Sacred Art of Chant: Preparing to Practice*
Thomas Keating	*Intimacy with God: An Introduction to Centering Prayer*

Gabriel Roth with John Loudon — *Maps to Ecstasy: A Healing Journey for the Untamed Spirit (5 Rhythms Dance as Meditation Practice)*

Alexander J. Shaia — "Sandplay in Spiritual Direction: Beyond Insight or Centering." *Presence Journal, June 2001*, available at www.quadratos.com/books/

Practice IV—Absorb the Deeper Rhythms

I go among the trees and sit still . . .
As we sing, the day turns, the trees move.

Wendell Berry

The four paths, the sequence of each day, and the order of the four seasons are significantly connected. God breathes creation into these cycles, and they are a daily death and resurrection, the ever-present mirror of the Christ in our lives. Our common conversation reflects this. We talk of how we slept and how "our day" is going. The weather is our most common topic.

Our fourth-path practice is to behold this truth—our connection with the rhythms of everyday life—with greater depth and mindfulness. The recommended discipline is a simple one—like Luke's gospel. Go outside once a day, take a deep breath, and reflect on our connections with the natural rhythms. (For greater resonance with our ancestors, do this at sunset or sunrise.)

Ancient traditions celebrated the beginnings of days and years in times of dark and quiet. We do not think this way today, but it used to be that when the sun disappeared it was the time to make ready. Sabbath begins at dusk, and autumn was always considered the first season of the year, the time when it was possible to see nature preparing for her long winter sleep.

This timing came more naturally to earlier, agrarian cultures, which viewed everything in terms of the crop cycle. Thus, the Jewish New Year begins in autumn, followed closely by the harvest festival of Sukkot. Autumn marked the ending of one crop's death, and the anticipation of the next one's life—the year's turning.

It would help us if we could once again match ourselves to early evening and autumn as natural expressions of the first path and the changing part of a universal cycle. After all, in the evening our bodies decelerate (or try to in our busy lives). We review our day and make plans for the next. In autumn, we watch the leaves lose their green and transition through color into brown. Some plants begin to go dormant and others to die.

Nonetheless, we realize that we will see many of them resurrect into new life come spring, while others will decay into rich compost for future growth. The turning of new life continues unceasingly. When we take a breath every autumn day, we can ask what challenges face us and with what willingness we face them. Are we attempting to cling to the green of the season past? Or are we willing to change—even if it means transformation into an unknown reality?

Our nighttime slumber and the arrival of winter's cold reflect the second path to us. Both are intended to slow us and grow us. Our metabolism and our brain both require time to regroup.

Long nights and winter snowfalls are mirrors for us. They can be a picture of interminable suffering and restlessness when we are unable to feel at peace. The gasp of night and the breath of winter can feel difficult to take in, and a yearning for warmth and love may overtake us trying to quell our lack of peace.

Or, can we instead see winter as a time of nothing stirring on the surface except the occasional storm, yet with tremendous work of growth being accomplished out of sight and underground? The second path holds pondering and terrible suffering or patient endurance. Quiescence is necessary for the life of an abundant spring to germinate and grow.

At last—or at least it seems so—our dark-accustomed eyes blink open and the first green shoots appear. The sun comes up, and the cycle releases spring! We breathe, stretch, wiggle our toes, enjoy, and notice anew. In spring, we exult in the bright colors of the flowers, in warmth and possibilities, yet there is tumult also. Sudden rainstorms pelt, air masses collide and bring tornadoes, and early heat creates flooding.

Each day as we awake, "it's always something," as the saying goes. This is the third path when our awareness is continually stretched. Quadratos asks us to become sensitive and aware. Everything is part of the whole—the embrace of someone we love, the contempt of an embittered relative, the transcendent, exquisite sunrise and the flood that devastates lives. When we take our daily breath in this third-path practice, we ask ourselves how to grow in understanding and acceptance of the complexities of this truth.

Almost without our notice, the freshness of the day turns and spring becomes summer. The revelations of the third path become the attentive labor of the fourth. Equipped with more knowledge, yet a bit road- weary, we allow wisdom to measure our pace and our actions. The sun is overhead and the summer days are long. When we take our summer breath, our questions have a different rhythm. They are more difficult.

Sometimes they snag on the exhale of our good labor, or maybe the shallow inhale of our sanctimony. "Am I doing only for myself and nothing for others?" or "Am I doing everything for others and nothing for myself?" or even "Does the life I am living match up with the beliefs I hold? Too much? Too little?"

These are the questions of living and learning the balance and maturity of the fourth path, and we see them best reflected when the sun is high and the summer is hot.

Early evening, nighttime, morning, afternoon—autumn, winter, spring, and summer—these natural cycles of four bring the Journey of Quadratos into a fresh intimacy for us. The processes we witness outwardly we also see in- wardly. Each day and every season holds both gift and challenge. The mind- fulness of a daily breath will help remind us to ask where and who we are.

Readings

Rob Bell	*What We Talk About, When We Talk About God*
Thomas Berry	*The Great Work: Our Way into the Future*
Nora Gallagher	*Things Seen and Unseen: A Year Lived in Faith*
China Galland	*Longing for Darkness: Tara and the Black Madonna*
J. Ruth Gendler	*Changing Light: The Eternal Cycle of Night and Day*
Joan Halifax	*The Fruitful Darkness: Reconnecting with the Body of the Earth*
Paul Bogard (editor)	*Let There Be Night*
Jan L. Richardson	*Night Visions: Searching the Shadows of Advent and Christmas*
Jan L. Richardson	*In Wisdom's Path: Discovering the Sacred in Every Season*
Brian Swimme	*The Hidden Heart of the Cosmos: Humanity and the New Story*

Practice V—Expand into Risk

And the day came when the risk to remain tight in a bud was more painful than the risk it took to blossom.
Anaïs Nin

Having made at least one turn of Quadratos' fourfold cycle, we are certainly familiar with risk. We may not yet greet it as a friend, but we now recognize it as a necessary component of our journey. We have engaged in it not once, but many times along our way.

This fourth-path practice has a strong message: risk-taking is not over, now or ever. The paths of the Quadratos cycle never end any more than the recurring cycle itself does. We can enter into each new path and enjoy continuing growth, or we can attempt to ignore the call for change from this universal pattern and inevitably regress. Those are our simple choices.

EIGHT—EIGHT ESSENTIAL AND CONTINUING PRACTICES

With the forward choice we gain vitality and joy, but at the price of continued vulnerability. When we "opt out" of our growth as individuals, the result is some variety of withering—we grow rigid, narrow, timid, fantastical, or depressed.

If we continue the journey, our major question becomes knowing when to risk and finding ways to support our courage. Clarissa Pinkola Estes, author and Jungian psychologist, writes in *Women Who Run with the Wolves*, "Climb the highest tree. Walk out on its thinnest limb. Let it break."

This is a terrific metaphor about maximizing human potential, but it could also be seen as a recommendation for recklessness. How do we discern the difference between an adventuresome spirit and downright stupidity? The quality of our daily lives is deeply affected by the answer to this question.

Furthermore, the consequences of our actions today—even of our words—are a great deal more far-reaching than they have ever been. We can travel literally with a virus by plane or train or figuratively with one via the Internet; in either case, we can infect millions, and others can do the same to us.

Words we speak and write and images we create arrive instantaneously in every corner of the planet. We can inflict great damage and are in physical and emotional jeopardy in ways we have never known and are not prepared for. We have no precedent for being so exposed, so known to each other, with such great responsibility for interdependence.

At the same time, on a personal level many lack the support systems they used to find in families, neighborhoods, and social and fraternal organizations. Yet, in some ways this is progress, as difficult as that may be to accept.

A lot of the unwritten rules that undergirded those same families, neighborhoods, and organizations were precisely the ones that ruled ancient tribes. Strong support was provided to members, but it came in return for unquestioning allegiance—and the willingness to shun, hurt, fight, and even kill those outside of and rejected by the head of the group.

Some church groups have begun innovative programs to help fill the gaps in community, but most people languish with no connections. Internet sites such as Facebook and Instagram are enormously successful, partially because they provide some sense of being a neighborhood, albeit in cyberspace; but by and large these are not real people on the ground putting their physical arms around each other for a hug.

No substantial new ways or groups have yet been developed to fill these voids. As a result, many of us feel lonely and uncertain particularly in the areas of relationships and discerning appropriate levels of responsibility.

In this tentative environment when, how, and to whom do we risk saying the words, "I want," "I need," "I love"? Or go further and make the commitments of "I have" and "I do"? How do we foster the growth we desire—in ourselves and in the larger world? Is there a guidebook we can follow?

The Journey of Quadratos is that guide, and the eight practices form a concrete and ongoing process we can use. Yet we acknowledge that it is very difficult to go it alone. In each of the practices, making the effort to join with others who also engage in the same activities will pay large dividends.

It is likely that somewhere, when lifting a paintbrush or while in the parking lot of a labyrinth, we will encounter a kindred soul. That encounter can become the kernel of a friendship which can lead to like-minded others, and even the formation of a Quadratos group.

No matter what we do in this regard however, moments of trial are still unavoidable. We will face something new, and we will feel that unmistakable, uncomfortable tightness in the chest or belly or cranium. That is the ego-self letting us know it is frightened, digging its heels right into that particular body part—wailing, "I don't want to take a risk!"

And that is our signal to pull out the tools we have placed in reserve for precisely this moment. This is when we talk with those trusted friends we have developed. And we pray, walk, grab some clay, or draw—and pray some more. Gradually trepidation lessens, equanimity arises and we move through our sense of peril.

Alternatively, our inner voice and counselors instead help us to discover that the signal to stop is—this time—accurate, wise, and protective, and we possibly *are* being foolhardy and misguided. If that is the case, then we either pause for more information or stop our course completely.

Regardless of the direction in which we move, the decision is completely ours, and we are able to make it with serenity and finality. We have developed a fourth-path practice to deal with risk, and we are certain that our process is solid. We have no regrets, and we know we will find the next challenge a bit easier because of our experience.

Readings

Joan D. Chittister	*Scarred by Struggle, Transformed by Hope*
Roger Housden	*Ten Poems to Set You Free*
Henri J. M. Nouwen	*The Inner Voice of Love: A Journey through Anguish to Freedom*

Practice VI–Learn to Let Go

Your desire must be disciplined, and what you want
to happen in time, sacrificed.

Rumi

Another way to state this practice in more psychological terms would be, "Don't be attached to results." It is possible that next to truth-speaking, this principle affects an emotionally and spiritually mature life more substantially than all the other practices, yet no action or striving whatsoever is required.

In fact, we are required *not* to strive or act. Luke gave a version of this practice when he assured his readers that *if* they lived a compassionate life and cared for each other, then despite every challenge they would find passion and joy in their communal life, and their Christian beliefs would ultimately not only endure but thrive. The modern version requires us to open ourselves to a realization having two parts.

First, we accept that positive results *will occur* provided we sincerely make our way through the universal spiritual paths of Quadratos and then continue our fourth-path practices. Stated in another way: we grasp that it is completely outside our power to control how "life" changes, but completely up to us to use our best efforts to improve ourselves—and that "life" will tend to improve if we do.

Second, we accept that we are not in any way in charge of the greater processes of life or the universe. The great cycles move through us—in their own time and with their own vast and inexplicable wisdom. We won't always understand why things happen. We won't always get the results we want. Good people unaccountably suffer, and bad people mysteriously thrive.

At the same time, it is possible for us to become so attuned to the visible face of the Christ in our lives that we discover miracles as ever-present and literally uncountable. We know deeply we are a significant part of the whole.

We also comprehend that every person and every living thing shares our significance equally—that we are part of the All that is animated by the creative, intelligent force of Spirit, of God, which is Love—and which will ultimately prevail.

However, understanding these matters intellectually does not make letting go or learning to detach simple or easy. In fact, letting go can be extremely difficult because we largely proceed through the same steps as if we were going to remain attached. We focus intensely, make decisions and plans, and take action. We do everything we would normally do, especially all of us who are really doers.

It differs only at the end—but then it *really* differs. At the very end no matter what plans, projects, prayers, or endeavors we are engaged in, small or large, we *give up*.

We examine everything we have done. We make sure we have been rigorous. We make certain we have been faithful in our process of Quadratos: setting out, enduring a time of meaningful struggle, coming to understanding, evaluating, allowing things to unfold and find maturity, praying frequently and going into silence, taking risks as we walk our truth, finding and using our true voice and our creativity, and breathing many times with the entire world to be certain our intentions are in service.

Then we stop abruptly. The time has come for us to take the final step. It is time for one last prayer—the words of letting go, the same prayer we recognize as Jesus' on the Mount of Olives (Matthew, Mark, and Luke): and so we pray, **"Yet, not my will but yours be done." (Luke 22:42)**

At this moment we release *all* of our efforts, our hopes, our doubts, and our fears—every single one of them—to the power we know is greater than ours. Perhaps our efforts will bear the fruit we desire. That depends on complexity and intelligence greater than ours.

Quite often, something entirely unexpected opens from our exertions and we get a pleasant surprise. Sometimes we are disappointed or left patiently waiting—as Nelson Mandela waited in prison for twenty-seven years.

Yet our inability to control the ending cannot change our actions. The course of our heart and conscience is unequivocal. We are asked to act and speak in the same way that Mary pronounced her transcendent canticle in Luke's gospel—as if we are completely certain everything that Jesus the Christ spoke as truth has already come to pass on this earth.

Readings

Beatrice Bruteau	*Radical Optimism: Practical Spirituality in an Uncertain World*
Alan Kreider	*The Patient Ferment of the Early Church*
J. Keith Miller	*A Hunger for Healing: Twelve Steps as a Classic Model for Christian Spiritual Growth*
Kathleen Dowling Singh	*The Grace in Dying: How We Are Transformed Spiritually As We Die*

Practice VII—Build the New Jeru-Shalom

Through our scientific and technological genius, we have made of this world a neighborhood and yet we have not had the ethical commitment to make of it a brotherhood. But somehow, and in some way, we have got to do this. We must all learn to live together as brothers or we will all perish together as fools. We are tied together in the single garment of destiny, caught in an inescapable network of mutuality. And whatever affects one directly affects all indirectly. For some strange reason I can never be what I ought to be until you are what you ought to be. And you can never be what you ought to be until I am what I ought to be. This is the way God's universe is made; this is the way it is structured.

Martin Luther King Jr.

This seventh practice doesn't seem, on its face, to require too much of us. It requests that we not isolate ourselves from others when we become fearful. Yet there are times when not holding ourselves separate can be very difficult indeed; when the mere asking for help from another human being is the hardest task we can set ourselves.

Yet, as Luke says, we will be greatly rewarded if we bring ourselves to "knock at midnight." Conversely, there are many occasions when extending our hand and heart in compassion to some surly, ungrateful opponent is the very last thing we want to do. It is through these apparently simple tasks that peace will ultimately be born.

The participants in any relationship or association that endures over an extended period take precisely these simple actions over and over and over again, whether it is a marriage, a community, a church synod, or the Congress of the United States.

We are sometimes able to observe such associations from a distance and assess whether or not people manage them with as much skill and success as they could. When the answer is no, we respectfully suggest that if they included the principles of Quadratos in their equation, they could improve matters substantially.

EIGHT—EIGHT ESSENTIAL AND CONTINUING PRACTICES

Why might that help? Because Quadratos provides awareness of three things: the real nature of "shalom," the stages of the universal cycle of change and growth, and the absolute necessity of carrying that growth outward into service. Grounded in Quadratos, we enter all relationships with the comprehension that Jeru-Shalom is a place that invites, mediates, and discovers the dynamic yet peaceful tension of opposites.

As we move through difficulty and challenge, we remain conscious of what is really happening in the *process* of relationship at all times. This helps us to not overreact. Furthermore, if we are practicing our journey, when our tendencies to move away from others overwhelm us (or when we try to control things or to move too close), we have a countervailing impulse. We are able to stop, make an assessment, and take appropriate and compassionate action—whether toward others or ourselves.

Spirit seen through the perspective of Quadratos reminds us that the whole is made up of All. We are held in love and significance but we are not held as *more* significant than others. We are not entitled to special treatment, to have our views heard over those of others, nor do we have a right to "win" over others.

It is our great human challenge to creatively discover ways through which all voices, all perspectives, and all needs in single communities, single countries, and on one globe can be heard and accommodated. We *all* belong.

This is precisely why the gospel map of transformation was originally given to us. And it is why it has been revealed again, this time supported by advances in psychology, sociology, and other sciences.

Jesus the Christ says, "Let anyone with ears to hear listen!" (Mark 4:9). The Gospels of Matthew and Mark led us up the mountain and through the sea to the epiphany in John. Then we walked through the lessons that taught us how to complete the process in Luke.

If we wish to build the new Jeru-Shalom, we must without fail walk Luke's roads. Genuine empathy arises through the activity of service. When we see through another's eyes, our separations disappear as the largely illusory divisions they actually are.

From this place of new understanding, we can join together and find the creative solutions that allow us to become authentic communities, sitting together in the mutual respect of Jeru-Shalom, the place of a true and diverse communion.

Readings

Peter Block	*Community: The Structure of Belonging*
M. Scott Peck	*The Different Drum: Community Making and Peace*
Toko-pa Turner	*Belonging—Remembering Ourselves Home*

Practice VIII—Make the Great Leap of Trust

But all shall be well, and all shall be well,
and all manner of thing shall be well.

Julian of Norwich

In each of the early Christian communities faced with the rigid strictures of tribe and the dramatic crises of history, trust between individuals and groups was a grave issue. And it could easily be said that one of the practical results we most need from the Journey of Quadratos is a capacity for the appropriate discernment of trust, which Practices IV and V specifically address. Trust may well be *the* issue of our time.

We often think fondly of the past, and when we do, most of us are yearning for two things: trust and simplicity. We remember when police officers and politicians ostensibly protected our interests, and when the word "pedophilia" was not a daily matter for the news, and unthinkable in the same sentence as "church." We could rely on what the doctor told us, walk into a store and buy something without comparison shopping, and a handy person could repair their own car without an advanced degree.

We have the sense that we used to have fewer decisions to make and that those decisions were somehow easier. We feel that formerly we were more able to rely on things, on institutions, and on people in some greater or stronger way than we do today, whether or not that is actually true. We are filled with apprehension and mistrust.

Fear lurks beneath the lack of trust we feel today. What do we fear? Is it pain, loneliness, loss of position, loss of respect? Is it possible that underneath all of these fears, real as they are, lies one core dread: the fear of not having love? *If we dig deeply enough, will we discover that our deepest fear is, What will I do if no one loves me?*

I believe it is the most powerful and painful fear we have. Why? Because it is our very first feeling. It is the primordial cry of the helpless infant who cannot feed itself and knows it will die without the parent who loves it.

It is why a baby smiles—with every gurgle begging, "Love me, feed me, and don't let me die." This fear is the terrible, painful truth with which we begin our lives, and we carry it with us to our graves—a gaping, psychological wound that no other human being ever fills for us, though we keep asking them to, over and over.

How then is it possible for us to find trust? In Western culture—with its excessive valuing of the individual—this generally seems to be with great difficulty. (Eastern culture has a different form, but nonetheless also wrestles with trust.) We learn at very young ages how physically vulnerable we are, other children teach us the ease of betrayal, and culture reiterates standing alone and depending only on yourself.

Sadly, our families, none of them trained as parents, are also frequently culpable in the lessons that breed our wariness. If the entire question of trust were left up to our egocentric, logical brains focused on self-protection, by adulthood we would believe only that the entire world is intrinsically unsafe. But in that eventuality, our lives would be barren and bitter. Therefore, the development of trust in Western culture is a great conundrum.

Fortunately for the emotional and spiritual quality of our existence, the signals of doubt are not an intellectual matter. They are carried by the body and its complex innate warning chemistries. We *feel* when someone or something is safe—or not. Our bodies and emotions are, therefore, what give us most of our options, and they generally get the deciding vote in choices about trust—which describe most of the significant choices in our lives.

However, because the brain's safeguards still need to be overridden, the act of trust requires courage. "Courage" derives from the French word for heart, *coeur*; it means to be heart-filled. The dilemma is, how do we fill ourselves with heart and gain the capacity to trust and overcome our fear without being just plain foolhardy?

The eight practices are precisely designed to complete the epiphany of the third path and make it into a more enduring and practical reality. Over time, the truth discovered through these practices fills the body and emotions and forges a spiritual connection powerful enough to overcome the natural anxieties that reside in most people; and that connection allows trust to form and find a home.

It is then possible for mind and heart to develop a belief system of faith and truly embody the trust that has been established—to make a "leap of faith," as the saying goes (even though there has been a whole process and actually no leap at all).

This is the heart—and truly the soul—of the entire journey. Once our minds and emotions are able to cross this chasm of terror, everything is changed forever. The infant's deep fear, which we have carried all our lives—the fear of feeling some terrible inner apocalypse—is stoked by the fuel of embodied despair, of being unloved.

Now that fear is entirely replaced by a *knowing* which fills us, *body, mind, heart and soul*—a luminous certainty that we are loved and accompanied from beyond our beginning; that we are in Union forever and will never be abandoned. In this wholly embodied vision of the Christ there are no outsiders, and the idea of us versus them becomes unnecessary, an outmoded illusion that we easily slip beyond.

Readings

Phil Cousineau	*The Art of Sacred Pilgrimage: The Seeker's Guide to Making Travel Sacred*
T. S. Eliot	*Four Quartets*
Brian Swimme and Mary Evelyn Tucker	*Journey of the Universe*
Pierre Teilhard de Chardin	*Hymn of the Universe*

Chapter 9
PARADIGMS AND PROMISES

Now that we have made our way through one cycle of Quadratos and its reflection in The Four-Gospel Journey, it is time to return to the beginning where many promises were made. There, I stated that Quadratos shows a way that both head and heart can absolutely trust the four Christian gospels as revelations of divine truth. I pledged that the four gospels read together form the experience of a universal guide to spiritual transformation.

Furthermore, I vowed that if you chose this experience, the vision and practice of your Christian faith would be renewed. Never again would the discovery of a new bit of information about Jesus' life or the history of the early Christian church cause you anxiety or dismay.

The promises did not stop with matters of faith. I went further. I said that if you followed this journey in a serious and committed manner your life would change. It would become better—perhaps even incredibly better—although I did not promise an overnight metamorphosis. It *would* take some time and some spiritual elbow grease as well. But eventually, equanimity would replace anxiety, compassion would supplant resentment—and instead of loneliness, curiosity, community, and joy would be the blessings of your life.

Now that you have taken those first tentative steps up Matthew's mountain, endured the bleak time in Mark's stormy sea, luxuriated in John's garden, and steadily marched along Luke's road, it is time for me to ask the question. Have these promises been kept?

A New Paradigm

You know the core premise—that the four gospels were selected *together* to be used as a process for inner transformation. This is *quite* different from Christianity's prevailing view. Quadratos believes that the four gospels were initially selected because they held a pattern incorporating wisdom already known to be powerful—and therefore certain to move a great and glorious faith forward.

The more common view—that the gospels were four separate stories of Jesus' life and teachings—seems unlikely to accomplish this purpose as successfully. Since there were dozens of gospels available to pick from, the "separate stories" view deems a matter as important as the choosing of the gospels to be less like making a serious plan and more like a committee squabbling and then settling on "the best of the bunch."

If, however, we instead choose to comprehend the four gospels as one continuous story of renewal divided into four chapters—as an integrated and sequential account of transformation through Jesus the Christ—then we have an entirely different picture. We can readily see the logical, serious, inspired blueprint for a great text that accompanies a great purpose.

We have an approach that provides a more logical and satisfying answer to the struggles of our heads and a deeper and more lyrical song for the rhythm of our hearts. It is this new and more fulfilling paradigm—the paradigm of Quadratos—that I offer to you. It is the story of Jesus the Christ who lives *eternally* within time.

Quadratos also provides a base for spiritual renewal on a larger scale, because it moves Christianity away from its current focus on dogma and historicity into practice. It is through spiritual practices that advance us toward a maturity of heart and mind that we will discover new lives in community and religious tradition.

The dilemmas of our faith will not be solved through continually looking for answers using the same principles we currently follow. New pieces of papyri, new translations, or new pronouncements from our various denominations are not going to solve the significant problems we face. It is my firm belief that our answers lie in a different precept altogether.

I understand that certainty of this new paradigm—indicated rather than explicit in early Christian writings—may feel difficult. We know that formal church support always lags behind. And Quadratos is *not* a reworking of the gospels as we have known them.

Quadratos *is* a paradigm shift, and its philosophical basis is *discontinuous* from that of many current writers and scholars. Therefore, how do you assess whether this is wishful thinking or a sound new frontier?

NINE—PARADIGMS AND PROMISES

Anytime a pattern is suggested—whether looking at clouds or at masses of statistics—the easy criticism suggests that a nonexistent design is being discerned or some negligible linkage is being made larger because the writer has an emotional longing for connection. Could that be the case with Quadratos?

I think not. I have shown a great deal of historical evidence and have searched for the deep patterns revealed by its details, rather than focusing on the details for their own sake. Unlike many biblical historians, I see no merit in using merely the narrow strictures of historical and theological documents that have so often been abridged and edited for political reasons, abuses of power and self-serving purposes.

Quadratos is based solidly on spiritual, psychological, anthropological, and sociological studies and patterns. They have appeared and demonstrated their worth over significant periods of time. These results are bolstered by like patterns in nature, hard science and art. The great rhythm revealed in Quadratos is universal. To quote Albert Einstein, "God doesn't play dice with the world."

Yet I am not relying only on intellectual constructs. The designs of four-ness that I have shown are solid and human-based. Many of them are permanent and match up with the patterns of our bodies and our very planet. Taken together, they provide compelling evidence that a pattern in Christianity based on four-ness is far more logical than one that is not.

Therefore, the words of Genesis 2:10—*"A river flows out of Eden to water the garden, and from there it divides and becomes four branches"*—do not surprise us. Quadratos is a newly recovered and valid foundation of Christianity. Simultaneously, it provides a fresh paradigm that makes the ancient heart of our faith conscious within us.

Quadratos, therefore, unequivocally states that Christianity made a right choice in choosing exactly four gospel texts. Furthermore, of all the available choices I logically believe—and faithfully trust—that these specific four texts were precisely the correct texts to choose.

Theses texts formed the ancient reading cycle, which was a purposeful plan for spiritual growth. Our certainty is not based on the biographical details of Jesus' life alone, but also on the way the four accounts of that life express an eternal truth that can be found throughout the millennia of human history—the universal journey of transformation.

Keeping Promises

And what of personal promises made in the early chapters of this book—promises that go well beyond the questions of theology? If you are reading this book for the first time, there is obviously no tangible way to know if your faith has, indeed, been rejuvenated. It takes a while to discover the improvement in a life.

Here is what we do know. We know that the message of Quadratos has been communicated to thousands upon thousands of people through lectures, workshops, and retreats every year for many years now. We know that its influence has spread sufficiently that Quadratos is used in the training of clergy, spiritual directors from diverse faiths, and psychotherapists using various modalities.

There are also multiple programs and groups at work within churches and outside of them, nationally and internationally, including grief and loss support groups, death and dying seminars, and creativity training. Quadratos is being used as essential reading for those in spiritual direction, psychotherapy, sermon writing, crafting worship services, baptism preparation, and developing rites of passage or pilgrimage journeys, as well as for parents wishing to understand the cycle of attachment with adoptive children. Legions of people in these and other areas have successfully incorporated this process into their lives.

I would like to offer a suggestion to you now. Make the fourfold journey and its practices a part of your life and see what happens. I am confident that if you seriously engage this process, you will find both your life in faith and your life in general revitalized.

Why? Because The Four-Gospel Journey is based on sound psychological and spiritual principles, and provides a true opening to a living, dynamic Jesus the Christ. I have experienced deep transformation myself and continue to do so as the gospel journey forms the spiritual and creative home for my life. I have watched the same process unfold in the lives of many others.

The Journey of Quadratos is critically relevant to this time in history because it offers tools and answers we need now. I believe that its advance from individuals to the general population will continue to follow the same pattern it has been doing—which is the same as that of any other timely shift in perspective, including its predecessors, the gospels themselves.

Change occurs from the bottom up. Each person whose life has improved tells another person or probably several people. Some of them try the program, and it works for them; then *they* share it—and the word spreads again and again and again and again. It doesn't take as long as one might suspect.

These days it is called "viral networking," and the mainstream is closer than we often think. Once the new perspective has been widely absorbed, we will look back and wonder why anyone ever thought the gospels had become irrelevant or out of date, and why they were presented only as four separate and profound stories of Jesus' life.

Your Journey

So, if all the promises are either clearly met or likely, the question now becomes this: how will you as an individual respond to the revelation of this profound new journey? When your belly begins to fill up with truth, or an angel's voice comes announcing visions to your innermost self, is it Zechariah's fear that will answer the swelling or Elizabeth's and Mary's willing acceptance?

Will you be able to quiet your uncertainties and discern the greater pattern—even when your friends or communities are not yet aware? Because, regardless of what happens broadly or in any church or in any other person's words or experience, each and every individual still must find his or her own way. We are in the process of transformation here which is certainly no quick fix. Reading this book is just a beginning.

Deep understanding takes a serious commitment of time and a Bible close at hand—not to mention the help of others. And each path still has to be lived out in the real world by each individual seeker, exploring and experiencing, praying and dancing its myriad joys and sorrows, trials and gifts, errors and answers. Then, and only then, will we truly know how to put this into practice in our lives.

For Quadratos to work in our lives it needs the qualities of the resurrection story in The Gospel of Luke. It needs to operate in the real stuff of our day-to-day experience, where we arise and eat and work, laugh and struggle. In Luke, Jesus explicitly did not reappear as a ghost, and he made sure all the apostles touched him and watched him eat.

This was a message to the early Christians, and it is a message to us today: Jesus the Christ is alive and alive in a very specific way. We are not striving for a life that we "spiritualize," as though it is a layer we somehow add to ourselves. We are striving to recognize that our lives and our spirit are already together and attempting to live out that truth. This is what the Journey of Quadratos brings to us.

In addition to our hoped-for changes, we also reap an unexpected bonus from Quadratos. It turns out that the periods of intense anxiety and chaos we undergo along the way, as well as the times of sweet calm, are clear and identifiable parts of the journey's pattern. Hence the names of the paths become our everyday "shorthand" for this remarkable plan of Spirit and its perpetual cycle of testing and growth.

When we hit an extended tough time and we know that it is a "Mark moment," we also know that it will pass—and that prayer is our succor. A call to render service arrives, and we yield to it as a loving message from Luke that yanks us out of our self-absorption. The journey falls into our practice, our thought—and our language.

NINE—PARADIGMS AND PROMISES

Inevitably, this book has focused on our individual spiritual journey. I am bringing the Journey of Quadratos to you for the first time. However, our personal journey in the Christ means little if it does not result in greater emphasis on *how we belong to each other* in the Christ, and how we form and live in communities that announce the truths of Jeru-Shalom.

From that long-ago moment after the fire when my Sitto pronounced the words "No hate" around the big family table, that has been my primary objective, and it continues to be. Yet this is only one volume; and though I have said much about community, there is a great deal more to be written on that topic than I have been able to cover in this book. Even defining *community* from the new paradigm would take many chapters.

After all, when we honor the reality of the Christ we are talking about eliminating the boundaries between our bodies and our minds and our hearts. When we fully absorb the epiphany we received in John's gospel and then act on it, we abolish dualism and joyously welcome complexity and paradox.

The application of these principles sharpens discernment and we discover new unities, such as the fact that dark holds light and female holds male and life holds death. Walls of every kind come down: those between biology and mathematics and anthropology and music and physics and art and language and theology and many more.

Many of the specific ways in which I think and hope that Quadratos can be applied to community are going to have to wait for further books. However, to accompany *Radical Transformation,* there are six *Heart and Mind Community Guides* to aid a circle—as small as two—in making The Four-Gospel Journey both separately and together. To be apprised of future books, guides and other coming works, go to the "Connect with Quadratos" page that follows.

We have redefined and re-proposed the ways in which we see and talk and move through our lives. I reiterate: Quadratos is a complete metamorphosis. It will require an unflinching decision on our part to live our lives through its lens.

As the great theologian Paul Tillich wrote in *Systematic Theology*, "Decision is a risk rooted in the courage of being free." Quadratos frees us, individually and collectively, to be closer to our greater purpose, closer to real harmony, closer to God.

Last Thoughts

Compared to our lives today, first-century Christians lived a simple, uncomplicated life. However, they faced terrific challenges, and they had to use every bit of strength and determination they could muster to live their new, radical faith in the face of fierce oppression by the Roman Empire.

In the twenty-first century, insofar as externals go, our daily lives are infinitely more complex than those of the early Christians. Yet our inner challenges haven't changed an iota. As we have discussed, trust is very difficult for us. We are just as beset by fear and anxiety and challenge—sometimes oppression—as they were. This entire book has asked the question, How did they manage? And, how can we?

They chanted the gospels. They meditated on them. They moved their bodies along with their rhythms. They studied them. And the gospels spread from person to person, gradually covering the world, because when people prayed the words and earnestly applied them, grace opened, and their hearts and minds expanded. Love and vitality increased in their lives.

The Quadratos approach refreshes those eternal texts of inspiration. It revitalizes and returns them to their primary role as agents of transformation.

Nothing on earth is needed today more than transformation. As a species, humanity has made great and genuine progress. We are physically healthier, and in some respects we are psychologically and emotionally healthier also.

Despite all the appalling and brutal things we still perpetrate upon one another, we have had an authentic increase in self-awareness. It is difficult for us to realize that only slightly more than one hundred years ago, women could not vote, small children worked in factories, and families packed a picnic and went on outings to hangings.

Today, many of us are willing to acknowledge our shortcomings, and even when the most egregious sins are discovered, not to despair but seek genuine correction and support others to do so. Yet too many of our emotional, moral, and spiritual paths are still murky and tenuous.

In 1945 *within weeks of each other*, two immense and public proclamations of power were made, though of very different kinds: atomic bombs were dropped on Hiroshima and Nagasaki and the Nuremberg trials were opened. This is an astonishing irony.

We announced the capacity to annihilate ourselves and simultaneously asserted that the individual has an unambiguous moral responsibility for all of humankind. In retrospect, the timing of those two events seems an almost surreal conjunction. And it sharply and unequivocally points to the kind of moral quandaries with which we are increasingly faced. These are precisely the deep and heavy burdens for which spiritual transformation is an absolute necessity.

Our world is complicated and dangerous. It dazzles us with its beauty and tantalizes with the immensity of possibility it holds out to us. Yet we could well incinerate ourselves at any second, or set in motion the ingredients of irreversible, lingering planetary suicide.

We *are* growing up as a species, but at this point in history, most of our progress has been focused on the externals—on science and technology—through using our intellectual skills. Attention to the other aspects of our humanity has languished, unattended since perhaps the Renaissance. And our psychological and spiritual development lags *far* behind.

Each day we experience constant unexpected intimacies, intrusions, demands, and confusions, without any real guidance or inner wisdom. This maelstrom with a void at the center brings us daily and frighteningly closer to virtual—or even real—Armageddon.

In the great arc of our humanity, it is as though we are in those impossible, painful teenage years. Before us stretches every potential: glory, love, thousands of poignant moments, success—as well as mediocrity, failure, and utter destruction.

Rationalism has stripped us of our parental, squabbling gods way up on Mount Olympus or in Valhalla. In a sense we feel orphaned, parentless. We have a relationship with one God who tells us that we have free will. We must choose our way, and that way must be to our greater purpose.

I hope that by now I have provided enough information for you to believe that, in fact, your life will be improved by the Journey of Quadratos. And perhaps that is reason enough for you to thoroughly study and engage in its practices.

But I would like to present you with another motive. This one is both critical and timeless. It has been around for a couple of millennia now and it has not changed. It has to do with our greater purpose—that mysterious part of us that we all refer to, search for, but never quite seem to find in its entirety.

I believe it is the same impulse that causes us to help others, work for charities, accomplish important things for humanity, and have hopes for our children's lives. We want to know that our lives have purpose and meaning, know that our time on this earth has not been wasted. But is there a still greater purpose?

Jesus the Christ teaches us through his dynamism and eternal life that much of what the world accepts is only illusion. Among the truths he gives us are the understandings that all are already One and there is no death.

He also gives us the solemn charge to humbly share the experience of our transformation and the example of our lives with others, so that steadily our entire world might be freed of illusion and become more one with each other and with God.

Yes—through sharing, we do expand our small humanity, and toward that end, our work takes many forms. It tells stories, dances, and paints paintings. It shepherds groups, both small and large, in worship and in song. It brings matter and spirit together and helps to guard the health of our home, the living planet.

It speaks up against injustice and runs for office. It leads without waiting for a leader to arise. It doesn't place responsibility on anyone else, and never expects a plaque on a wall. These labors are never lonely, because God's Advocate is by our side at every precious moment.

And thanks to Mary's prescience, we know that it is through the humble endeavors of this journey, the reality of the Christ, and the presence of grace that we will ultimately be led to rescue the earth and save ourselves.

Are we concerned that our lives will be too short for the task—that we will never see results? No, never. We know with certainty that life is eternal and God's time is the only one worth marking. We have our greater purpose and it is very clear.

We are focused on the noble work with which Christians were charged two thousand years ago and which hasn't changed: follow the journey, understand and know God, follow the journey, grow and live with God, follow the journey, pass it on and serve God—and do this with all our heart and soul and strength and mind.

Jesus the Christ prays,

> *"I ask not only on behalf of these, but also on behalf of those who will believe in me through their word, that they may all be one. As you, Father, are in me and I am in you, may they also be in us, so that the world may believe that you have sent me.*
>
> *The glory that you have given me, I have given them, so that they may be one, as we are one, I in them and you in me, that they may become completely one, so that the world may know that you have sent me and have loved them even as you have loved me." (John 17:20-23)*

CONNECT WITH QUADRATOS

www.quadratos.com

Our website is the meeting place for the Quadratos community. You can read reflections on each of the four paths or particular gospel passages, find links on the *Interviews* page to a host of podcasts on Quadratos, watch films, learn about upcoming talks, retreats and courses, as well as purchase other books and resource materials including:

- *Heart and Mind Community: Six-in-One Guide, Convener Text*
  A series of six sequential guides—in a one volume compendium—that follow the chapters of this book. The Guide series offers an in-depth and transformative experience for a community of two or more. Each Guide contains eight to eleven sessions, with reflective questions and prayers for that portion of the Path, as well as practices for the Quadratos Journey. An *Information Packet* about the Guide is available on the website as a free download.

- *Gateway to Oneness: Re-imaging Us as Christians*
  Scripture texts, prayers and rituals for Easter set in a cosmic, unitive expression for study, personal prayer or communal celebration. Purchase a personal study text or an annual use permit for communal, public worship.

- Handcrafted Quadratos Notebooks; mugs, prayer cards/bookmarks for each path, Q mousepad, remembrance bands, tote bags, postcards, posters and other items.

If you are interested in inviting Alexander John to speak or lead a retreat, all needed information is available on the Quadratos website. Click on the *Alexander John* tab and then *Invite*.

BIBLIOGRAPHY

Allen, Pat. *Art is a Way of Knowing: A Guide to Self-Knowledge and Spiritual Fulfillment through Creativity*. Boston, MA: Shambhala,1995.

Armstrong, Karen. *A History of God: The 4000-Year Quest of Judaism, Christianity and Islam*. New York: Alfred A. Knopf, 1993.

_____.*The Great Transformation: The Beginning of Our Religious Traditions*. New York: Knopf Doubleday, 2006.

Andrus, Marc Handley. *The Mandala of Christ: An Exploration of a Christian Mandalic Process in the Early Christian Period*. academic paper, California Institute of Integral Studies, 2013.

Andrus, Marc and Matthew Fox. *Stations of the Cosmic Christ*. 2016.

Arnold, Patrick M. *Wildmen, Warriors, and Kings: Masculine Spirituality and the Bible*. New York: Crossroad, 1992.

Arrien, Angeles. *The Fourfold Way: Walking the Paths of the Warrior, Teacher, Healer, and Visionary*. San Francisco: HarperSanFrancisco, 1993.

Artress, Lauren. *Walking a Sacred Path: Rediscovering the Labyrinth as a Spiritual Practice*. New York: Riverhead Trade, 1995.

_____.*The Sacred Path Companion: A Guide to Walking the Labyrinth to Heal and Transform*. New York: Riverhead Trade, 2006.

Athanasius. *The Life of Anthony and The Letter to Marcellinus*. Translated by Robert C. Gregg. New York: Paulist, 1980.

Augustine of Hippo. *Selected Writings*. Translated by Mary T. Clark. New York: Paulist, 1984.

Bass, Diana Butler, and Joseph Stewart-Sicking. *From Nomads to Pilgrims: Stories from Practicing Congregations*. Herndon, VA: Alban Institute, 2006.

Bass, Diana Butler. *Christianity for the Rest of Us: How the Neighborhood Church Is Transforming the Faith*. San Francisco: HarperSanFrancisco, 2006.

_____.*A People's History of Christianity: The Other Side of the Story*. San Francisco: HarperOne, 2009.

Bass, Dorothy C., ed. *Practicing Our Faith: A Way of Life for a Searching People*. San Francisco: Jossey-Bass, 1997.

Bell, Rob. *What We Talk About When We Talk About God*. San Francisco: HarperOne, 2013.

_____. *What Is the Bible?* San Francisco: HarperOne, 2017.

_____. with Kristen Bell. *The Zimzum of Love: A New Way of Understanding Marriage*. San Francisco: HarperOne, 2014.

Benedict, St. *The Rule of St. Benedict*. Edited by Timothy Fry. New York: Vintage, 1998.

Berry, Thomas. *The Great Work: Our Way into the Future*. New York: Three Rivers, 2000.

Berry, Wendell. *A Timbered Choir: The Sabbath Poems, 1979–1997*. New York: Counterpoint, 1998.

Block, Peter. *Community: The Structure of Belonging*. San Francisco: Berrett-Koehler, 2008.

Bogard, Paul, editor. *Let There Be Night: Testimony on Behalf of the Dark*. Las Vegas: University of Nevada Press, 2008.

Bolen, Jean Shinoda. *Crossing to Avalon: A Woman's Midlife Pilgrimage*. San Francisco: HarperSanFrancisco, 1994.

Bonneau, Normand. *The Sunday Lectionary: Ritual Word, Paschal Shape*. Collegeville, MN: Liturgical Press, 1998.

Boorstein, Sylvia. *It's Easier Than You Think: The Buddhist Way to Happiness*. San Francisco: HarperSanFrancisco, 1995.

Borg, Marcus J. *Meeting Jesus Again for the First Time: The Historical Jesus and the Heart of Contemporary Faith*. San Francisco: HarperSanFrancisco, 1995

_____. *The Heart of Christianity: Rediscovering a Life of Faith*. San Francisco: HarperSanFrancisco, 2003.

Borg, Marcus J., and John Dominic Crossan. *The Last Week: A Day-by-Day Account of Jesus's Final Week in Jerusalem*. San Francisco: HarperSanFrancisco, 2006.

Bosnak, Robert. *Tracks in the Wilderness of Dreaming: Exploring Interior Landscape Through Practical Dreamwork*. New York: Delacorte, 1996.

Bourgeault, Cynthia. *The Holy Trinity and the Law of Three*. Boston: Shambhala, 2013.

_____.Chanting the Psalms: *A Practical Guide with Instructional CD*. Boston: New Seeds, 2006.

Bradshaw, Paul F. *The Search for the Origins of Christian Worship: Sources and Methods for the Study of Early Liturgy*. New York: Oxford University Press, 1992.

Bradshaw, Paul F., and Lawrence A. Hoffman, eds. *Passover and Easter: Origin and History to Modern Times*. Notre Dame, IN: University of Notre Dame Press, 1999.

Brown, Raymond E. *Jesus God and Man*. New York: Macmillan, 1967.

_____."Symposium on The Gospel of John"—course notes. Birmingham, Alabama, 1977.

Brown, Raymond E., and Francis J. Moloney. *An Introduction to The Gospel of John*. New Haven, CT: Anchor Yale Bible Reference Library, 2003.

Bruteau, Beatrice. *Radical Optimism: Practical Spirituality in an Uncertain World*. Boulder, CO: Sentient, 1997.

Campbell, Joseph. *The Masks of God: Creative Mythology*. New York: Viking Compass, 1970.

_____.*The Masks of God: Occidental Mythology*. New York: Viking Compass, 1970.

_____.*The Masks of God: Oriental Mythology*. New York: Viking Compass, 1970.

_____.*The Masks of God: Primitive Mythology*. New York: Viking Compass, 1970.

_____.*The Hero with a Thousand Faces*. Princeton University Press, 1973.

_____.*Thou Art That: Transforming Religious Metaphor*. Edited by Eugene Kennedy. Novato, CA: New World Library, 2001.

Candolini, Gernot. *Labyrinths: Walking Toward the Center*. Munich, Germany: Claudius Verlag, 2004.

Caprio, Betsy. *Star Trek: Good News in Modern Images*. Kansas City: Sheed Andrews McMeel, 1978.

Carroll, James. *Jerusalem, Jerusalem: How the Ancient City Ignited Our Modern World*. Boston: Houghton Mifflin Harcourt, 2011.

Casey, Michael. *Sacred Reading: The Ancient Art of Lectio Divina*. Liguori, MO: Liguori, 1996.

Catholic Encyclopedia. Digital version compiled and © Catholic Online.

Catholic Encyclopedia © Catholic Encyclopedia. New York: Robert Appleton Company—vol. 1: 1907; vol. 2: 1907; vol. 3: 1908; vol. 4: 1908; vol. 5: 1909; vol. 6: 1909; vol. 7: 1910; vol. 8: 1910; vol. 9: 1910; vol. 10: 1911; vol. 11: 1911; vol. 12: 1911; vol. 13: 1912; vol. 14: 1912; vol. 15: 1912.

Chittister, Joan D. *Scarred by Struggle, Transformed by Hope.* Grand Rapids, MI: Eerdmans, 2005.

Clément, Olivier. *The Roots of Christian Mysticism.* London: New City Press, 1993.

Clift, Jean Dalby, and Wallace B. Clift. *Symbols of Transformation in Dreams.* New York: Crossroad, 1984.

Cooper, David A. *God Is a Verb: Kabbalah and the Practice of Mystical Judaism.* New York: Riverhead Books, 1997.

Cousineau, Phil. *The Art of Sacred Pilgrimage: The Seeker's Guide to Making Travel Sacred.* Berkeley, CA: Conari, 2000.

_____. *Once and Future Myths: The Power of Ancient Stories in Modern Times.* Berkeley: Conari, 2001.

Crossan, John Dominic. *The Historical Jesus: The Life of a Mediterranean Jewish Peasant.* New York: HarperCollins, 1992.

Dalai Lama, His Holiness the. *Buddha Heart, Buddha Mind: Living the Four Noble Truths.* Chestnut Ridge, NY: Crossroad, 2000.

Dalai Lama, Desmond Tutu and David Abrams. *The Book of Joy: Lasting Happiness in a Changing World.* NY: Penguin, 2016

Daniélou, Alain. *The Myths and Gods of India: The Classic Work on Hindu Polytheism.* Rochester, VT: Inner Traditions International, 1991.

Daniélou, Jean, S.J. *The Bible and the Liturgy.* Ann Arbor, MI: Servant Books, 1956.

Donovan, Vincent J. *Christianity Rediscovered.* Maryknoll, NY: Orbis Books, 1982.

Doty, William G. *Mythography: The Study of Myths and Rituals.* Tuscaloosa: University of Alabama Press, 1986.

Douglas-Klotz, Neil. *Prayers of the Cosmos: Meditations on the Aramaic Words of Jesus.* San Francisco: HarperSanFrancisco, 1990.

_____. *The Hidden Gospel: Decoding the Spiritual Message of the Aramaic Jesus*. Wheaton, IL: Quest Books, 1999.

Driver, Tom F. *Liberating Rites: Understanding the Transformative Power of Ritual*. Boulder, CO: Westview, 1998.

Duggan, Robert, ed. *Conversion and the Catechumenate*. New York: Paulist, 1984.

Dujarier, Michel. *A History of the Catechumenate: The First Six Centuries*. New York: William H. Sadlier, 1979.

_____. *The Rites of Christian Initiation: Historical and Pastoral Reflections*. New York: William H. Sadlier, 1979.

Dunne, John S. *The Way of All the Earth: Experiments in Truth and Religion*. New York: Macmillan, 1972.

_____. *Time and Myth: Meditations on Storytelling as an Exploration of Life and Death*. New York: Doubleday, 1973.

_____. *A Search for God in Time and Memory*. Notre Dame, IN: University of Notre Dame Press, 1977.

_____. *The Reasons of the Heart: A Journey into Solitude and Back Again into the Human Circle*. New York: Macmillan, 1978.

Edinger, Edward F. *The Bible and the Psyche: Individuation Symbolism in the Old Testament*. Toronto: Inner City Books, 1986.

_____. *The Christian Archetype: A Jungian Commentary on the Life of Christ*. Toronto: Inner City Books, 1987.

_____. *Archetype of the Apocalypse: A Jungian Study of the Book of Revelation*. Peru, IL: Open Court, 1999.

Ehrenreich, Barbara. *Blood Rites: Origins and History of the Passions of War*. New York: Henry Holt, 1997.

Ehrman, Bart D. *Misquoting Jesus*. San Francisco: HarperSanFrancisco, 2005.

_____. *Jesus Interrupted*. San Francisco: HarperOne, 2009.

Eliade, Mircea. *Rites and Symbols of Initiation: The Mysteries of Birth and Rebirth*. New York: Harper & Row, 1958.

Eliot, T. S. *Four Quartets*. New York: Harvest Books, 1968.

Ephrem the Syrian. *Hymns*. Translated by Kathleen E. McVey. New York: Paulist, 1989.

Estes, Clarissa Pinkola. *Women Who Run With the Wolves: Myths and Stories of the Wild Woman*. New York: Ballantine Books, 1992.

Eusebius. *Ecclesiastical History*. Books I–V and 6–10; vols. 153 and 265 in Loeb Classical Library. Cambridge, MA: Harvard University Press, 1926.

Fischer, Norman. *Opening to You: Zen-Inspired Translations of the Psalms*. New York: Viking, 2002.

Fowler, James W. *Stages of Faith: The Psychology of Human Development and the Quest for Meaning*. San Francisco: Harper & Row, 1981.

Fox, Matthew. *Breakthrough: Meister Eckhart's Creation Spirituality in New Translation*. New York: Image Book, 1980.

———. Original Blessing: *A Primer in Creation Spirituality*. Santa Fe, NM: Bear & Company, 1983.

Francis, St., and St. Clare. *The Complete Works*. Translated by Regis J. Armstrong and Ignatius C. Brady. New York: Paulist, 1982.

Frost, Seena B. *SoulCollage Evolving: An Intuitive Collage Process for Self-Discovery and Community*. Santa Cruz, CA: Hanford Mead Publishers, 2012.

Gallagher, Nora. *Things Seen and Unseen: A Year Lived in Faith*. New York: Alfred A. Knopf, 1998

———. *Practicing Resurrection: A Memoir of Work, Doubt, Discernment, and Moments of Grace*. New York: Alfred A. Knopf, 2003.

Galland, China. *Longing for Darkness: Tara and the Black Madonna*. New York: Penguin Compass, 1990.

Gendler, J. Ruth. *Changing Light: The Eternal Cycle of Night and Day*. New York: Perennial, 1993.

Gold, Peter. *Navajo and Tibetan Sacred Wisdom: The Circle of the Spirit*. Rochester, VT: Inner Traditions, 1994.

Gregory of Nyssa. *The Life of Moses*. Translated by Everett Ferguson and Abraham J. Malerbe. New York: Paulist Press, 1978.

Griffith-Jones, Robin. *The Four Witnesses: The Rebel, The Rabbi, The Chronicler, and The Mystic*. San Francisco: HarperSanFrancisco, 2000.

Grimes, Ronald L. *Deeply into the Bone: Re-Inventing Rites of Passage*. Berkeley: University of California Press, 2000.

Groves, Richard F. and Henriette Anne Klauser. *The American Book of Dying: Lessons in Healing Spiritual Pain*. Berkeley: Ten Speed Press, 2005.

Halifax, Joan. *The Fruitful Darkness: Reconnecting with the Body of the Earth*. New York: HarperCollins, 1994.

Hall, Thelma. *Too Deep for Words: Rediscovering Lectio Divina*. New York: Paulist, 1988.

Harris, Bud. *The Father Quest: Rediscovering an Elemental Psychic Force*. Alexander, NC: Alexander Books, 1996.

Harris, Massimilla, and Bud Harris. *Like Gold through Fire: Understanding the Transforming Power of Suffering*. Alexander, NC: Alexander Books, 1996.

Henderson, Joseph L. *Thresholds of Initiation*. Middleton, CT: Wesleyan University Press, 1967.

Hernandez, Ana. *The Sacred Art of Chant: Preparing to Practice*. Woodstock, VT: Skylight Paths Publishing, 2004.

Hildegarde of Bingen. *Hildegarde of Bingen's Book of Divine Works*. Santa Fe, NM: Bear & Company, 1987.

Housden, Roger. *Ten Poems to Set You Free*. New York: Harmony Books, 2003.

http://www.blueletterbible.org lexicon/concordance KJV translation/concordance.

http://www.perseus.tufts.edu Greek language references and translation, Tufts University, Boston, MA.

Ibn 'Abbad of Ronda. *Letters on the Sufi Path*. Translated by John Renard. New York: Paulist, 1986.

Ibn Al'Arabi. *The Bezels of Wisdom*. Translated by R.W.J. Austin. New York: Paulist, 1980.

Ignatius, St. *The Spiritual Exercises of St. Ignatius of Loyola*. Whitefish, MT: Kessinger, 2007.

Irenaeus of Lyons, St. *Against Heresies*. Whitefish, MT: Kessinger, 2004.

Jaskolski, Helmut. *The Labyrinth: Symbol of Fear, Rebirth, and Liberation*. Boston: Shambhala, 1997.

John of the Cross. *Dark Night of the Soul*. Translated by Mirabai Starr. New York: Riverhead Books, 2002.

Johnson, Maxwell E. *The Rites of Christian Initiation: Their Evolution and Interpretation, Revised and Expanded Edition*. Collegeville, MN: Pueblo, 2007.

Johnson, Robert A. *Owning Your Own Shadow: Understanding the Dark Side of the Psyche*. San Francisco: HarperSanFrancisco, 1991.

_____. *Balancing Heaven and Earth*. San Francisco: HarperSanFrancisco, 1998.

Jones, Alan. *Soul Making: The Desert Way of Spirituality*. London: SCM, 1986.

_____. *Reimagining Christianity: Reconnect Your Spirit without Disconnecting Your Mind*. Hoboken, NJ: Wiley, 2005.

Julian of Norwich. *Revelations of Divine Love*. St. Meinrad, IN: Abbey, 1975.

Jung, C. G. *Symbols of Transformation: An Analysis of the Prelude to a Case of Schizophrenia*. Vol. 5 in *Collected Works*. Princeton, NJ: Princeton University Press, 1956.

_____. *Memories, Dreams, Reflections*. New York: Vintage Books, 1963.

_____. *Alchemical Studies*. Vol. 13 in Collected Works. Princeton, NJ: Princeton University Press, 1967.

_____. *Psychology and Alchemy*. Vol. 12 in *Collected Works*. Princeton, NJ: Princeton University Press, 1968.

_____. *The Symbolic Life: Miscellaneous Writings*. Vol. 18 in *Collected Works*. Princeton, NJ: Princeton University Press, 1989.

Kalff, Dora M. *Sandplay: A Psychotherapeutic Approach to the Psyche*. Oberlin, OH: Analytical Psychological Press, 2020.

Kalsched, Donald. *The Inner World of Trauma: Archetypal Defenses of the Personal Spirit*. New York: Routledge, 1996.

Kavanagh, Aidan. *The Shape of Baptism: The Rite of Christian Initiation*. New York: Pueblo, 1978.

_____. *On Liturgical Theology*. Collegeville, MN: Liturgical, 1981.

Kawai, Hayao. *Buddhism and the Art of Psychotherapy*. College Station, TX: Texas A&M University Press, 1996.

Keating, Thomas. *Intimacy with God: An Introduction to Centering Prayer*. New York: Crossroad, 1994.

_____. *The Human Condition*. New York: Paulist, 1999.

_____. *Open Mind, Open Heart: The Contemplative Dimension of the Gospel*. New York: Continuum, 2006.

Kelly, Henry Ansgar. *The Devil at Baptism: Ritual, Theology and Drama*. Ithaca, NY: Cornell University Press, 1985.

Kelsey, Morton T. *Encounter with God*. Minneapolis, MN: Bethany Fellowship, 1972.

———. *The Other Side of Silence: A Guide to Christian Meditation*. New York: Paulist, 1976.

———. *Christo-Psychology*. New York: Crossroad, 1982.

———. *Companions on the Inner Way: The Art of Spiritual Guidance*. New York: Crossroad, 1983.

Kornfield, Jack. *A Path with Heart: A Guide through the Perils and Promises of Spiritual Life*. New York: Bantam Books, 1993.

Kreider, Alan. *The Patient Ferment of the Early Church*. Grand Rapids, MI: Baker Academic, 2016.

Lamott, Anne. *Bird by Bird: Some Instructions on Writing and Life*. New York: Anchor Books, 1995.

Lane, Belden C. *The Solace of Fierce Landscapes: Exploring Desert and Mountain Spirituality*. New York: Oxford University Press, 1998.

Levine, Peter A. *Waking the Tiger: Healing Trauma—The Innate Capacity to Transform Overwhelming Experiences*. Berkeley, CA: North Atlantic Books, 1997.

Lew, Alan. *This Is Real and You Are Completely Unprepared: The Days of Awe as a Journey of Transformation*. New York: Little, Brown, 2003.

Lizorkin-Eyzenberg, Eli. *The Jewish Gospel of John: Discovering Jesus, King of All Israel*: Tel Aviv, Israel: Jewish Studies for Christians, 2015.

Luke, Helen M. *Dark Wood to White Rose: Journey and Transformation in Dante's Divine Comedy*. New York: Parabola Books, 1989.

Mahdi, Louise, Steven Foster Carus, and Meredith Little, eds. *Betwixt and Between: Patterns of Masculine and Feminine Initiation*. La Salle, IL: Open Court, 1987.

McCann, I. Lisa, and Laurie Anne Pearlman. *Psychological Trauma and the Adult Survivor: Theory, Therapy and Transformation*. New York: Brunner/Mazel, 1990.

McGilchrist, Iain. *The Master and His Emissary*. New Haven: Yale University, 2009.

McLaren, Brian D. *Finding Our Way Again: The Return of the Ancient Practices*. Nashville, TN: Thomas Nelson, 2008.

_____. *The Secret Message of Jesus: Uncovering the Truth That Could Change Everything*. Nashville, TN: Thomas Nelson, 2006.

Meador, Betty DeShong. *Uncursing the Dark: Treasures from the Underworld*. Wilmette, IL: Chiron, 1992.

Merrill, Nan C. *Psalms for Praying: An Invitation to Wholeness*. New York: Continuum, 2007.

Merton, Thomas. *Seven Storey Mountain*. Ft. Washington, PA: Harvest Books, [1948] 1999.

_____. *No Man Is an Island*. New York: Harcourt, Brace, 1955.

_____. *The Hidden Ground of Love: The Letters of Thomas Merton on Religious Experience And Social Concerns*. New York: Farrar, Straus and Giroux, 1985.

Miller, J. Keith. *A Hunger for Healing: Twelve Steps as a Classic Model for Christian Spiritual Growth*. New York: HarperCollins e-books, 2011.

Moore, Robert, and Douglas Gillette. *King Warrior Magician Lover: Rediscovering the Archetypes of the Mature Masculine*. San Francisco: HarperSanFrancisco, 1990.

Moore, Thomas. *Original Self: Living with Paradox and Originality*. New York: Harper Perennial, 2001.

Murphy Center for Liturgical Research. *Made, Not Born: New Perspectives on Christian Initiation and the Catechumenate*. Notre Dame, IN: University of Notre Dame Press, 1976.

Neville, Gwen Kennedy, and John H. Westerhoff III. *Learning through Liturgy*. New York: Seabury Press, 1978

Newell, J. Philip. *Christ of the Celts: The Healing of Creation*. San Francisco, CA: Jossey-Bass, 2008.

Nouwen, Henri J. M. *Reaching Out: The Three Movements of the Spiritual Life*. New York: Doubleday, 1975.

_____. *The Inner Voice of Love: A Journey through Anguish to Freedom*. New York: Image Books, 1999.

O'Donohue, John. *Beauty: The Invisible Embrace*. New York: Harper Perennial, 2005.

Olivera, Bernardo. *How Far to Follow? The Martyrs of Atlas*. Petersham, MA: St. Bede's Publications, 1997.

O'Murchu, Diarmuid. *Quantum Theology: Spiritual Implications of the New Physics*. NY, NY: The Crossroad Publishing Co., 2004.

Origen. *On First Principles*. Book IV, translated by Rowan A. Greer. New York: Paulist Press, 1979.

Pagels, Elaine. *Beyond Belief: The Secret Gospel of Thomas*. New York: Vintage Books, 2003.

Paintner, Christine Valters. *Water, Wind, Earth & Fire: The Christian Practice of Praying with The Elements*. Notre Dame, IN: Sorin Books, 2010.

Palmer, Parker J. *The Courage to Teach: Exploring the Inner Landscape of a Teacher's Life*. San Francisco: Jossey-Bass, 1998.

Peat, David F. *The Blackwinged Night: Creativity in Nature and Mind*. Cambridge, MA: Perseus, 2000.

Peck, M. Scott. *The Road Less Traveled: A New Psychology of Love, Traditional Values and Spiritual Growth*. New York: Simon & Schuster, 1978.

_____. *The Different Drum: Community Making and Peace*. New York: Simon & Schuster, 1987.

Pennington, Basil M. *Lectio Divina: Renewing the Ancient Practice of Praying the Scriptures*. New York: Crossroad, 1998.

Perera, Sylvia Brinton. *Descent to the Goddess: A Way of Initiation for Women*. Toronto: Inner City Books, 1981.

Perry, John Weir. *Lord of the Four Quarters: The Mythology of Kingship*. New York: Paulist, 1991.

Pfatteicher, Philip H. *Liturgical Spirituality*. Valley Forge, PA: Trinity, 1997.

Pope Benedict XVI. *Jesus of Nazareth: From the Baptism in the Jordan to the Transfiguration*. Translated by Adrian J. Walker. New York: Doubleday, 2007.

Pope John XXIII. *Journal of a Soul*. Translated by Dorothy White. New York: McGraw-Hill, 1965.

Ramshaw, Gail. *Treasures Old and New: Images in the Lectionary*. Minneapolis, MN: Augsburg Fortress, 2002.

Richardson, Jan L. *Night Vision: Searching the Shadows of Advent and Christmas*. Orlando, FL: Wanton Gospeller, 2012.

_____. *In Wisdom's Path: Discovering the Sacred in Every Season*. Orlando, FL: Wanton Gospeller, 2012.

_____. *In the Sanctuary of Women: A Companion for Reflection and Prayer*. Nashville, TN: Upper Room Books, 2010.

Rohr, Richard. *Quest for the Grail*. New York: Crossroad, 1997.

_____. *Everything Belongs: The Gift of Contemplative Prayer*. Chestnut Ridge, NY: Crossroad, 2003.

_____. with Mike Morrell. *The Divine Dance: The Trinity and Your Transformation*. New Kensington, PA: Whitaker House, 2016.

_____. *The Universal Christ*. New York, Convergent Books, 2019.

Rosen, David H. *Transforming Depression: Healing the Soul Through Creativity*. New York: Penguin, 1993.

Roth, Gabriel, with John Loudon. *Maps to Ecstasy: A Healing Journey for the Untamed Spirit*. Novato, CA: Natraj Publishing, 1998.

Ruden, Sarah. *Paul Among The People: The Apostle Reinterpreted and Reimagined in His Own Time*. New York: Pantheon Books, 2010.

Rupp, Joyce and Marcrina Wiederkerhr. *The Circle of Life: The Heart's Journey Through the Seasons*. Notre Dame, IN: Sorin Books, 2005.

Rumi, Jalal al-Din. *The Soul of Rumi: A New Collection of Ecstatic Poems*. Translated by Coleman Barks. San Francisco: HarperSanFrancisco, 2001.

_____. *Safed Spirituality: Rules of Mystical Piety and the Beginning of Wisdom*. Translated by Lawrence Fine. New York: Paulist, 1984.

Sandner, Donald. Navaho *Symbols of Healing*. New York: Harvest Books, 1979.

Sanford, John A. *The Kingdom Within: A Study of the Inner Meaning of Jesus' Sayings*. New York: Lippincott, 1970.

_____. *Mystical Christianity: A Psychological Commentary on The Gospel of John*. New York: Crossroad, 1993.

Schachter-Shalomi, Zalman. *Paradigm Shift: From the Jewish Renewal Teachings of Reb Zalman Schachter-Shalomi*. Northvale, NJ: Jason Aronson, 1993.

Schmemann, Alexander. *Great Lent: Journey to Pascha*. Crestwood, NY: St. Vladimir's Seminary Press, 1969.

_____. *Of Water and the Spirit*. Crestwood, NY: St. Vladimir's Seminary Press, 1974.

Searle, Mark. *Christening: The Making of Christians*. Collegeville, MN: Liturgical, 1980.

_____. ed. *Sunday Morning: A Time for Worship*. Collegeville, MN: Liturgical, 1982.

Shaia, Alexander John. *Returning From Camino*, Second Edition. Santa Fe, NM: Quadratos LLC, 2019.

Shaia, Alexander J. "Sandplay in Spiritual Direction: Beyond Insight or Centering." *Presence Journal*, June 2001, available on www.quadratos.com/books/

Shaw, Martin. *A Branch from the Lightening Tree: Ecstatic Myth and the Grace of Wildness*. Ashland, Oregon: White Cloud Press, 2011.

_____. *Wolf Milk: Chthonic Memory in the Deep Wild*. Devon, England: Cista Mystica Press, 2019.

_____. *Courting the Wild Twin*. London: Chelsea Green Publishing, 2020.

Shea, John. *Stories of God: An Unauthorized Biography*. Chicago: Thomas More Press, 1978.

Singh, Kathleen Dowling. *The Grace in Dying: How We Are Transformed Spiritually As We Die*. San Francisco: HarperSanFrancisco, 1998.

Somé, Malidoma Patrice. *Ritual: Power, Healing and Community*. Portland, OR: Swan/Raven, 1993.

_____. *Of Water and the Spirit: Ritual, Magic and Initiation in the Life of an African Shaman, Second Edition*. London: Penguin Books, 1995.

Spong, John Shelby. *Liberating the Gospels: Reading the Bible with Jewish Eyes*. San Francisco: HarperSanFrancisco, 1996.

Starr, Mirabai. *Wild Mercy: Living the Fierce and Tender Wisdom of the Women Mystics*. Boulder CO: Sounds True, 2019.

Stein, Murray. *Transformation: Emergence of the Self*. College Station, TX: Texas A&M University Press, 1998.

Stewart-Sicking, Joseph A. and Alexander J. Shaia. "Facing Change: Lessons from The Gospel of Matthew." *Human Development*, 33(2), 25-29, 2011.

Storm, Hyemeyohsts. *Song of Heyoehkah*. San Francisco: Harper & Row, 1981.

Swimme, Brian, and Thomas Berry. *The Universe Story: From the Primordial Flaring Forth to the Ecozoic Era: A Celebration of the Unfolding of the Cosmos*. San Francisco: HarperSanFrancisco, 1992.

Swimme, Brian. *The Hidden Heart of the Cosmos: Humanity and the New Story*. Maryknoll, NY: Orbis Books, 1999.

Swimme, Brian and Mary Evelyn Tucker. *Journey of the Universe*. New Haven, CT: Yale University Press, 2011.

Symposium on Christian Initiation. *Becoming a Catholic Christian*. New York: William H. Sadlier, 1978.

Talley, Thomas J. *The Origins of the Liturgical Year*. Collegeville, MN: Liturgical, 1991.

Teilhard de Chardin, Pierre. *Hymn of the Universe*. New York: Harper Perennial, 1972.

Teresa of Avila. *The Interior Castle*. Translated by Mirabai Starr. New York: Riverhead Books, 2003.

Tickle, Phyllis. *The Great Emergence: How Christianity Is Changing and Why*. Grand Rapids, MI: Baker Books, 2008.

Turner, Victor. *The Ritual Process: Structure and Anti-Structure*. Ithaca, NY: Cornell University Press, 1969.

_____. *Twenty-Four Hours a Day*. Center City, MN: Hazelden, nd.

_____. *The Forest of Symbols: Aspects of Ndembu Ritual*. Ithaca, NY: Cornell University Press, 1970.

Turner, Toko-pa. *Belonging: Remembering Ourselves Home*. 2017.

Ulman, Richard B., and Doris Brothers. *The Shattered Self: A Psychoanalytic Study of Trauma*. Hillsdale, NJ: Analytic Press, 1988.

van der Kolk, Bessel A. *Psychological Trauma*. Washington, DC: American Psychiatric Press, 1987.

van Gennep, Arnold. *The Rites of Passage*. Chicago: University of Chicago Press, 1960.

Warren, Rick. *The Purpose Driven Life*. Grand Rapids, MI: Zondervan, 2002.

Weinrib, Estelle L. *Images of the Self: The Sandplay Therapy Process*. Boston: Sigo, 1983.

West, Fritz. *Scripture and Memory: The Ecumenical Hermeneutic of the Three-Year Lectionaries*. Collegeville, MN: Liturgical Press, 1997.

West, Geoffrey B. "The Scale of the Tree of Life from Molecules and Cells to Whales and Ecosystems." Stanley Ulam Memorial Lectures, Santa Fe Institute, Santa Fe, NM, 2001.

West, Geoffrey B., and James H. Brown. "Life's Universal Scaling Laws." *Physics Today*. September 2004.

Whitaker, E. C. *Documents of the Baptismal Liturgy*. London: Hollen Street, 1970.

Whiting, Lindsay. *Living into Art: Journeys through Collage*. Montclair, NJ: Paper Lantern Press, 2008.

Whyte, David. *River Flow: New and Selected Poems*. Langley, WA: Many Rivers, 2007.

Williamson, John. *The Oak King, the Holy King, and the Unicorn: The Myths and Symbolism of the Unicorn Tapestries*. New York: Harper& Row, 1986.

Wills, Gary. *What Jesus Meant*. New York: Viking, 2006.

Wirth, Steven. *The Path of Contemplative Dialogue: Engaging the Collective Spirit*. Open Source, www.contemplativedialogue.org.

Wuthnow, Robert. *Creative Spirituality: The Way of the Artist*. Berkeley: University of California Press, 2001.

Yarnold, Edward. *The Awe Inspiring Rites of Initiation: Baptismal Homilies of the Fourth Century*. Slough, UK: St. Paul Publications, 1972.

Zoja, Luigi. Drugs, *Addiction and Initiation: The Modern Search for Ritual*. Boston: Sigo, 1989.

Zolbrod, Paul G. Diné Bahané: *The Navajo Creation Story*. Albuquerque: University of New Mexico Press, 1984.

INDEX A
SCRIPTURE CITED LISTED ALPHABETICALLY BY BOOK OF THE BIBLE

1 Corinthians
    8:6 **31**
    10:4 **31, 211**
1 Kings
    17:8–16 **362**
2 Samuel
    11 **81**
Acts of the Apostles
    314–315
Colossians
    1:15–17 **31, 208**
Daniel
    7:13 **113**
Deuteronomy
    6:5–6 **325**
Exodus
    12:1–6 **258**
Genesis
    1:1 **211**
    1:2 **153–155, 230**
    2:7 **278**
    2:10 **421**
    22 **71**
    38 **81**
Hebrews
    11:26 **31**
Isaiah
    3:5–6 **333**
    11:3b–6 **291**
    40:3 **144**
    42:4 **144**

John
    1:1–2 **209**
    1:1–5 **213**
    1:5 **216**
    1:10–13 **213**
    1:13 **211**
    1:14 **209, 213**
    1:16–18 **213**
    1:29–34 **220**
    2:1–11 **223**
    3:1–10 **228–228**
    3:16–18 **229**
    4:3–14 **231**
    4:21–24 **232**
    4:39 **232**
    9:13–21 **234**
    9:38 **234**
    9:39–41 **235**
    11:32–45 **236–237**
    12:12–15 **241**
    13:1–15 **244**
    14:3 **285**
    14:16–17 **51, 246**
    15:1–2 **246**
    15:12–13 **246**
    15:14–16 **246**
    16:20–21 **246**
    16:32–33 **246–247**
    17:20–23 **429**
    17:21b–26 **247**
    17:26 **246**

18:1–11 **251–252**
18:12–27 **254–255**
18:28 **256**
18:33–38 **256**
19:1–3 **256–257**
19:9–11 **257**
19:13–14 **260**
19:16–18 **260–261**
19:25b–30 **262–263**
19:32–34 **263**
19:38–42 **264**
20:1–16 **274–275**
20:19–23 **279**
20:24–31 **284**
21:9–18 **291-292**

Luke
1:1–4 **316**
1:5–25 **317–318**
1:26–38 **319–320**
1:39–40 **320**
1:46–55 **320–321**
2:1–19 **323**

2:39–52 **325–326**
3:1–17 **334–335**
4:1–13 **339**
4:14–30 **340–341**
6:12–16 **342**
6:17–36 **343–344**
6:46–49 **344**
10:25–28 **53–54**
10:25–37 **351–352**
11:5–10 **353**
15:1–10 **354**
15:11–32 **355–356**
17:20–21 **356**
19:29–44 **360–361**

22:14–38 **363–364**
22:39–62 **365–366**
22:42 **409**
22:63–71 **367**
23:1–12 **367–368**
23:26–31 **369**
23:32–43 **370**
23:44–49 **371**
24:1–12 **377**
24:13–35 **377–378**
24:36–53 **378–379**

Mark
1:1 **143**
1:2–3 **144**
1:4–5 **144**
1:7–8 **145**
1:9–11 **145**
1:12–13 **146**
1:14–15 **146**
1:35–39 **149**
4:35–41 **151**
8:17–18 **50, 152**

8:27 **155, 174**
8:27–36 **155**
9:2–10 **156**
9:42–50 **158**
11:15–18 **161–162**
11:27–33 **162**
12:1–12 **163**
13:7–13 **164**
13:30–31 **164**
13:37 **165**
14:17–21 **168**
14:26–31 **168**
14:32–38 **169**
14:66–72 **170**

SCRIPTURE CITED LISTED ALPHABETICALLY BY BOOK OF THE BIBLE

15:6–15 **170–171**
15:16–20 **171–172**
15:21 **172**
15:22–40 **174–175**
16:1–8 **178**

Matthew
  1:1 **79**
  1:2 **81**
  1:3 **81**
  1:6 **82**
  1:16 **83**

  1:18–19 **84**
  1:20–22 **48**
  1:20–25 **85**
  2:1–9 **86–87**
  2:10–12 **87–88**
  2:13–23 **90**
  3:1–3 **92**
  3:4–10 **93–94**
  3:13–17 **94–95**
  3:17–4:1 **97**

  4:2–4 **97**
  4:5–7 **98**
  4:8–11 **98**
  5:1–12 **103**
  5:17 **104**
  5:21–22 **104**
  5:27–28 **104**
  5:33–35 **104**
  5:38–42 **104–105**
  5:43–45 **105**
  26:1–5 **108**
  26:6–7 **109**
  26:14–16 **109**
  26:17–19 **110**
  26:20–25 **110**

26:30–35 **111**
26:36–41 **112**
26:47–50 **113**
26:59–66 **114**
26:69–75 **114–115**
27:3–5 **116**
27:20–31 **118**
27:33–34 **119**
27:39–44 **119–120**
27:46–50 **120**
27:50–52 **121**

28:1–2 **123**
28:5–7 **123**
28:9–10 **123**
28:16–20 **125**

Psalms
  19 **xi**
  22 **120, 172, 173, 180–182, 184, 261, 371**
  22:29–31 **173**
  69 **261**

  91 **338**
  121 **127**
  122 **293**
  126 **191**
  131 **381**
  133 **381**

INDEX B
SCRIPTURE CITED LISTED ALPHABETICALLY BY CHAPTER/PAGE IN
RADICAL TRANSFORMATION

Chapter 2—The Keys
1 Corinthians
    8:6 **31**
    10:4 **31**

Colossians
    1:15–17 **31**
Hebrews
    11:26 **31**

Chapter 3—The Fourfold Journey of Transformation
John
    14:16–17 **51**
Luke
    10:25–28 **53-54**
Mark
    8:17–18 **50**
Matthew
    1:20–22 **48**

Chapter 4—Climbing the Great Mountain of Matthew/ 1st Path
2 Samuel
    11 **81**
Daniel
    7:13 **113**
Genesis
    22 **71**
    38 **81**
Mark
    1:1 **143**
Matthew
    1:1 **79**

1:2 **81**
1:3 **81**
1:6 **82**
1:16 **83**
1:18–19 **84**
1:20–25 **85**
2:1–9 **86-87**
2:10–12 **87-88**
2:13–23 **90**
3:1–3 **92**
3:4–10 **93-94**
3:13–17 **94-95**
3:17–4:1 **97**
4:2–4 **97**
4:5–7 **98**
4:8–11 **98**
5:1–12 **103**
5:17 **104**
5:21–22 **104**
5:27–28 **104**
5:33–35 **104**
5:38–42 **104-105**
5:43–45 **105**
26:1–5 **108**
26:6–7 **109**
26:14–16 **109**
26:17–19 **110**
26:20–25 **110**
26:30–35 **111**

26:36–41 **112**
26:47–50 **113**
26:59–66 **114**
26:69–75 **114–115**
27:3–5 **116**
27:20–31 **118**
27:33–34 **119**
27:39–44 **119–120**
27:46–50 **120**
27:50–52 **121**
28:1–2 **123**
28:5–7 **123**
28:9–10 **123**
28:16–20 **125**

Psalms
22 **120**

Chapter 5—Crossing Mark's Stormy Sea / 2nd Path

Isaiah
40:3 **144**
42:4 **144**

Mark
1:1 **143**
1:2–3 **144**
1:4–5 **144**
1:7–8 **145**
1:9–11 **145**
1:12–13 **146**
1:14–15 **146**
1:35–39 **149**
4:35–41 **151**
8:17–18 **152**
8:27 **155, 174**
8:27–36 **155**
9:2–10 **156**
9:42–50 **158**
11:15–18 **161–162**
11:27–33 **162**
12:1–12 **163**
13:7–13 **164**
13:30–31 **164**
13:37 **165**
14:17–21 **168**
14:26–31 **168**
14:32–38 **169**
14:66–72 **170**
15:6–15 **170–171**
15:16–20 **171–172**
15:21 **172**
15:22–40 **174–175**
16:1–8 **178**

Psalms
22 **120, 172, 173, 180–181, 184**
22:29–31 **173**

Chapter 6—Being in John's Glorious Garden / 3rd Path

1 Corinthians
10:4 **211**

Colossians
1:15–17 **208**

Exodus
12:1–6 **258**

Genesis
1:1 **211**
1:2 **230**
2:7 **278**

Isaiah
11:3b–6 **291**

John
1:1–2 **209**
1:1–5 **213**
1:5 **216**
1:10–13 **213**
1:13 **211**

1:14 **209, 213**
1:16–18 **213**
1:29–34 **220**

2:1–11 **223**
3:1–10 **227–228**
3:16–18 **229**
4:3–14 **231**
4:21–24 **232**

4:39 **232**
9:13–21 **234**
9:38 **234**
9:39–41 **235**
11:32–45 **236–237**
12:12–15 **241**
13:1–15 **244**
14:3 **285**
14:16–17 **246**
15:1–2 **246**
15:12–13 **246**
15:14–16 **246**
16:20–21 **246**
16:32–33 **246–247**
17:21b–26 **247**
17:26 **246**
18:1–11 **251–252**
18:12–27 **254–255**
18:28 **256**
18:33–38 **256**
19:1–3 **256–257**
19:9–11 **257**
19:13–14 **260**
19:16–18 **260–261**
19:25b–30 **262–263**
19:32–34 **263**
19:38–42 **264**
20:1–16 **274–275**

20:19–23 **279**
20:24–31 **284**
21:9–18 **291–292**

Psalms
   22 **261**
   69 **261**
   122 **293**
   126 **191**

Chapter 7—Walking Luke's Road of Riches/ 4th Path
1 Kings
   17:8–16 **362**
Acts of the Apostles
   314–315
Deuteronomy
   6:5–6 **325**
Isaiah
   3:5–6 **333**
John
   1:5 **216**
Luke
   1:1–4 **316**
   1:5–25 **317–318**
   1:26–38 **319–320**
   1:39–40 **320**
   1:46–55 **320–321**
   2:1–19 **323**
   2:39–52 **325–326**
   3:1–17 **334–335**
   4:1–13 **339**
   4:14–30 **340–341**
   6:12–16 **342**
   6:17–36 **343–344**
   6:46–49 **344**
   10:25–37 **351–352**
   11:5–10 **353**
   15:1–10 **354**

15:11–32 **355-356**
17:20–21 **356**
19:29–44 **360-361**
22:14–38 **363-364**
22:39–62 **365-366**
22:63–71 **367**
23:1–12 **367-368**
23:26–31 **369**
23:32–43 **370**
23:44–49 **371**
24:1–12 **377**
24:13–35 **377-378**
24:36–53 **378-379**

Psalms
22 **371**
131 **381**
133 **381**

Chapter 8—Eight Essential and Continuing Practices
Luke
22:42 **409**

Chapter 9—Paradigms and Promises
Genesis
2:10 **421**
John
17:20–23 **429**

NORTHERN HEMISPHERE

Third Path ~ John / Revelation

Being in the Glorious Garden
How do we receive joy and experience union?

Receiving the Gift
Ecstatic, Calm,
Visionary, Zealous

Spring – East
First Light to Mid-Morning
The Eagle (*visionary sight*)

Fourth Path ~ Luke / Acts

Walking the Road of Riches
How do we mature in service?

Serving Life / Community
Gratitude, Integration of Opposites,
Patience, Speak Truth with Love

Summer – South
Mid-Morning to Fading Light
The Ox (*perseverance*)

Second Path ~ Mark

Crossing the Stormy Sea
How do we move
through suffering?

Enduring all Obstacles
Strained by Opposites,
Exhaustion, Doubt,
Loneliness

Winter – North
Late Evening to First Light
The Lion (*noble strength*)

First Path ~Matthew

Climbing the Great Mountain
How do we face
change?

Hearing the Summons
Shock, Unease,
Anxiety, Betrayal

Autumn – West
Fading Light to Late Evening
The Angel (*announces new journey*)

©Alexander John Shaia, PhD.
www.quadratos.com
All Rights Reserved

SOUTHERN HEMISPHERE

Third Path ~ John / Revelation
Being in the Glorious Garden
How do we receive joy and experience union?

Receiving the Gift
Ecstatic, Calm,
Visionary, Zealous

Spring – East
First Light to Mid-Morning
The Eagle (*visionary sight*)

Fourth Path ~ Luke / Acts
Walking the Road of Riches
How do we mature in service?

Serving Life / Community
Gratitude, Integration of Opposites,
Patience, Speak Truth with Love

Summer – North
Mid-Morning to Fading Light
The Ox (*perseverance*)

Second Path ~ Mark
Crossing the Stormy Sea
How do we move through suffering?

Enduring all Obstacles
Strained by Opposites,
Exhaustion, Doubt,
Loneliness

Winter – South
Late Evening to First Light
The Lion (*noble strength*)

First Path ~ Matthew
Climbing the Great Mountain
How do we face change?

Hearing the Summons
Shock, Unease,
Anxiety, Betrayal

Autumn – West
Fading Light to Late Evening
The Angel (*announces new journey*)

©Alexander John Shaia, PhD.
www.quadratos.com
All Rights Reserved

ACKNOWLEDGEMENTS

To my sitto, jiddo, parents, brothers, nephews, great nieces and great nephew, and extended Lebanese family—my deepest gratitude to you for maintaining a big table and always keeping my place at it open. To the Maronite Eastern Rite Catholic tradition—I had no idea of the magnitude of the gift I received as a child, to be steeped in a non-Western, poetic, mystical and Aramaic world, and I am thankful for it.

To Morton Kelsey, Joseph Campbell, Mark Searle and all of my formative professors at the University of Notre Dame, I hope my work may be a worthy continuation of yours. To my many teachers, especially Eva Maria Sanchez, Christiane Brusselmans, James Dunning, Raymond Brown, Angeles Arrien, Betsy Caprio, Josie Abbenante, Dora M. Kalff and colleagues in the International Society for Sandplay Therapy and Sandplay Therapists of America as well the many authors who pointed the way. My work is built upon your skill and efforts that we might grow in awareness. And to my former parishioners, Sandplay patients and spiritual directees, you allowed me the honor of witnessing your journey. In the fire and grace of your lives, you taught me the deep truths of Quadratos.

To my collaborator, Michelle Gaugy, there are no words to express the honor of working with you and my gratitude for your contributions to Quadratos—its logic, beautiful prose and your faithful presence with me and the material in the times we could not see a way forward.

My profound thanks to the many who contributed to the prior editions of this book; those who donated monies for the initial book (*Beyond the Biography of Jesus, Vol.1*) to be published, with tremendous gratitude to Peter Honsberger and team at Cold Tree Press for their trust in me and this work; Michael Maudlin and team at HarperOne for the second book (*The Hidden Power of the Gospels*) as well as Tom Grady, Melissa Weiner at Stray Dog Media, Nicole Reinecker at Neek Design, Connie Cox, an untiring copy editor doing whatever was needed, and Megan Stewart-Sicking who did likewise in organizing conferences and speaking events.

Appreciation also for Sarah Louise Ricketts who graciously formatted the initial Kindle edition of *Heart and Mind*. My esteem for Lynda Helmer's tireless efforts as copy editor and cover designer for the Second Edition of *Heart and Mind*. And there are no adequate words for Joy Jaber, who as she lay terminally ill went through the text with an eagle-eye, correcting typos and subtle errors. Likewise, my appreciation for Eddie Cruz, Rafael Polendo, Ryan Sprenger and Nora Sophia who with skill and patience have helped to bring this hardcover edition of *Radical Transformation* to publication. Cheers to one and all!

Immense gratitude for my U.S. colleagues, especially those in San Antonio, Santa Fe, Olympia, Sacramento, Saratoga, San Carlos, Santa Barbara, St. Helena, Burlingame, Baltimore, and the Bread of Life Center and its two-year Quadratos Immersion Study. Now the work has spread to Australia, China, New Zealand, the UK, Ireland, Germany, Spain, other parts of the EU, the Middle East and Asia. My deep respect for all pioneers who are taking forward the practice of *Heart and Mind*.

And a grateful bow to Donna Nicolson who pioneered the first online Heart and Mind Community. Following upon her work is that of Annie Sempill. No adequate words exist for Annie's evident skill and radiant heart. By her efforts, online Heart and Mind Communities span the planet.

Equally, the work of Quadratos is sustained by those praying *Gateway to Oneness*—Christianity's ancestral Easter. May our practice and prayer "That All Be One" come true.

To those who wrestle and challenge the concepts within Quadratos, your questioning is a gift—offering all of us the promise of an ever-more true wisdom, compassion and understanding.

To each person in the worldwide family of Quadratos—you are deeply held in my heart and daily prayer. You are pilgrims and pioneers, helping all of us to go beyond what we have known. Sisters and brothers—lead on. You are inhabiting fresh ways of being, knowing and relating. Together you are giving birth to a new heaven and earth—a vibrant Jeru-Shalom for all peoples.

In'shallah
Ah'mein!

AUTHOR

Alexander John Shaia, PhD, is a thoughtful and poetic man, living the ancient rhythms of his Lebanese and Aramaic heritage. With deep conviction, he invites us into a practice of spirituality (and Christianity) for the twenty-first century—one that crosses traditional boundaries, encourages vital thinking and inhabits a genuine community of the heart.

As a spiritual director, educator, anthropologist, psychologist, liturgist, and senior Teaching Member of the International Society for Sandplay Therapy, Alexander John is known as an original, cross-discipline thinker and passionate professional speaker. He founded Quadratos, LLC as well as the Blue Door Retreat in Santa Fe, New Mexico. He travels internationally, lecturing on Quadratos, and leading seminars and retreats including Gateway to Oneness: Re-imaging Us as Christians. Each year, Alexander mentors an intimate band of pilgrims on the Camino, the West's most ancient path of transformation. See www.quadratos.com for more about his work and offerings.

When not on the road, home is in the beloved mountains near Santa Fe or an old fishing village along the wild Galician coast. An ideal day finds him with his dog, a book of poetry and in the presence of ancient stones.

He would be delighted to hear from you. Write him at info@quadratos.com and/or connect through his Facebook page, Alexander John Shaia—Author and Quadratos on Instagram.

COLLABORATOR

Michelle L. Gaugy is a writer, speaker on topics of art and culture, an art consultant to artists and art galleries, and the owner of an art gallery in Santa Fe, New Mexico. She is also the former president of the Awakening Museum and Foundation, an interfaith center of spiritual art. She travels as much as her two small poodles, Dora and Gala, will allow. She can be reached at mgaugy@gmail.com.